ROCKETO™

Journey to the Hidden Sea

Volume 2

Frank Espinosa

Co-Writer: Marie Taylor

Logo Design & Production: Masanori Hase

Image Comics Publisher: Erik Larsen President: Todd McFarlane CEO: Marc Silvestri Vice-President: Jim Valentino Executive Director: Eric Stephenson Director of Marketing: Mark Haven Britt Accounts Manager: Thao Le
Accounting Assistant: Rosemary Cao Administrative Assistant: Traci Hui Traffic Manager: Joe Keatinge Production Manager: Allen Hui Production Artist: Jonathan Chan Production Artist: Drew Gill Production Artist: Chris Giarrusso

ROCKETO, VOL 2: JOURNEY TO THE HIDDEN SEA. Published by Image Comics, Inc., Office of publication: 1942 University Avenue, Suite 305, Berkeley, California 94704.
PRINTED IN CANADA

INTRODUCTION

I love Rocketo. Rocketo is one of those books that is a culmination of the best skills and vision that comics have to offer. The creation of a new world map filled with amazing wonders is a staple of fantasy lore, and the pulp magazine hero who takes us there is standard stuff that we all know, but it demands our attention when it's done this well. Frank Espinosa is one of the brightest new talents to grace comics, and by that I mean that I fully appreciate his time and efforts gracing this medium. Frank could have just as easily kept his skills in the animation field alone, where he's just come from. Frank spent many years guiding other talented artists with work he both illustrated and animated for Warner Bros. Consumer Products. This is where I got to know Frank and had the privilege to see Rocketo in development some time ago. What I've seen of Frank's vision for the series, the number of epic stories he has planned and the volume of artwork generated that he's yet to show, is nothing short of stunning.

Artistically, Frank has accomplished a wonderful hybrid style, combining the best figure modeling of animated feature films and the more liberated expressionist line of European comics. With resemblance to the classic comic strips of Chester Gould and Alex Raymond to the kinetic energy of Jack Kirby's work, Frank's style transcends the ages of the comic book. His look is inspired by the past and pushing us forward graphically into the future. His line only indicates the purity of his subject's gesture and position without always holding in the form to a rigid contour. Color is employed at an amazing level of accent only, restrained to a limited palate of mostly only two colors used at a single time. These innovations are put to an exceptional effect, creating a mood and graphic experience not likely to be found elsewhere. At his core there is Frank's strength of drawing keeping these bold steps together, making the images hold up for closer scrutiny. Coupled with his boundless creativity, Rocketo's artwork is married with a story of impressive tone, execution, and class. The panoramic format of this work is well-suited to the epic nature of events it documents, and it makes this new retro-future Earth seem all the more inviting.

It's a rare thing to find that craftsman who tells a passionate tale with such quality as both writer and artist and who has the commitment to make the journey. I know I'll be there to follow him on that journey, absorbing the inspirations that his labors bring.

ALEX ROSS
2005

It has been 2000 years since the Great Shattering of the planet Earth.
New men have been created for this New World.
Among them are the Mappers who explore the unknown continents,
chart the depths of oceans, navigating new jungles and deserts,
guiding others in the discovery of their world.

These are the journeys of Rocketo Garrison.

7

REUNIONS

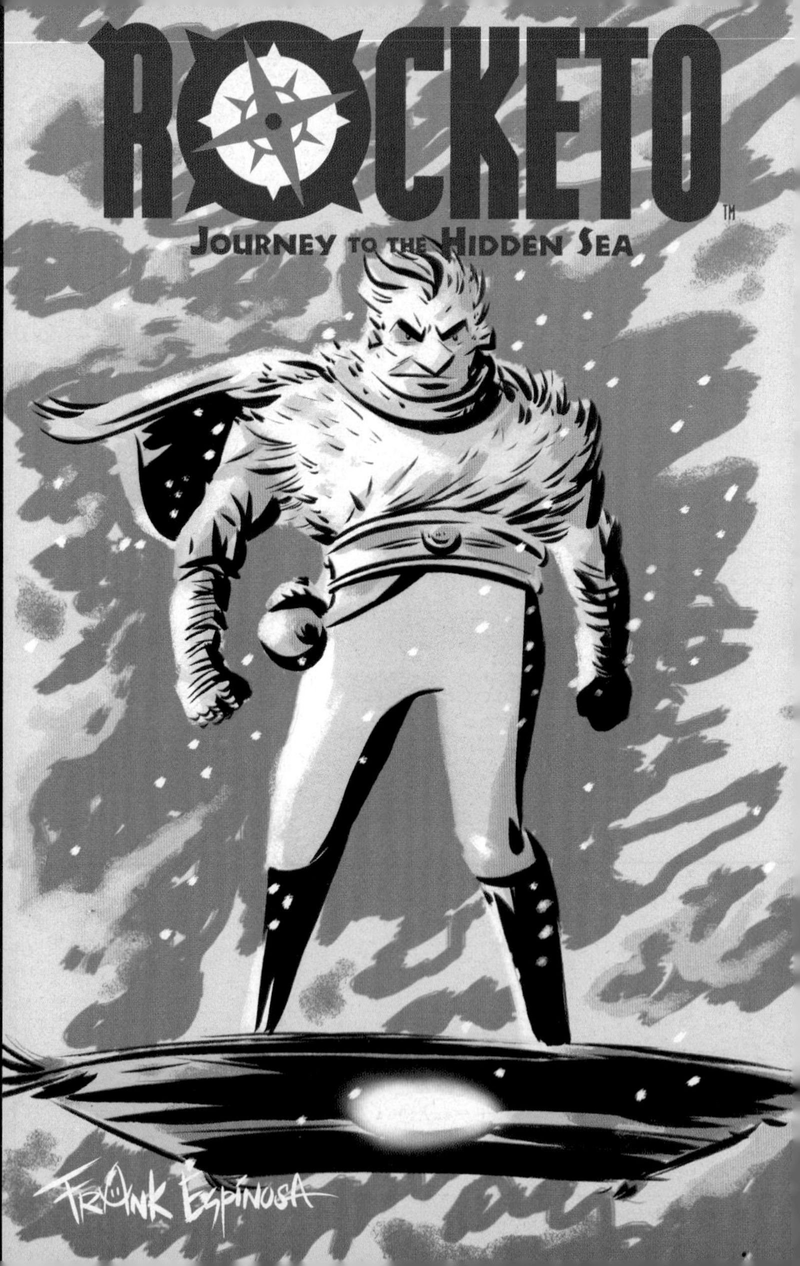
ROCKETO™
JOURNEY TO THE HIDDEN SEA
FRANK ESPINOSA

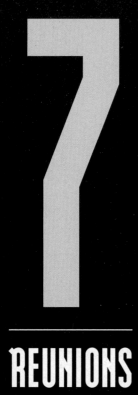

SOMEWHERE IN THE HIDDEN SEA, 1917 NW TIME...

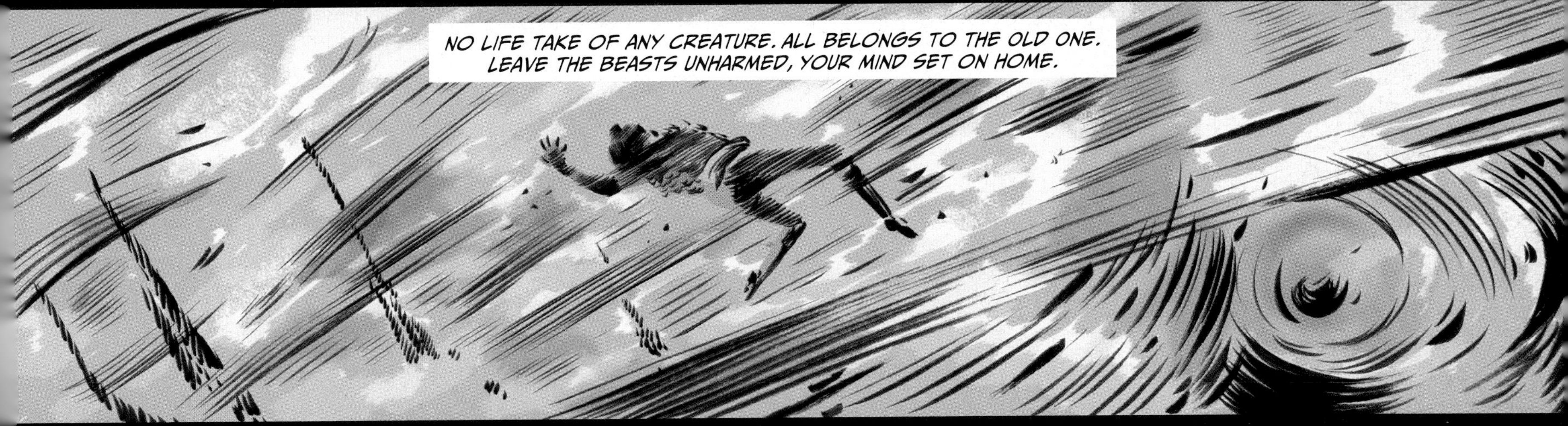
NO LIFE TAKE OF ANY CREATURE. ALL BELONGS TO THE OLD ONE.
LEAVE THE BEASTS UNHARMED, YOUR MIND SET ON HOME.

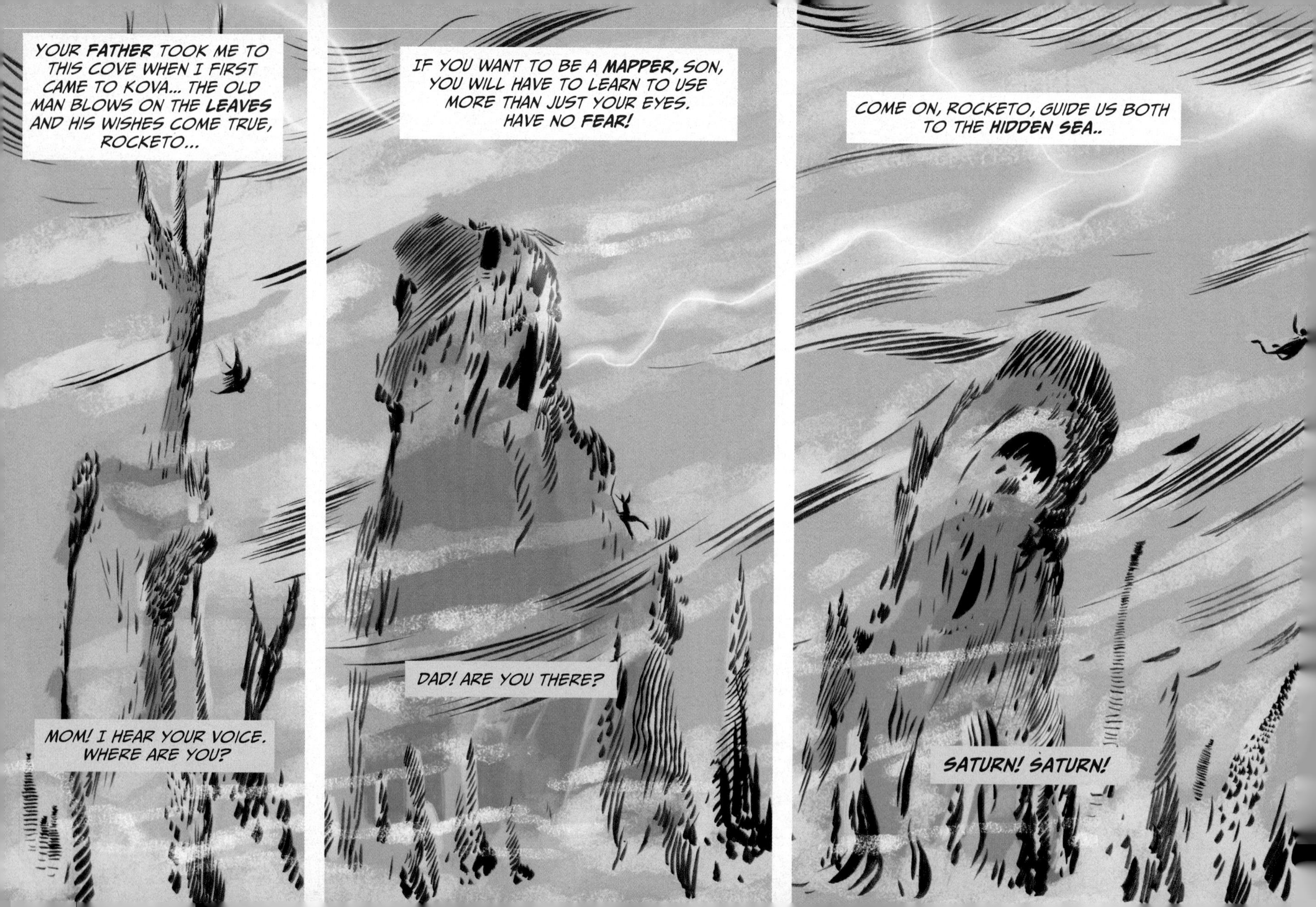
YOUR FATHER TOOK ME TO THIS COVE WHEN I FIRST CAME TO KOVA... THE OLD MAN BLOWS ON THE LEAVES AND HIS WISHES COME TRUE, ROCKETO...
MOM! I HEAR YOUR VOICE. WHERE ARE YOU?
IF YOU WANT TO BE A MAPPER, SON, YOU WILL HAVE TO LEARN TO USE MORE THAN JUST YOUR EYES. HAVE NO FEAR!
DAD! ARE YOU THERE?
COME ON, ROCKETO, GUIDE US BOTH TO THE HIDDEN SEA..
SATURN! SATURN!

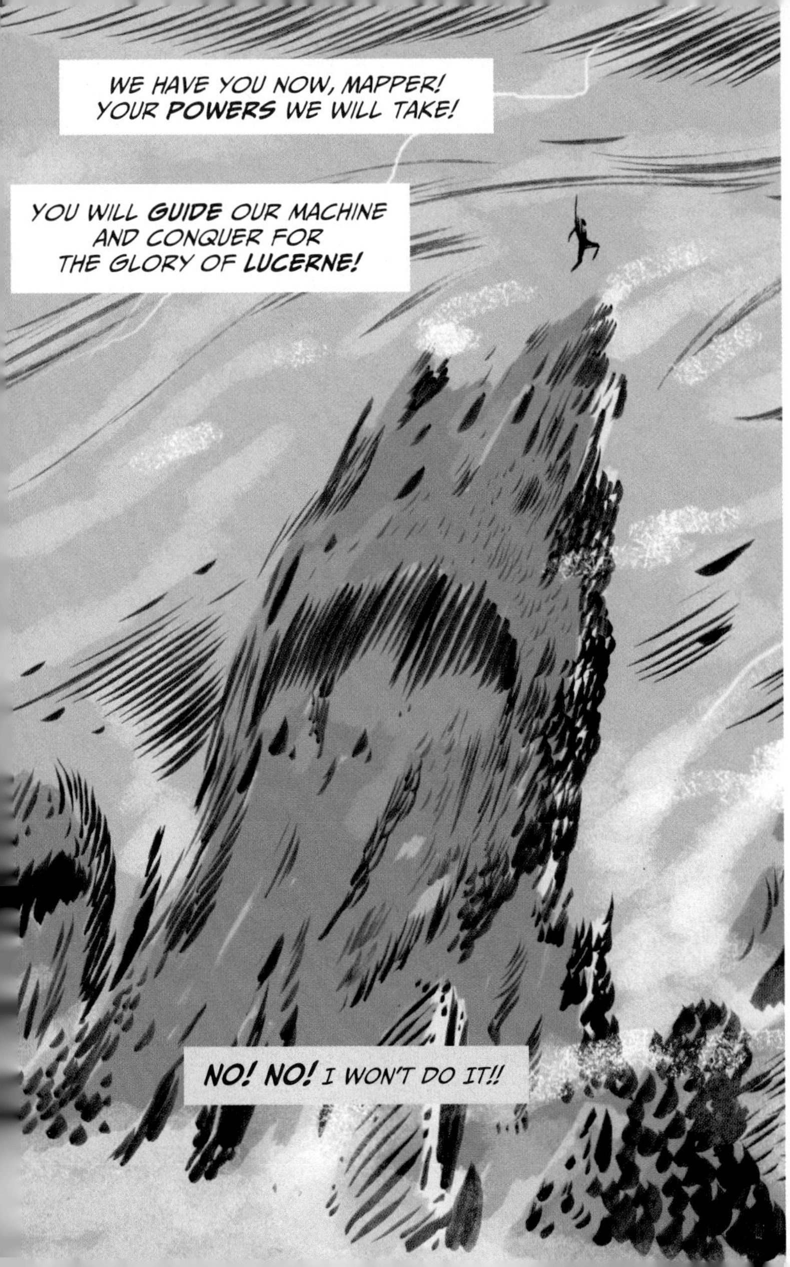
WE HAVE YOU NOW, MAPPER! YOUR POWERS WE WILL TAKE!
YOU WILL GUIDE OUR MACHINE AND CONQUER FOR THE GLORY OF LUCERNE!
NO! NO! I WON'T DO IT!!

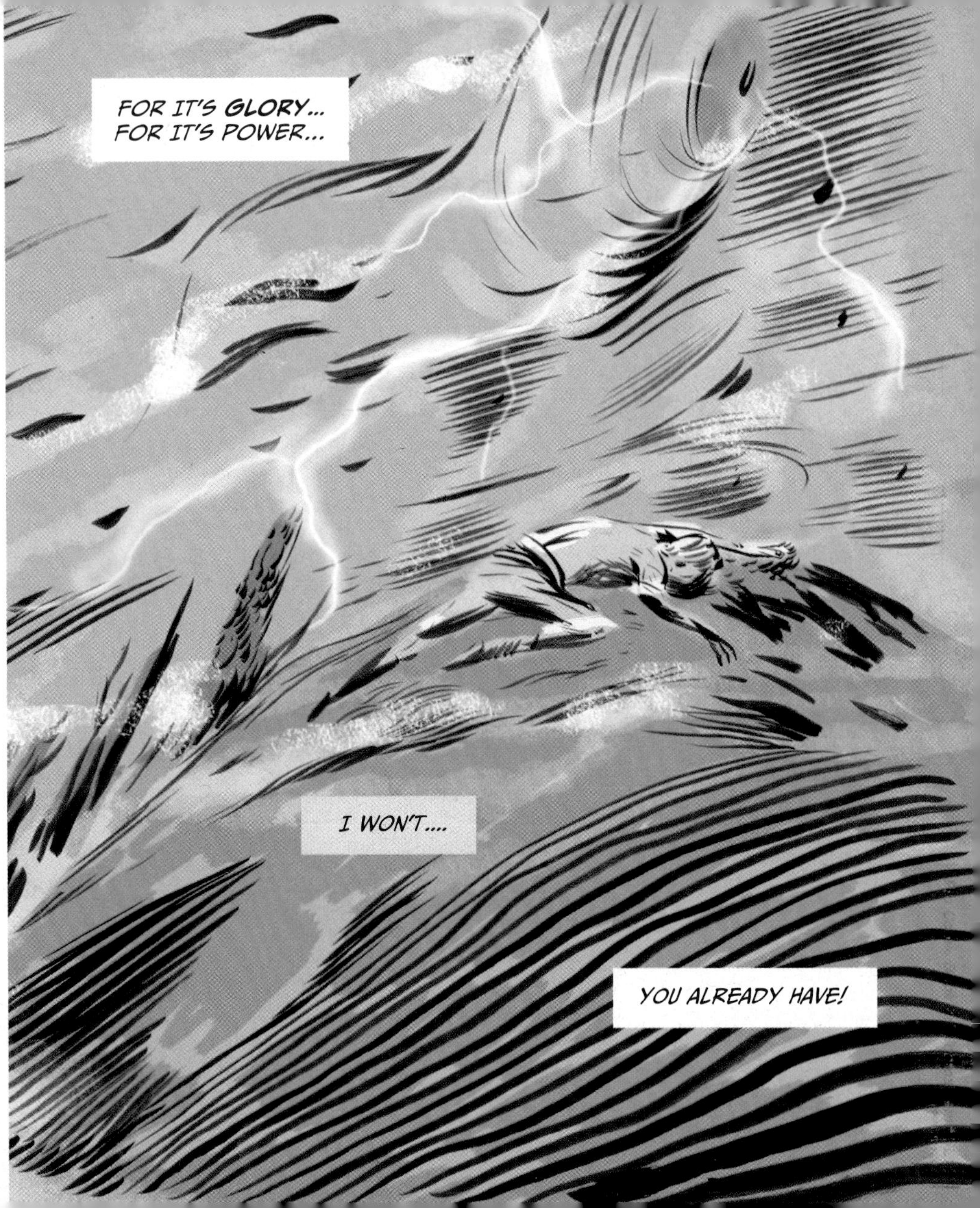
FOR IT'S GLORY... FOR IT'S POWER...
I WON'T....
YOU ALREADY HAVE!

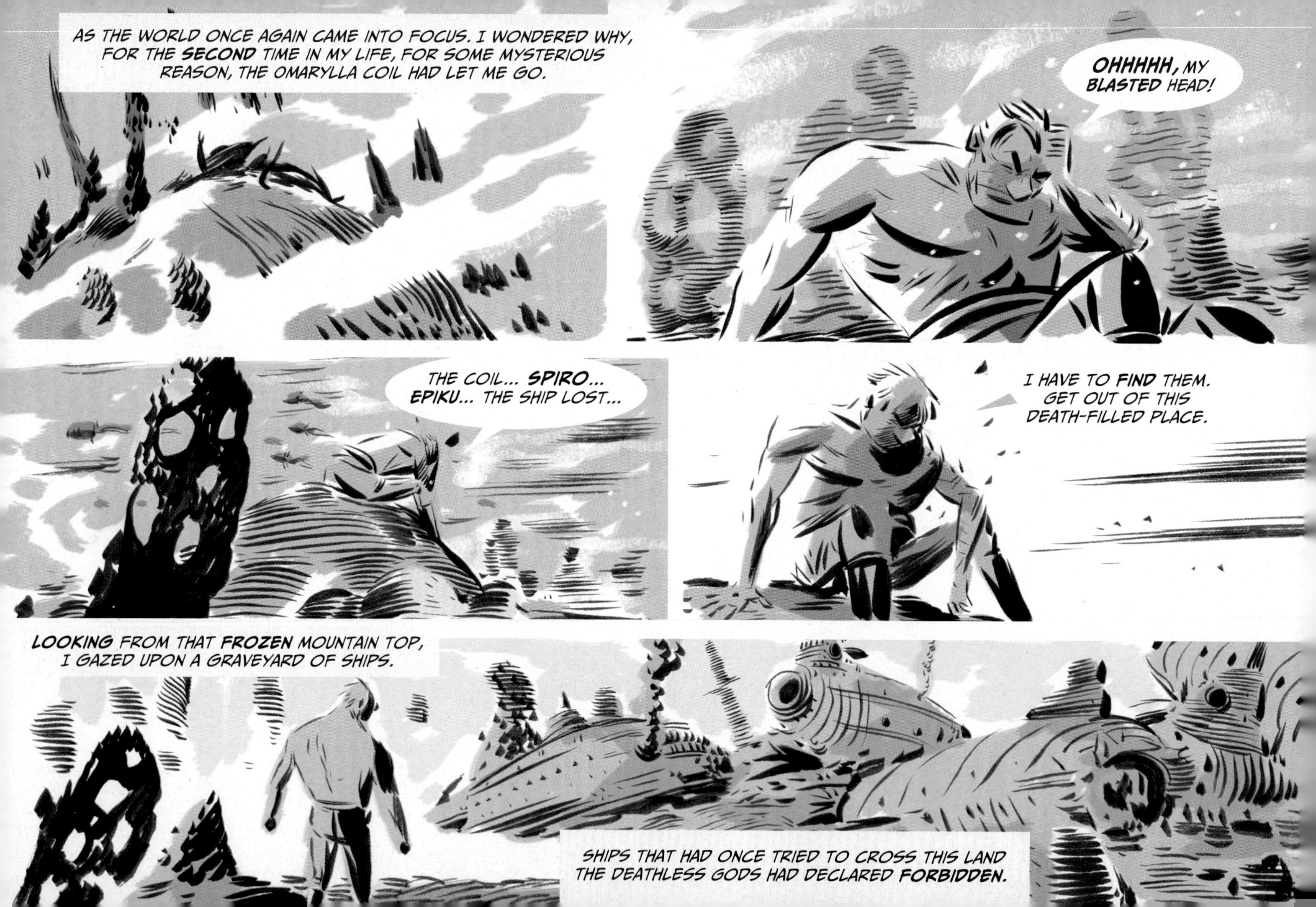
AS THE WORLD ONCE AGAIN CAME INTO FOCUS. I WONDERED WHY, FOR THE **SECOND** TIME IN MY LIFE, FOR SOME MYSTERIOUS REASON, THE OMARYLLA COIL HAD LET ME GO.
OHHHHH, MY **BLASTED** HEAD!
THE COIL... **SPIRO...** **EPIKU...** THE SHIP LOST...
I HAVE TO **FIND** THEM. GET OUT OF THIS DEATH-FILLED PLACE.
LOOKING FROM THAT **FROZEN** MOUNTAIN TOP, I GAZED UPON A GRAVEYARD OF SHIPS.
SHIPS THAT HAD ONCE TRIED TO CROSS THIS LAND THE DEATHLESS GODS HAD DECLARED **FORBIDDEN.**

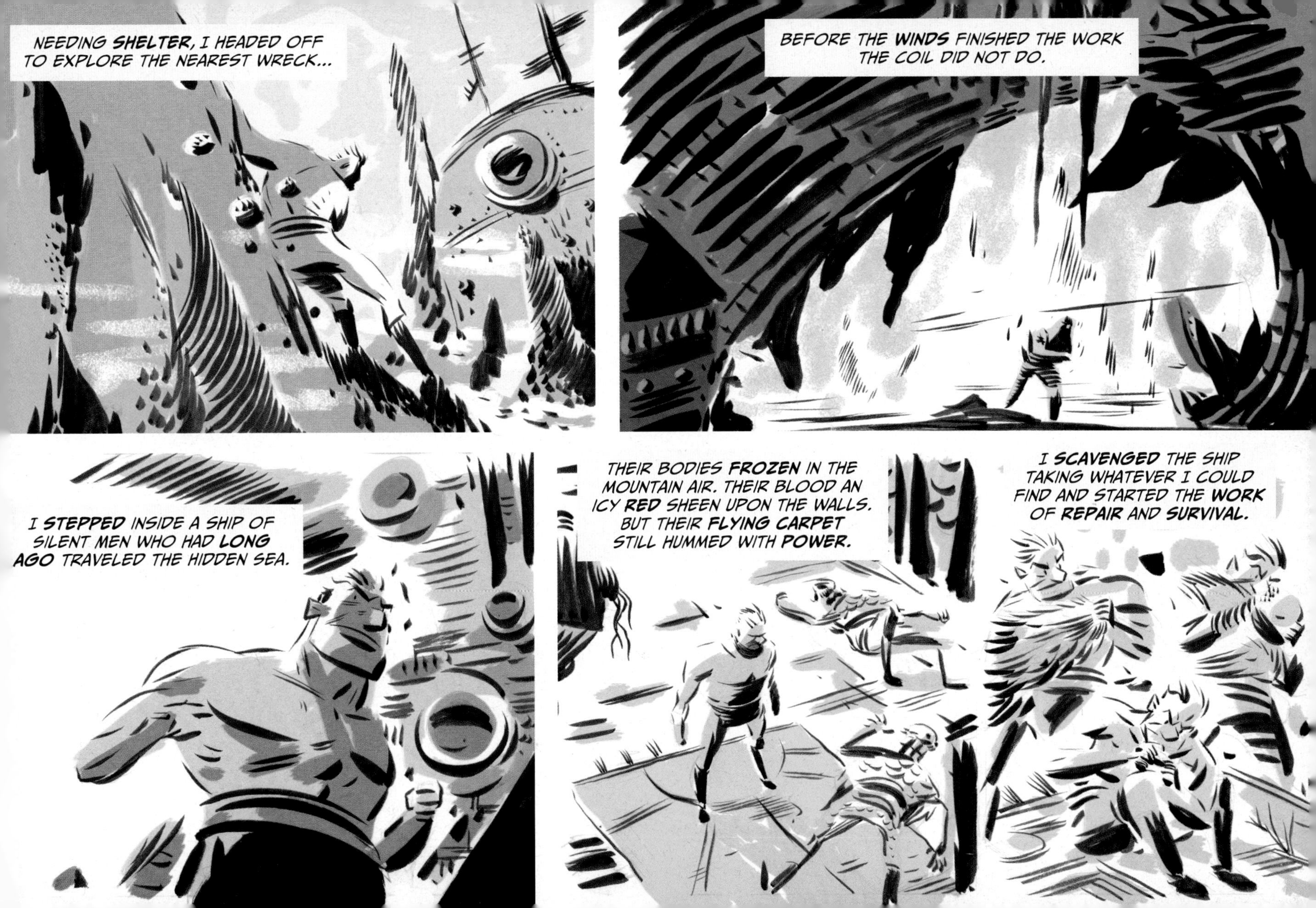
NEEDING **SHELTER**, I HEADED OFF TO EXPLORE THE NEAREST WRECK...
BEFORE THE **WINDS** FINISHED THE WORK THE COIL DID NOT DO.
I **STEPPED** INSIDE A SHIP OF SILENT MEN WHO HAD **LONG AGO** TRAVELED THE HIDDEN SEA.
THEIR BODIES **FROZEN** IN THE MOUNTAIN AIR. THEIR BLOOD AN ICY **RED** SHEEN UPON THE WALLS. BUT THEIR **FLYING CARPET** STILL HUMMED WITH **POWER.**
I **SCAVENGED** THE SHIP TAKING WHATEVER I COULD FIND AND STARTED THE **WORK** OF **REPAIR** AND **SURVIVAL.**

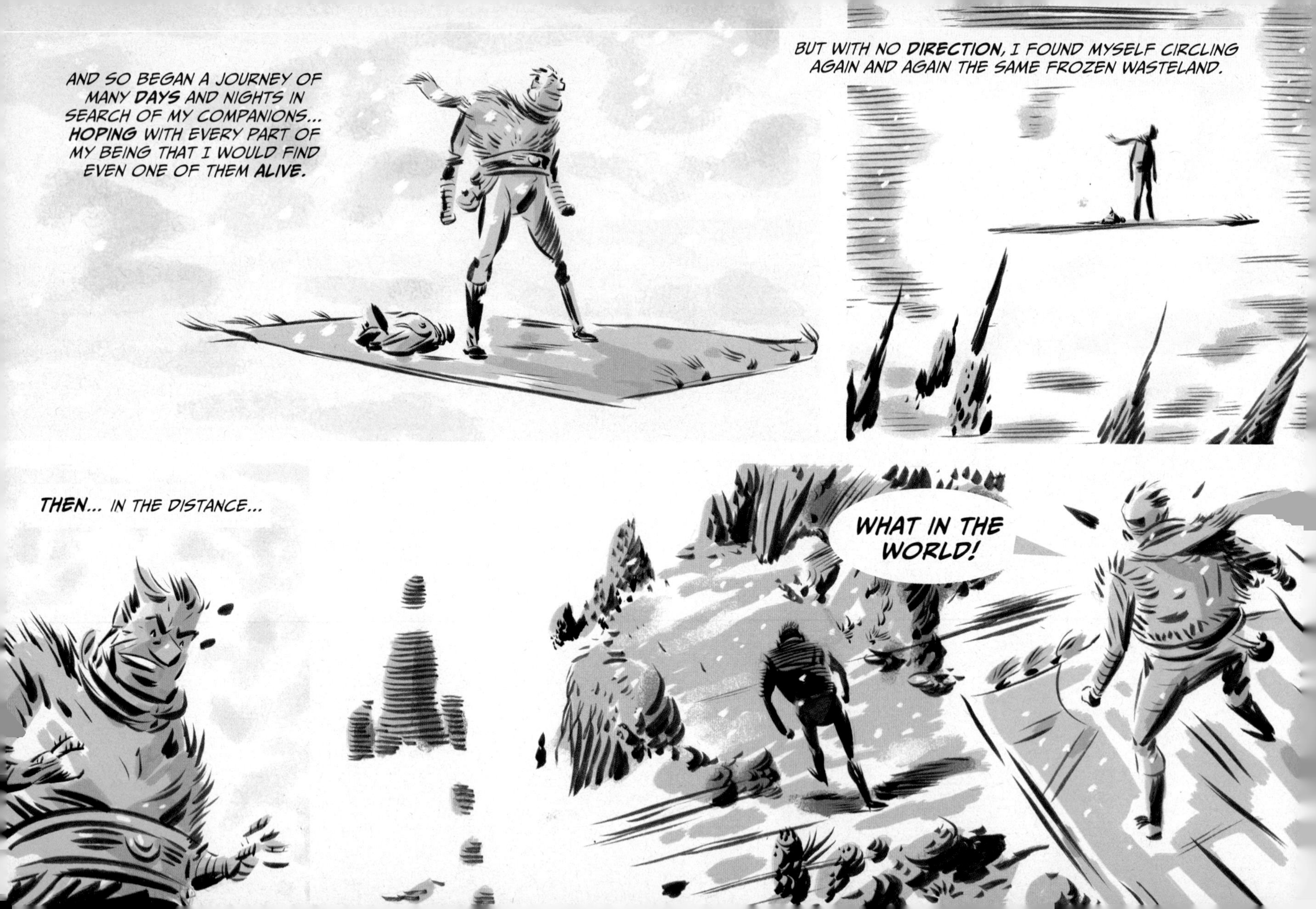
AND SO BEGAN A JOURNEY OF MANY DAYS AND NIGHTS IN SEARCH OF MY COMPANIONS... HOPING WITH EVERY PART OF MY BEING THAT I WOULD FIND EVEN ONE OF THEM ALIVE.
BUT WITH NO DIRECTION, I FOUND MYSELF CIRCLING AGAIN AND AGAIN THE SAME FROZEN WASTELAND.
THEN... IN THE DISTANCE...
WHAT IN THE WORLD!

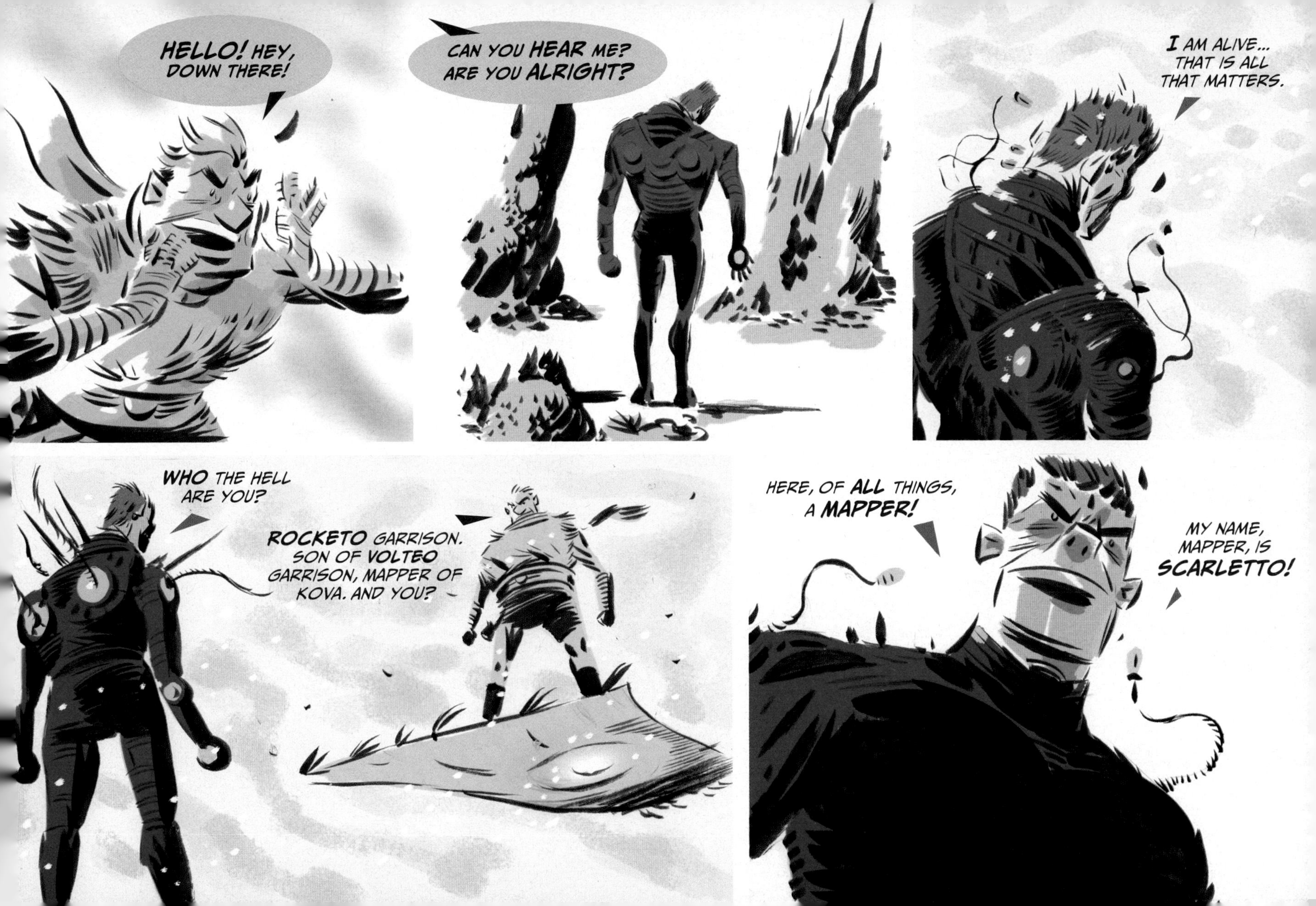
HELLO! HEY, DOWN THERE!
CAN YOU HEAR ME? ARE YOU ALRIGHT?
I AM ALIVE... THAT IS ALL THAT MATTERS.
WHO THE HELL ARE YOU?
ROCKETO GARRISON. SON OF VOLTEO GARRISON, MAPPER OF KOVA. AND YOU?
HERE, OF ALL THINGS, A MAPPER!
MY NAME, MAPPER, IS SCARLETTO!

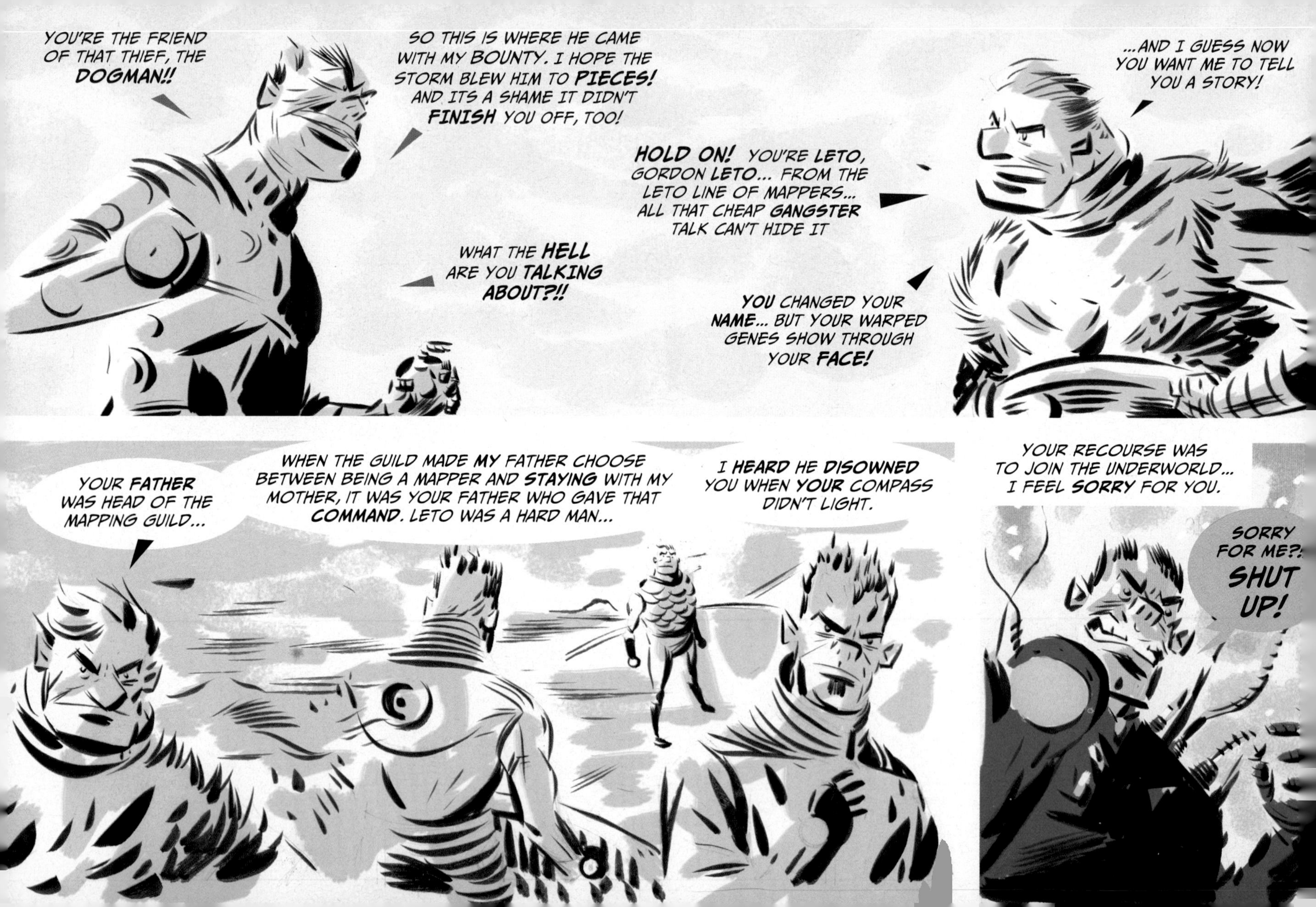
YOU'RE THE FRIEND OF THAT THIEF, THE DOGMAN!!
SO THIS IS WHERE HE CAME WITH MY BOUNTY. I HOPE THE STORM BLEW HIM TO PIECES! AND ITS A SHAME IT DIDN'T FINISH YOU OFF, TOO!
WHAT THE HELL ARE YOU TALKING ABOUT?!!
...AND I GUESS NOW YOU WANT ME TO TELL YOU A STORY!
HOLD ON! YOU'RE LETO, GORDON LETO... FROM THE LETO LINE OF MAPPERS... ALL THAT CHEAP GANGSTER TALK CAN'T HIDE IT
YOU CHANGED YOUR NAME... BUT YOUR WARPED GENES SHOW THROUGH YOUR FACE!
YOUR FATHER WAS HEAD OF THE MAPPING GUILD...
WHEN THE GUILD MADE MY FATHER CHOOSE BETWEEN BEING A MAPPER AND STAYING WITH MY MOTHER, IT WAS YOUR FATHER WHO GAVE THAT COMMAND. LETO WAS A HARD MAN...
I HEARD HE DISOWNED YOU WHEN YOUR COMPASS DIDN'T LIGHT.
YOUR RECOURSE WAS TO JOIN THE UNDERWORLD... I FEEL SORRY FOR YOU.
SORRY FOR ME?! SHUT UP!

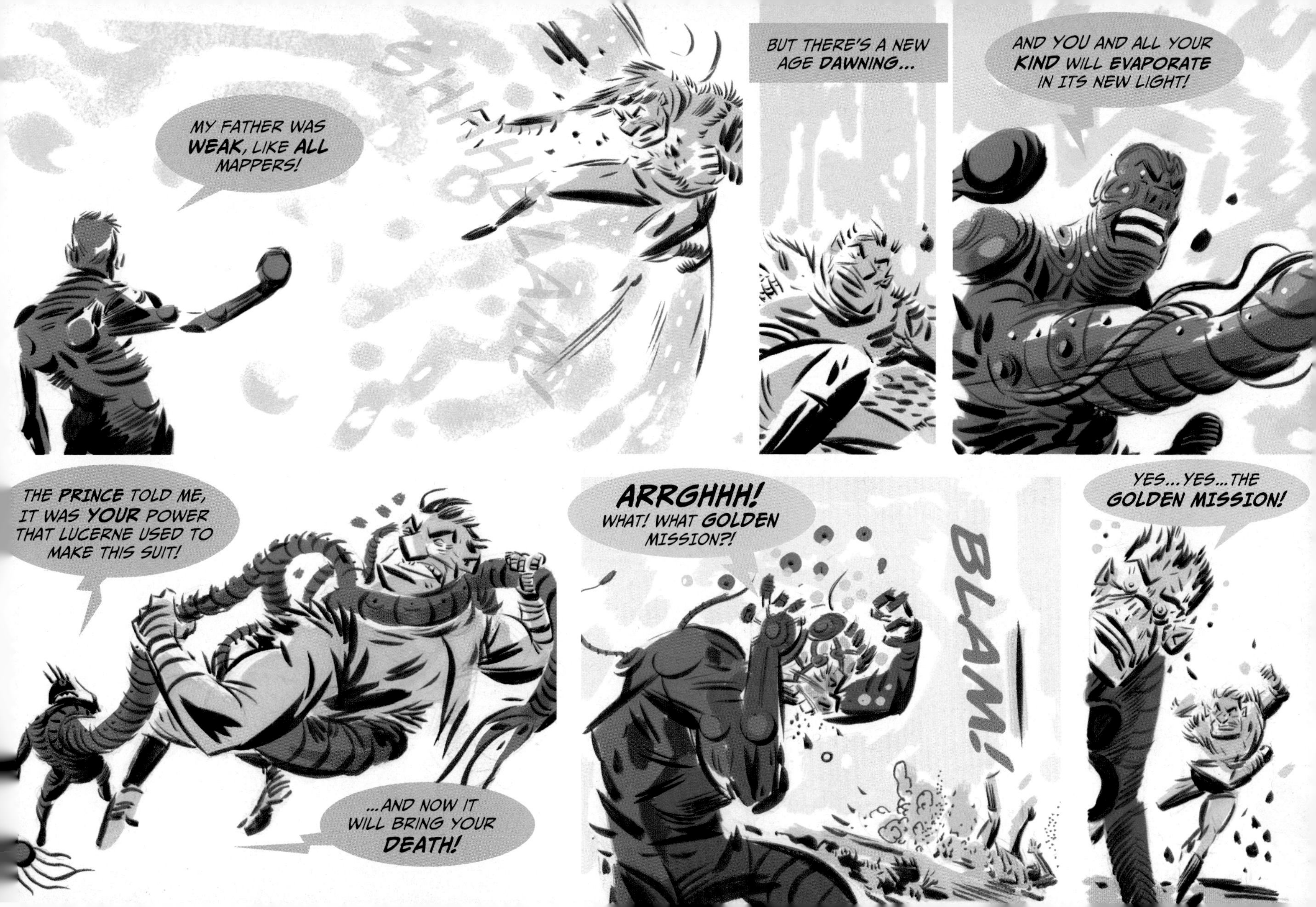
MY FATHER WAS WEAK, LIKE ALL MAPPERS!
SHHHBLAM!
BUT THERE'S A NEW AGE DAWNING...
AND YOU AND ALL YOUR KIND WILL EVAPORATE IN ITS NEW LIGHT!
THE PRINCE TOLD ME, IT WAS YOUR POWER THAT LUCERNE USED TO MAKE THIS SUIT!
...AND NOW IT WILL BRING YOUR DEATH!
ARRGHHH! WHAT! WHAT GOLDEN MISSION?!
BLAM!
YES...YES...THE GOLDEN MISSION!

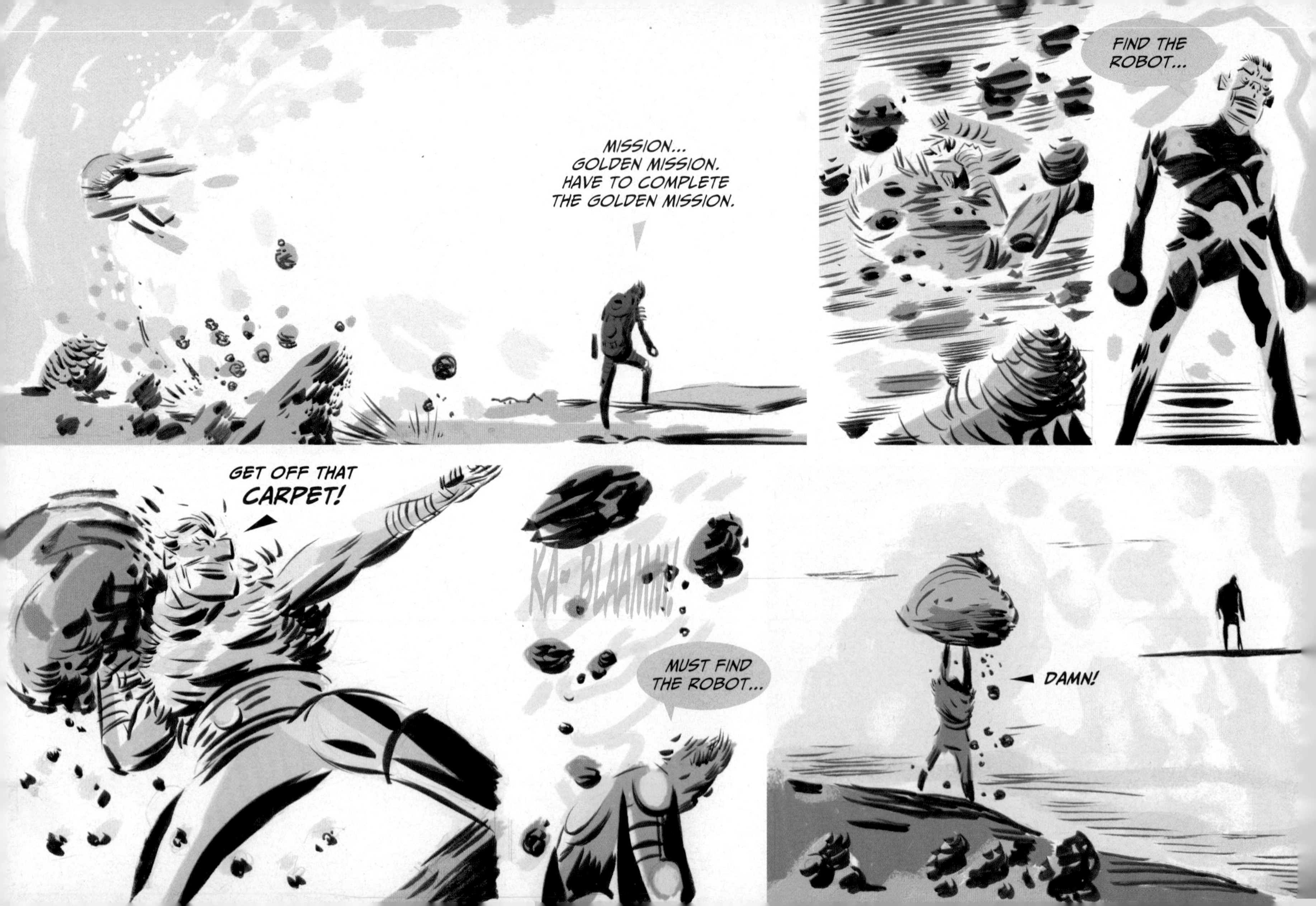
MISSION... GOLDEN MISSION. HAVE TO COMPLETE THE GOLDEN MISSION.
FIND THE ROBOT...
GET OFF THAT CARPET!
KA- BLAAMM!
MUST FIND THE ROBOT...
DAMN!

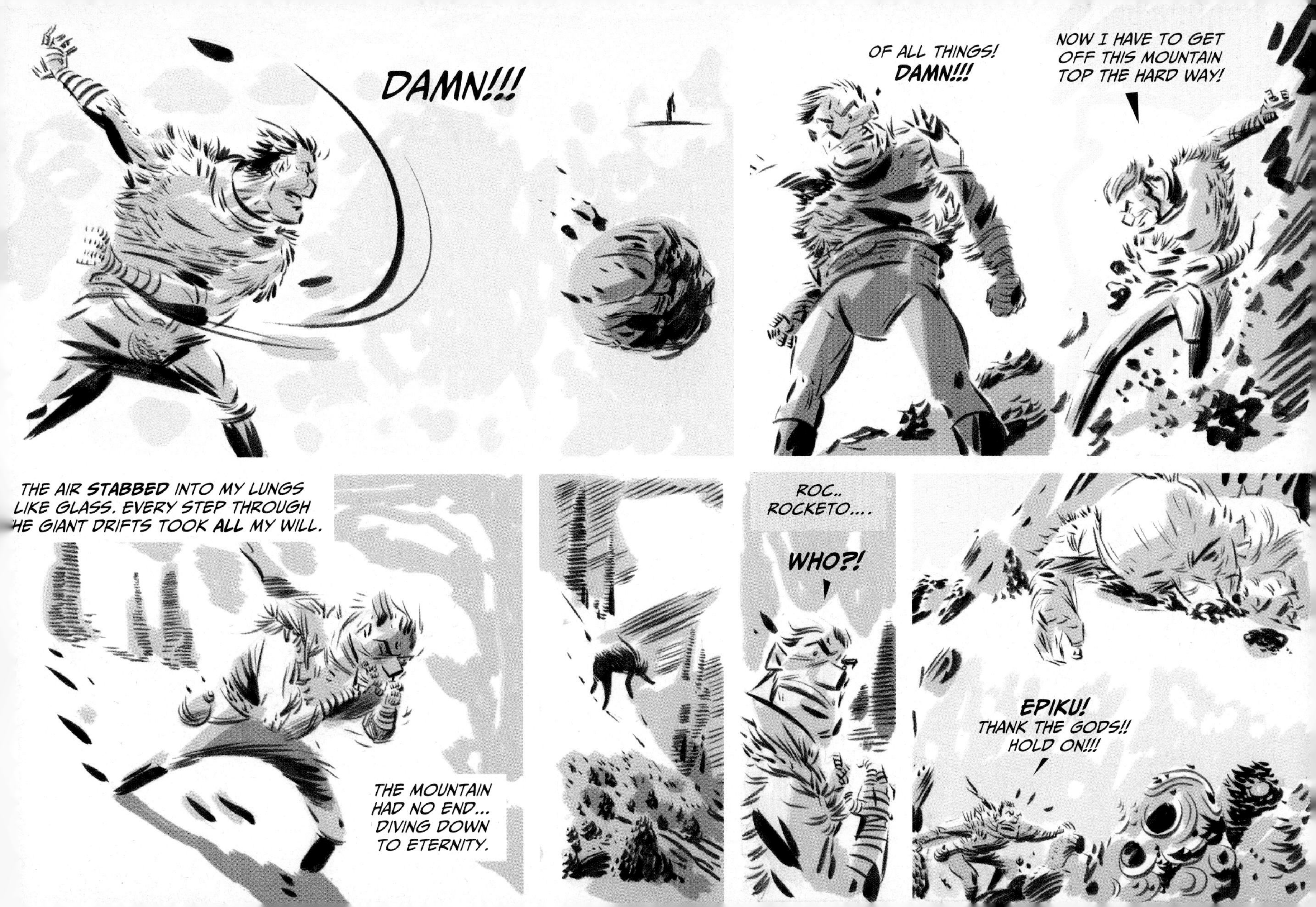
DAMN!!!
OF ALL THINGS! DAMN!!!
NOW I HAVE TO GET OFF THIS MOUNTAIN TOP THE HARD WAY!
THE AIR STABBED INTO MY LUNGS LIKE GLASS. EVERY STEP THROUGH THE GIANT DRIFTS TOOK ALL MY WILL.
THE MOUNTAIN HAD NO END... DIVING DOWN TO ETERNITY.
ROC.. ROCKETO....
WHO?!
EPIKU! THANK THE GODS!! HOLD ON!!!

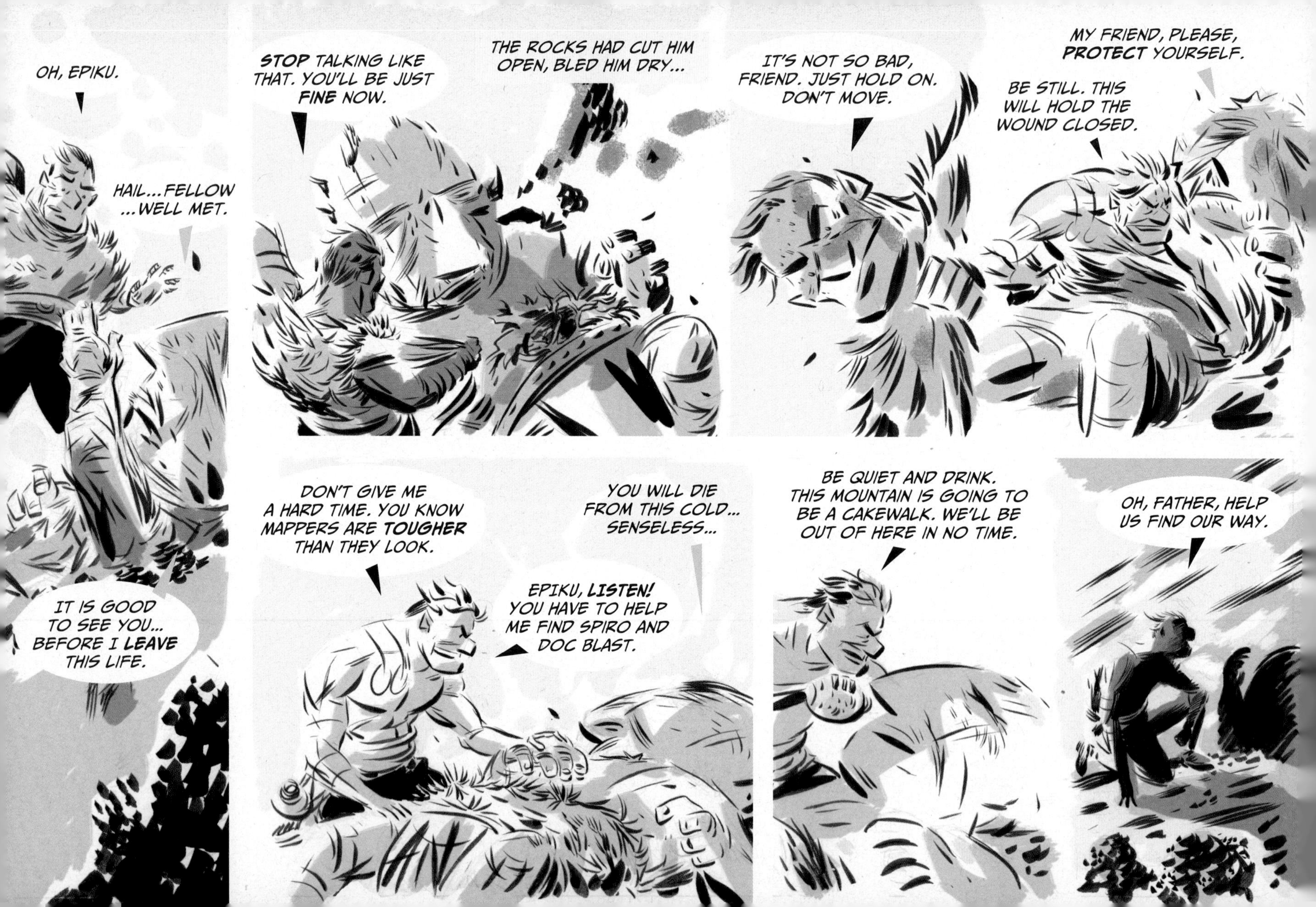

OH, EPIKU.
HAIL...FELLOW ...WELL MET.
IT IS GOOD TO SEE YOU... BEFORE I LEAVE THIS LIFE.
STOP TALKING LIKE THAT. YOU'LL BE JUST FINE NOW.
THE ROCKS HAD CUT HIM OPEN, BLED HIM DRY...
IT'S NOT SO BAD, FRIEND. JUST HOLD ON. DON'T MOVE.
MY FRIEND, PLEASE, PROTECT YOURSELF.
BE STILL. THIS WILL HOLD THE WOUND CLOSED.
DON'T GIVE ME A HARD TIME. YOU KNOW MAPPERS ARE TOUGHER THAN THEY LOOK.
YOU WILL DIE FROM THIS COLD... SENSELESS...
EPIKU, LISTEN! YOU HAVE TO HELP ME FIND SPIRO AND DOC BLAST.
BE QUIET AND DRINK. THIS MOUNTAIN IS GOING TO BE A CAKEWALK. WE'LL BE OUT OF HERE IN NO TIME.
OH, FATHER, HELP US FIND OUR WAY.

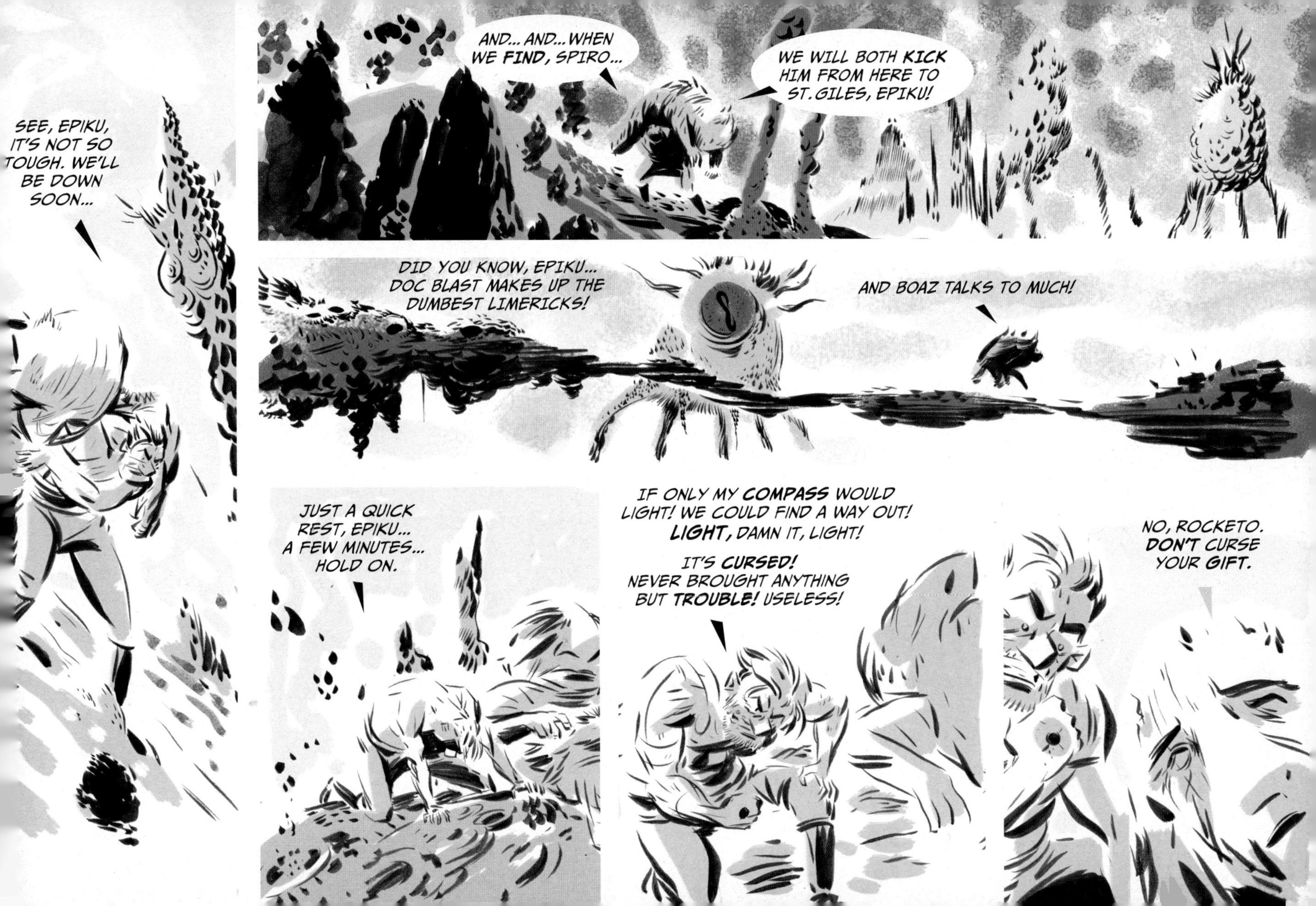
SEE, EPIKU, IT'S NOT SO TOUGH. WE'LL BE DOWN SOON...
AND... AND... WHEN WE FIND, SPIRO...
WE WILL BOTH KICK HIM FROM HERE TO ST. GILES, EPIKU!
DID YOU KNOW, EPIKU... DOC BLAST MAKES UP THE DUMBEST LIMERICKS!
AND BOAZ TALKS TO MUCH!
JUST A QUICK REST, EPIKU... A FEW MINUTES... HOLD ON.
IF ONLY MY COMPASS WOULD LIGHT! WE COULD FIND A WAY OUT! LIGHT, DAMN IT, LIGHT!
IT'S CURSED! NEVER BROUGHT ANYTHING BUT TROUBLE! USELESS!
NO, ROCKETO. DON'T CURSE YOUR GIFT.

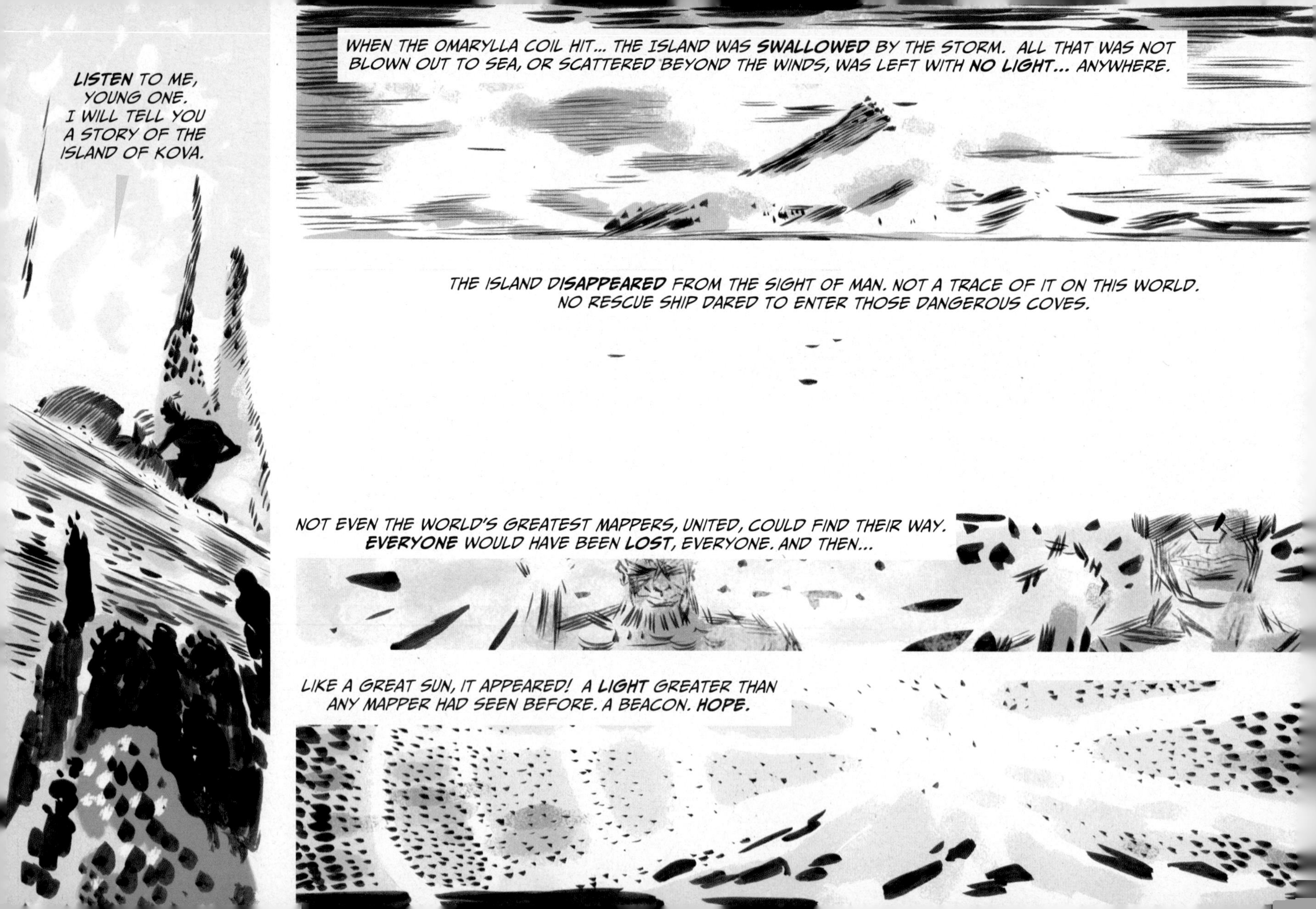
LISTEN TO ME, YOUNG ONE. I WILL TELL YOU A STORY OF THE ISLAND OF KOVA.
WHEN THE OMARYLLA COIL HIT... THE ISLAND WAS SWALLOWED BY THE STORM. ALL THAT WAS NOT BLOWN OUT TO SEA, OR SCATTERED BEYOND THE WINDS, WAS LEFT WITH NO LIGHT... ANYWHERE.
THE ISLAND DISAPPEARED FROM THE SIGHT OF MAN. NOT A TRACE OF IT ON THIS WORLD. NO RESCUE SHIP DARED TO ENTER THOSE DANGEROUS COVES.
NOT EVEN THE WORLD'S GREATEST MAPPERS, UNITED, COULD FIND THEIR WAY. EVERYONE WOULD HAVE BEEN LOST, EVERYONE. AND THEN...
LIKE A GREAT SUN, IT APPEARED! A LIGHT GREATER THAN ANY MAPPER HAD SEEN BEFORE. A BEACON. HOPE.

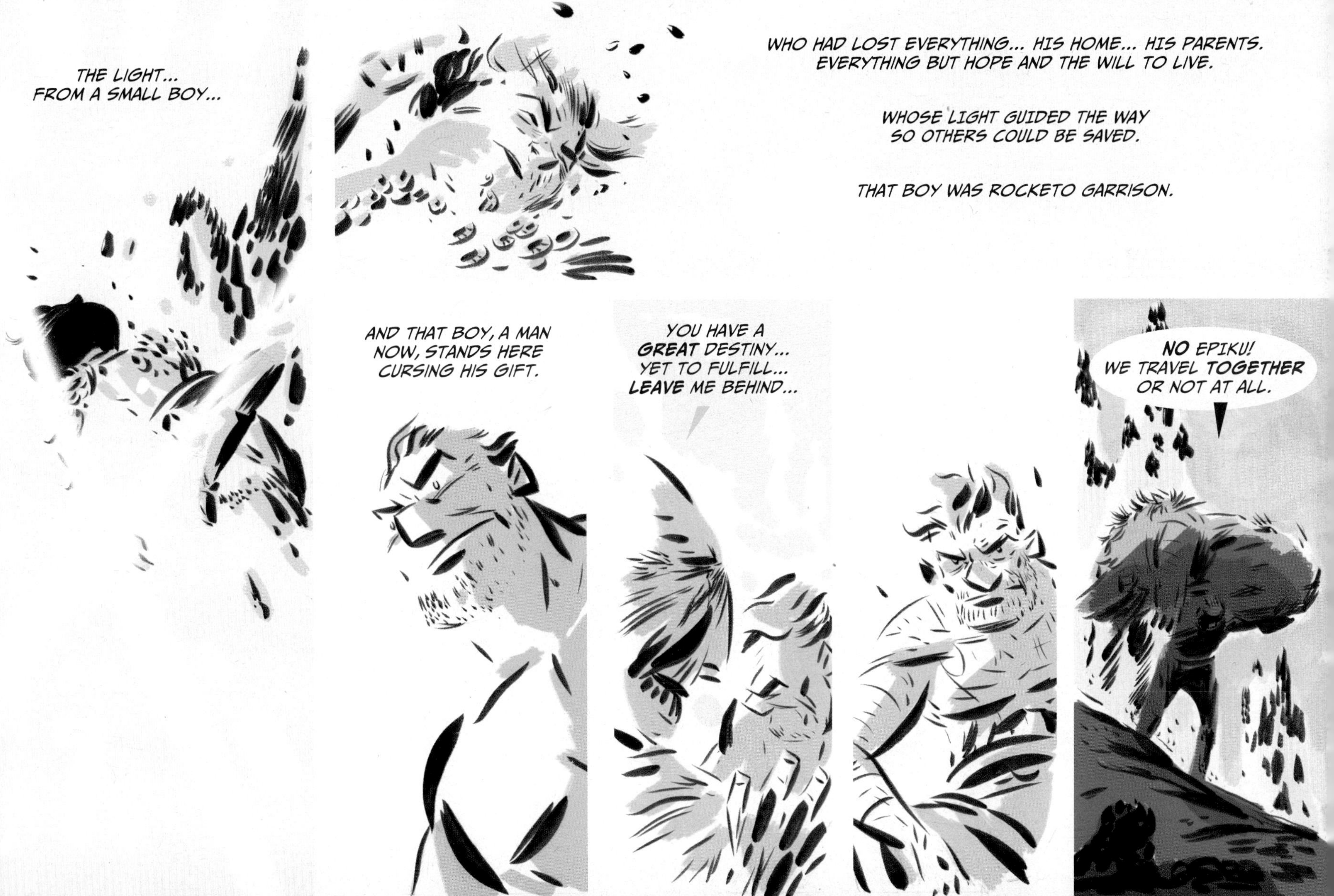
THE LIGHT... FROM A SMALL BOY...
WHO HAD LOST EVERYTHING... HIS HOME... HIS PARENTS. EVERYTHING BUT HOPE AND THE WILL TO LIVE.
WHOSE LIGHT GUIDED THE WAY SO OTHERS COULD BE SAVED.
THAT BOY WAS ROCKETO GARRISON.
AND THAT BOY, A MAN NOW, STANDS HERE CURSING HIS GIFT.
YOU HAVE A **GREAT** DESTINY... YET TO FULFILL... **LEAVE** ME BEHIND...
NO EPIKU! WE TRAVEL **TOGETHER** OR NOT AT ALL.

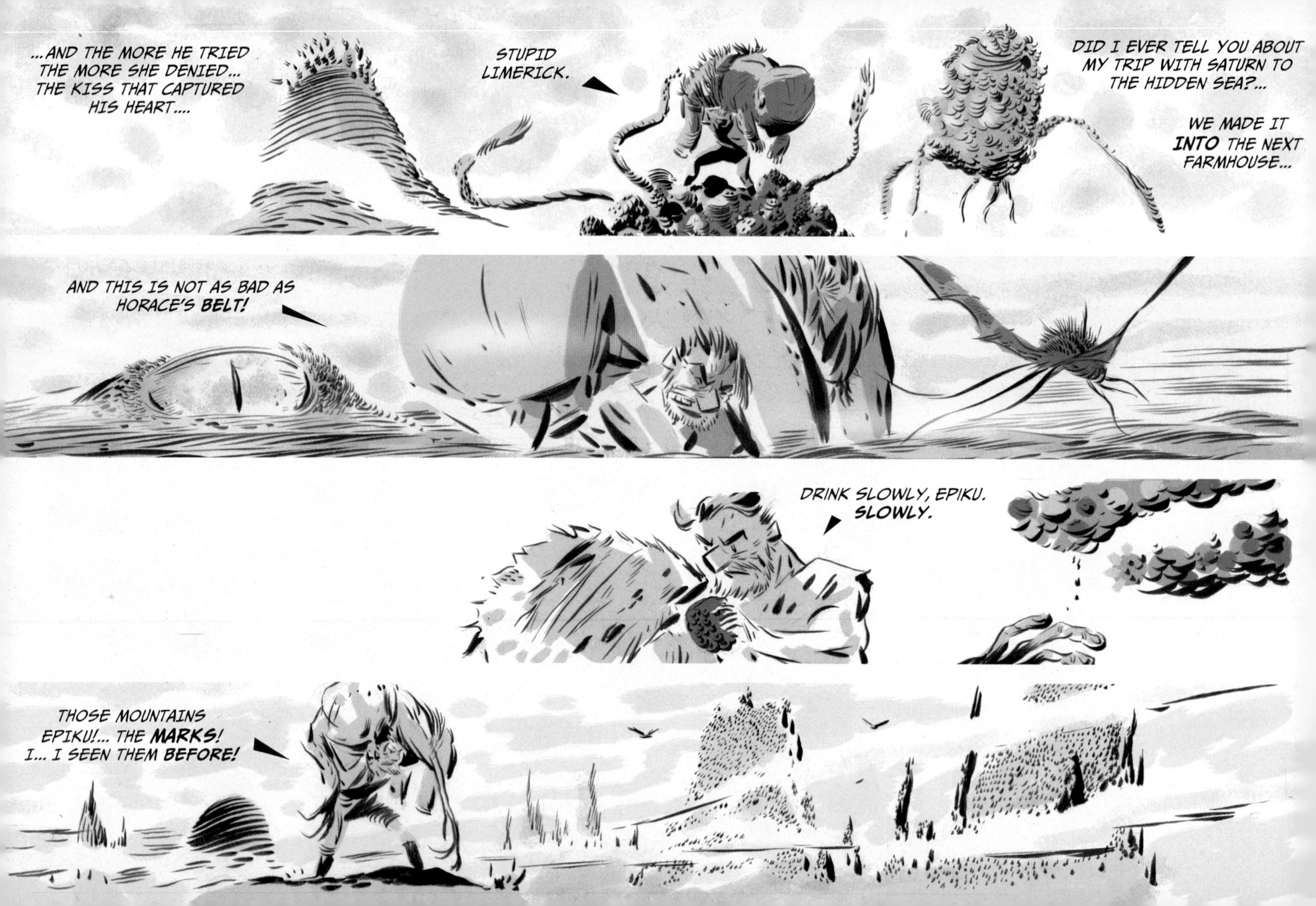
...AND THE MORE HE TRIED THE MORE SHE DENIED... THE KISS THAT CAPTURED HIS HEART....
STUPID LIMERICK.
DID I EVER TELL YOU ABOUT MY TRIP WITH SATURN TO THE HIDDEN SEA?...
WE MADE IT INTO THE NEXT FARMHOUSE...
AND THIS IS NOT AS BAD AS HORACE'S BELT!
DRINK SLOWLY, EPIKU. SLOWLY.
THOSE MOUNTAINS EPIKU!... THE MARKS! I... I SEEN THEM BEFORE!

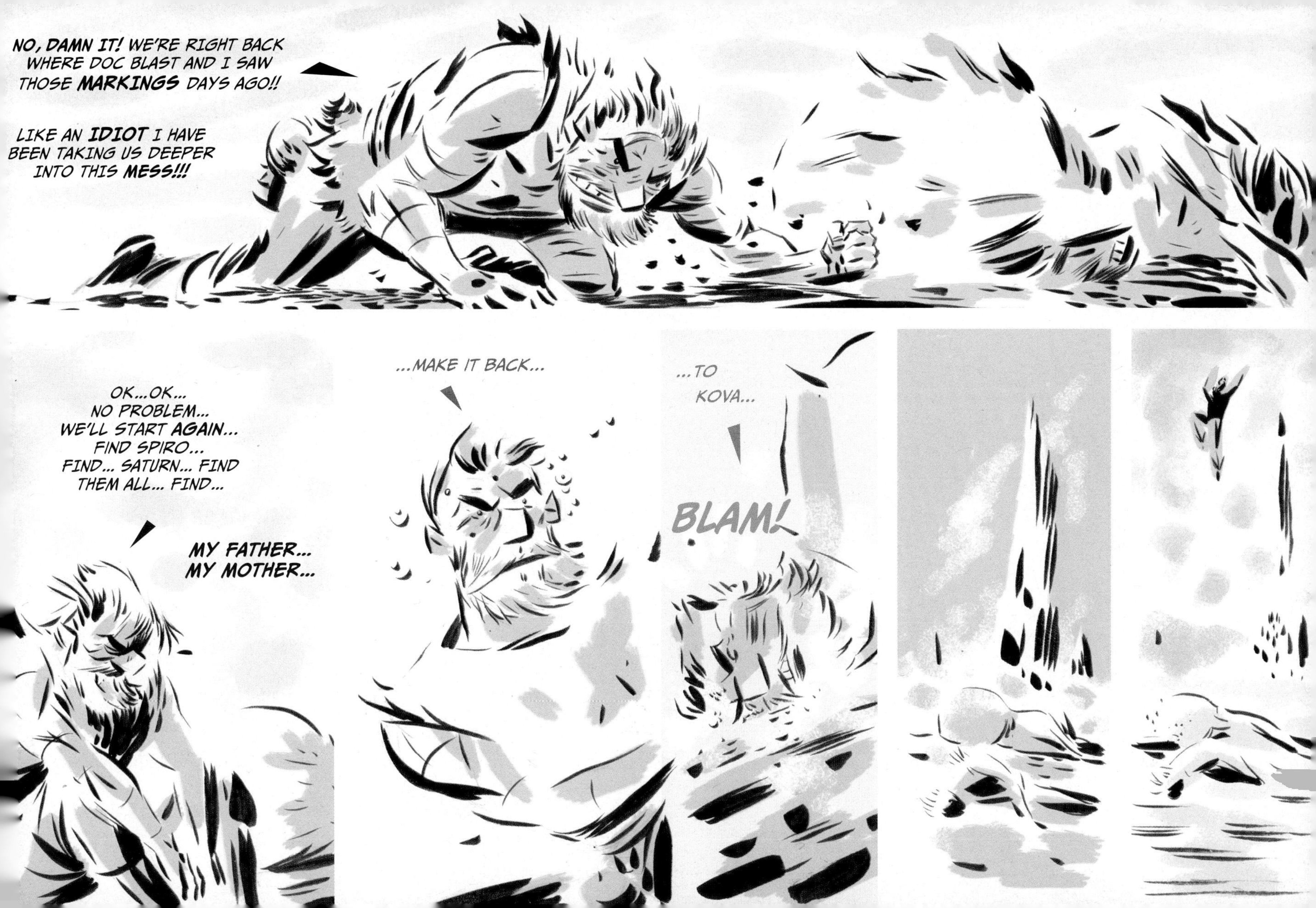
NO, DAMN IT! WE'RE RIGHT BACK WHERE DOC BLAST AND I SAW THOSE MARKINGS DAYS AGO!!
LIKE AN IDIOT I HAVE BEEN TAKING US DEEPER INTO THIS MESS!!!
OK...OK... NO PROBLEM... WE'LL START AGAIN... FIND SPIRO... FIND... SATURN... FIND THEM ALL... FIND...
MY FATHER... MY MOTHER...
...MAKE IT BACK...
...TO KOVA...
BLAM!

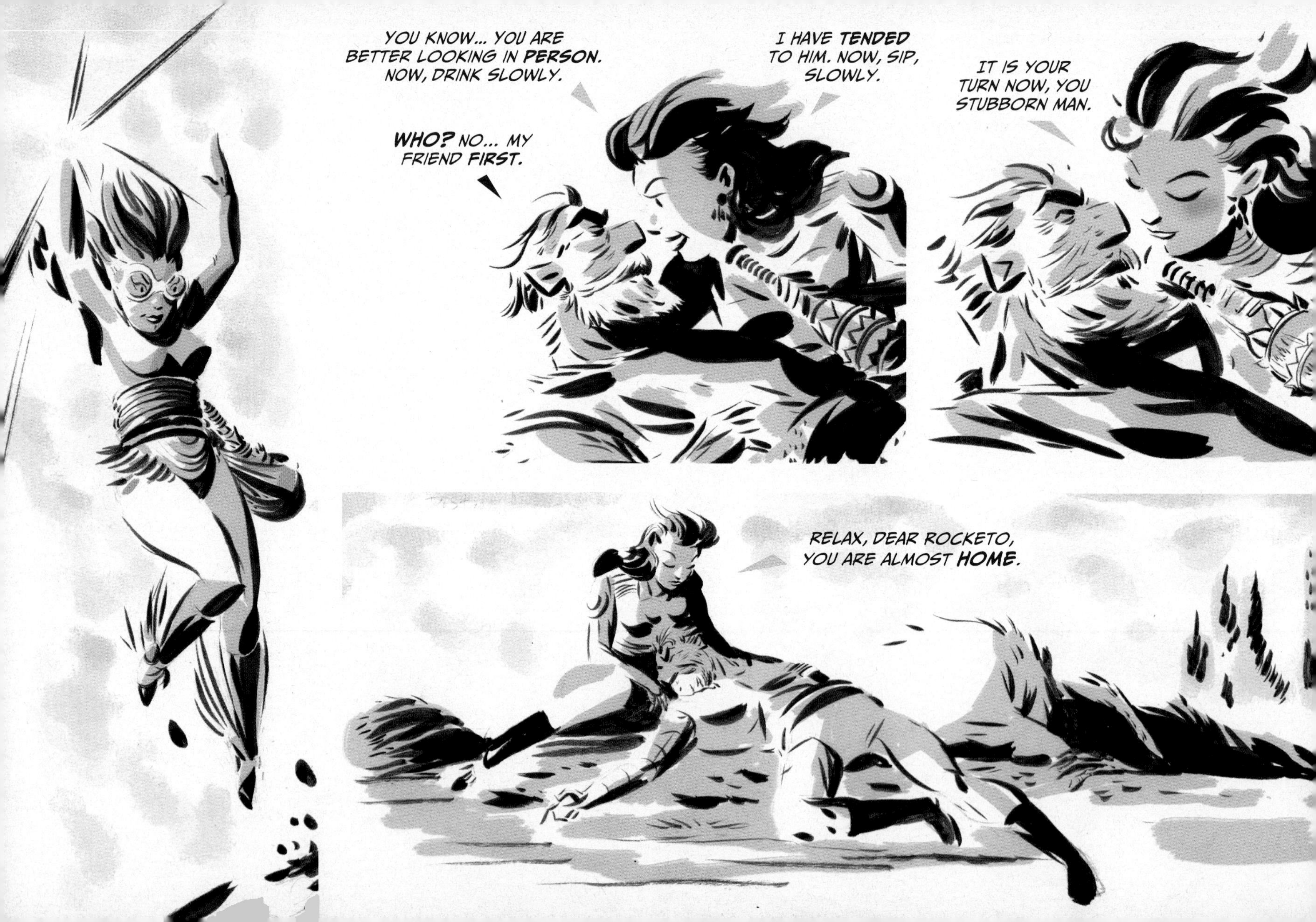
YOU KNOW... YOU ARE BETTER LOOKING IN PERSON. NOW, DRINK SLOWLY.
WHO? NO... MY FRIEND FIRST.
I HAVE TENDED TO HIM. NOW, SIP, SLOWLY.
IT IS YOUR TURN NOW, YOU STUBBORN MAN.
RELAX, DEAR ROCKETO, YOU ARE ALMOST HOME.

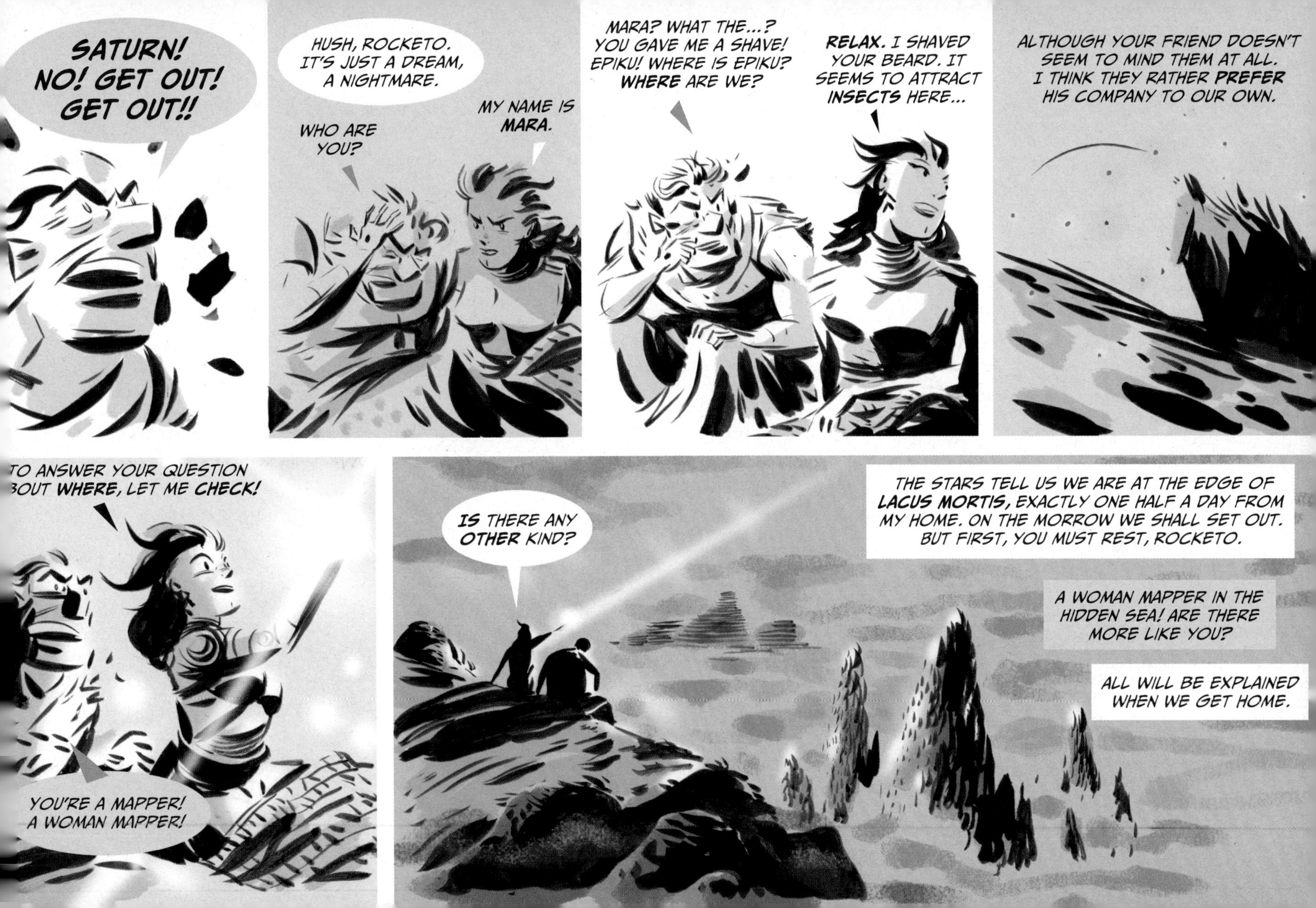
SATURN! NO! GET OUT! GET OUT!!
HUSH, ROCKETO. IT'S JUST A DREAM, A NIGHTMARE.
WHO ARE YOU?
MY NAME IS MARA.
MARA? WHAT THE...? YOU GAVE ME A SHAVE! EPIKU! WHERE IS EPIKU? WHERE ARE WE?
RELAX. I SHAVED YOUR BEARD. IT SEEMS TO ATTRACT INSECTS HERE...
ALTHOUGH YOUR FRIEND DOESN'T SEEM TO MIND THEM AT ALL. I THINK THEY RATHER PREFER HIS COMPANY TO OUR OWN.
TO ANSWER YOUR QUESTION BOUT WHERE, LET ME CHECK!
YOU'RE A MAPPER! A WOMAN MAPPER!
IS THERE ANY OTHER KIND?
THE STARS TELL US WE ARE AT THE EDGE OF LACUS MORTIS, EXACTLY ONE HALF A DAY FROM MY HOME. ON THE MORROW WE SHALL SET OUT. BUT FIRST, YOU MUST REST, ROCKETO.
A WOMAN MAPPER IN THE HIDDEN SEA! ARE THERE MORE LIKE YOU?
ALL WILL BE EXPLAINED WHEN WE GET HOME.

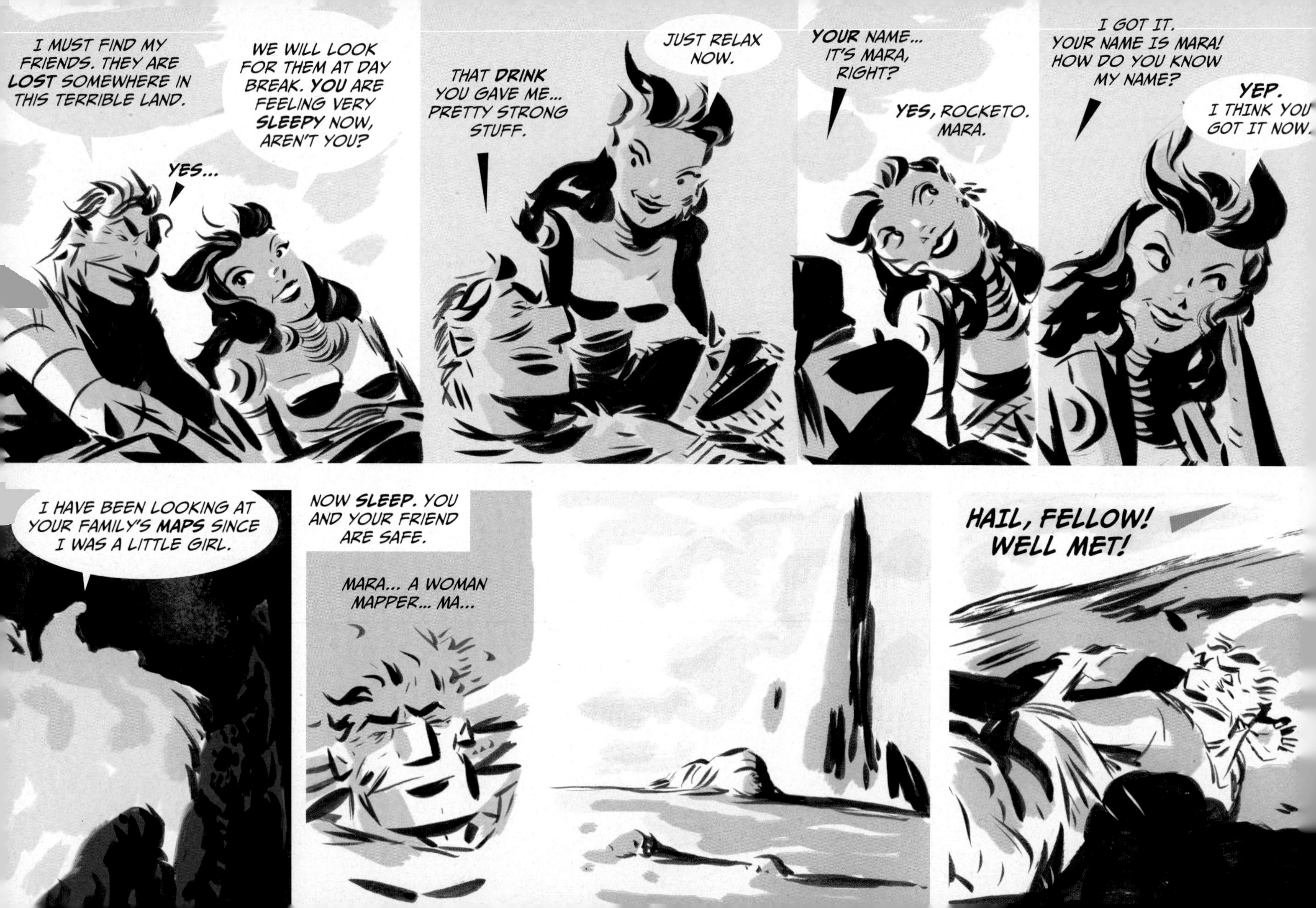

I MUST FIND MY FRIENDS. THEY ARE LOST SOMEWHERE IN THIS TERRIBLE LAND.
WE WILL LOOK FOR THEM AT DAY BREAK. YOU ARE FEELING VERY SLEEPY NOW, AREN'T YOU?
YES...
THAT DRINK YOU GAVE ME... PRETTY STRONG STUFF.
JUST RELAX NOW.
YOUR NAME... IT'S MARA, RIGHT?
YES, ROCKETO. MARA.
I GOT IT. YOUR NAME IS MARA! HOW DO YOU KNOW MY NAME?
YEP. I THINK YOU GOT IT NOW.
I HAVE BEEN LOOKING AT YOUR FAMILY'S MAPS SINCE I WAS A LITTLE GIRL.
NOW SLEEP. YOU AND YOUR FRIEND ARE SAFE.
MARA... A WOMAN MAPPER... MA...
HAIL, FELLOW! WELL MET!

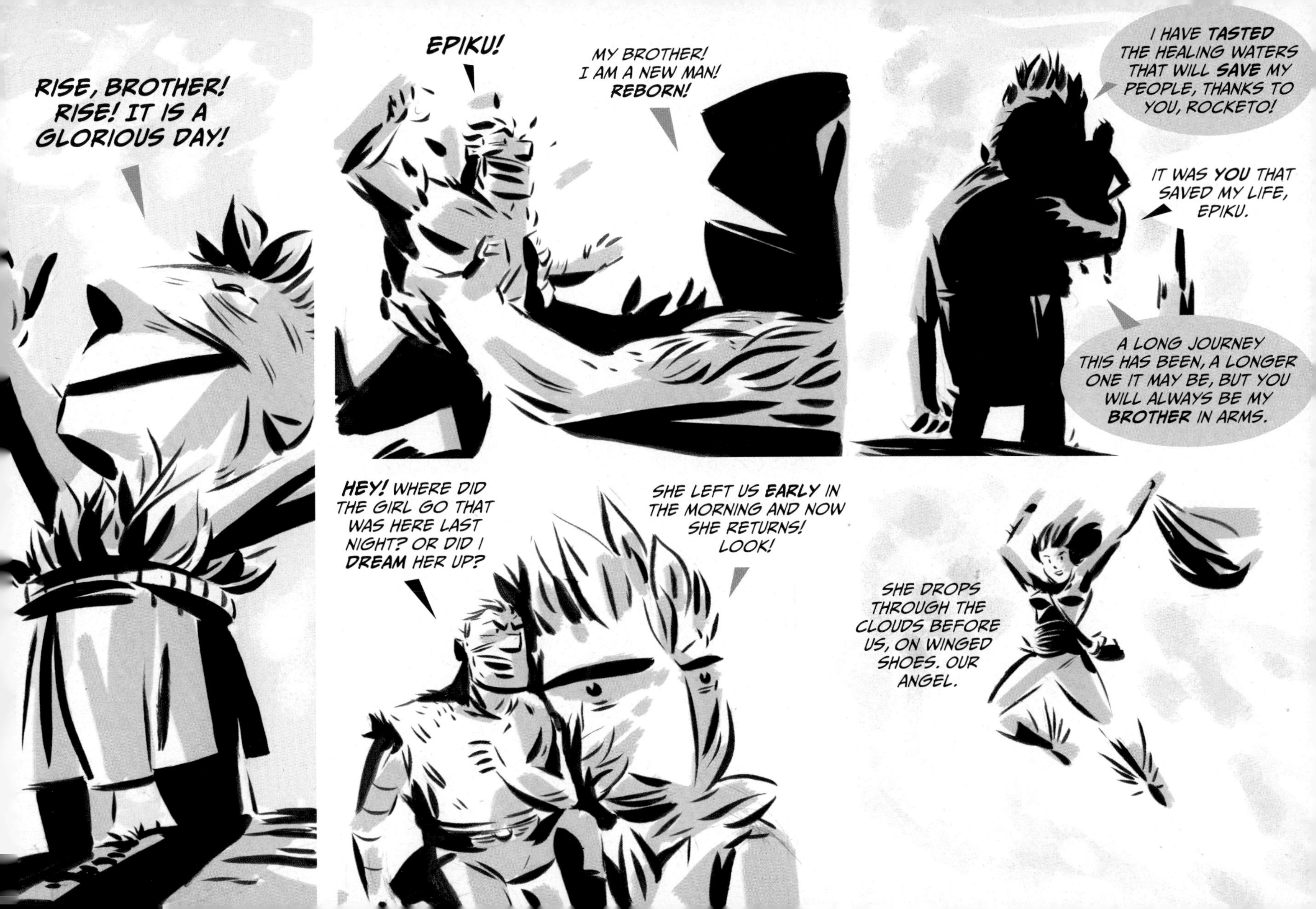
RISE, BROTHER! RISE! IT IS A GLORIOUS DAY!
EPIKU!
MY BROTHER! I AM A NEW MAN! REBORN!
I HAVE TASTED THE HEALING WATERS THAT WILL SAVE MY PEOPLE, THANKS TO YOU, ROCKETO!
IT WAS YOU THAT SAVED MY LIFE, EPIKU.
A LONG JOURNEY THIS HAS BEEN, A LONGER ONE IT MAY BE, BUT YOU WILL ALWAYS BE MY BROTHER IN ARMS.
HEY! WHERE DID THE GIRL GO THAT WAS HERE LAST NIGHT? OR DID I DREAM HER UP?
SHE LEFT US EARLY IN THE MORNING AND NOW SHE RETURNS! LOOK!
SHE DROPS THROUGH THE CLOUDS BEFORE US, ON WINGED SHOES. OUR ANGEL.

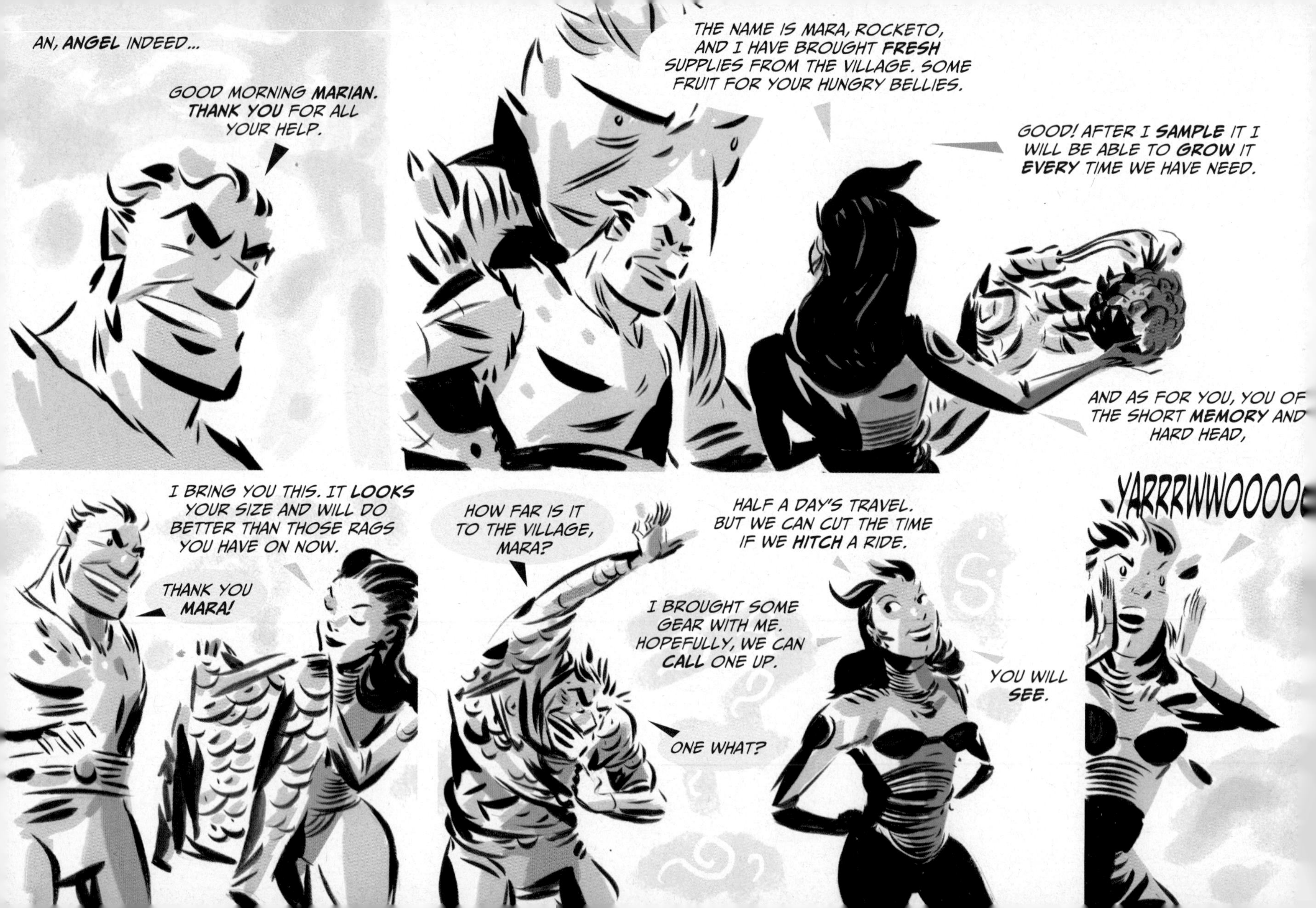

AN, ANGEL INDEED...
GOOD MORNING MARIAN. THANK YOU FOR ALL YOUR HELP.
THE NAME IS MARA, ROCKETO, AND I HAVE BROUGHT FRESH SUPPLIES FROM THE VILLAGE. SOME FRUIT FOR YOUR HUNGRY BELLIES.
GOOD! AFTER I SAMPLE IT I WILL BE ABLE TO GROW IT EVERY TIME WE HAVE NEED.
AND AS FOR YOU, YOU OF THE SHORT MEMORY AND HARD HEAD,
I BRING YOU THIS. IT LOOKS YOUR SIZE AND WILL DO BETTER THAN THOSE RAGS YOU HAVE ON NOW.
THANK YOU MARA!
HOW FAR IS IT TO THE VILLAGE, MARA?
HALF A DAY'S TRAVEL. BUT WE CAN CUT THE TIME IF WE HITCH A RIDE.
I BROUGHT SOME GEAR WITH ME. HOPEFULLY, WE CAN CALL ONE UP.
ONE WHAT?
YOU WILL SEE.
YARRRWWOOOOO

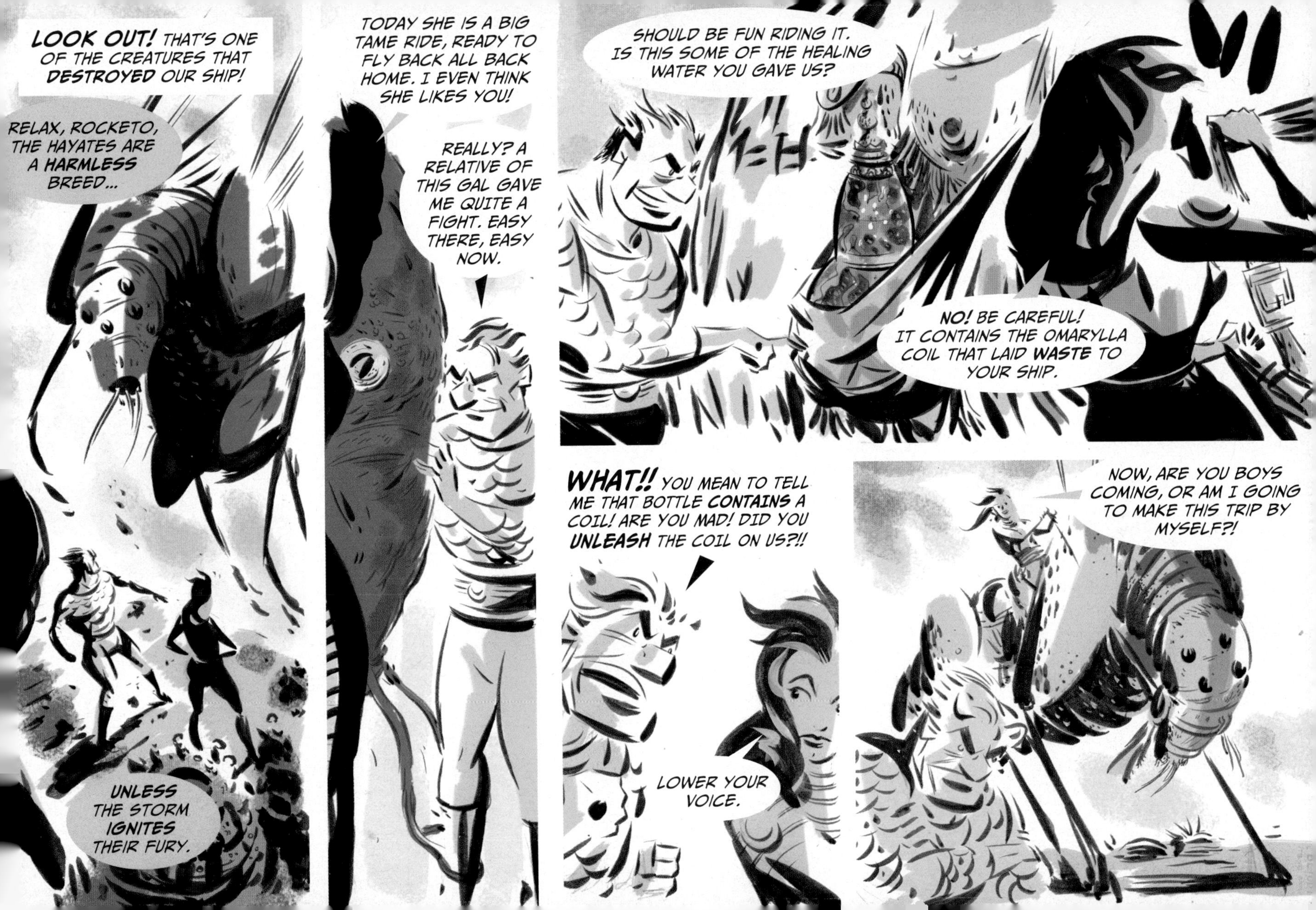

LOOK OUT! THAT'S ONE OF THE CREATURES THAT DESTROYED OUR SHIP!
RELAX, ROCKETO, THE HAYATES ARE A HARMLESS BREED...
UNLESS THE STORM IGNITES THEIR FURY.
TODAY SHE IS A BIG TAME RIDE, READY TO FLY BACK ALL BACK HOME. I EVEN THINK SHE LIKES YOU!
REALLY? A RELATIVE OF THIS GAL GAVE ME QUITE A FIGHT. EASY THERE, EASY NOW.
SHOULD BE FUN RIDING IT. IS THIS SOME OF THE HEALING WATER YOU GAVE US?
NO! BE CAREFUL! IT CONTAINS THE OMARYLLA COIL THAT LAID WASTE TO YOUR SHIP.
WHAT!! YOU MEAN TO TELL ME THAT BOTTLE CONTAINS A COIL! ARE YOU MAD! DID YOU UNLEASH THE COIL ON US?!!
LOWER YOUR VOICE.
NOW, ARE YOU BOYS COMING, OR AM I GOING TO MAKE THIS TRIP BY MYSELF?!

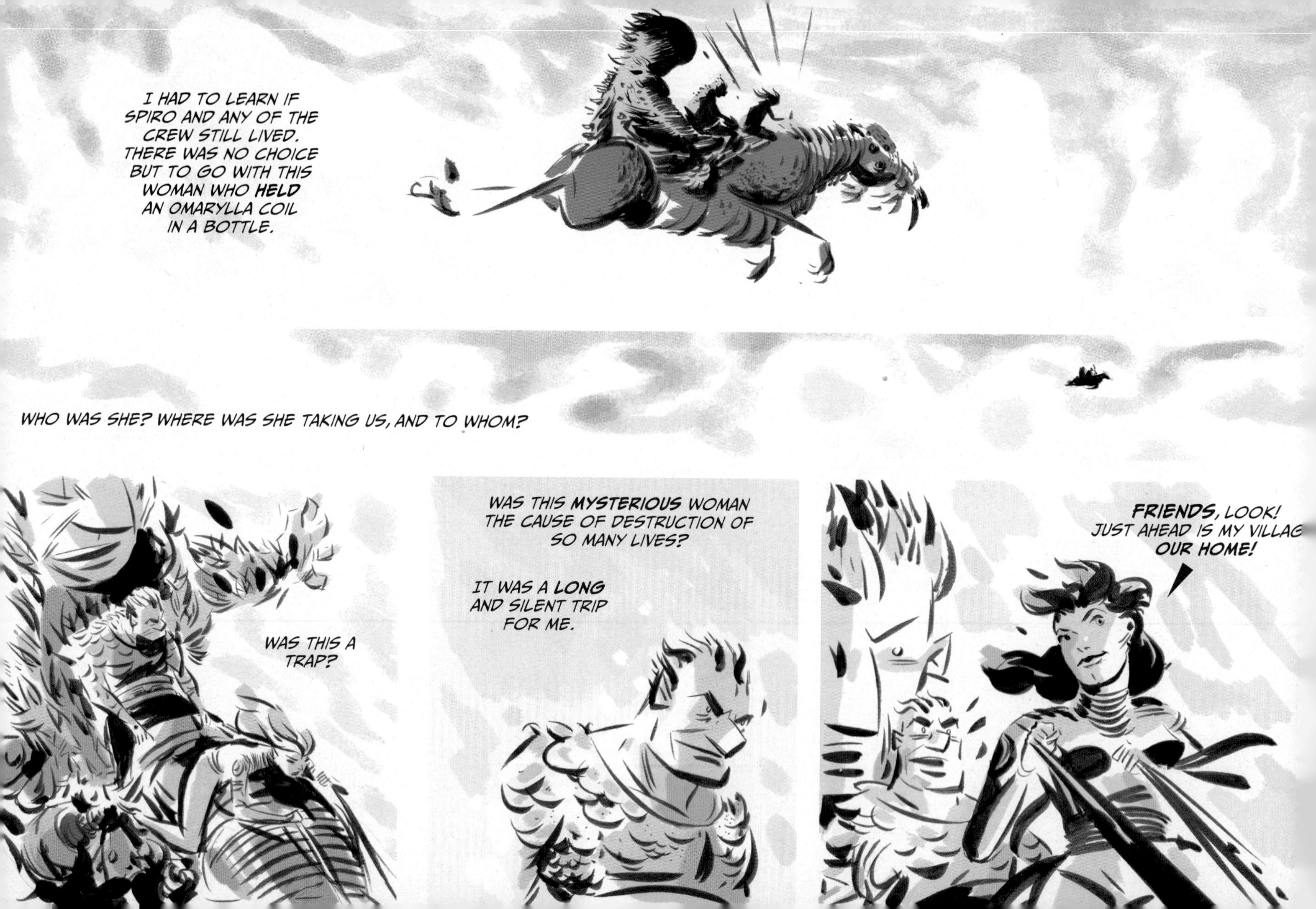
I HAD TO LEARN IF SPIRO AND ANY OF THE CREW STILL LIVED. THERE WAS NO CHOICE BUT TO GO WITH THIS WOMAN WHO **HELD** AN OMARYLLA COIL IN A BOTTLE.
WHO WAS SHE? WHERE WAS SHE TAKING US, AND TO WHOM?
WAS THIS A TRAP?
WAS THIS **MYSTERIOUS** WOMAN THE CAUSE OF DESTRUCTION OF SO MANY LIVES?
IT WAS A **LONG** AND SILENT TRIP FOR ME.
FRIENDS, LOOK! JUST AHEAD IS MY VILLAG
OUR HOME!

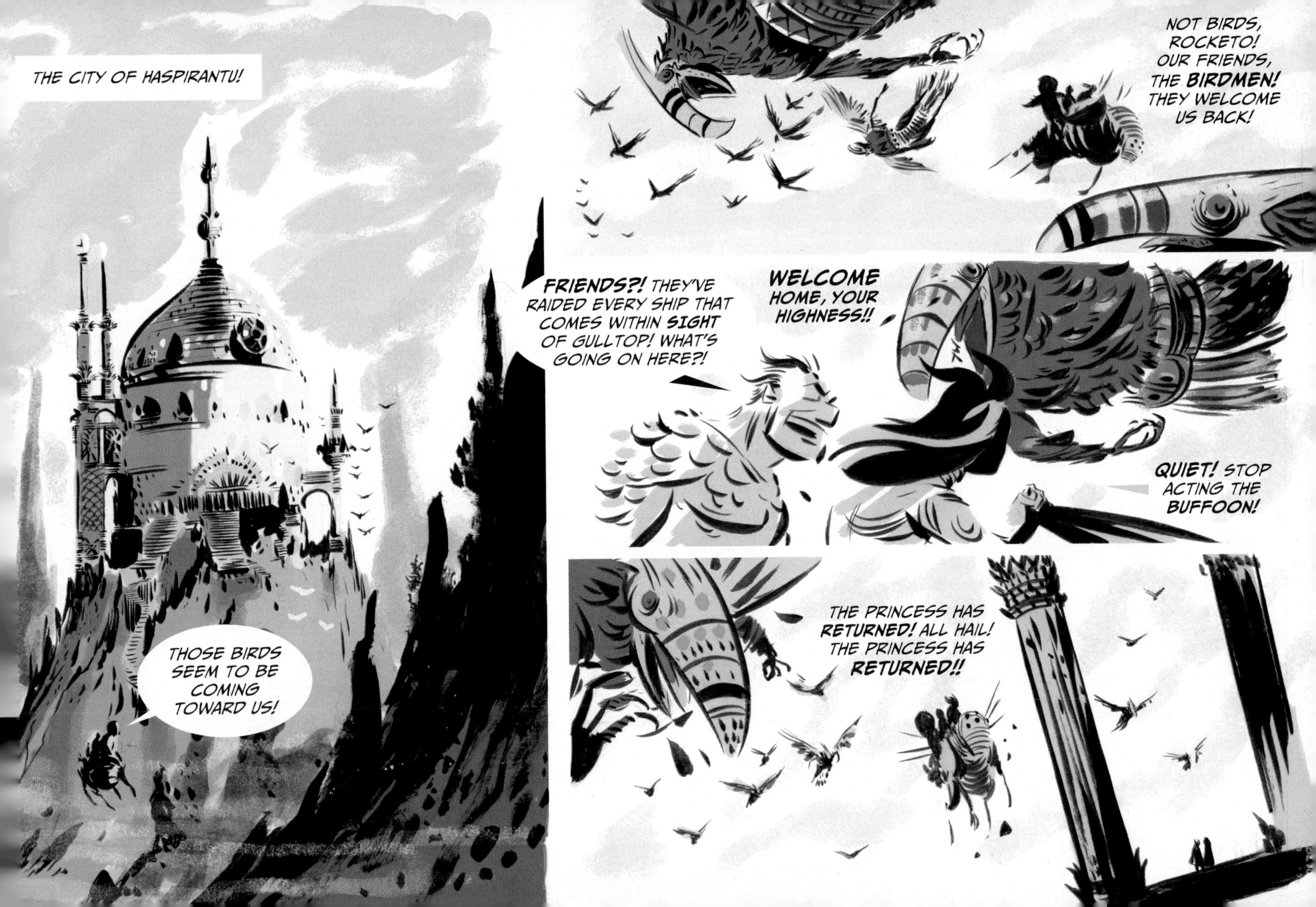
THE CITY OF HASPIRANTU!
THOSE BIRDS SEEM TO BE COMING TOWARD US!
NOT BIRDS, ROCKETO! OUR FRIENDS, THE BIRDMEN! THEY WELCOME US BACK!
FRIENDS?! THEY'VE RAIDED EVERY SHIP THAT COMES WITHIN SIGHT OF GULLTOP! WHAT'S GOING ON HERE?!
WELCOME HOME, YOUR HIGHNESS!!
QUIET! STOP ACTING THE BUFFOON!
THE PRINCESS HAS RETURNED! ALL HAIL! THE PRINCESS HAS RETURNED!!

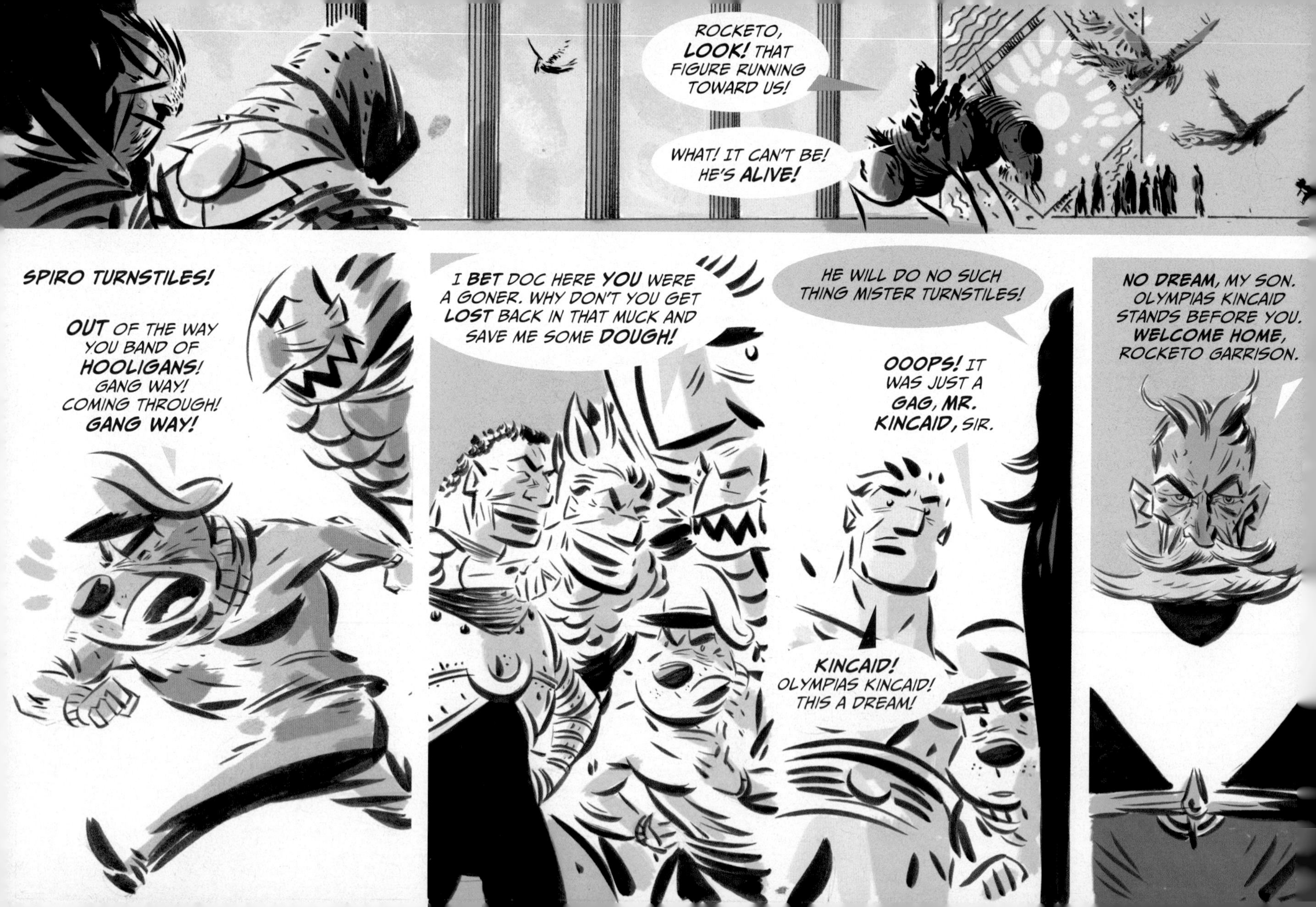
ROCKETO, LOOK! THAT FIGURE RUNNING TOWARD US!
WHAT! IT CAN'T BE! HE'S ALIVE!
SPIRO TURNSTILES!
OUT OF THE WAY YOU BAND OF HOOLIGANS! GANG WAY! COMING THROUGH! GANG WAY!
I BET DOC HERE YOU WERE A GONER. WHY DON'T YOU GET LOST BACK IN THAT MUCK AND SAVE ME SOME DOUGH!
HE WILL DO NO SUCH THING MISTER TURNSTILES!
OOOPS! IT WAS JUST A GAG, MR. KINCAID, SIR.
KINCAID! OLYMPIAS KINCAID! THIS A DREAM!
NO DREAM, MY SON. OLYMPIAS KINCAID STANDS BEFORE YOU. WELCOME HOME, ROCKETO GARRISON.

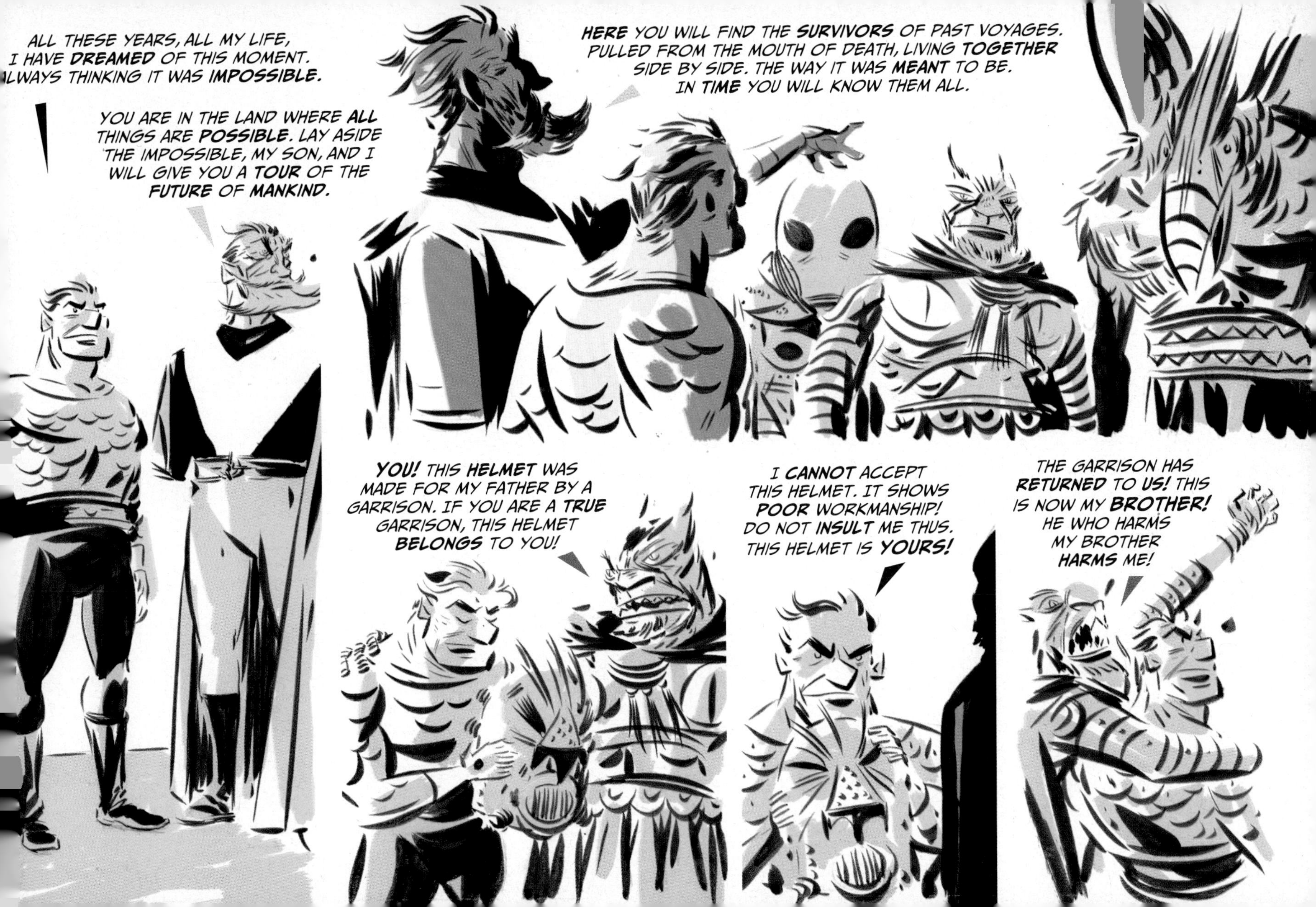
ALL THESE YEARS, ALL MY LIFE, I HAVE DREAMED OF THIS MOMENT. ALWAYS THINKING IT WAS IMPOSSIBLE.
YOU ARE IN THE LAND WHERE ALL THINGS ARE POSSIBLE. LAY ASIDE THE IMPOSSIBLE, MY SON, AND I WILL GIVE YOU A TOUR OF THE FUTURE OF MANKIND.
HERE YOU WILL FIND THE SURVIVORS OF PAST VOYAGES. PULLED FROM THE MOUTH OF DEATH, LIVING TOGETHER SIDE BY SIDE. THE WAY IT WAS MEANT TO BE. IN TIME YOU WILL KNOW THEM ALL.
YOU! THIS HELMET WAS MADE FOR MY FATHER BY A GARRISON. IF YOU ARE A TRUE GARRISON, THIS HELMET BELONGS TO YOU!
I CANNOT ACCEPT THIS HELMET. IT SHOWS POOR WORKMANSHIP! DO NOT INSULT ME THUS. THIS HELMET IS YOURS!
THE GARRISON HAS RETURNED TO US! THIS IS NOW MY BROTHER! HE WHO HARMS MY BROTHER HARMS ME!

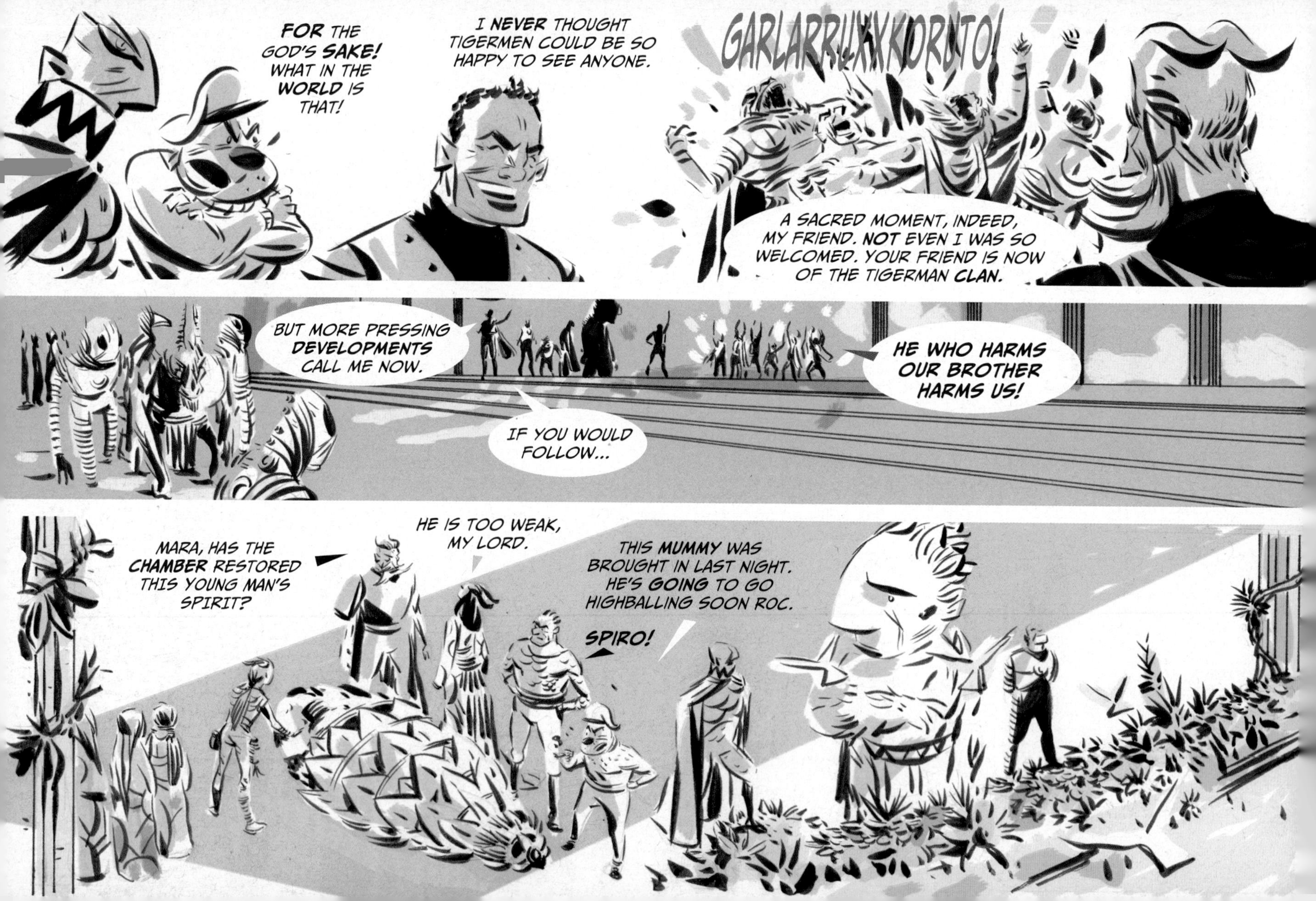
FOR THE GOD'S SAKE! WHAT IN THE WORLD IS THAT!
I NEVER THOUGHT TIGERMEN COULD BE SO HAPPY TO SEE ANYONE.
GARLARRUXXKORUTO!
A SACRED MOMENT, INDEED, MY FRIEND. NOT EVEN I WAS SO WELCOMED. YOUR FRIEND IS NOW OF THE TIGERMAN CLAN.
BUT MORE PRESSING DEVELOPMENTS CALL ME NOW.
IF YOU WOULD FOLLOW...
HE WHO HARMS OUR BROTHER HARMS US!
MARA, HAS THE CHAMBER RESTORED THIS YOUNG MAN'S SPIRIT?
HE IS TOO WEAK, MY LORD.
THIS MUMMY WAS BROUGHT IN LAST NIGHT. HE'S GOING TO GO HIGHBALLING SOON ROC.
SPIRO!

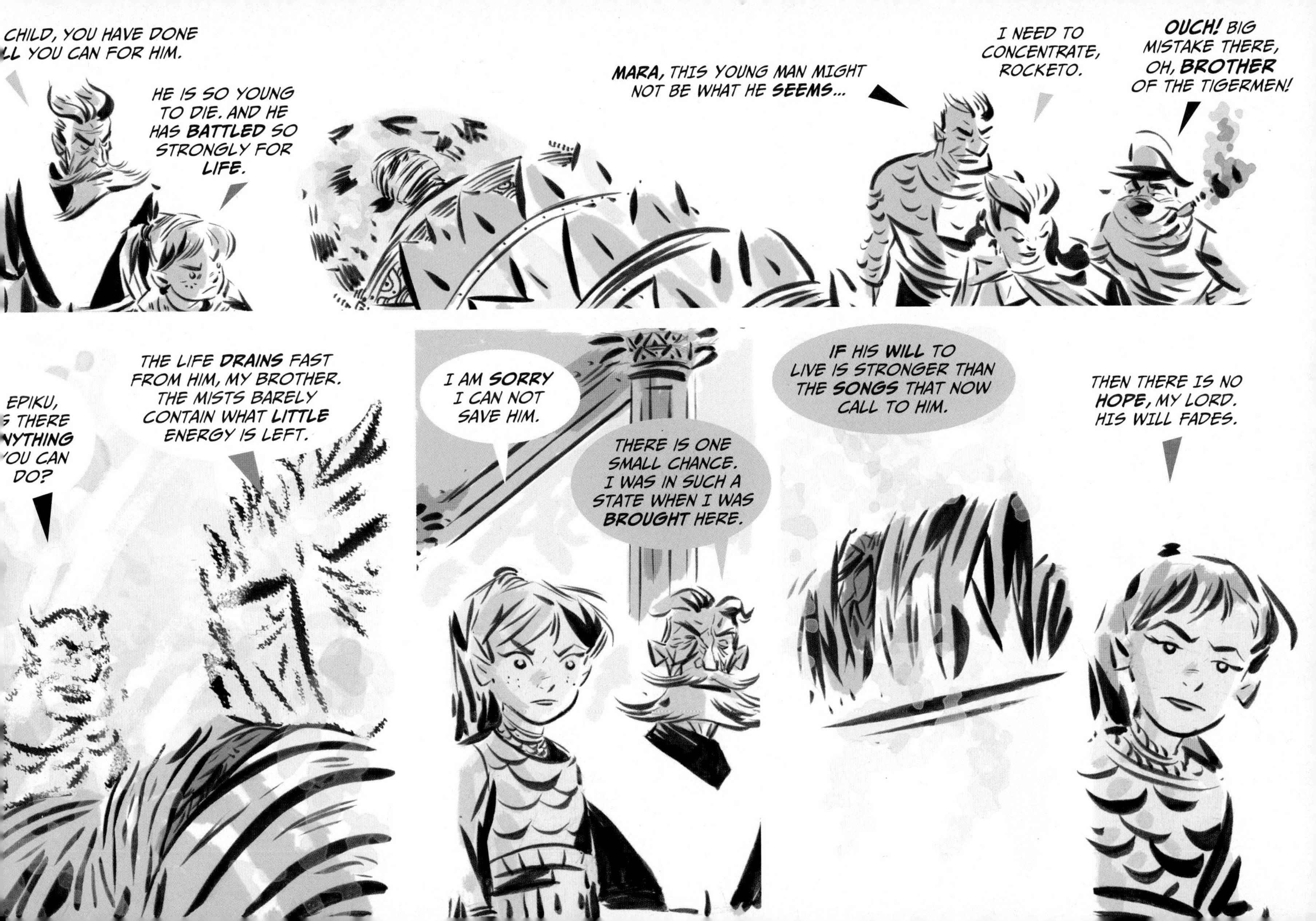
CHILD, YOU HAVE DONE
LL YOU CAN FOR HIM.
HE IS SO YOUNG TO DIE. AND HE HAS BATTLED SO STRONGLY FOR LIFE.
MARA, THIS YOUNG MAN MIGHT NOT BE WHAT HE SEEMS...
I NEED TO CONCENTRATE, ROCKETO.
OUCH! BIG MISTAKE THERE, OH, BROTHER OF THE TIGERMEN!
EPIKU, S THERE NYTHING YOU CAN DO?
THE LIFE DRAINS FAST FROM HIM, MY BROTHER. THE MISTS BARELY CONTAIN WHAT LITTLE ENERGY IS LEFT.
I AM SORRY I CAN NOT SAVE HIM.
THERE IS ONE SMALL CHANCE. I WAS IN SUCH A STATE WHEN I WAS BROUGHT HERE.
IF HIS WILL TO LIVE IS STRONGER THAN THE SONGS THAT NOW CALL TO HIM.
THEN THERE IS NO HOPE, MY LORD. HIS WILL FADES.

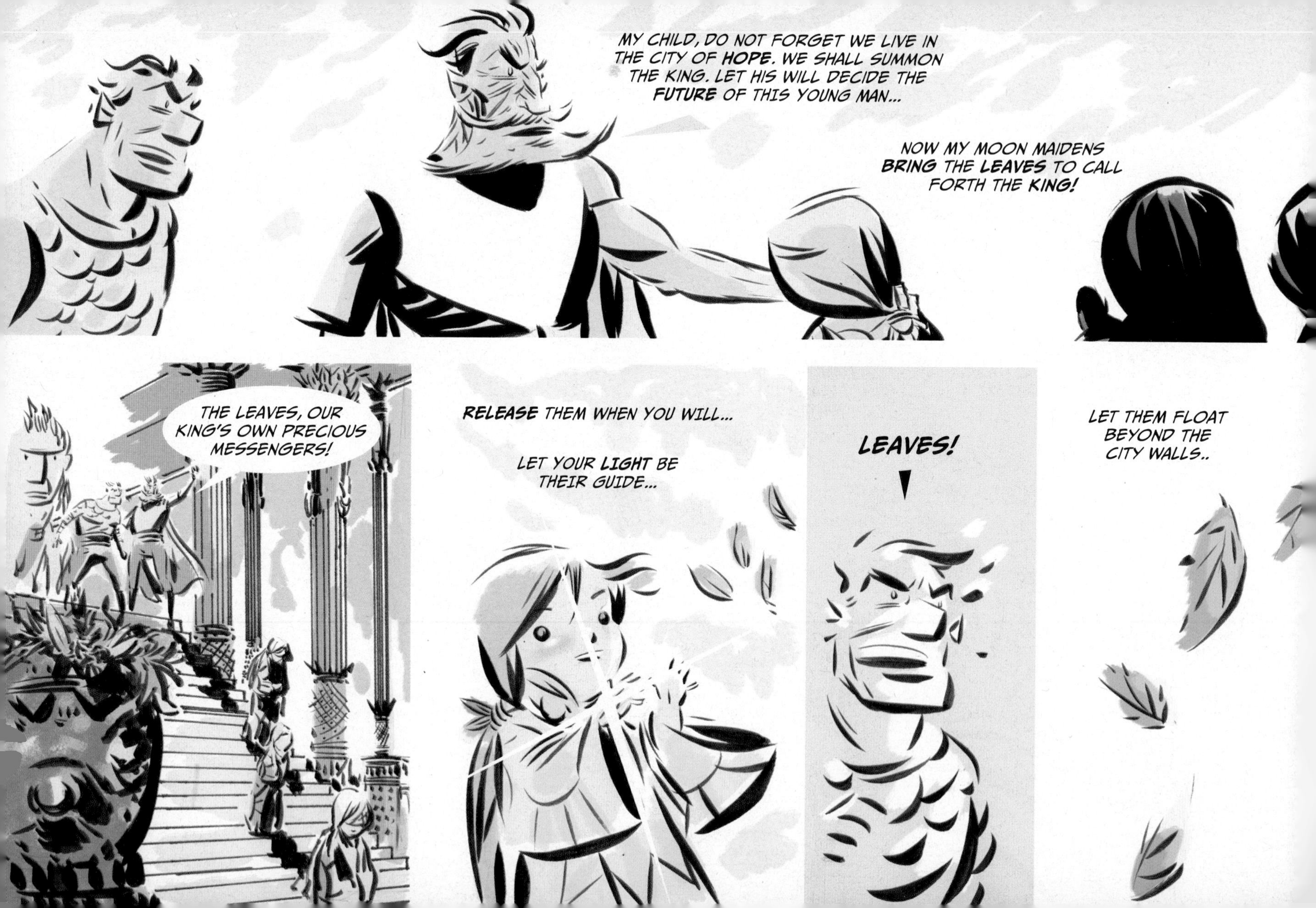
MY CHILD, DO NOT FORGET WE LIVE IN THE CITY OF HOPE. WE SHALL SUMMON THE KING. LET HIS WILL DECIDE THE FUTURE OF THIS YOUNG MAN...
NOW MY MOON MAIDENS BRING THE LEAVES TO CALL FORTH THE KING!
THE LEAVES, OUR KING'S OWN PRECIOUS MESSENGERS!
RELEASE THEM WHEN YOU WILL...
LET YOUR LIGHT BE THEIR GUIDE...
LEAVES!
LET THEM FLOAT BEYOND THE CITY WALLS..

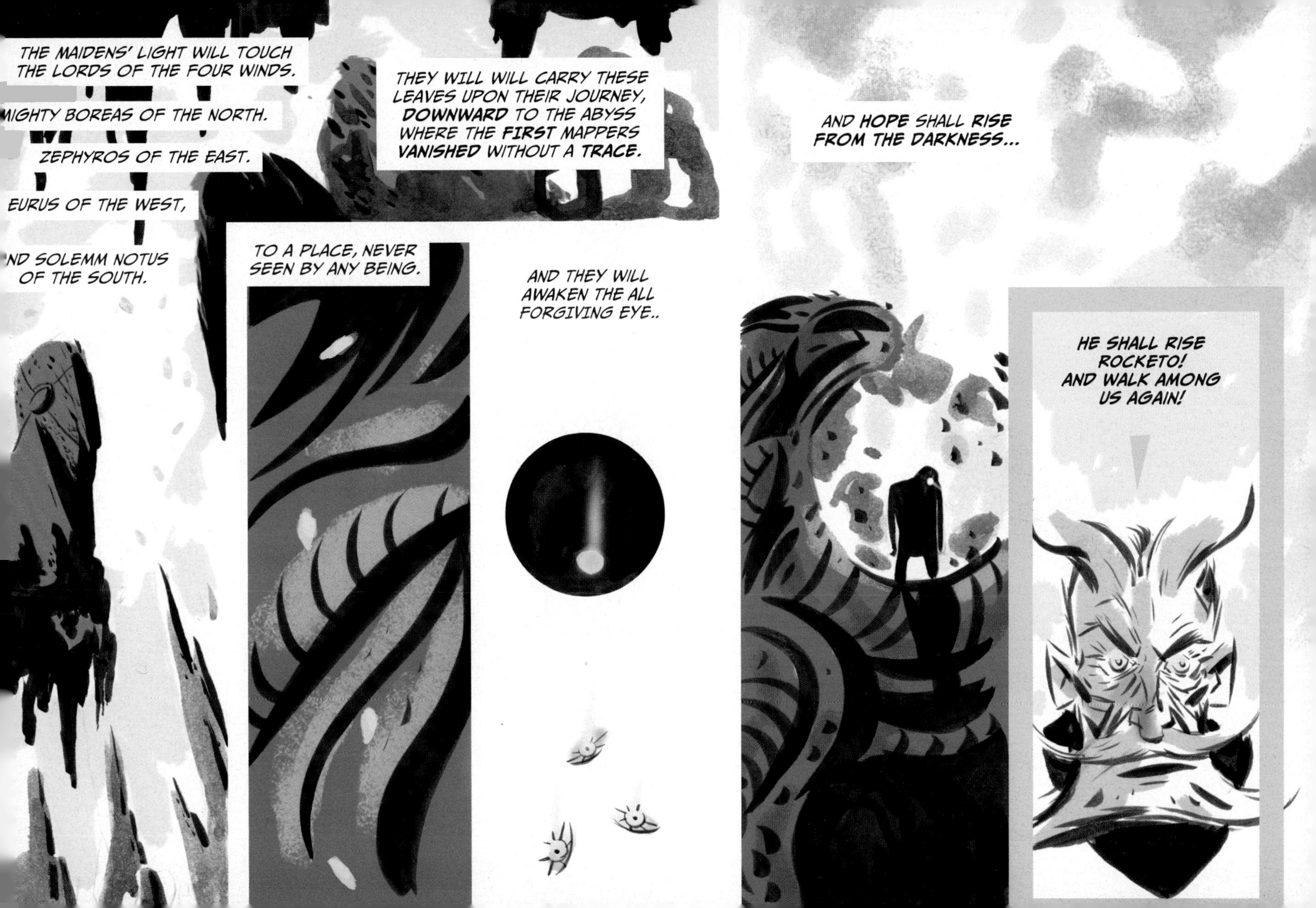
THE MAIDENS' LIGHT WILL TOUCH THE LORDS OF THE FOUR WINDS.
MIGHTY BOREAS OF THE NORTH.
ZEPHYROS OF THE EAST.
EURUS OF THE WEST,
ND SOLEMM NOTUS OF THE SOUTH.
THEY WILL WILL CARRY THESE LEAVES UPON THEIR JOURNEY, DOWNWARD TO THE ABYSS WHERE THE FIRST MAPPERS VANISHED WITHOUT A TRACE.
TO A PLACE, NEVER SEEN BY ANY BEING.
AND THEY WILL AWAKEN THE ALL FORGIVING EYE..
AND HOPE SHALL RISE FROM THE DARKNESS...
HE SHALL RISE ROCKETO! AND WALK AMONG US AGAIN!

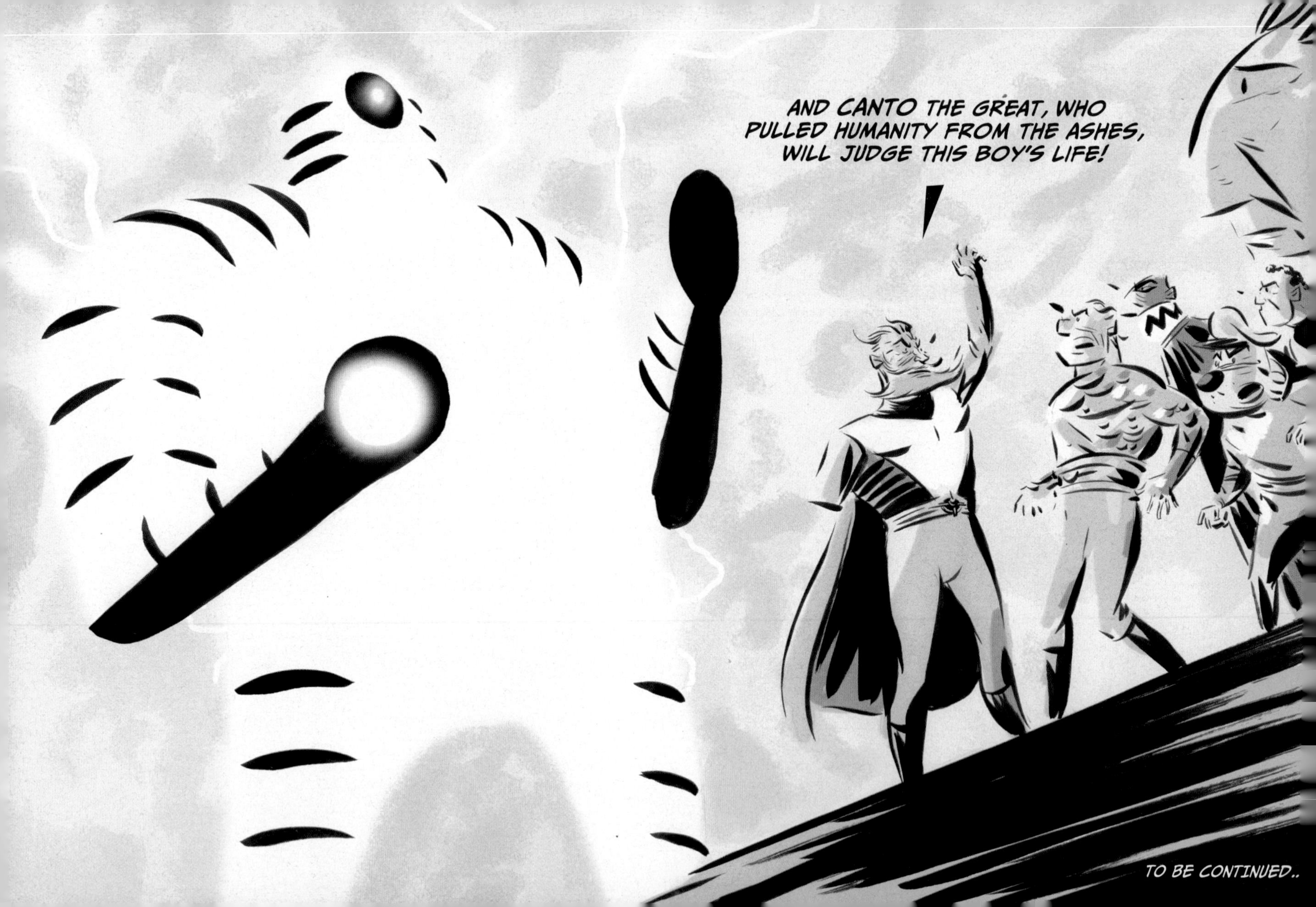
AND CANTO THE GREAT, WHO PULLED HUMANITY FROM THE ASHES, WILL JUDGE THIS BOY'S LIFE!
TO BE CONTINUED..

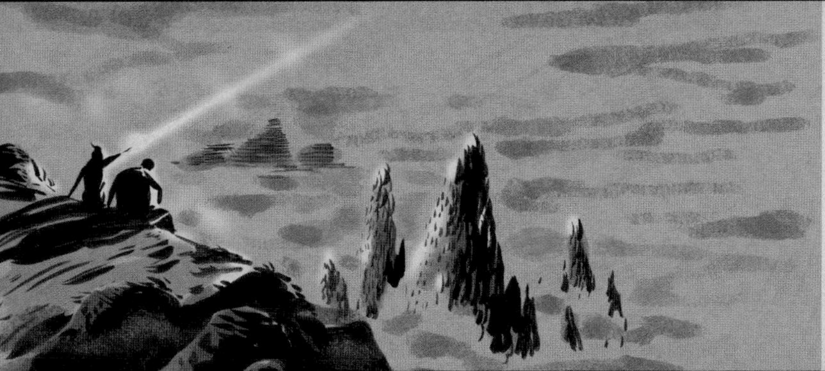

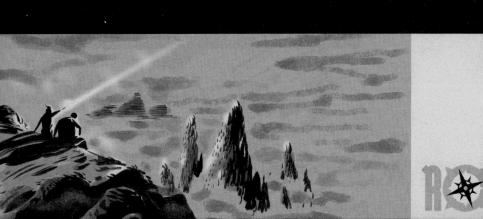

ROCKETO

8

REVELATIONS

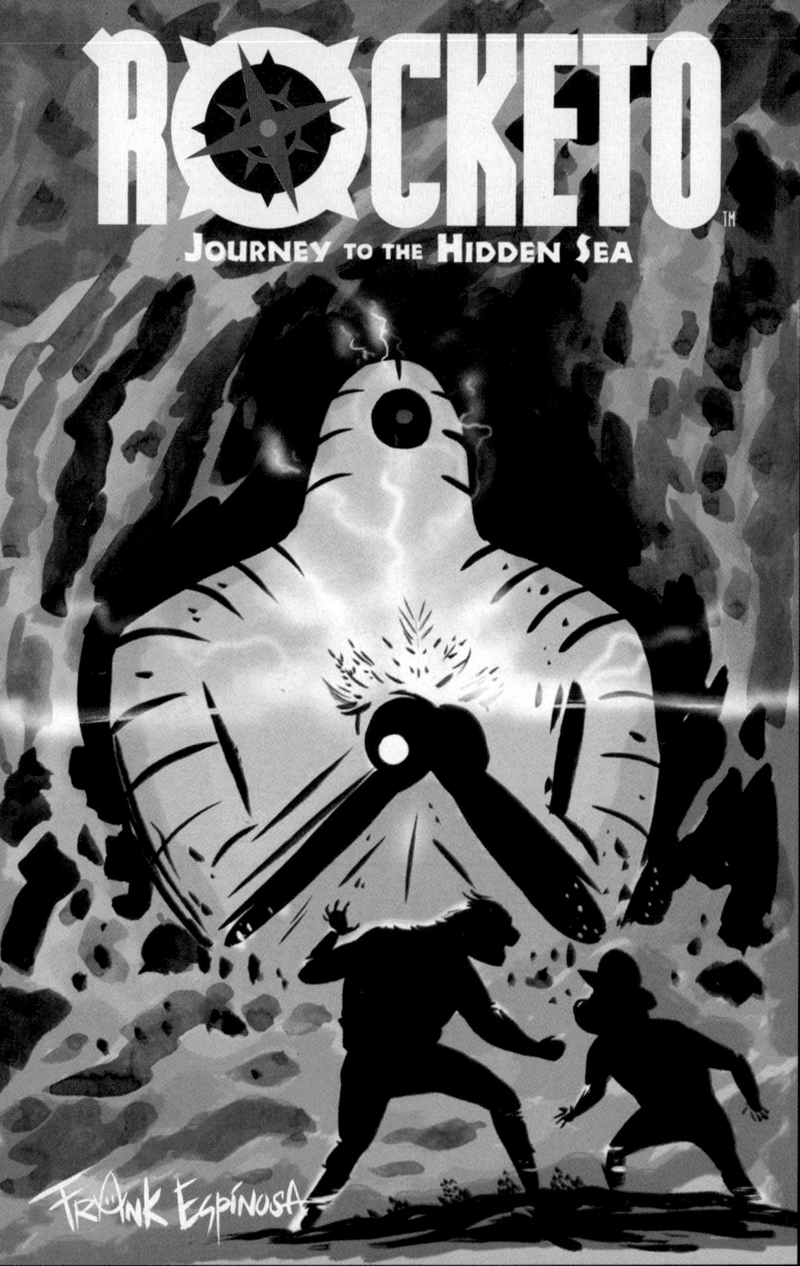
ROCKETO™
JOURNEY TO THE HIDDEN SEA
FRANK ESPINOSA

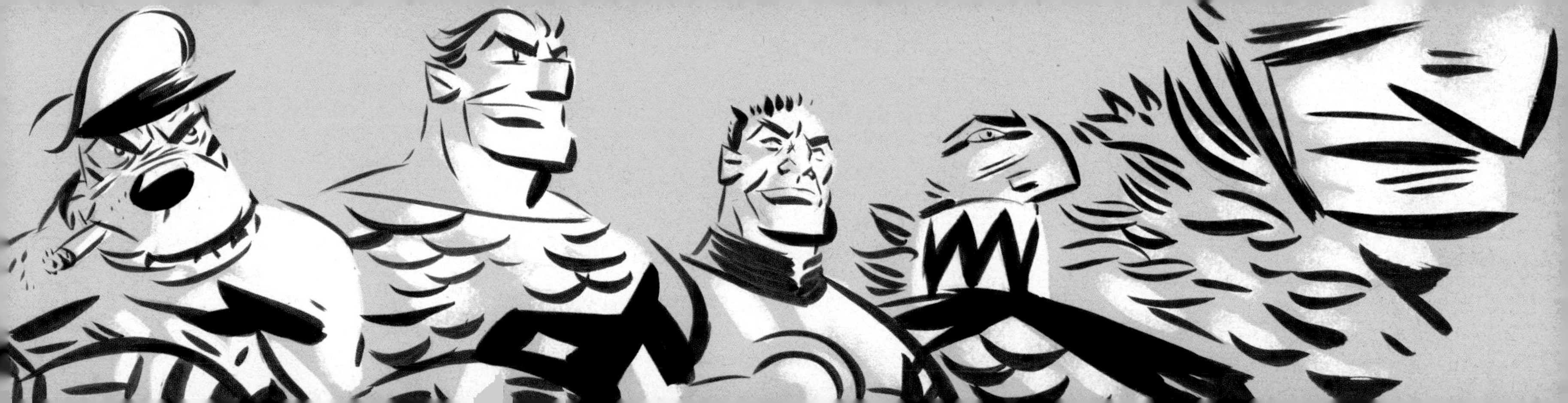

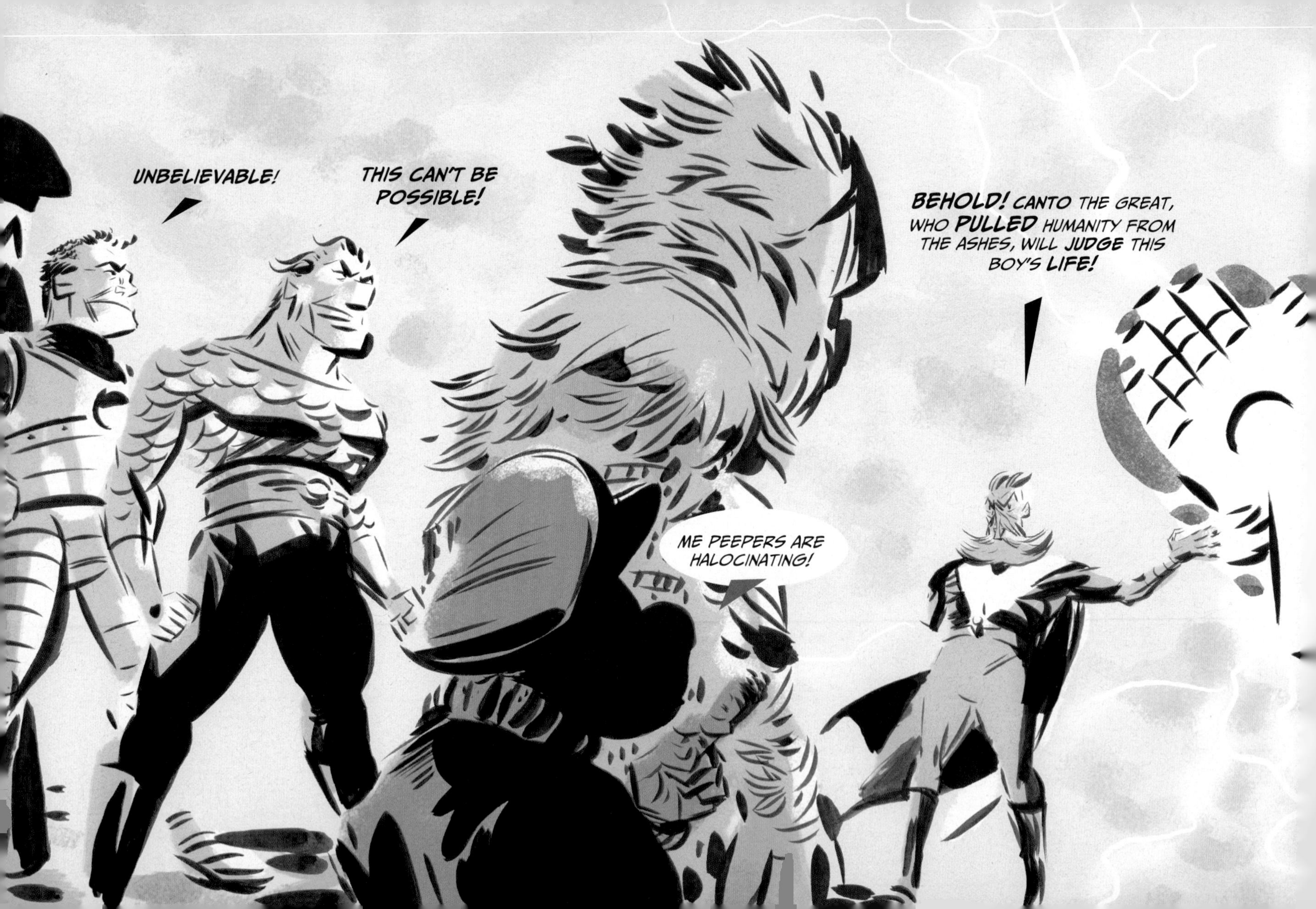
UNBELIEVABLE!
THIS CAN'T BE POSSIBLE!
ME PEEPERS ARE HALOCINATING!
BEHOLD! CANTO THE GREAT, WHO PULLED HUMANITY FROM THE ASHES, WILL JUDGE THIS BOY'S LIFE!

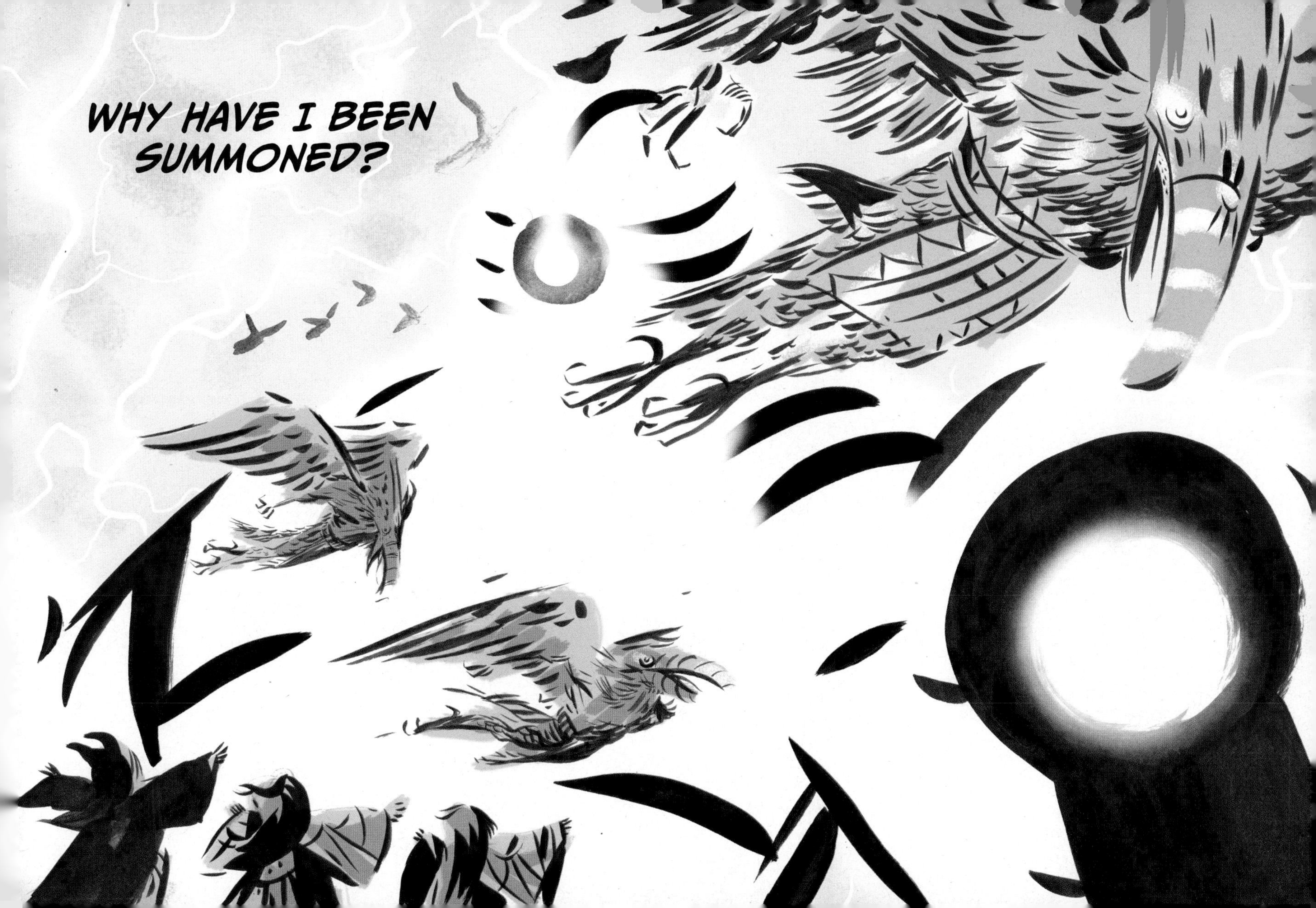
WHY HAVE I BEEN SUMMONED?

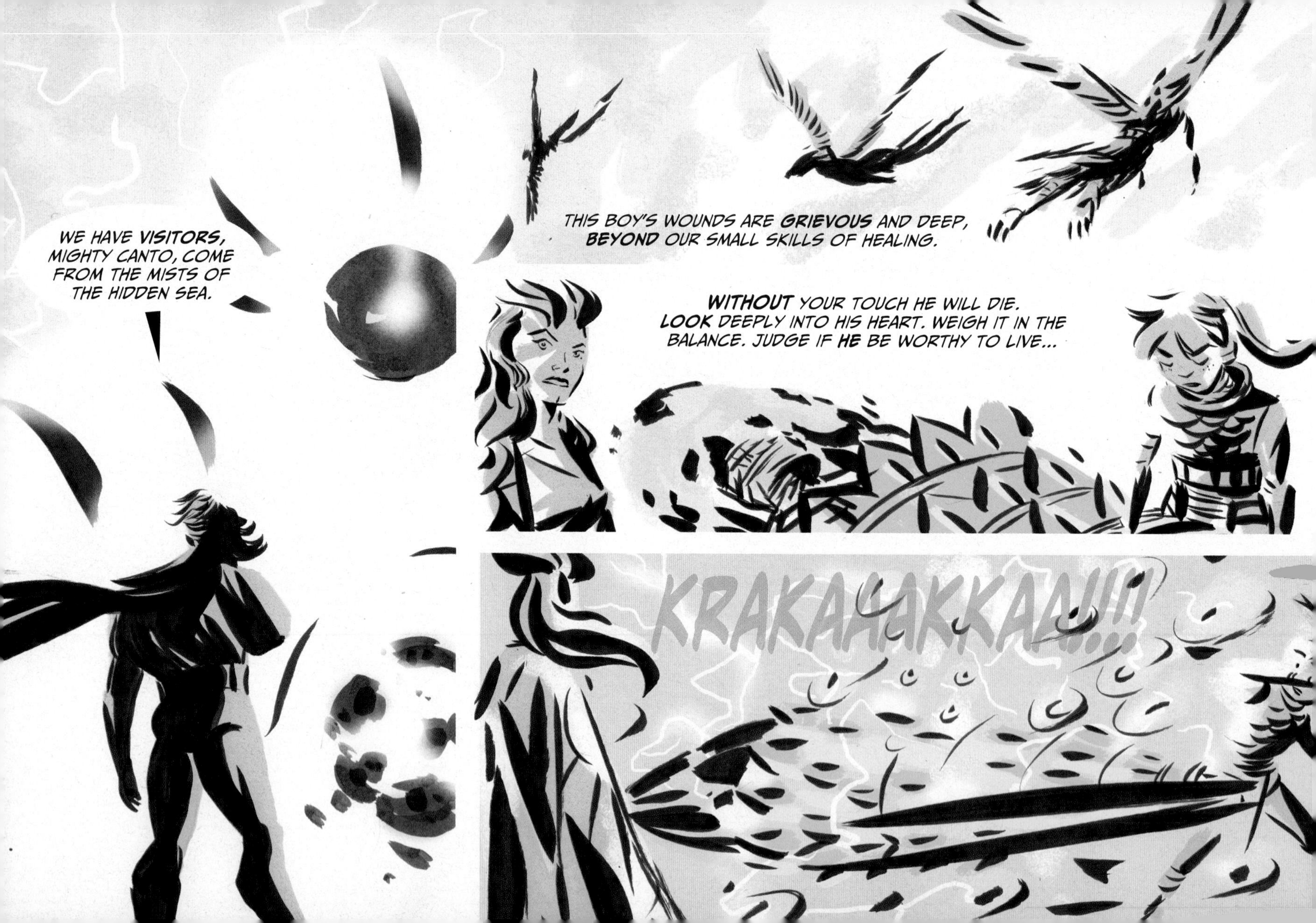
WE HAVE VISITORS, MIGHTY CANTO, COME FROM THE MISTS OF THE HIDDEN SEA.
THIS BOY'S WOUNDS ARE GRIEVOUS AND DEEP, BEYOND OUR SMALL SKILLS OF HEALING.
WITHOUT YOUR TOUCH HE WILL DIE. LOOK DEEPLY INTO HIS HEART. WEIGH IT IN THE BALANCE. JUDGE IF HE BE WORTHY TO LIVE...
KRAKAAAKKAA!!!

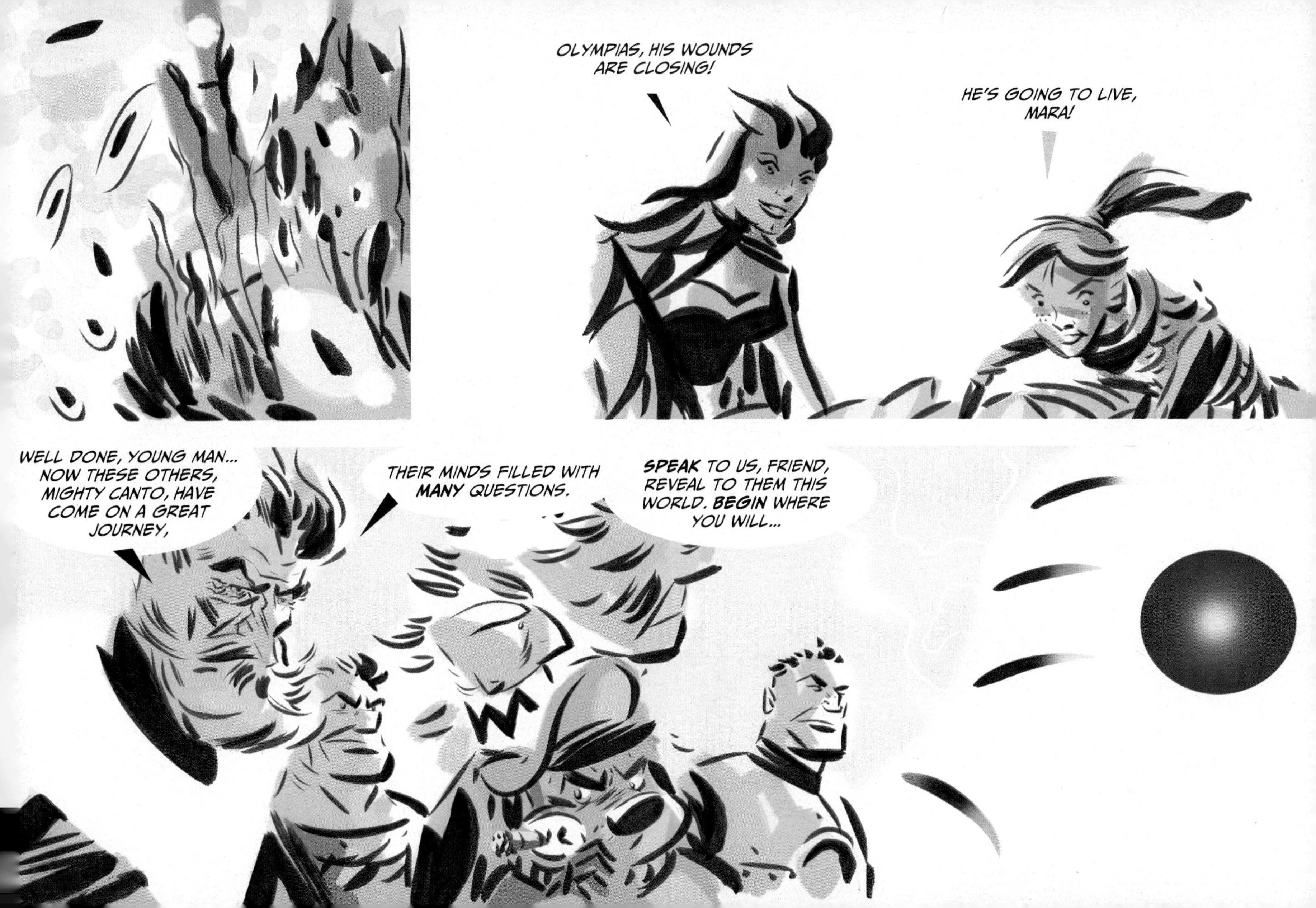
OLYMPIAS, HIS WOUNDS ARE CLOSING!
HE'S GOING TO LIVE, MARA!
WELL DONE, YOUNG MAN... NOW THESE OTHERS, MIGHTY CANTO, HAVE COME ON A GREAT JOURNEY,
THEIR MINDS FILLED WITH **MANY** QUESTIONS.
SPEAK TO US, FRIEND, REVEAL TO THEM THIS WORLD. **BEGIN** WHERE YOU WILL...

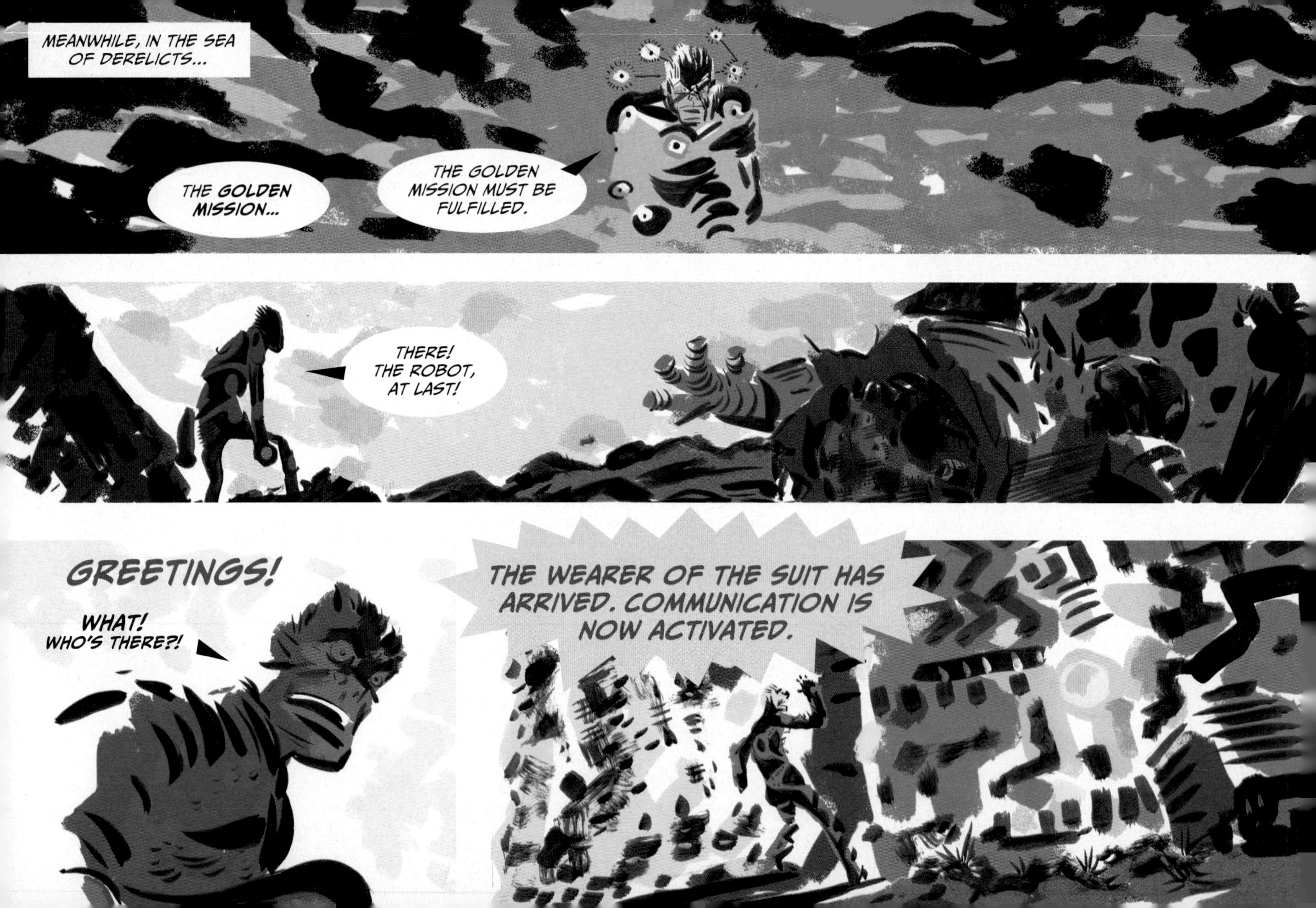
MEANWHILE, IN THE SEA OF DERELICTS...
THE GOLDEN MISSION...
THE GOLDEN MISSION MUST BE FULFILLED.
THERE! THE ROBOT, AT LAST!
GREETINGS!
WHAT! WHO'S THERE?!
THE WEARER OF THE SUIT HAS ARRIVED. COMMUNICATION IS NOW ACTIVATED.

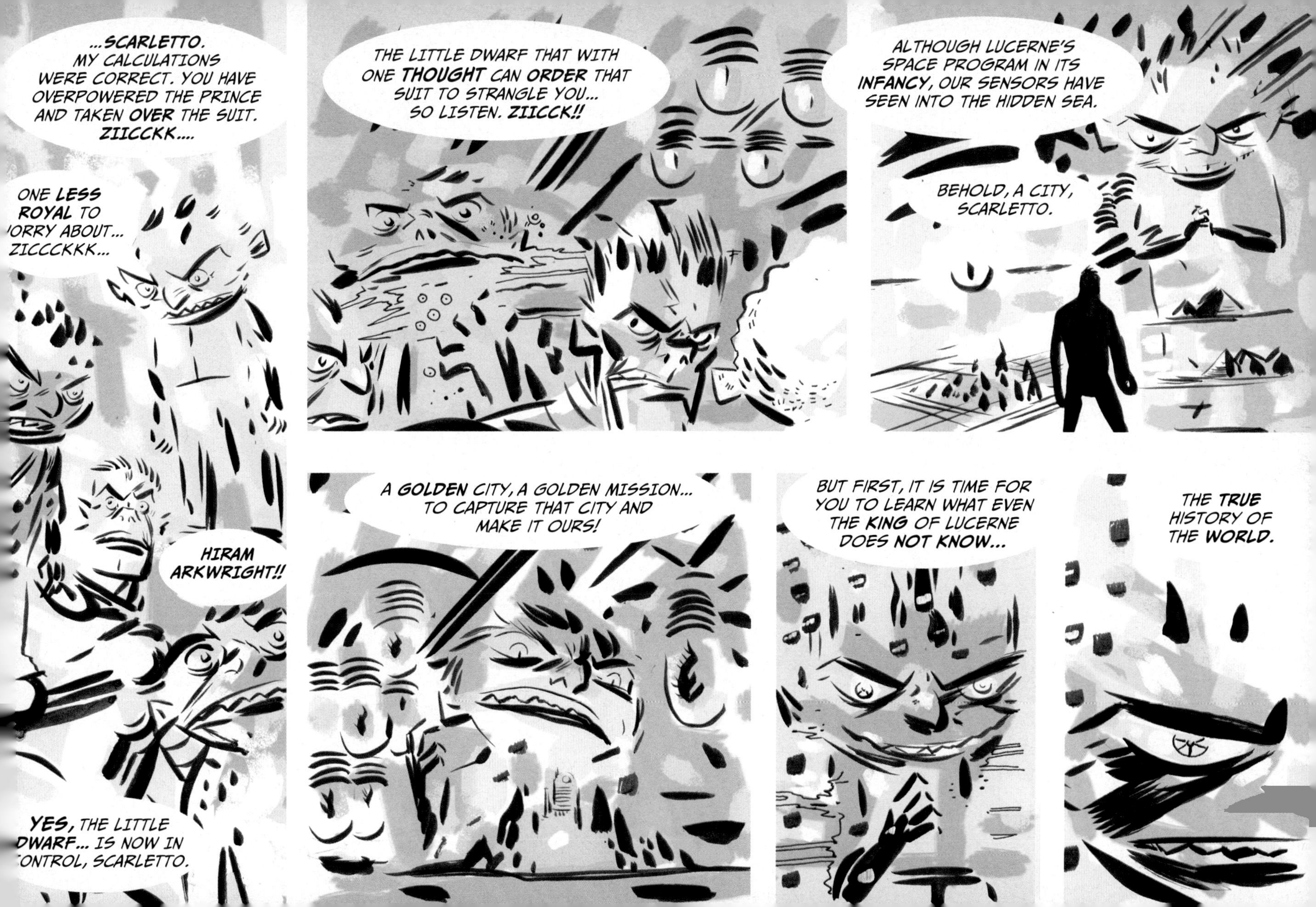
...SCARLETTO. MY CALCULATIONS WERE CORRECT. YOU HAVE OVERPOWERED THE PRINCE AND TAKEN OVER THE SUIT. ZIICCKK....
ONE LESS ROYAL TO WORRY ABOUT... ZICCCKKK...
HIRAM ARKWRIGHT!!
YES, THE LITTLE DWARF... IS NOW IN CONTROL, SCARLETTO.
THE LITTLE DWARF THAT WITH ONE THOUGHT CAN ORDER THAT SUIT TO STRANGLE YOU... SO LISTEN. ZIICCK!!
ALTHOUGH LUCERNE'S SPACE PROGRAM IN ITS INFANCY, OUR SENSORS HAVE SEEN INTO THE HIDDEN SEA.
BEHOLD, A CITY, SCARLETTO.
A GOLDEN CITY, A GOLDEN MISSION... TO CAPTURE THAT CITY AND MAKE IT OURS!
BUT FIRST, IT IS TIME FOR YOU TO LEARN WHAT EVEN THE KING OF LUCERNE DOES NOT KNOW...
THE TRUE HISTORY OF THE WORLD.

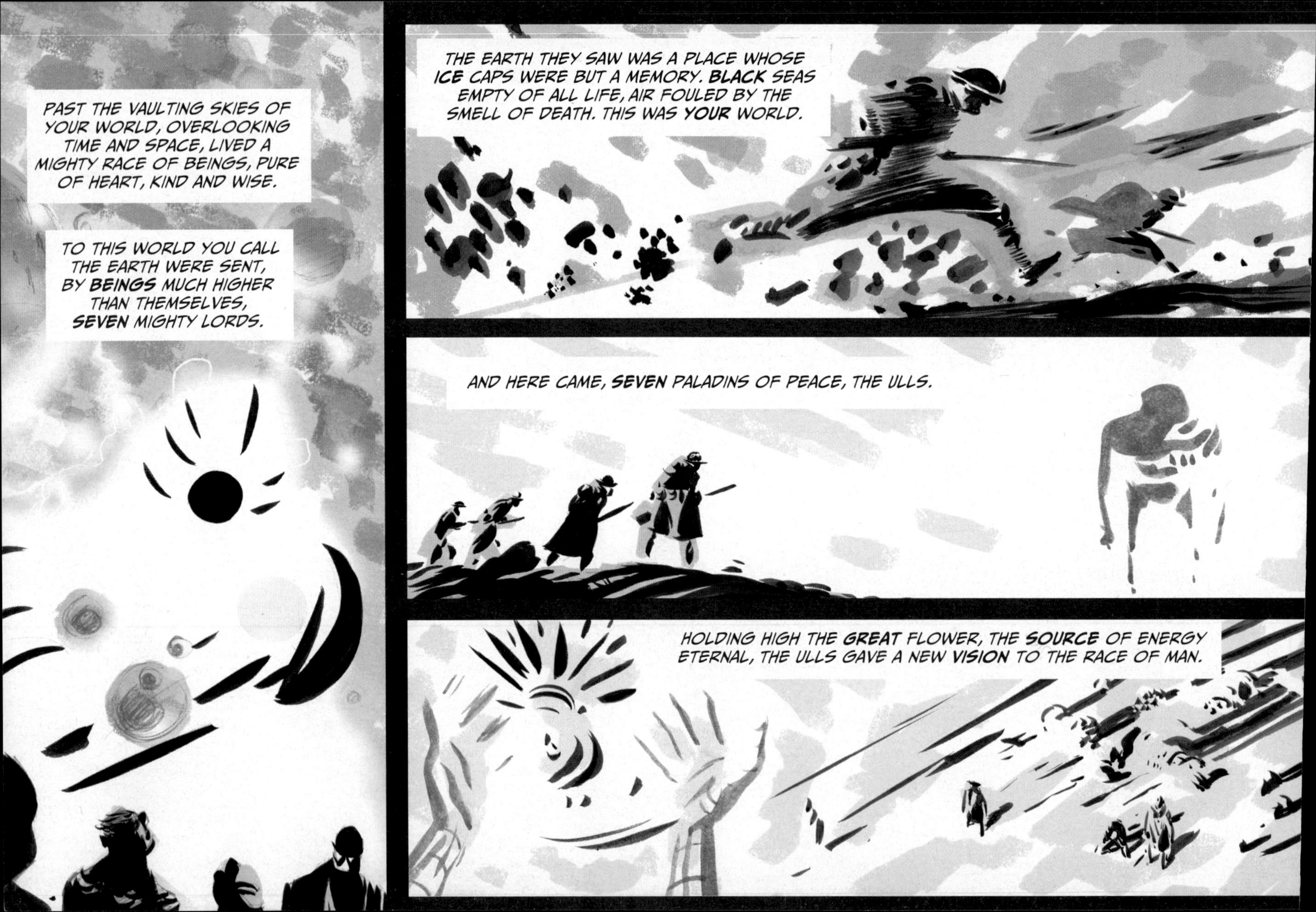
PAST THE VAULTING SKIES OF YOUR WORLD, OVERLOOKING TIME AND SPACE, LIVED A MIGHTY RACE OF BEINGS, PURE OF HEART, KIND AND WISE.
TO THIS WORLD YOU CALL THE EARTH WERE SENT, BY BEINGS MUCH HIGHER THAN THEMSELVES, SEVEN MIGHTY LORDS.
THE EARTH THEY SAW WAS A PLACE WHOSE ICE CAPS WERE BUT A MEMORY. BLACK SEAS EMPTY OF ALL LIFE, AIR FOULED BY THE SMELL OF DEATH. THIS WAS YOUR WORLD.
AND HERE CAME, SEVEN PALADINS OF PEACE, THE ULLS.
HOLDING HIGH THE GREAT FLOWER, THE SOURCE OF ENERGY ETERNAL, THE ULLS GAVE A NEW VISION TO THE RACE OF MAN.

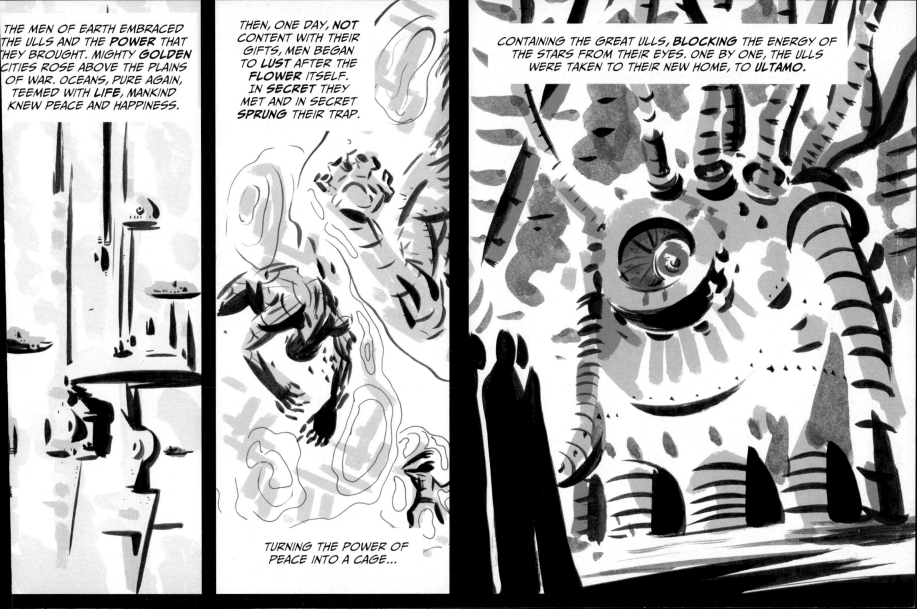

THE MEN OF EARTH EMBRACED THE ULLS AND THE **POWER** THAT THEY BROUGHT. MIGHTY **GOLDEN** CITIES ROSE ABOVE THE PLAINS OF WAR. OCEANS, PURE AGAIN, TEEMED WITH **LIFE**, MANKIND KNEW PEACE AND HAPPINESS.

THEN, ONE DAY, **NOT** CONTENT WITH THEIR GIFTS, MEN BEGAN TO **LUST** AFTER THE **FLOWER** ITSELF. IN **SECRET** THEY MET AND IN SECRET **SPRUNG** THEIR TRAP.

TURNING THE POWER OF PEACE INTO A CAGE...

CONTAINING THE GREAT ULLS, **BLOCKING** THE ENERGY OF THE STARS FROM THEIR EYES. ONE BY ONE, THE ULLS WERE TAKEN TO THEIR NEW HOME, TO **ULTAMO.**

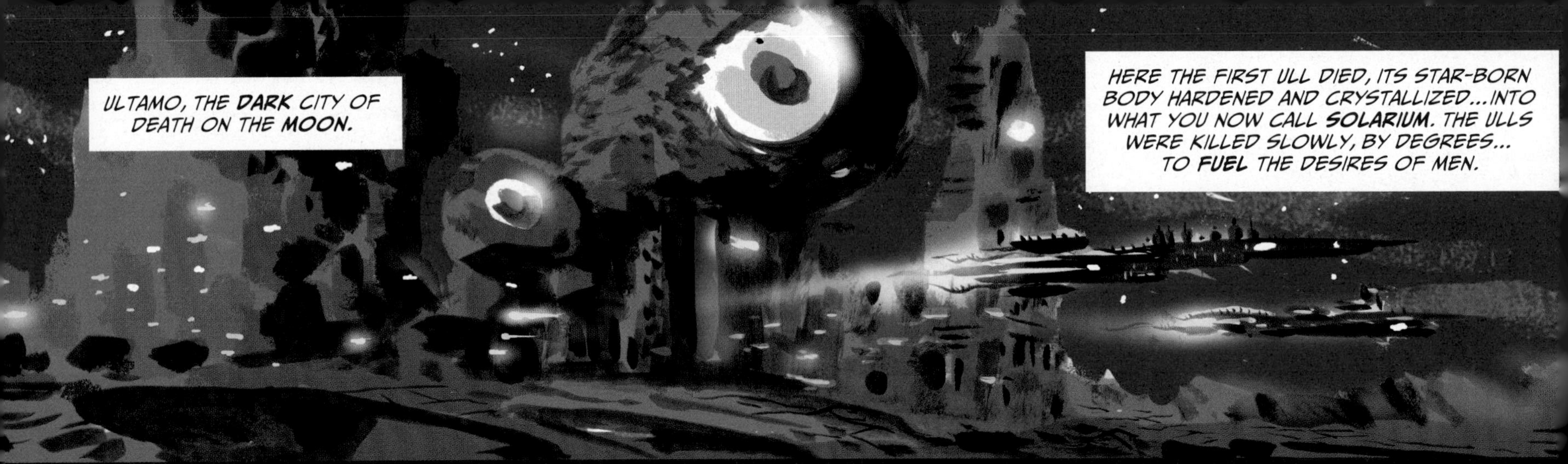
ULTAMO, THE DARK CITY OF DEATH ON THE MOON.
HERE THE FIRST ULL DIED, ITS STAR-BORN BODY HARDENED AND CRYSTALLIZED... INTO WHAT YOU NOW CALL SOLARIUM. THE ULLS WERE KILLED SLOWLY, BY DEGREES... TO FUEL THE DESIRES OF MEN.

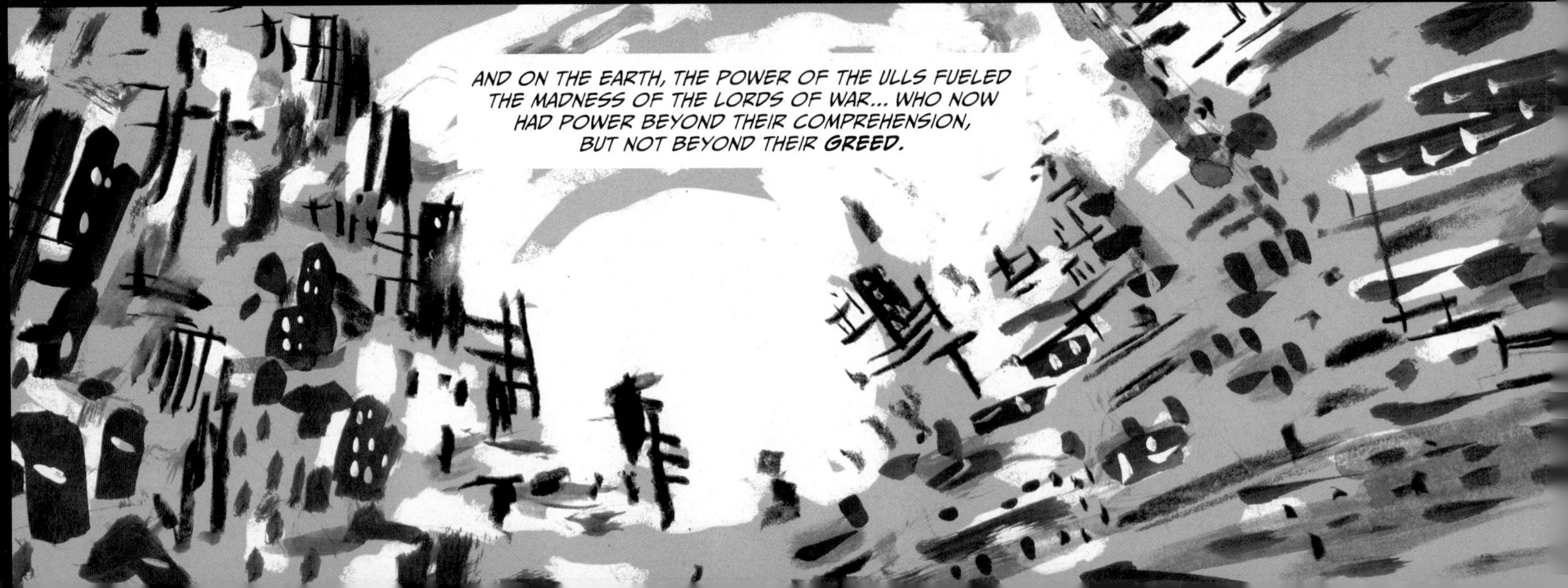
AND ON THE EARTH, THE POWER OF THE ULLS FUELED THE MADNESS OF THE LORDS OF WAR... WHO NOW HAD POWER BEYOND THEIR COMPREHENSION, BUT NOT BEYOND THEIR GREED.

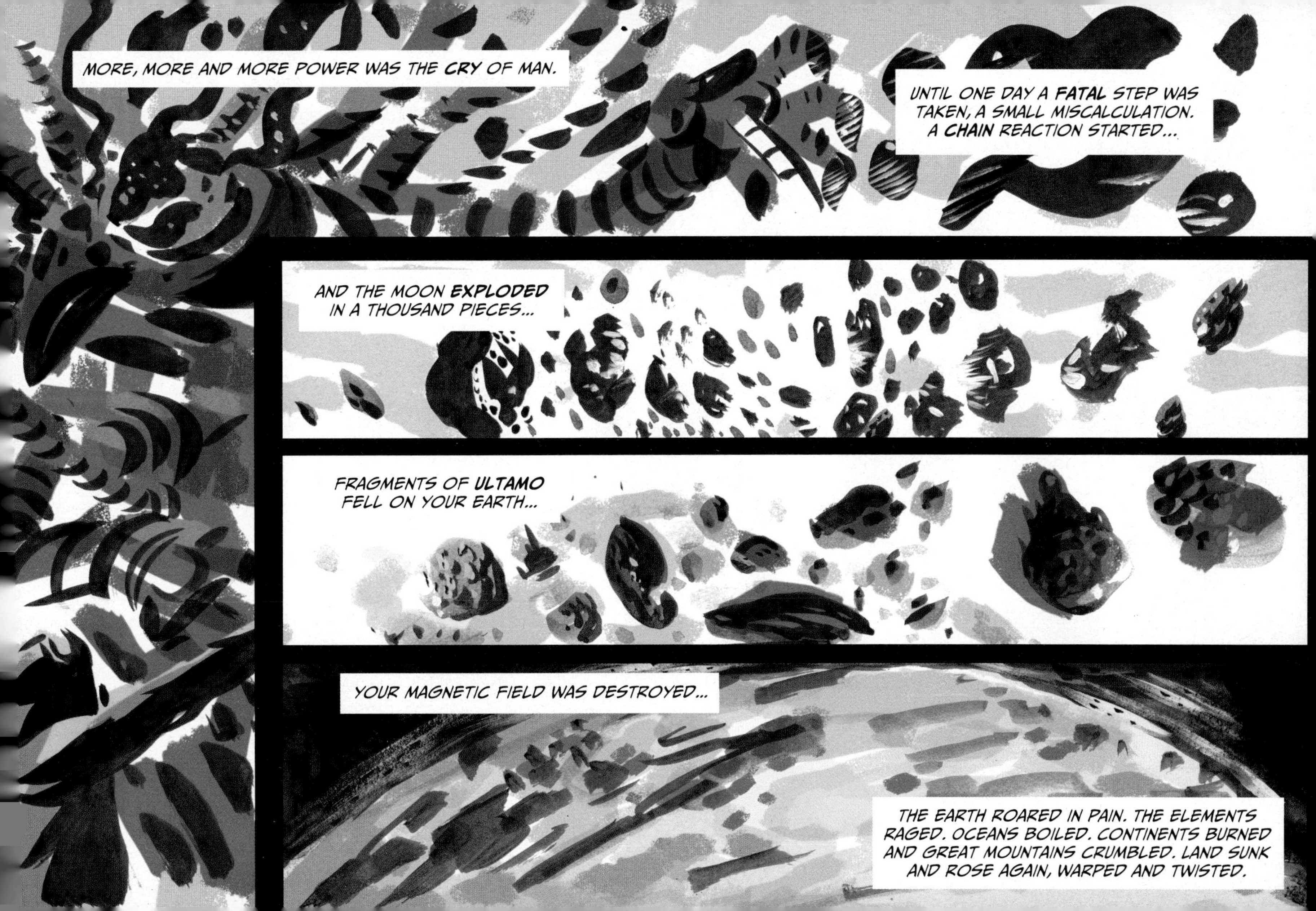
MORE, MORE AND MORE POWER WAS THE CRY OF MAN.
UNTIL ONE DAY A FATAL STEP WAS TAKEN, A SMALL MISCALCULATION. A CHAIN REACTION STARTED...
AND THE MOON EXPLODED IN A THOUSAND PIECES...
FRAGMENTS OF ULTAMO FELL ON YOUR EARTH...
YOUR MAGNETIC FIELD WAS DESTROYED...
THE EARTH ROARED IN PAIN. THE ELEMENTS RAGED. OCEANS BOILED. CONTINENTS BURNED AND GREAT MOUNTAINS CRUMBLED. LAND SUNK AND ROSE AGAIN, WARPED AND TWISTED.

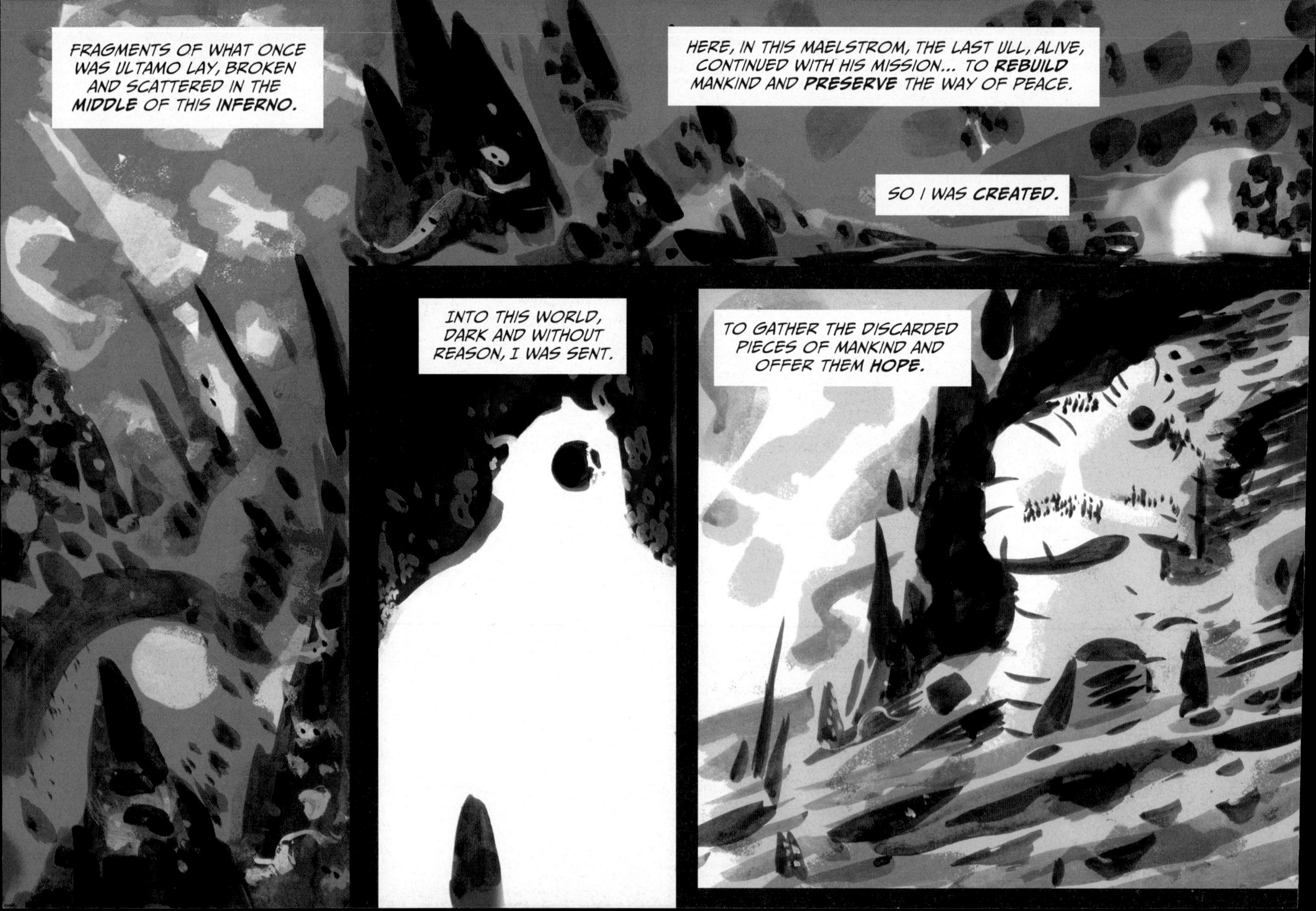
FRAGMENTS OF WHAT ONCE WAS ULTAMO LAY, BROKEN AND SCATTERED IN THE **MIDDLE** OF THIS **INFERNO.**
HERE, IN THIS MAELSTROM, THE LAST ULL, ALIVE, CONTINUED WITH HIS MISSION... TO **REBUILD** MANKIND AND **PRESERVE** THE WAY OF PEACE.
SO I WAS **CREATED.**
INTO THIS WORLD, DARK AND WITHOUT REASON, I WAS SENT.
TO GATHER THE DISCARDED PIECES OF MANKIND AND OFFER THEM **HOPE.**

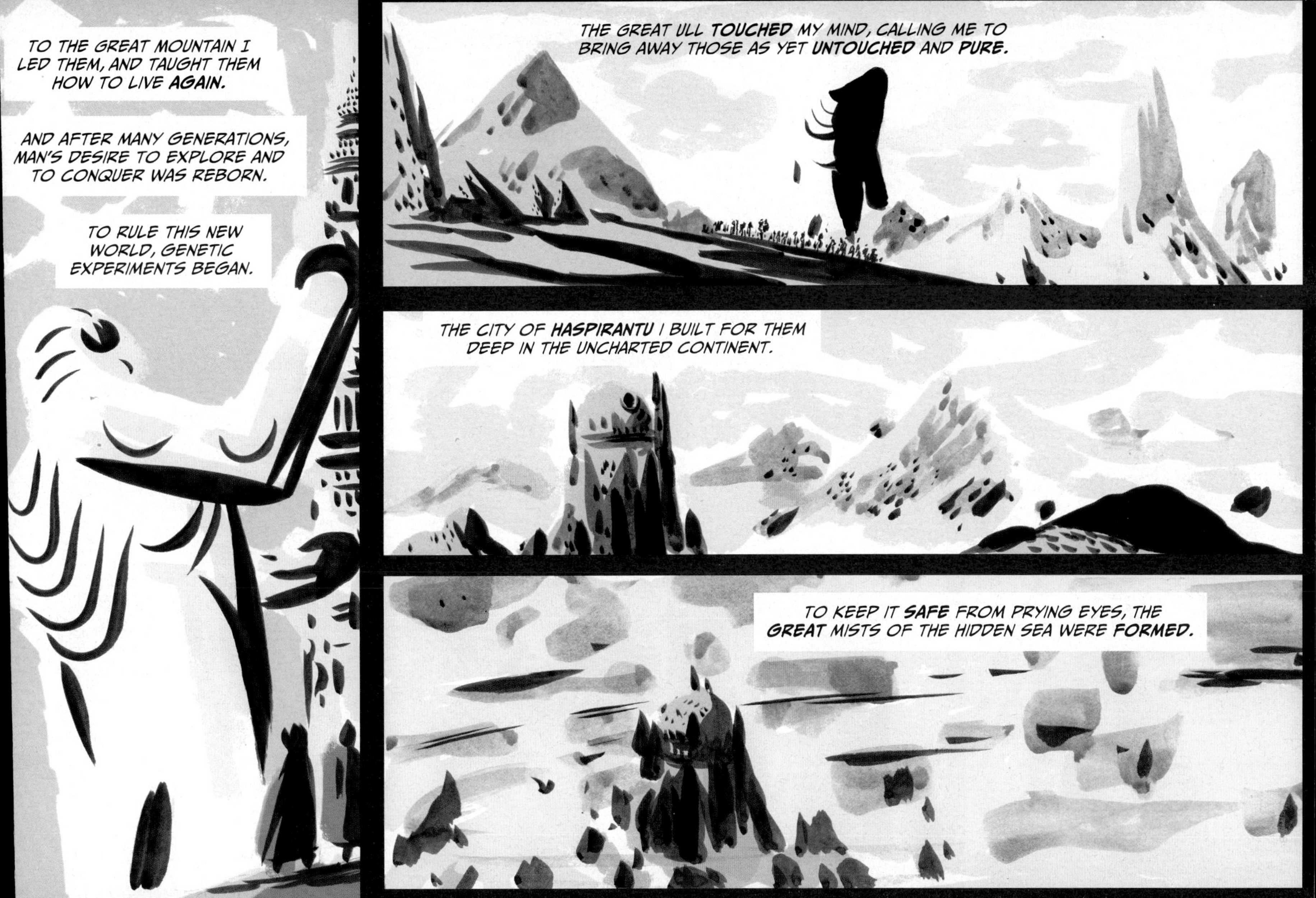
TO THE GREAT MOUNTAIN I LED THEM, AND TAUGHT THEM HOW TO LIVE AGAIN.
AND AFTER MANY GENERATIONS, MAN'S DESIRE TO EXPLORE AND TO CONQUER WAS REBORN.
TO RULE THIS NEW WORLD, GENETIC EXPERIMENTS BEGAN.
THE GREAT ULL TOUCHED MY MIND, CALLING ME TO BRING AWAY THOSE AS YET UNTOUCHED AND PURE.
THE CITY OF HASPIRANTU I BUILT FOR THEM DEEP IN THE UNCHARTED CONTINENT.
TO KEEP IT SAFE FROM PRYING EYES, THE GREAT MISTS OF THE HIDDEN SEA WERE FORMED.

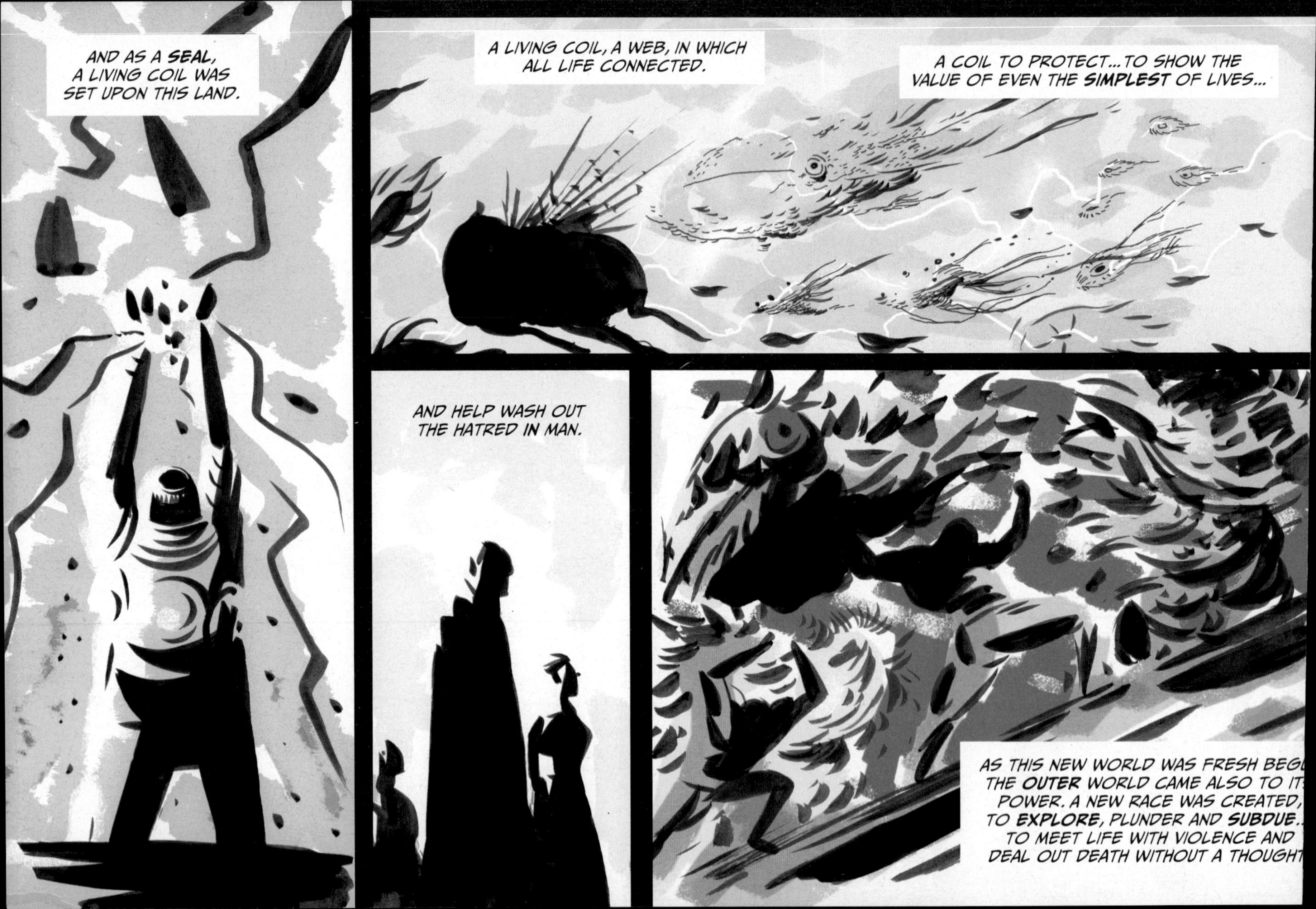
AND AS A SEAL, A LIVING COIL WAS SET UPON THIS LAND.
A LIVING COIL, A WEB, IN WHICH ALL LIFE CONNECTED.
A COIL TO PROTECT...TO SHOW THE VALUE OF EVEN THE SIMPLEST OF LIVES...
AND HELP WASH OUT THE HATRED IN MAN.
AS THIS NEW WORLD WAS FRESH BEG
THE OUTER WORLD CAME ALSO TO IT
POWER. A NEW RACE WAS CREATED,
TO EXPLORE, PLUNDER AND SUBDUE..
TO MEET LIFE WITH VIOLENCE AND
DEAL OUT DEATH WITHOUT A THOUGHT

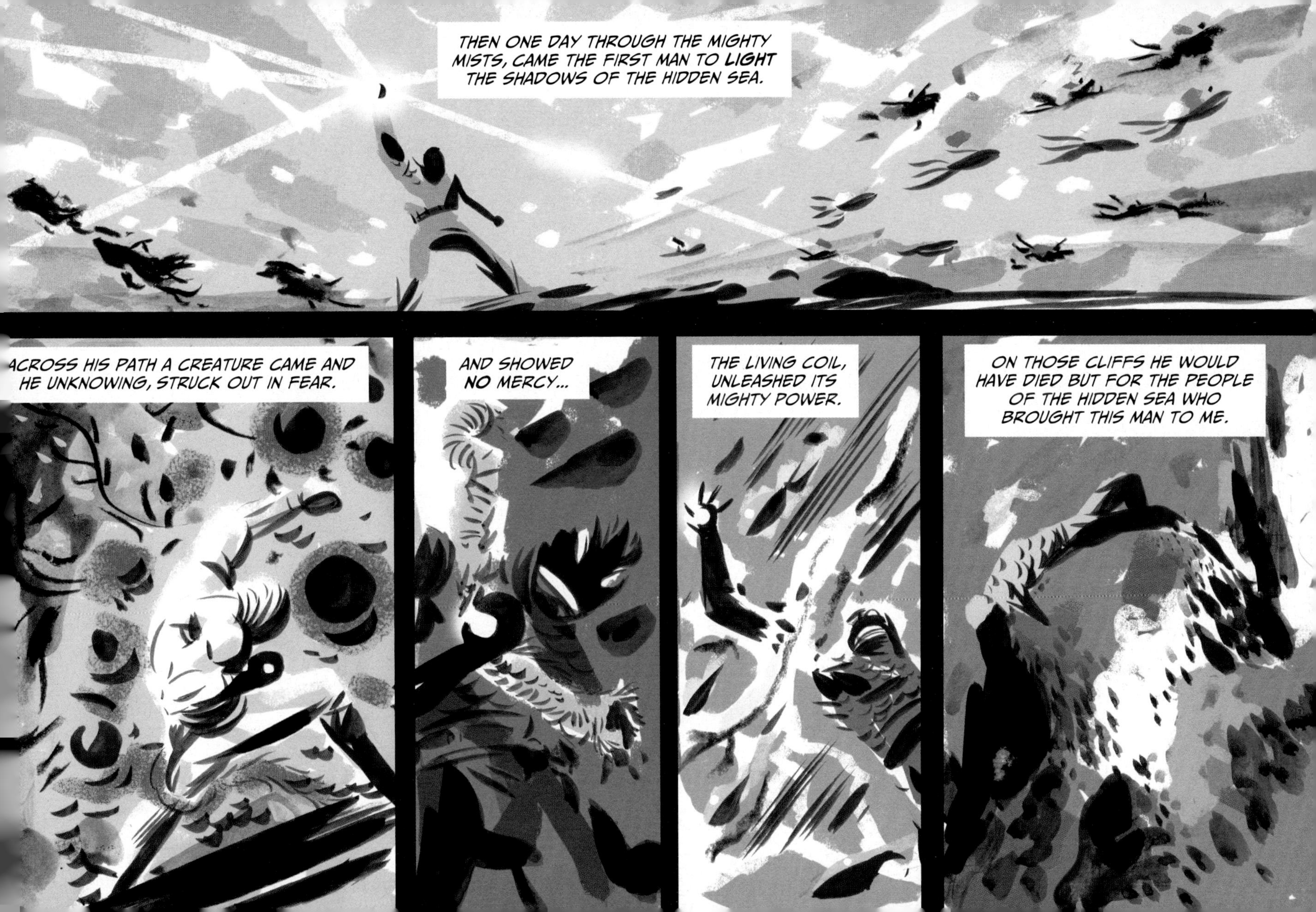
THEN ONE DAY THROUGH THE MIGHTY MISTS, CAME THE FIRST MAN TO LIGHT THE SHADOWS OF THE HIDDEN SEA.
ACROSS HIS PATH A CREATURE CAME AND HE UNKNOWING, STRUCK OUT IN FEAR.
AND SHOWED NO MERCY...
THE LIVING COIL, UNLEASHED ITS MIGHTY POWER.
ON THOSE CLIFFS HE WOULD HAVE DIED BUT FOR THE PEOPLE OF THE HIDDEN SEA WHO BROUGHT THIS MAN TO ME.

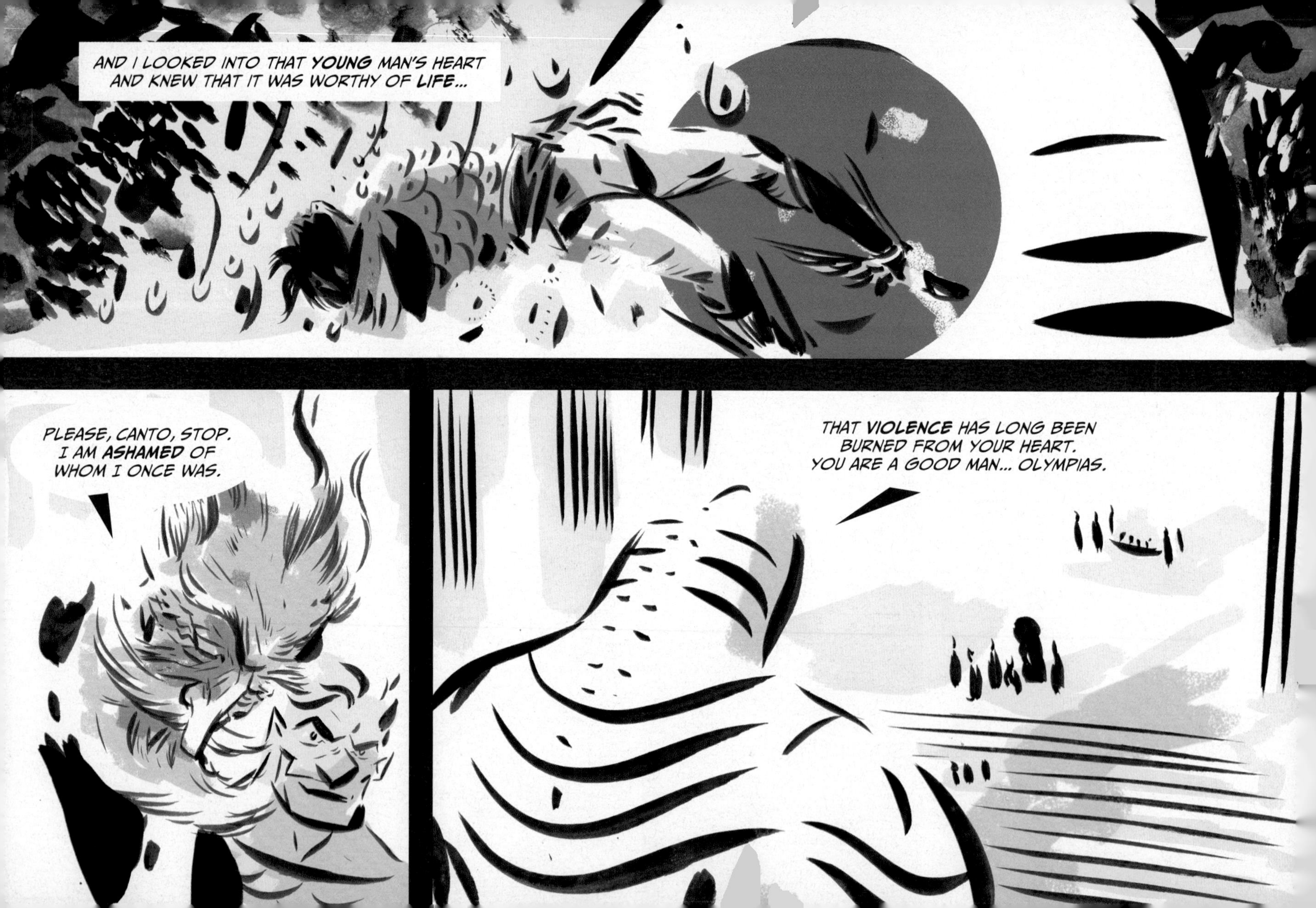
AND I LOOKED INTO THAT YOUNG MAN'S HEART AND KNEW THAT IT WAS WORTHY OF LIFE...
PLEASE, CANTO, STOP. I AM ASHAMED OF WHOM I ONCE WAS.
THAT VIOLENCE HAS LONG BEEN BURNED FROM YOUR HEART. YOU ARE A GOOD MAN... OLYMPIAS.

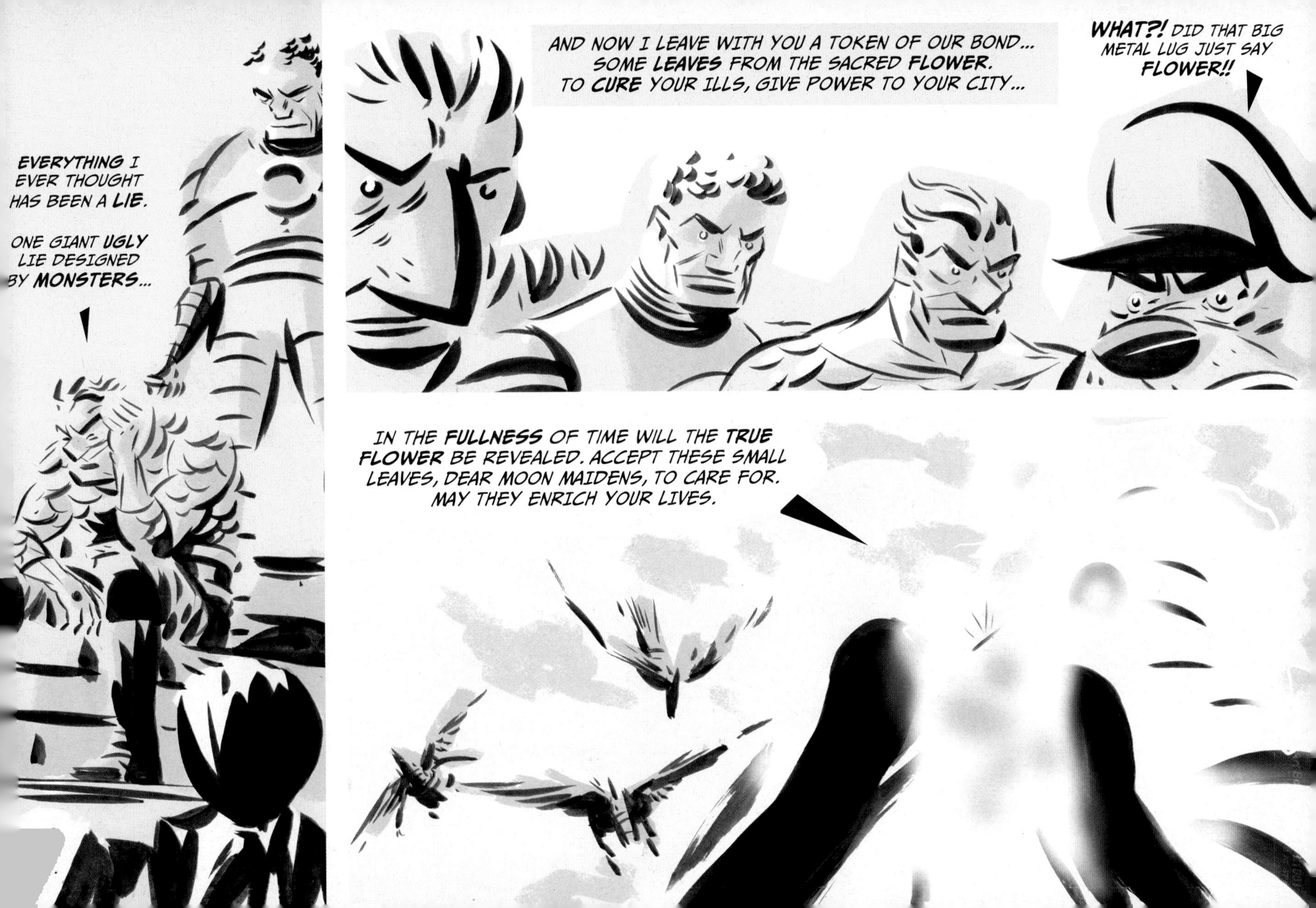

EVERYTHING I EVER THOUGHT HAS BEEN A LIE.
ONE GIANT UGLY LIE DESIGNED BY MONSTERS...
AND NOW I LEAVE WITH YOU A TOKEN OF OUR BOND... SOME LEAVES FROM THE SACRED FLOWER. TO CURE YOUR ILLS, GIVE POWER TO YOUR CITY...
WHAT?! DID THAT BIG METAL LUG JUST SAY FLOWER!!
IN THE FULLNESS OF TIME WILL THE TRUE FLOWER BE REVEALED. ACCEPT THESE SMALL LEAVES, DEAR MOON MAIDENS, TO CARE FOR. MAY THEY ENRICH YOUR LIVES.

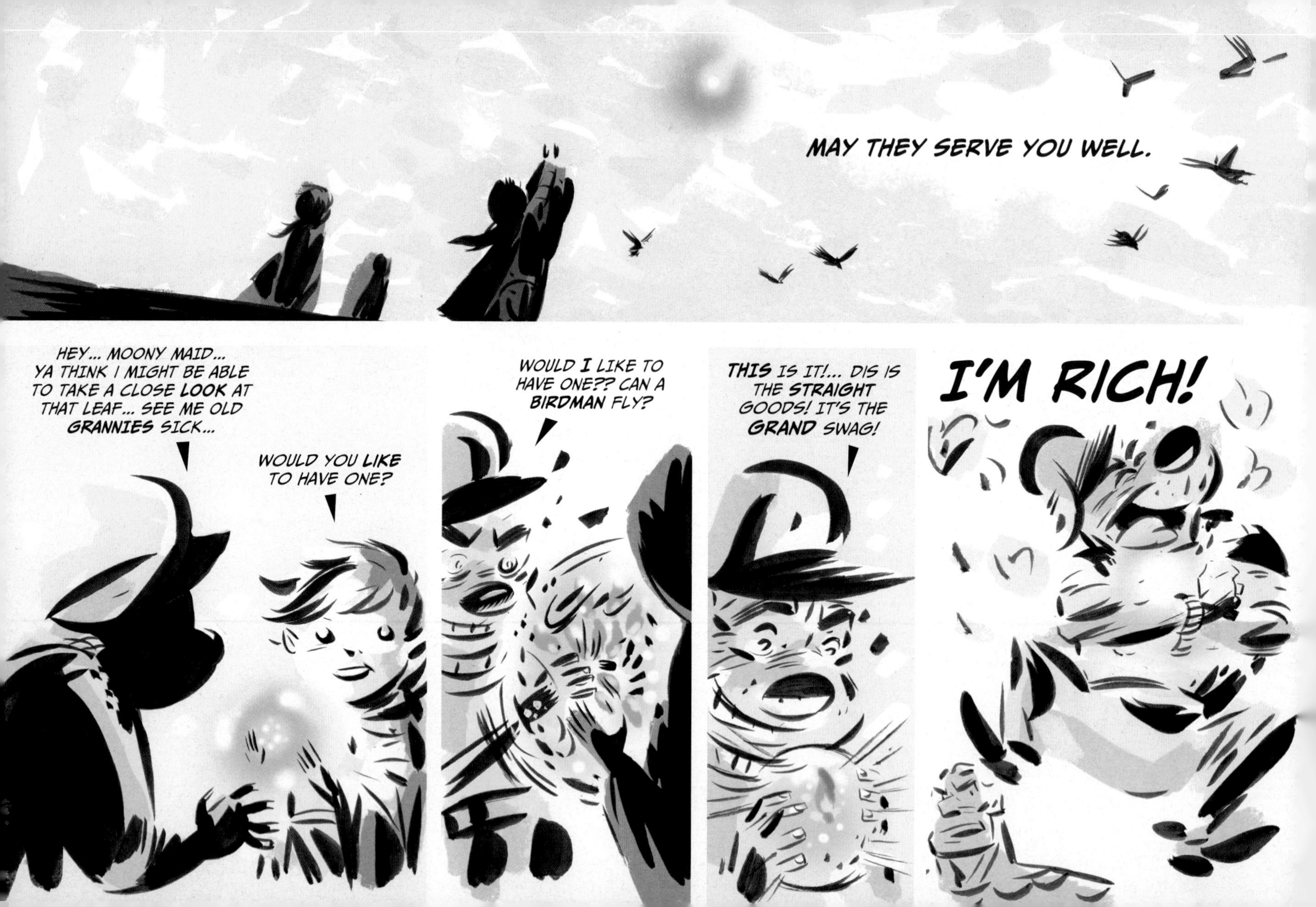
MAY THEY SERVE YOU WELL.
HEY... MOONY MAID... YA THINK I MIGHT BE ABLE TO TAKE A CLOSE LOOK AT THAT LEAF... SEE ME OLD GRANNIES SICK...
WOULD YOU LIKE TO HAVE ONE?
WOULD I LIKE TO HAVE ONE?? CAN A BIRDMAN FLY?
THIS IS IT!... DIS IS THE STRAIGHT GOODS! IT'S THE GRAND SWAG!
I'M RICH!

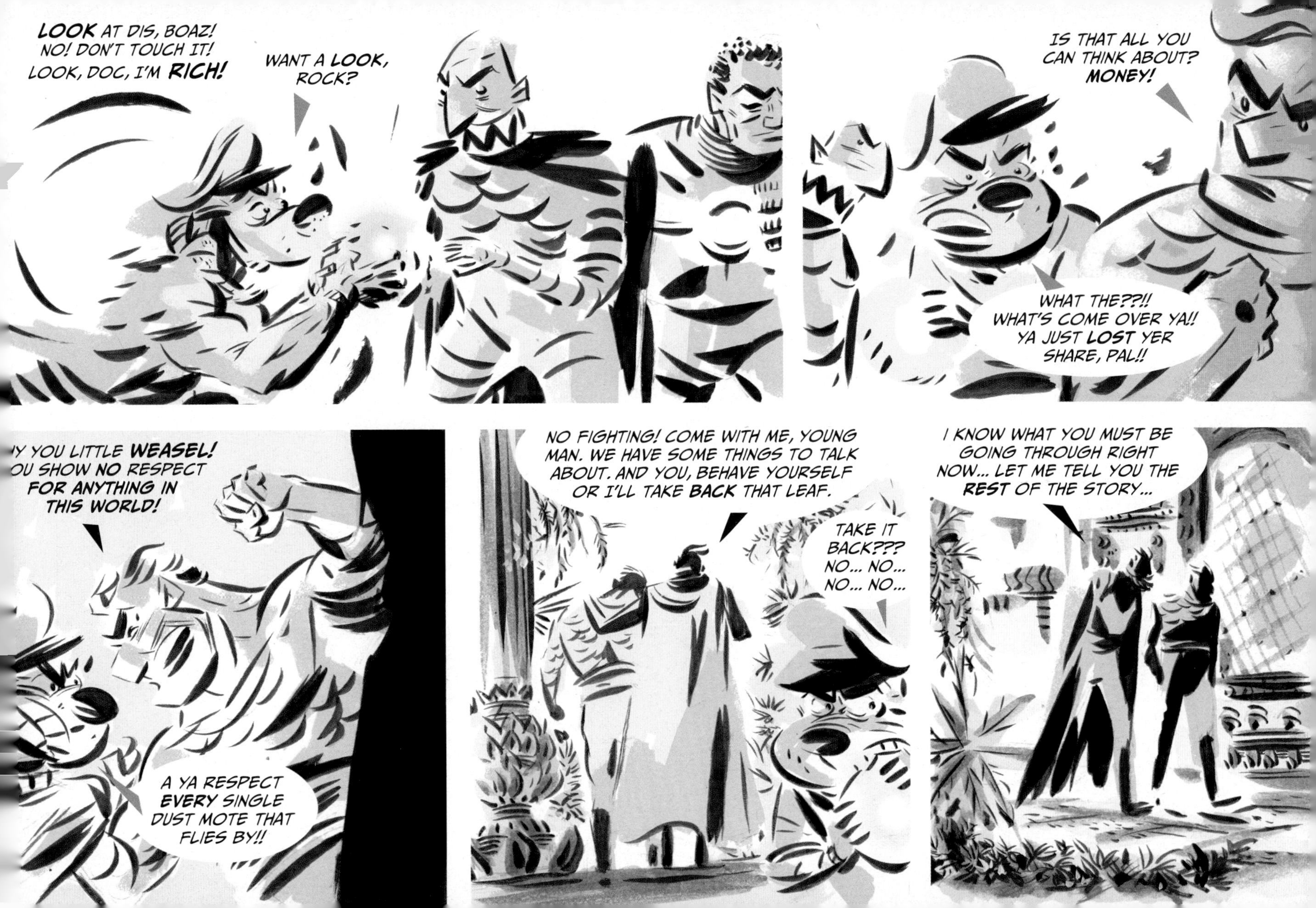
LOOK AT DIS, BOAZ! NO! DON'T TOUCH IT! LOOK, DOC, I'M RICH!
WANT A LOOK, ROCK?
IS THAT ALL YOU CAN THINK ABOUT? MONEY!
WHAT THE??!! WHAT'S COME OVER YA!! YA JUST LOST YER SHARE, PAL!!
Y YOU LITTLE WEASEL! OU SHOW NO RESPECT FOR ANYTHING IN THIS WORLD!
A YA RESPECT EVERY SINGLE DUST MOTE THAT FLIES BY!!
NO FIGHTING! COME WITH ME, YOUNG MAN. WE HAVE SOME THINGS TO TALK ABOUT. AND YOU, BEHAVE YOURSELF OR I'LL TAKE BACK THAT LEAF.
TAKE IT BACK??? NO... NO... NO... NO...
I KNOW WHAT YOU MUST BE GOING THROUGH RIGHT NOW... LET ME TELL YOU THE REST OF THE STORY...

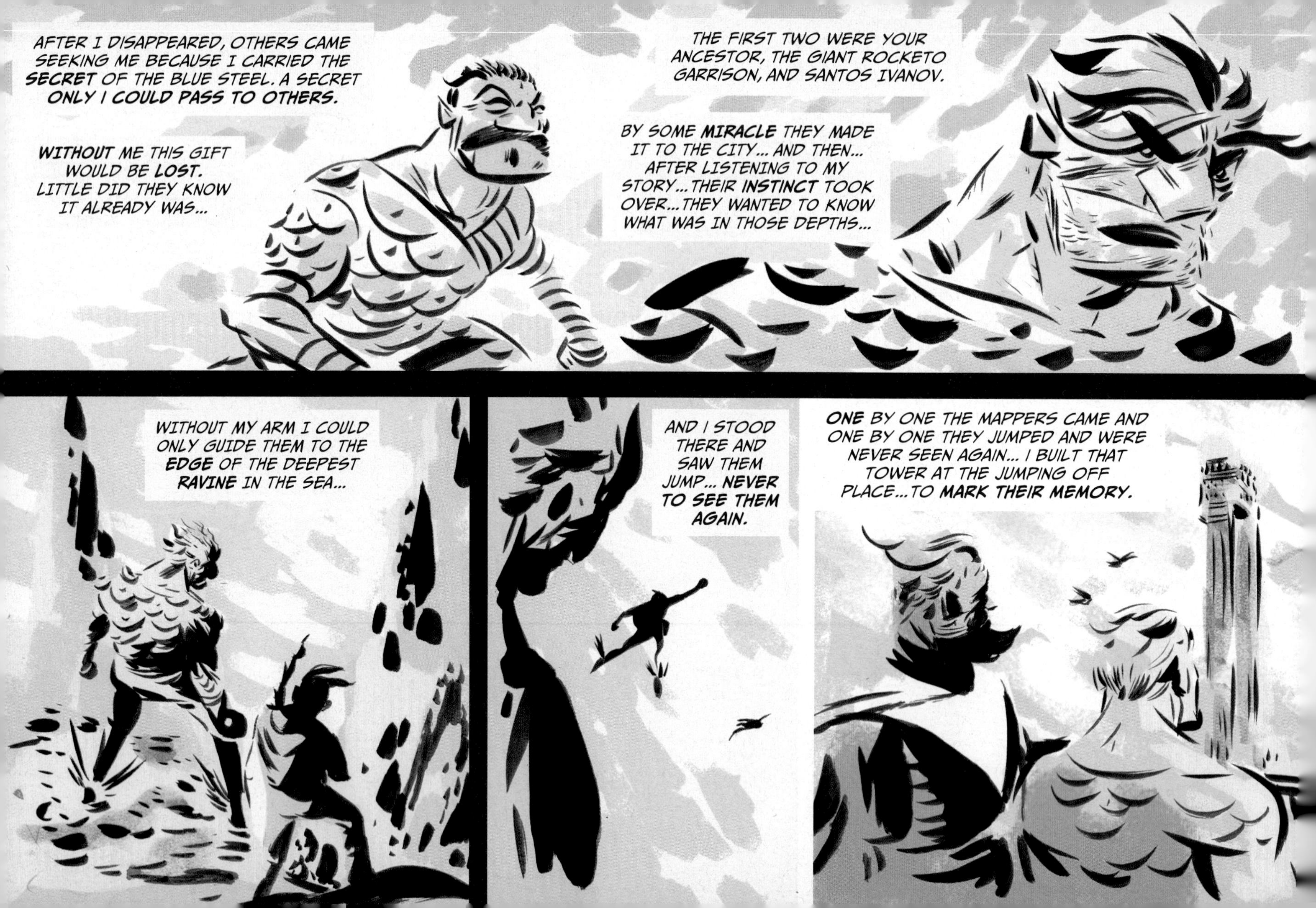

AFTER I DISAPPEARED, OTHERS CAME SEEKING ME BECAUSE I CARRIED THE **SECRET** OF THE BLUE STEEL. A SECRET **ONLY** I **COULD PASS TO OTHERS.**
WITHOUT ME THIS GIFT WOULD BE **LOST.** LITTLE DID THEY KNOW IT ALREADY WAS...
THE FIRST TWO WERE YOUR ANCESTOR, THE GIANT ROCKETO GARRISON, AND SANTOS IVANOV.
BY SOME **MIRACLE** THEY MADE IT TO THE CITY... AND THEN... AFTER LISTENING TO MY STORY...THEIR **INSTINCT** TOOK OVER...THEY WANTED TO KNOW WHAT WAS IN THOSE DEPTHS...
WITHOUT MY ARM I COULD ONLY GUIDE THEM TO THE **EDGE** OF THE DEEPEST **RAVINE** IN THE SEA...
AND I STOOD THERE AND SAW THEM JUMP... **NEVER TO SEE THEM AGAIN.**
ONE BY ONE THE MAPPERS CAME AND ONE BY ONE THEY JUMPED AND WERE NEVER SEEN AGAIN... I BUILT THAT TOWER AT THE JUMPING OFF PLACE...TO **MARK THEIR MEMORY.**

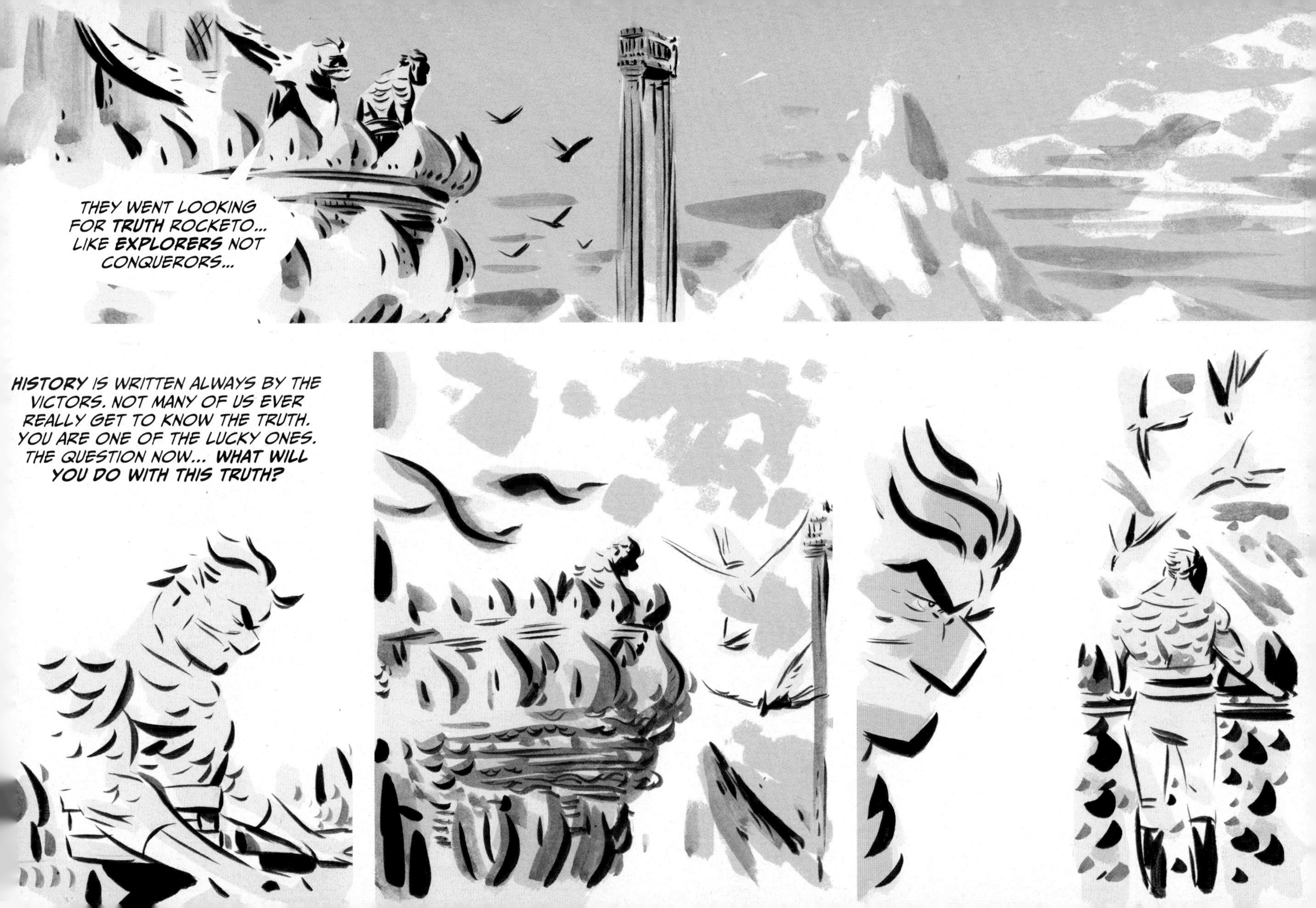
THEY WENT LOOKING FOR TRUTH ROCKETO... LIKE EXPLORERS NOT CONQUERORS...
HISTORY IS WRITTEN ALWAYS BY THE VICTORS. NOT MANY OF US EVER REALLY GET TO KNOW THE TRUTH. YOU ARE ONE OF THE LUCKY ONES. THE QUESTION NOW... WHAT WILL YOU DO WITH THIS TRUTH?

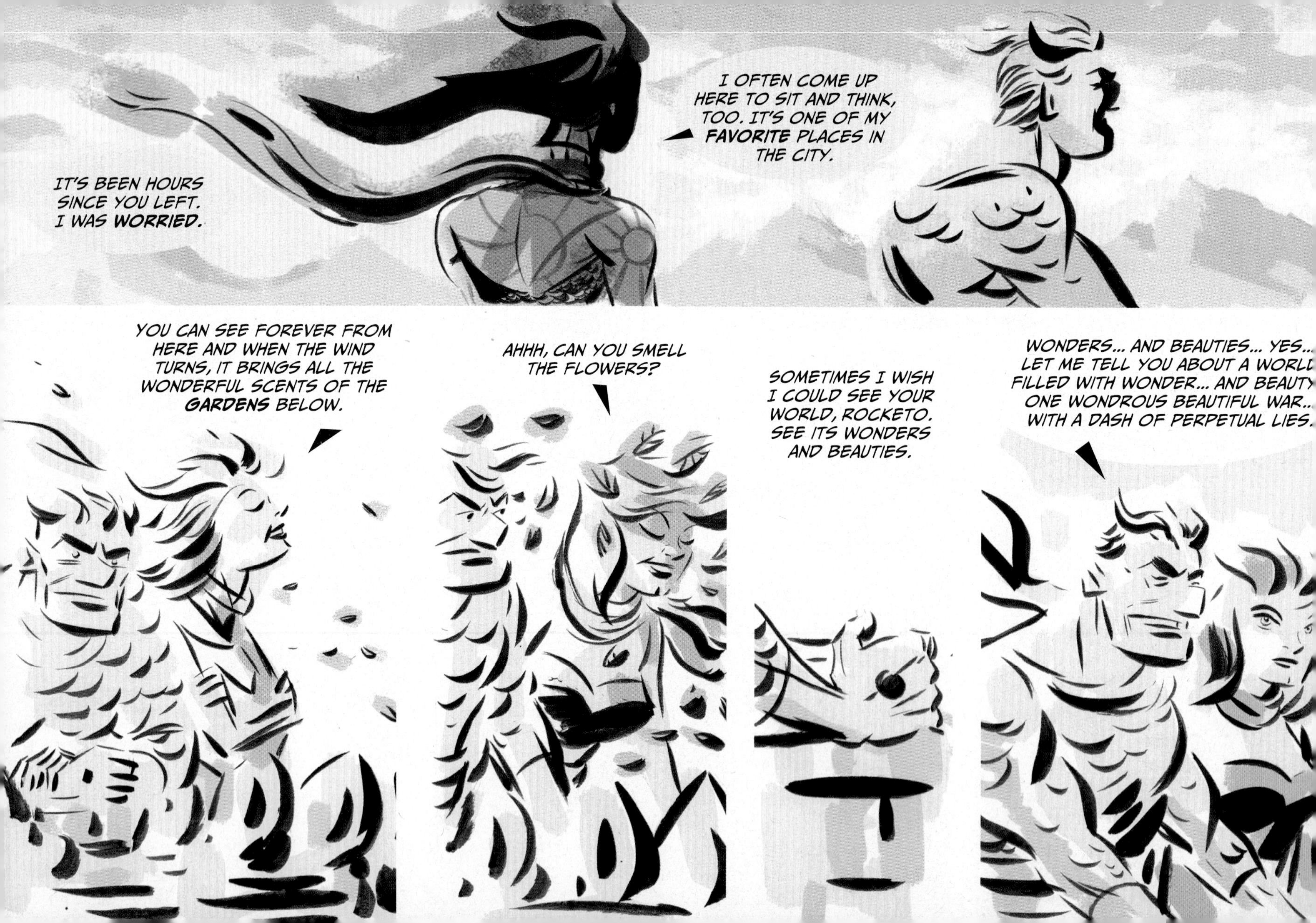
IT'S BEEN HOURS SINCE YOU LEFT. I WAS **WORRIED.**
I OFTEN COME UP HERE TO SIT AND THINK, TOO. IT'S ONE OF MY **FAVORITE** PLACES IN THE CITY.
YOU CAN SEE FOREVER FROM HERE AND WHEN THE WIND TURNS, IT BRINGS ALL THE WONDERFUL SCENTS OF THE **GARDENS** BELOW.
AHHH, CAN YOU SMELL THE FLOWERS?
SOMETIMES I WISH I COULD SEE YOUR WORLD, ROCKETO. SEE ITS WONDERS AND BEAUTIES.
WONDERS... AND BEAUTIES... YES... LET ME TELL YOU ABOUT A WORL FILLED WITH WONDER... AND BEAUTY ONE WONDROUS BEAUTIFUL WAR... WITH A DASH OF PERPETUAL LIES.

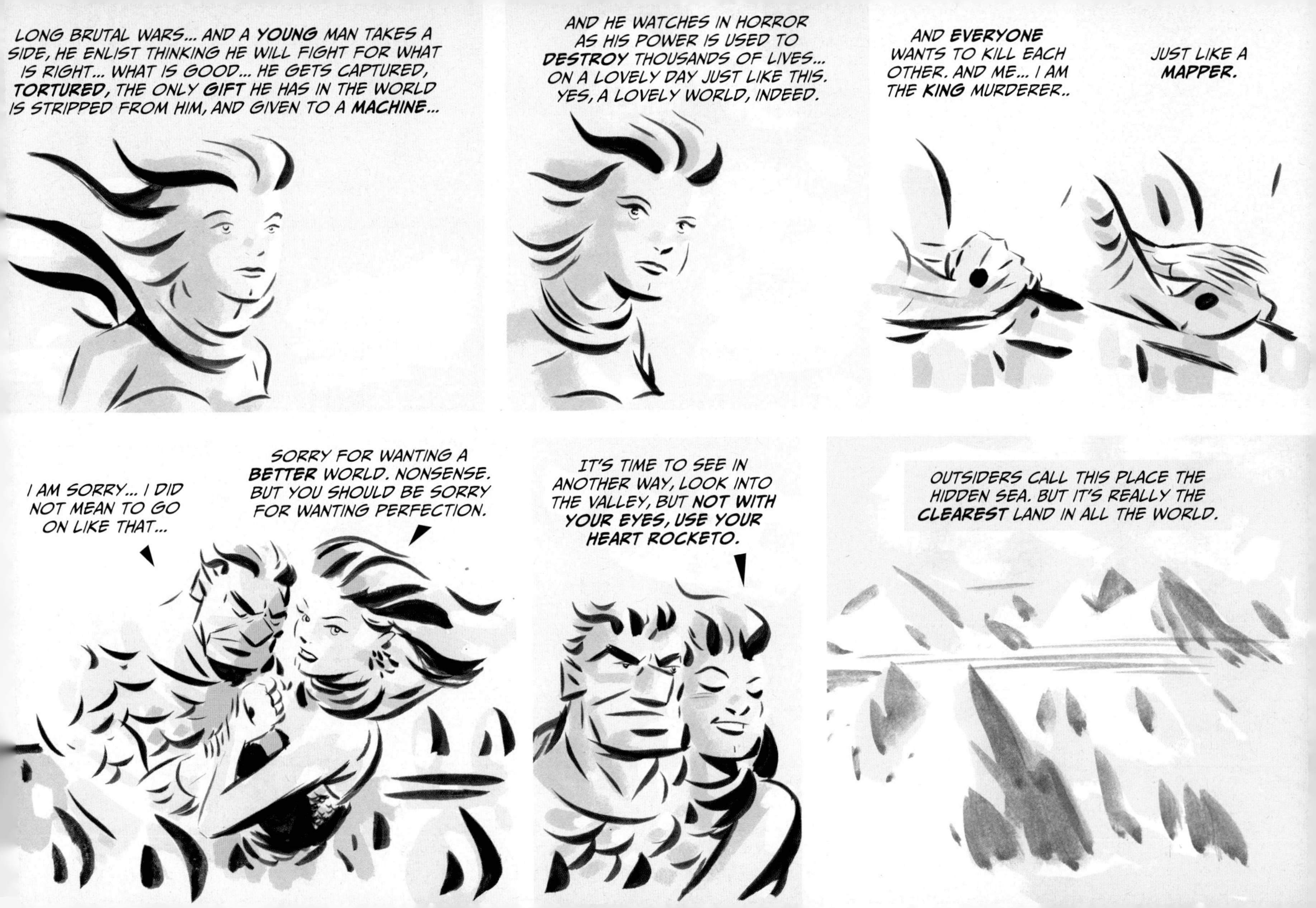
LONG BRUTAL WARS... AND A YOUNG MAN TAKES A SIDE, HE ENLIST THINKING HE WILL FIGHT FOR WHAT IS RIGHT... WHAT IS GOOD... HE GETS CAPTURED, TORTURED, THE ONLY GIFT HE HAS IN THE WORLD IS STRIPPED FROM HIM, AND GIVEN TO A MACHINE...
AND HE WATCHES IN HORROR AS HIS POWER IS USED TO DESTROY THOUSANDS OF LIVES... ON A LOVELY DAY JUST LIKE THIS. YES, A LOVELY WORLD, INDEED.
AND EVERYONE WANTS TO KILL EACH OTHER. AND ME... I AM THE KING MURDERER..
JUST LIKE A MAPPER.
I AM SORRY... I DID NOT MEAN TO GO ON LIKE THAT...
SORRY FOR WANTING A BETTER WORLD. NONSENSE. BUT YOU SHOULD BE SORRY FOR WANTING PERFECTION.
IT'S TIME TO SEE IN ANOTHER WAY, LOOK INTO THE VALLEY, BUT NOT WITH YOUR EYES, USE YOUR HEART ROCKETO.
OUTSIDERS CALL THIS PLACE THE HIDDEN SEA. BUT IT'S REALLY THE CLEAREST LAND IN ALL THE WORLD.

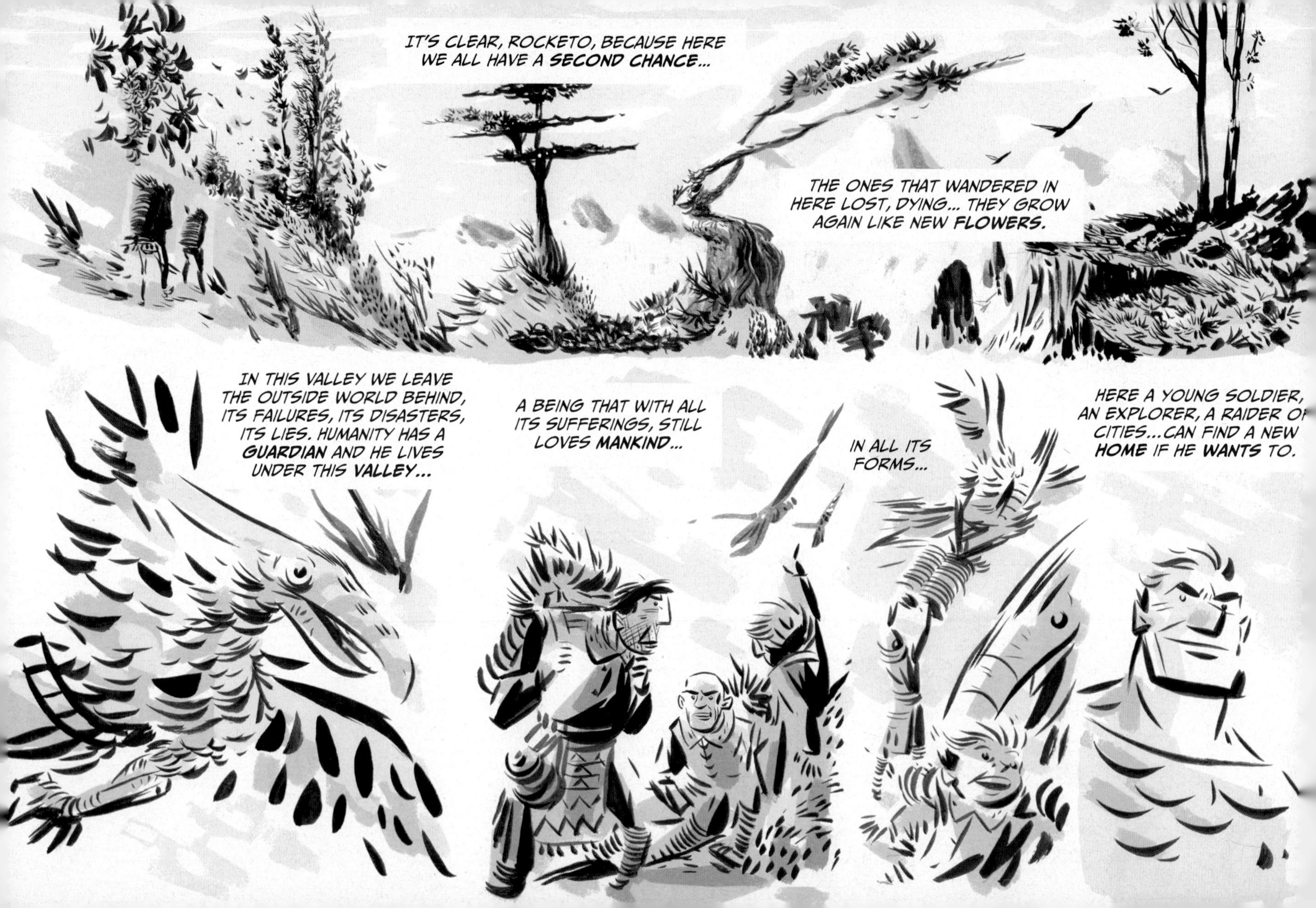
IT'S CLEAR, ROCKETO, BECAUSE HERE WE ALL HAVE A **SECOND CHANCE**...
THE ONES THAT WANDERED IN HERE LOST, DYING... THEY GROW AGAIN LIKE NEW **FLOWERS**.
IN THIS VALLEY WE LEAVE THE OUTSIDE WORLD BEHIND, ITS FAILURES, ITS DISASTERS, ITS LIES. HUMANITY HAS A **GUARDIAN** AND HE LIVES UNDER THIS **VALLEY**...
A BEING THAT WITH ALL ITS SUFFERINGS, STILL LOVES **MANKIND**...
IN ALL ITS FORMS...
HERE A YOUNG SOLDIER, AN EXPLORER, A RAIDER OF CITIES...CAN FIND A NEW **HOME** IF HE **WANTS** TO.

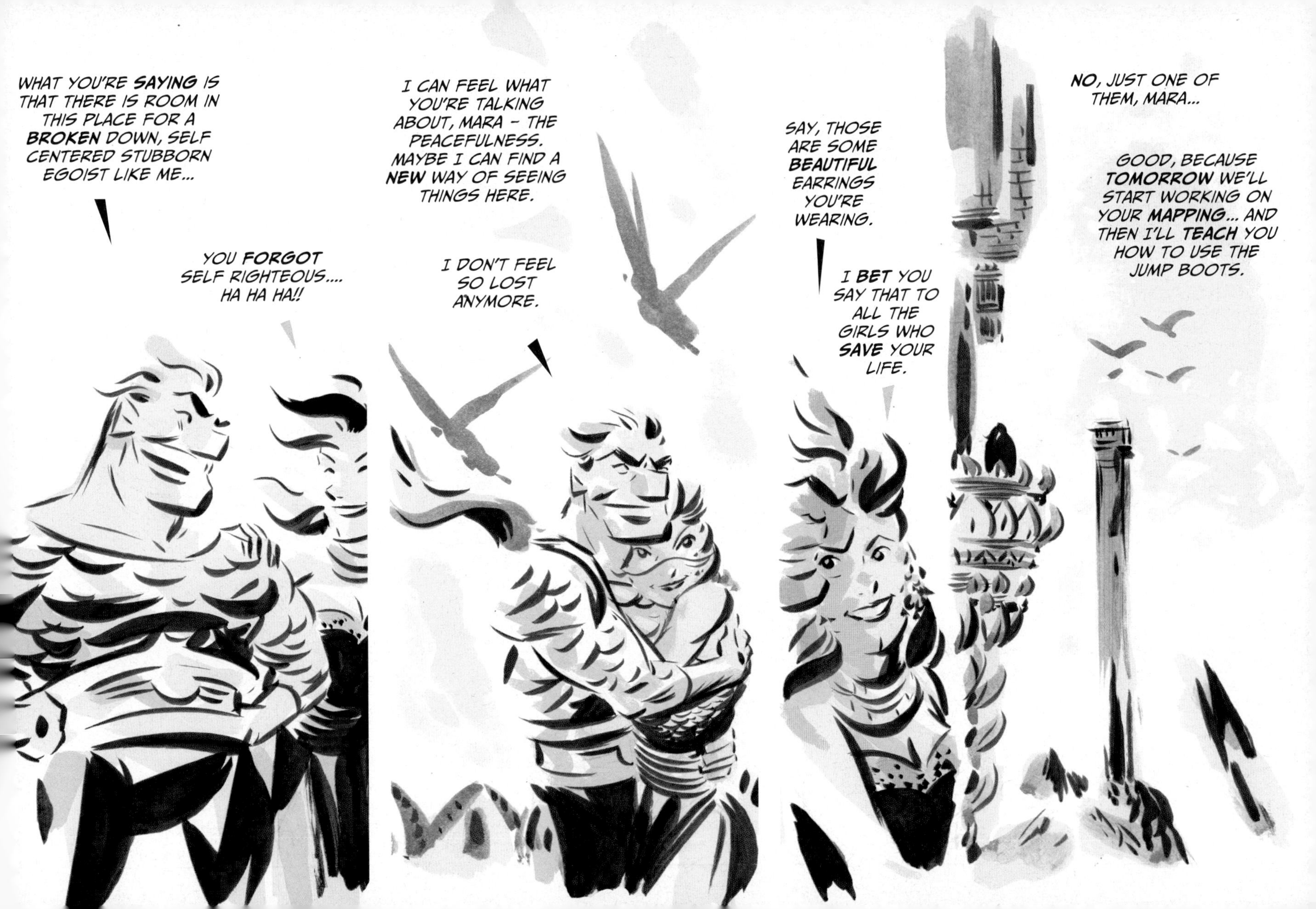
WHAT YOU'RE **SAYING** IS THAT THERE IS ROOM IN THIS PLACE FOR A **BROKEN** DOWN, SELF CENTERED STUBBORN EGOIST LIKE ME...
YOU **FORGOT** SELF RIGHTEOUS.... HA HA HA!!
I CAN FEEL WHAT YOU'RE TALKING ABOUT, MARA - THE PEACEFULNESS. MAYBE I CAN FIND A **NEW** WAY OF SEEING THINGS HERE.
I DON'T FEEL SO LOST ANYMORE.
SAY, THOSE ARE SOME **BEAUTIFUL** EARRINGS YOU'RE WEARING.
I **BET** YOU SAY THAT TO ALL THE GIRLS WHO **SAVE** YOUR LIFE.
NO, JUST ONE OF THEM, MARA...
GOOD, BECAUSE **TOMORROW** WE'LL START WORKING ON YOUR **MAPPING**... AND THEN I'LL **TEACH** YOU HOW TO USE THE JUMP BOOTS.

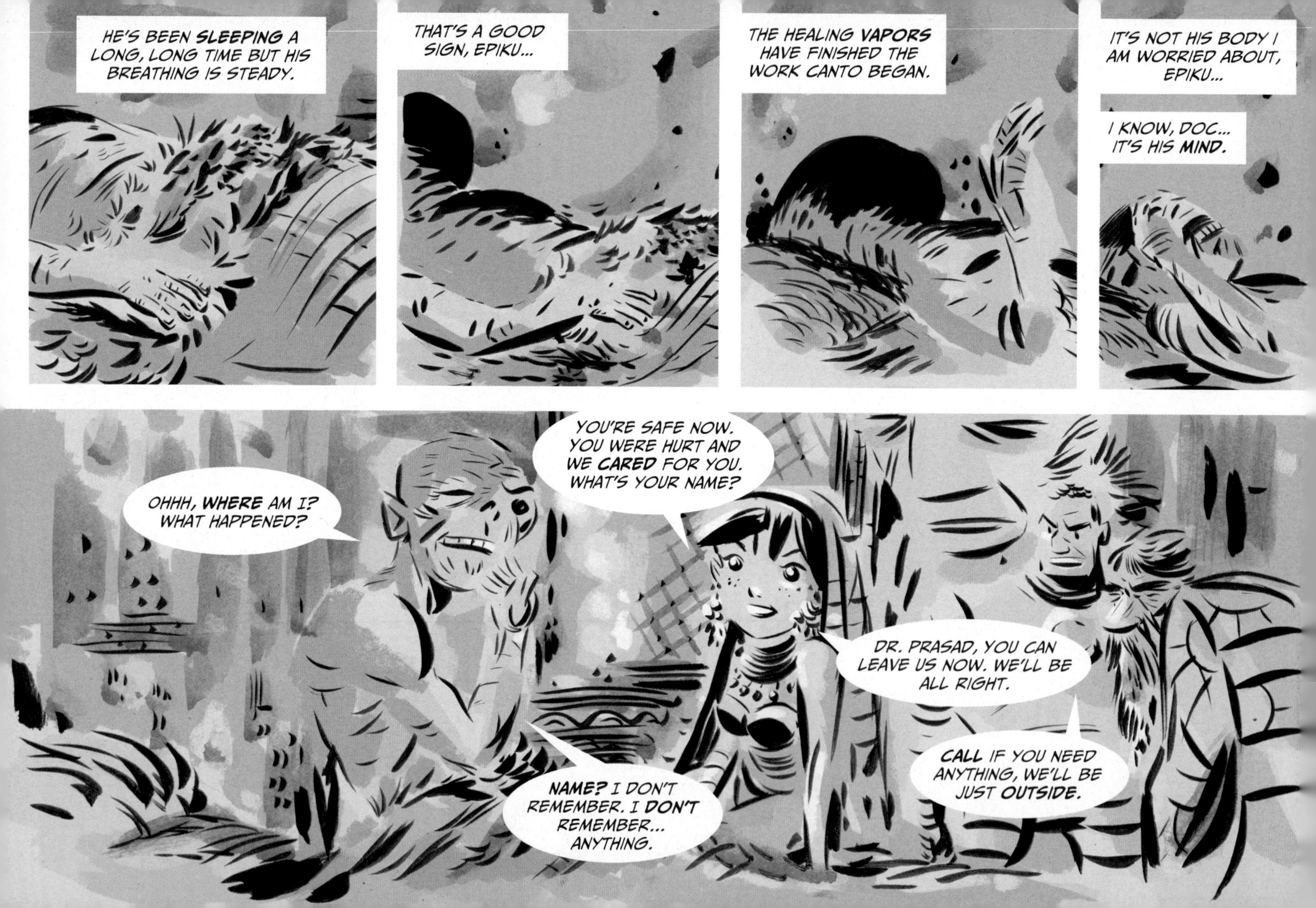
HE'S BEEN **SLEEPING** A LONG, LONG TIME BUT HIS BREATHING IS STEADY.
THAT'S A GOOD SIGN, EPIKU...
THE HEALING **VAPORS** HAVE FINISHED THE WORK CANTO BEGAN.
IT'S NOT HIS BODY I AM WORRIED ABOUT, EPIKU...
I KNOW, DOC... IT'S HIS **MIND.**
OHHH, **WHERE** AM I? WHAT HAPPENED?
YOU'RE SAFE NOW. YOU WERE HURT AND WE **CARED** FOR YOU. WHAT'S YOUR NAME?
NAME? I DON'T REMEMBER. I **DON'T** REMEMBER... ANYTHING.
DR. PRASAD, YOU CAN LEAVE US NOW. WE'LL BE ALL RIGHT.
CALL IF YOU NEED ANYTHING, WE'LL BE JUST **OUTSIDE.**

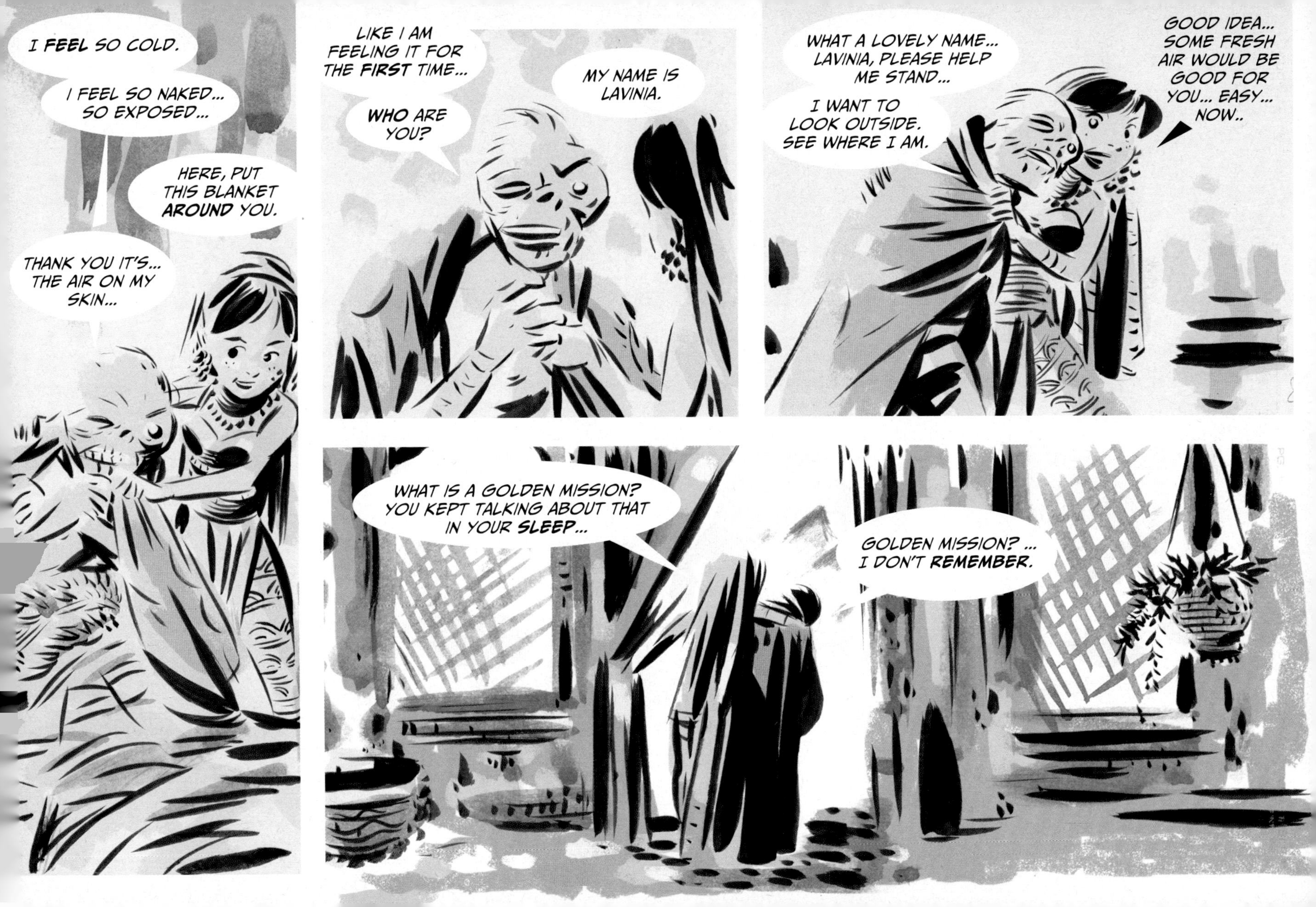
I FEEL SO COLD.
I FEEL SO NAKED... SO EXPOSED...
HERE, PUT THIS BLANKET AROUND YOU.
THANK YOU IT'S... THE AIR ON MY SKIN...
LIKE I AM FEELING IT FOR THE FIRST TIME...
WHO ARE YOU?
MY NAME IS LAVINIA.
WHAT A LOVELY NAME... LAVINIA, PLEASE HELP ME STAND...
I WANT TO LOOK OUTSIDE. SEE WHERE I AM.
GOOD IDEA... SOME FRESH AIR WOULD BE GOOD FOR YOU... EASY... NOW..
WHAT IS A GOLDEN MISSION? YOU KEPT TALKING ABOUT THAT IN YOUR SLEEP...
GOLDEN MISSION? ... I DON'T REMEMBER.

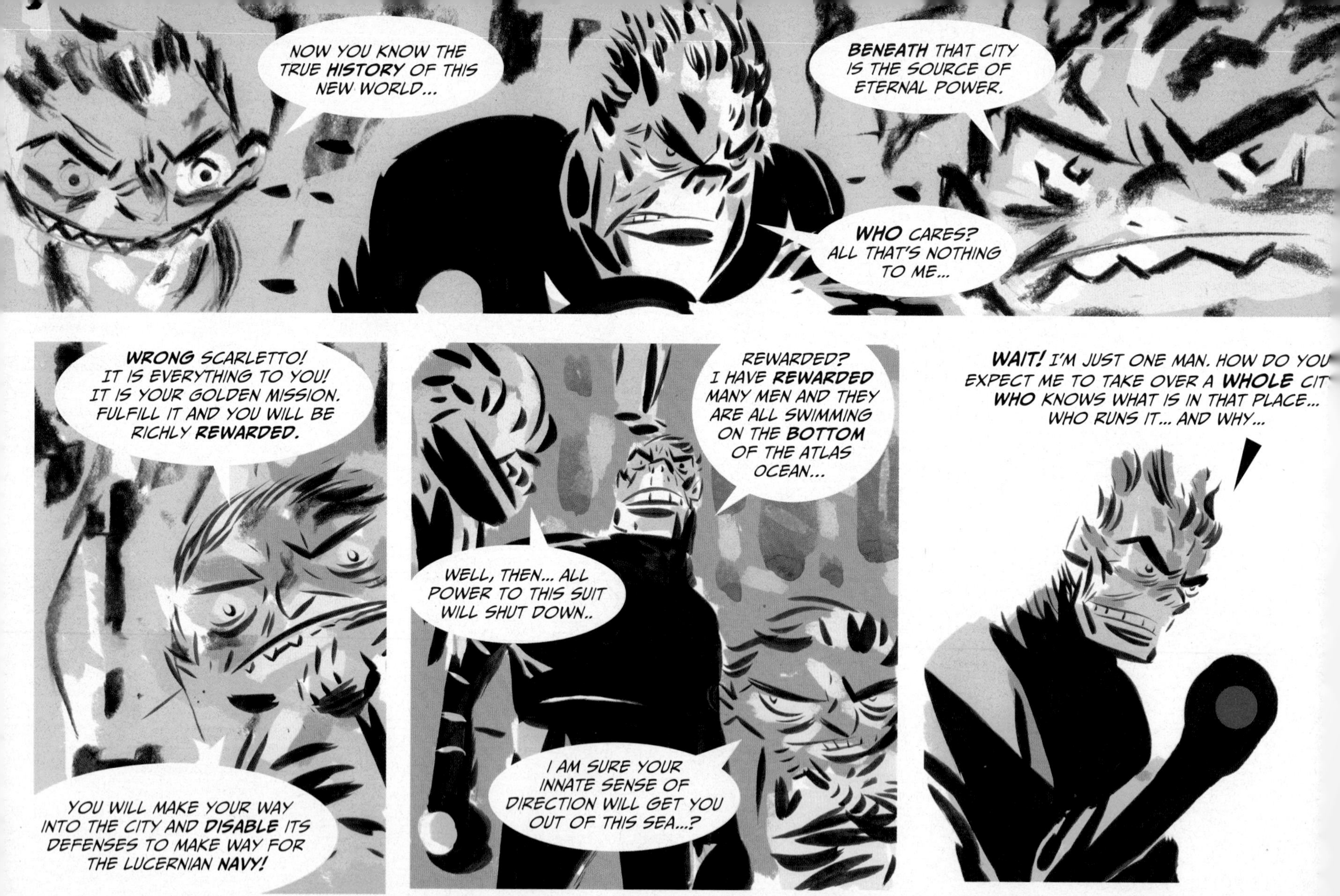
NOW YOU KNOW THE TRUE HISTORY OF THIS NEW WORLD...
BENEATH THAT CITY IS THE SOURCE OF ETERNAL POWER.
WHO CARES? ALL THAT'S NOTHING TO ME...
WRONG SCARLETTO! IT IS EVERYTHING TO YOU! IT IS YOUR GOLDEN MISSION. FULFILL IT AND YOU WILL BE RICHLY REWARDED.
YOU WILL MAKE YOUR WAY INTO THE CITY AND DISABLE ITS DEFENSES TO MAKE WAY FOR THE LUCERNIAN NAVY!
REWARDED? I HAVE REWARDED MANY MEN AND THEY ARE ALL SWIMMING ON THE BOTTOM OF THE ATLAS OCEAN...
WELL, THEN... ALL POWER TO THIS SUIT WILL SHUT DOWN..
I AM SURE YOUR INNATE SENSE OF DIRECTION WILL GET YOU OUT OF THIS SEA...?
WAIT! I'M JUST ONE MAN. HOW DO YOU EXPECT ME TO TAKE OVER A WHOLE CIT
WHO KNOWS WHAT IS IN THAT PLACE... WHO RUNS IT... AND WHY...

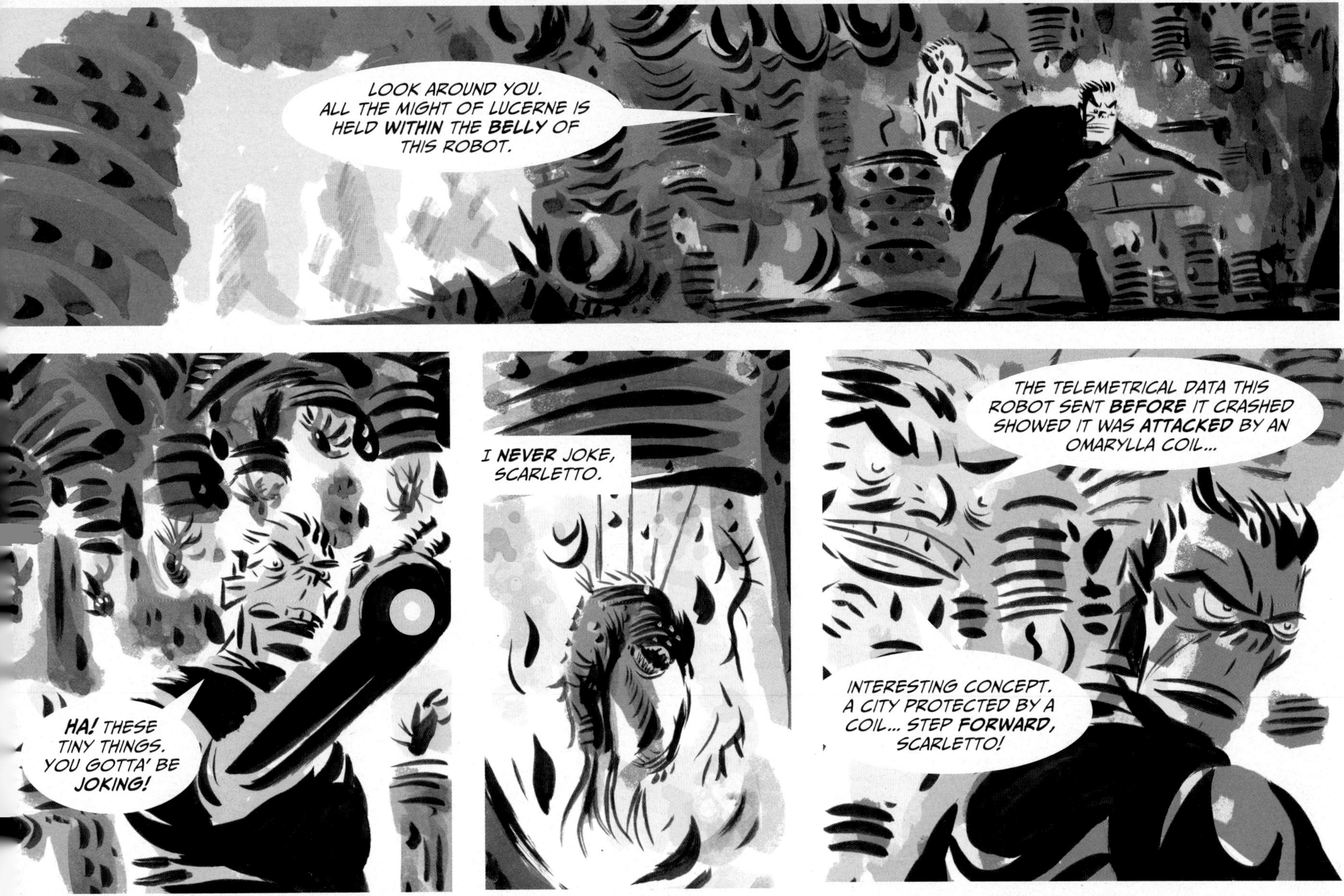
LOOK AROUND YOU. ALL THE MIGHT OF LUCERNE IS HELD **WITHIN** THE **BELLY** OF THIS ROBOT.
HA! THESE TINY THINGS. YOU GOTTA' BE **JOKING!**
I **NEVER** JOKE, SCARLETTO.
THE TELEMETRICAL DATA THIS ROBOT SENT **BEFORE** IT CRASHED SHOWED IT WAS **ATTACKED** BY AN OMARYLLA COIL...
INTERESTING CONCEPT. A CITY PROTECTED BY A COIL... STEP **FORWARD,** SCARLETTO!

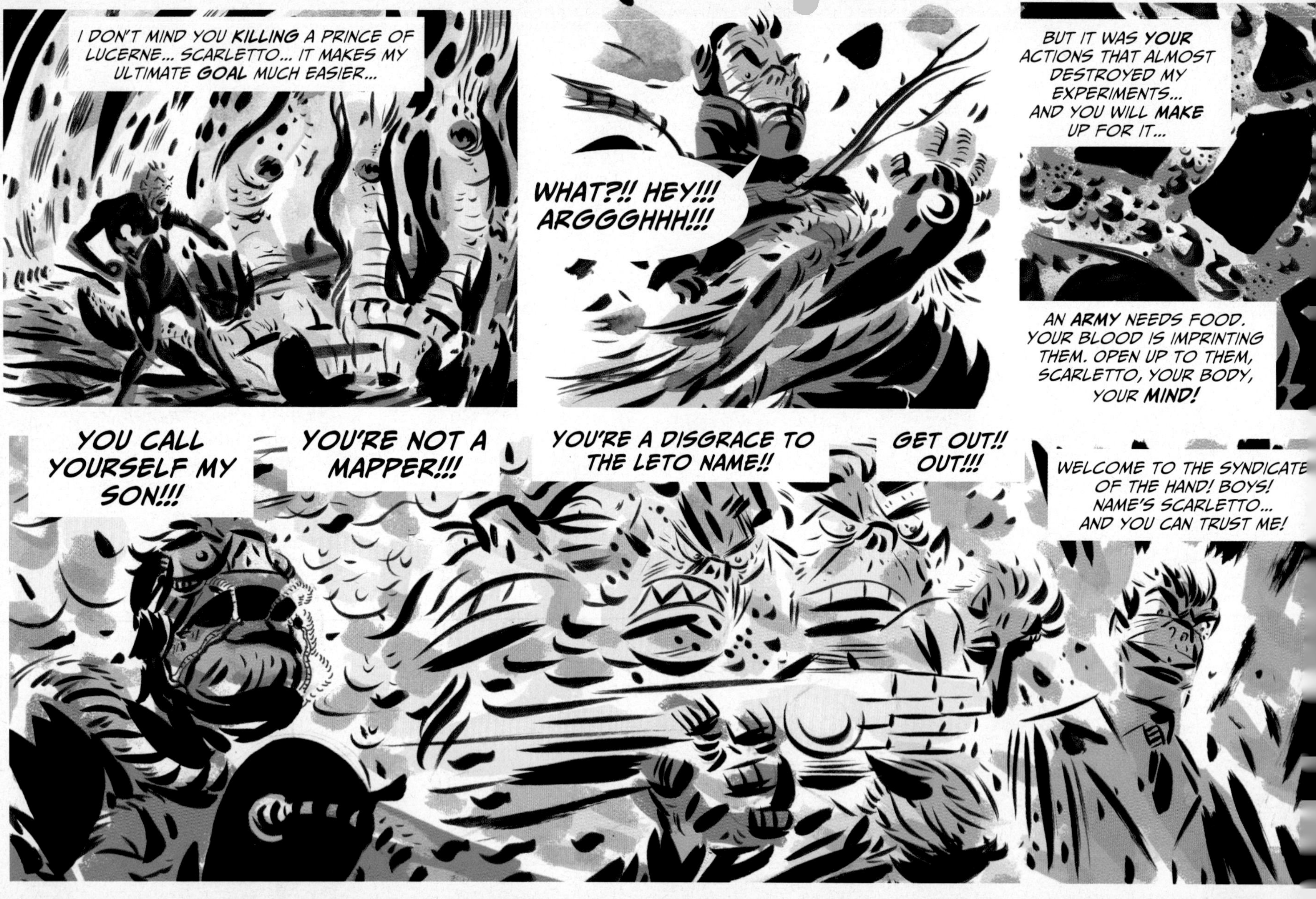
I DON'T MIND YOU KILLING A PRINCE OF LUCERNE... SCARLETTO... IT MAKES MY ULTIMATE GOAL MUCH EASIER...
WHAT?!! HEY!!! ARGGGHHH!!!
BUT IT WAS YOUR ACTIONS THAT ALMOST DESTROYED MY EXPERIMENTS... AND YOU WILL MAKE UP FOR IT...
AN ARMY NEEDS FOOD. YOUR BLOOD IS IMPRINTING THEM. OPEN UP TO THEM, SCARLETTO, YOUR BODY, YOUR MIND!
YOU CALL YOURSELF MY SON!!!
YOU'RE NOT A MAPPER!!!
YOU'RE A DISGRACE TO THE LETO NAME!!
GET OUT!! OUT!!!
WELCOME TO THE SYNDICATE OF THE HAND! BOYS! NAME'S SCARLETTO... AND YOU CAN TRUST ME!

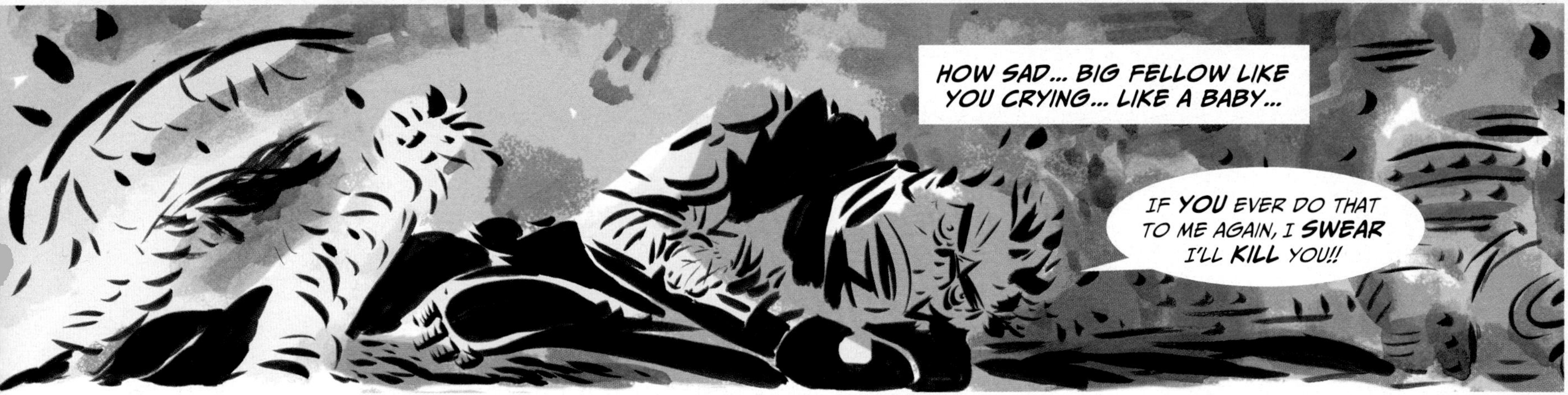
HOW SAD... BIG FELLOW LIKE YOU CRYING... LIKE A BABY...
IF **YOU** EVER DO THAT TO ME AGAIN, I **SWEAR** I'LL **KILL** YOU!!

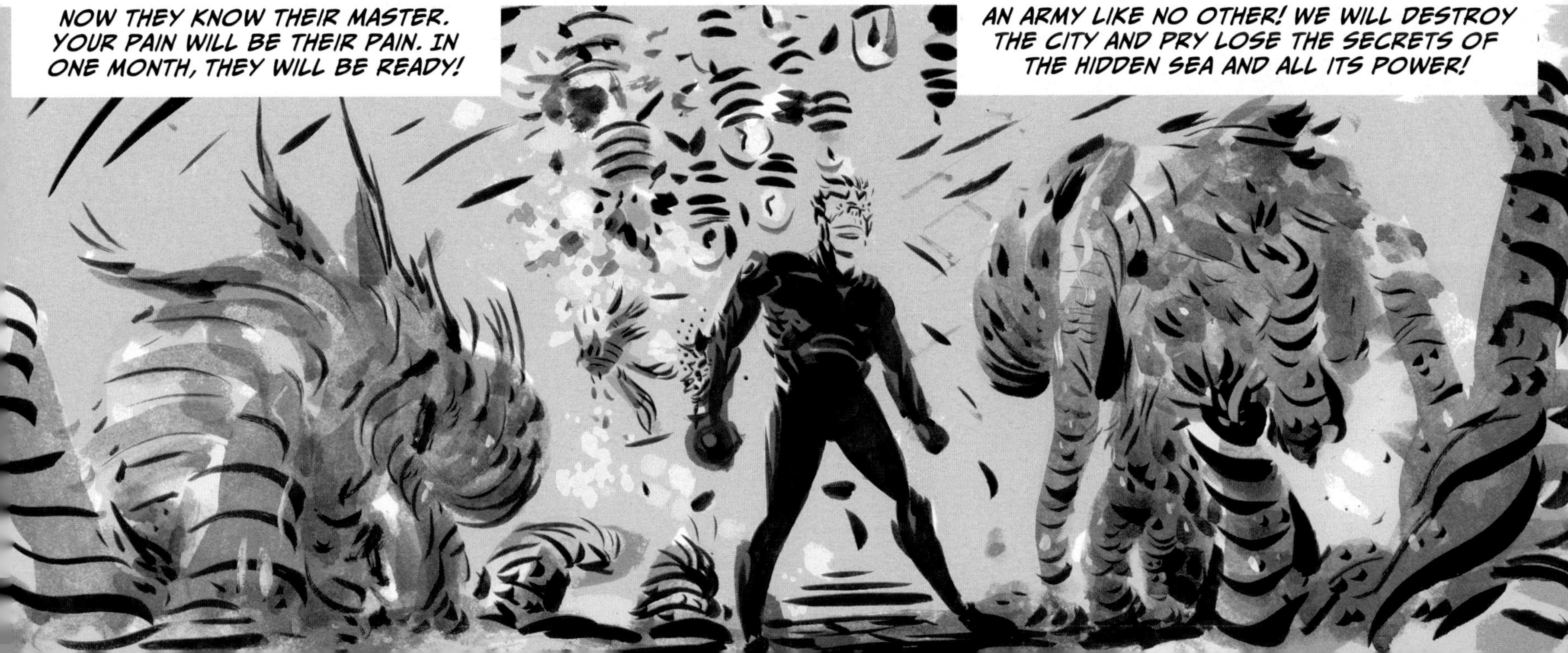
NOW THEY KNOW THEIR MASTER. YOUR PAIN WILL BE THEIR PAIN. IN ONE MONTH, THEY WILL BE READY!
AN ARMY LIKE NO OTHER! WE WILL DESTROY THE CITY AND PRY LOSE THE SECRETS OF THE HIDDEN SEA AND ALL ITS POWER!

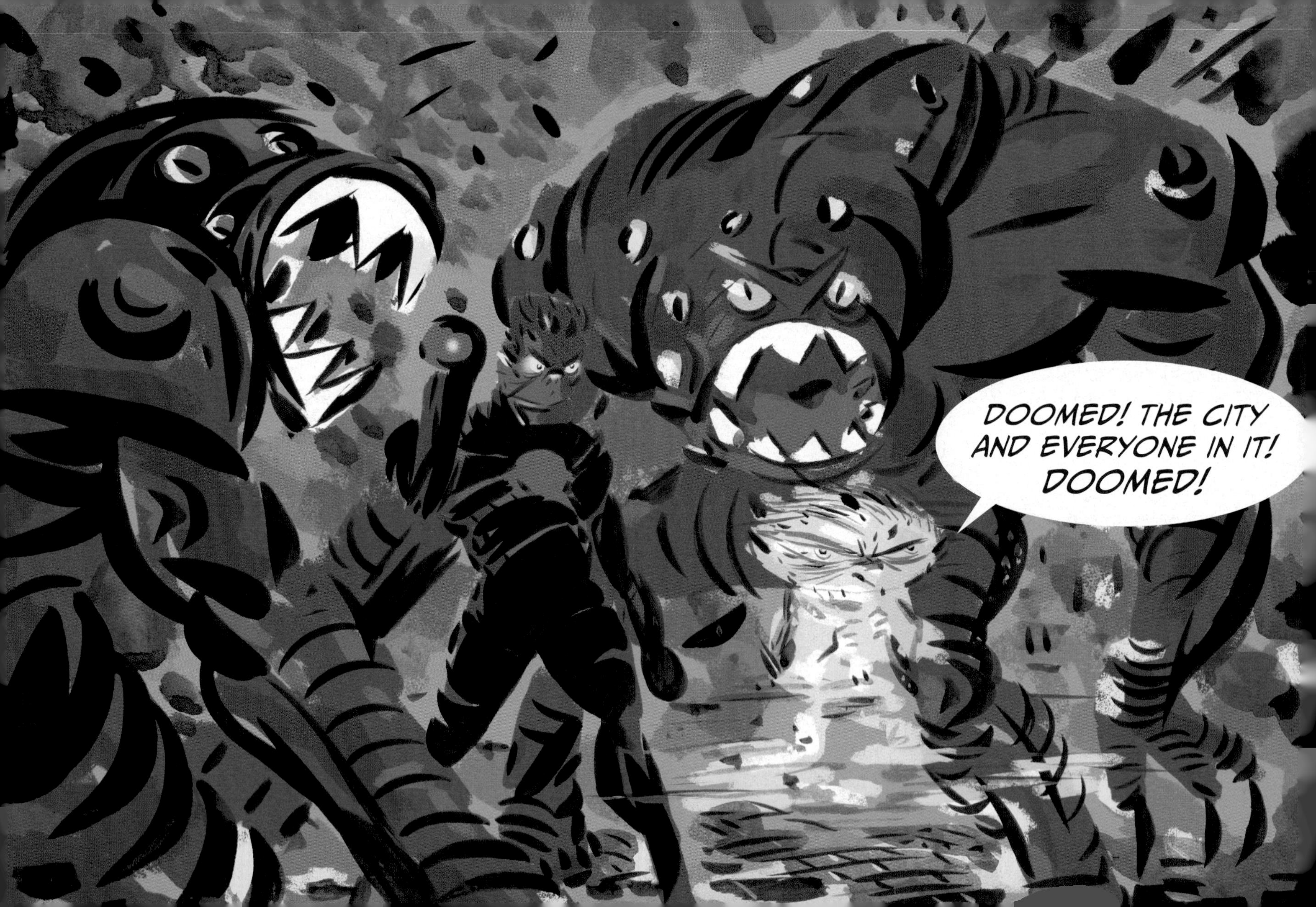
DOOMED! THE CITY AND EVERYONE IN IT! DOOMED!

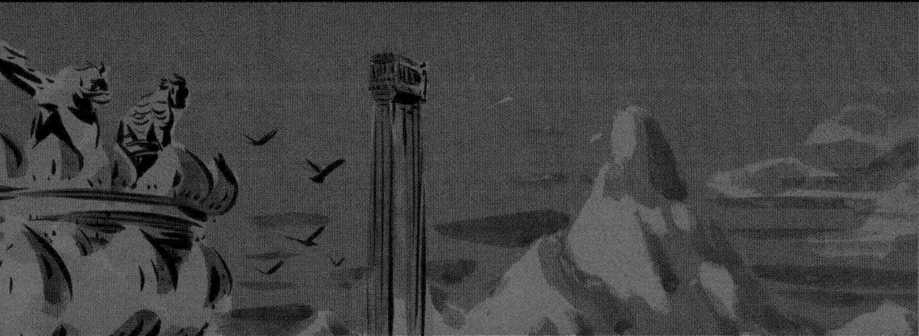

ROCKETO

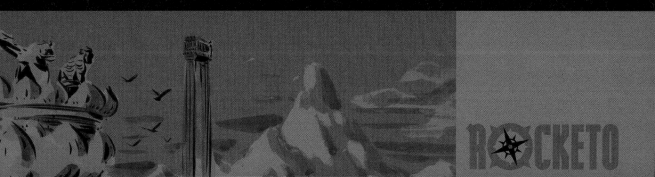

9

RESOLUTIONS

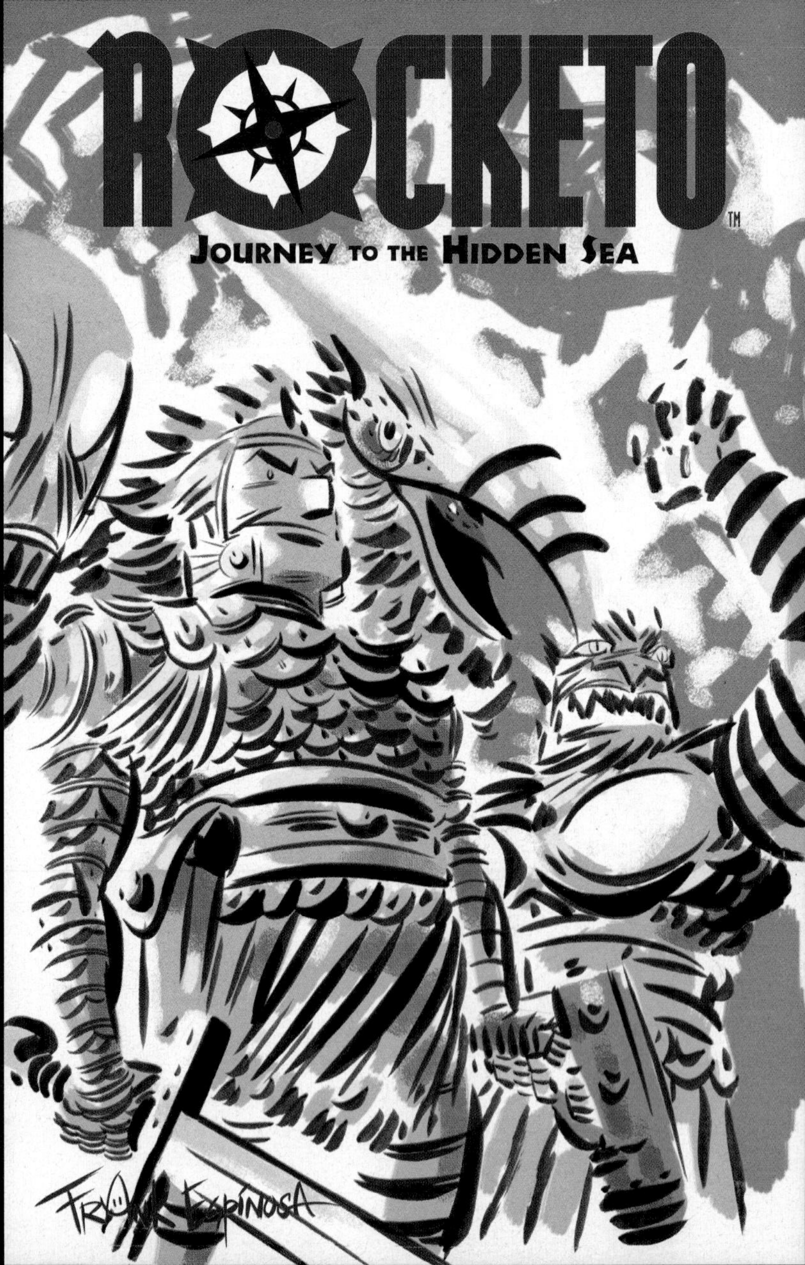
ROCKETO™
JOURNEY TO THE HIDDEN SEA

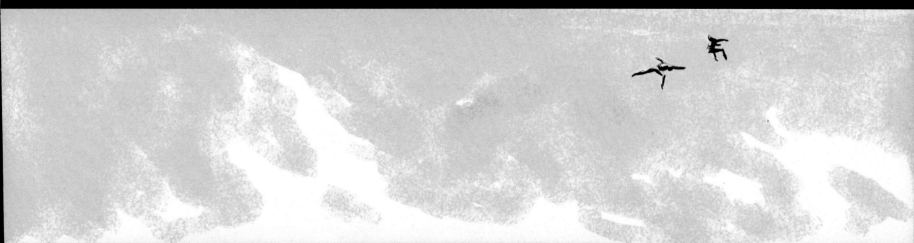

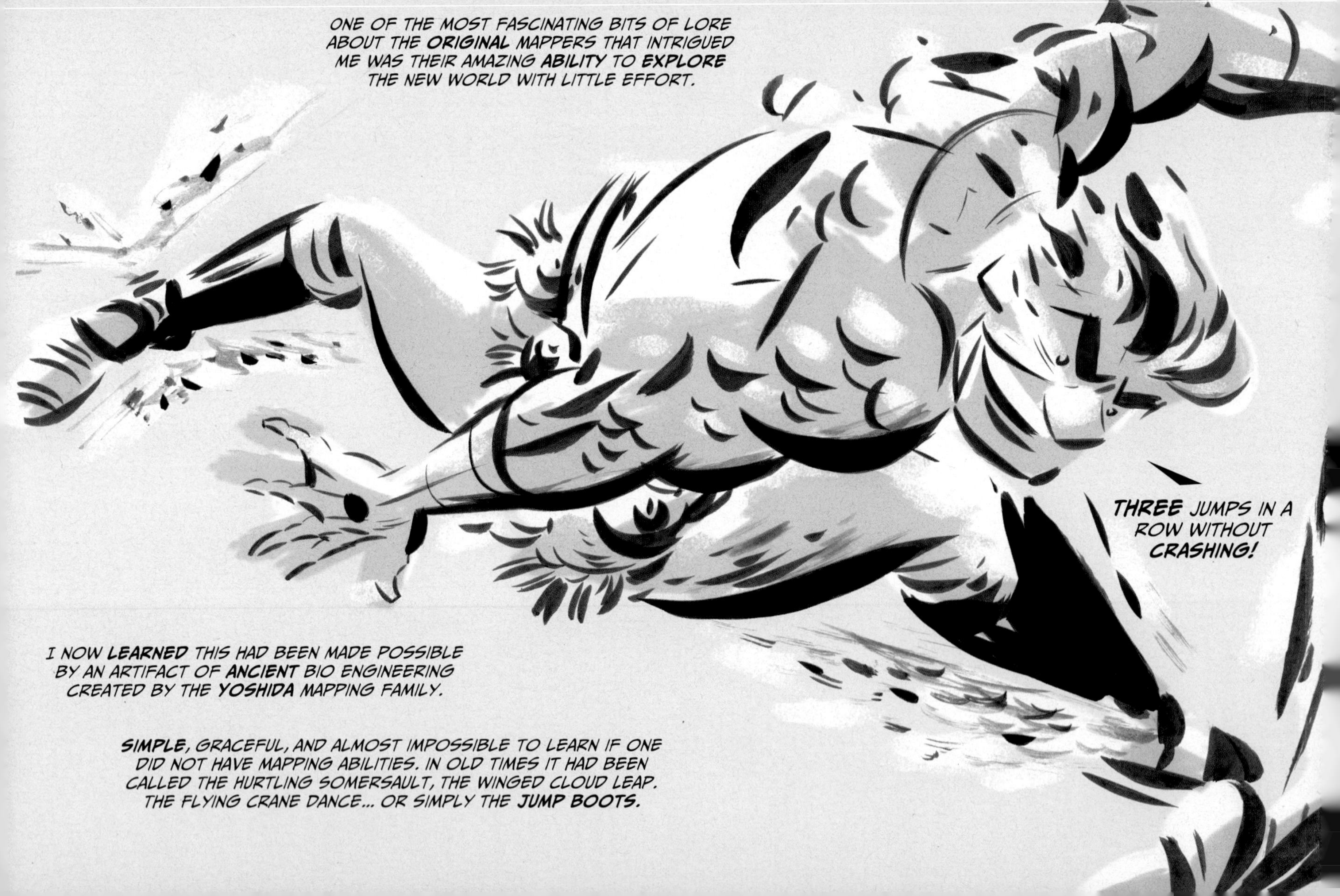
ONE OF THE MOST FASCINATING BITS OF LORE ABOUT THE ORIGINAL MAPPERS THAT INTRIGUED ME WAS THEIR AMAZING ABILITY TO EXPLORE THE NEW WORLD WITH LITTLE EFFORT.
THREE JUMPS IN A ROW WITHOUT CRASHING!
I NOW LEARNED THIS HAD BEEN MADE POSSIBLE BY AN ARTIFACT OF ANCIENT BIO ENGINEERING CREATED BY THE YOSHIDA MAPPING FAMILY.
SIMPLE, GRACEFUL, AND ALMOST IMPOSSIBLE TO LEARN IF ONE DID NOT HAVE MAPPING ABILITIES. IN OLD TIMES IT HAD BEEN CALLED THE HURTLING SOMERSAULT, THE WINGED CLOUD LEAP. THE FLYING CRANE DANCE... OR SIMPLY THE JUMP BOOTS.

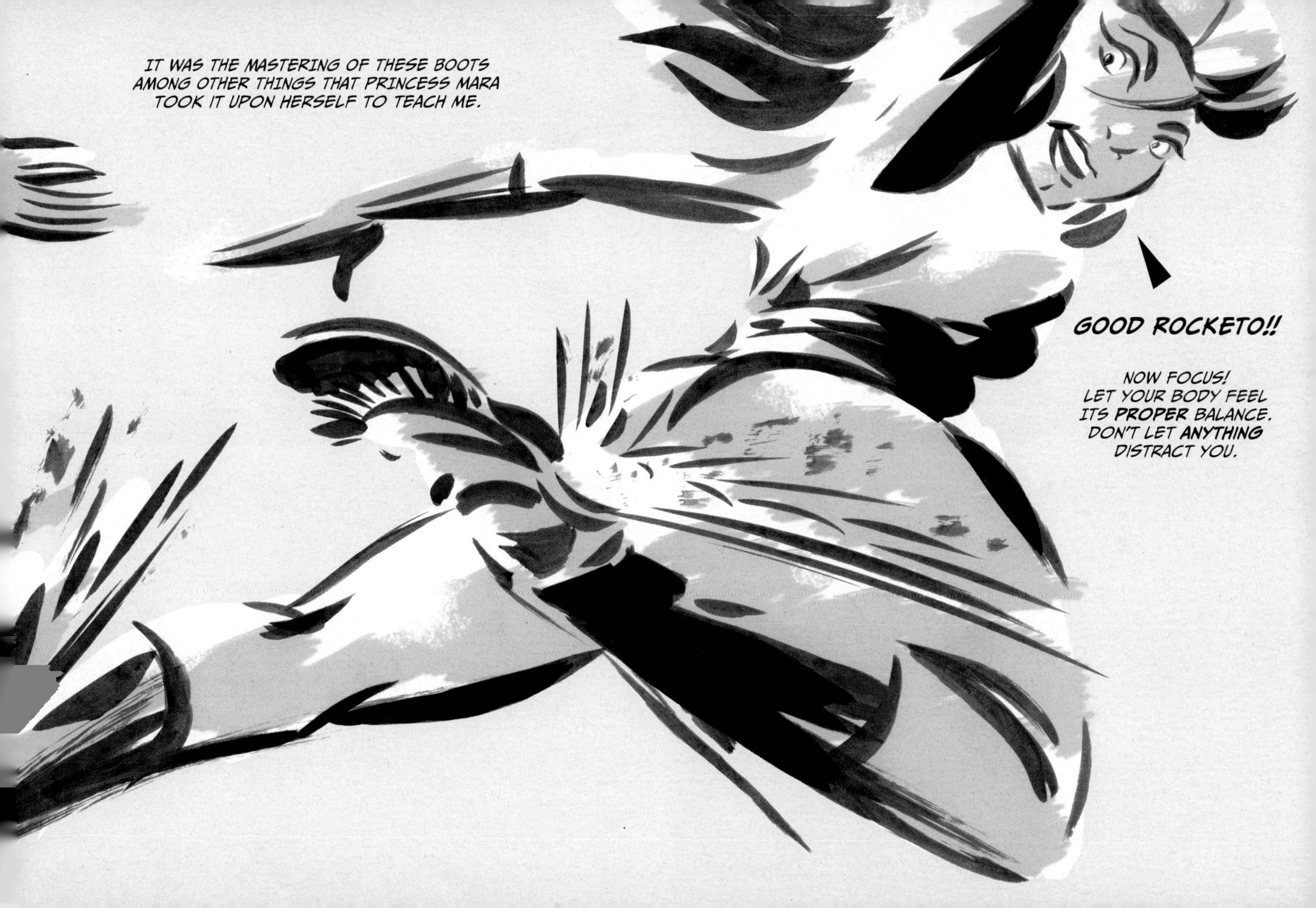
IT WAS THE MASTERING OF THESE BOOTS AMONG OTHER THINGS THAT PRINCESS MARA TOOK IT UPON HERSELF TO TEACH ME.
GOOD ROCKETO!!
NOW FOCUS! LET YOUR BODY FEEL ITS **PROPER** BALANCE. DON'T LET **ANYTHING** DISTRACT YOU.

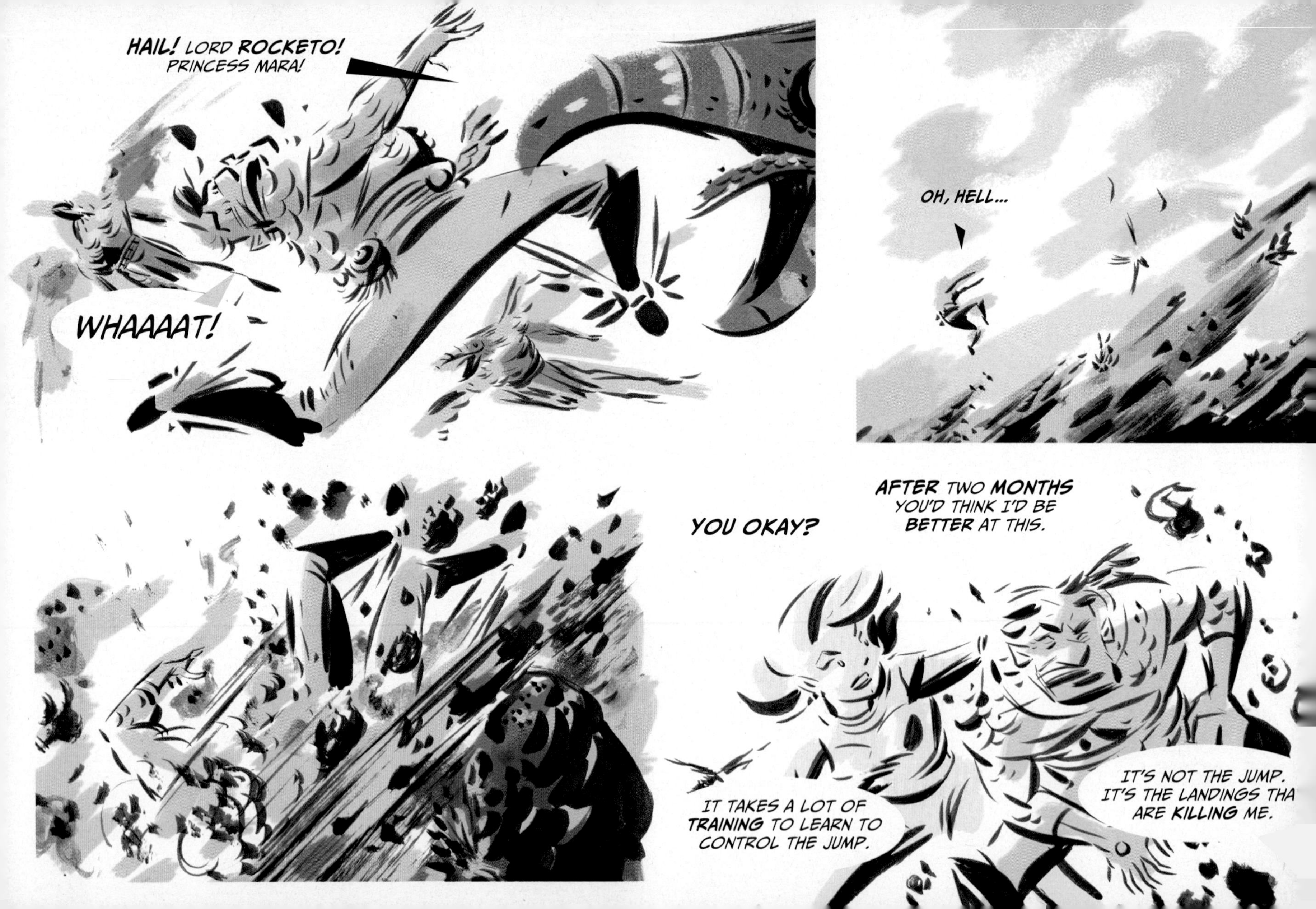
HAIL! LORD ROCKETO! PRINCESS MARA!
WHAAAAT!
OH, HELL...
YOU OKAY?
AFTER TWO MONTHS YOU'D THINK I'D BE BETTER AT THIS.
IT TAKES A LOT OF TRAINING TO LEARN TO CONTROL THE JUMP.
IT'S NOT THE JUMP. IT'S THE LANDINGS THA ARE KILLING ME.

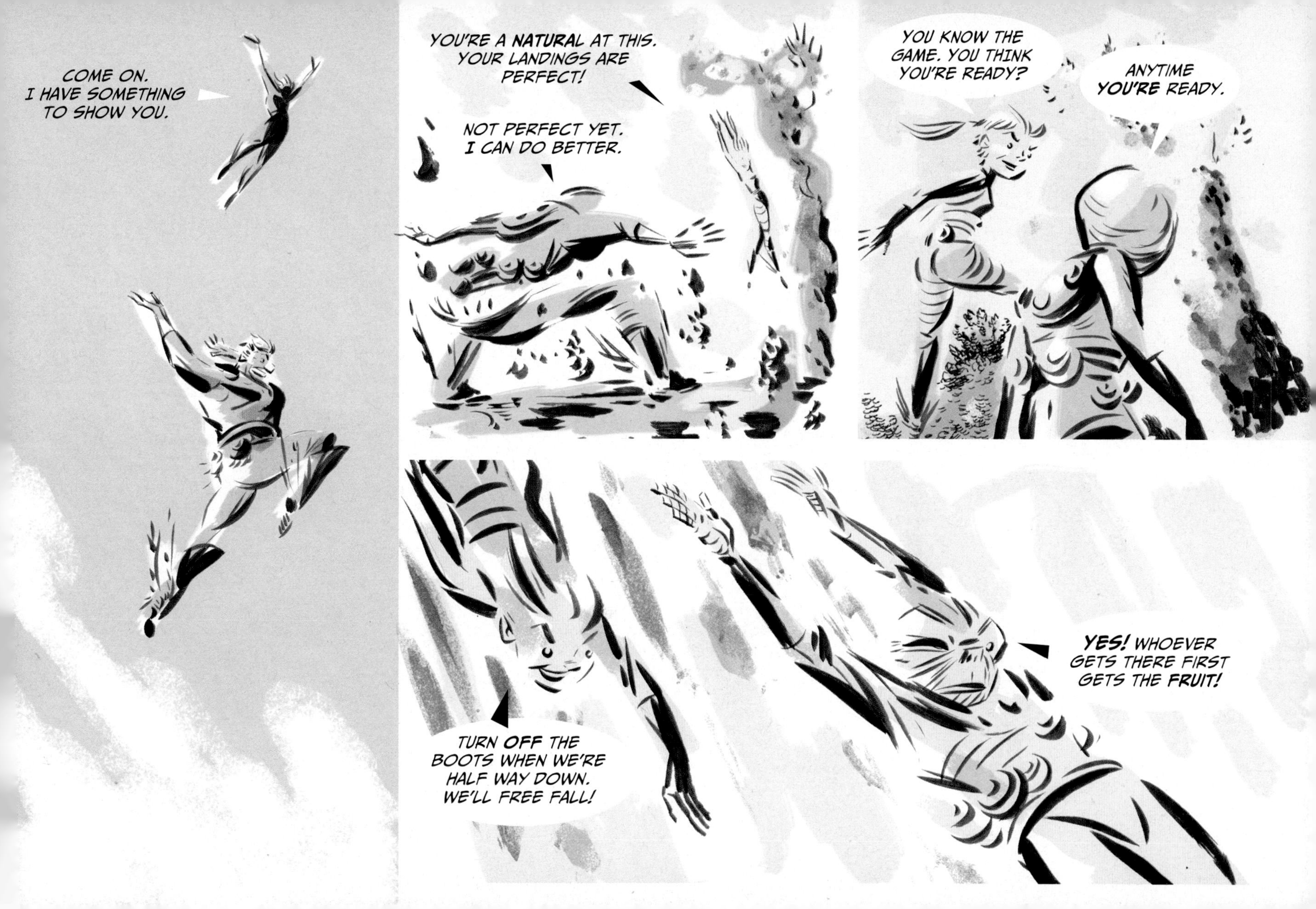
COME ON. I HAVE SOMETHING TO SHOW YOU.
YOU'RE A **NATURAL** AT THIS. YOUR LANDINGS ARE PERFECT!
NOT PERFECT YET. I CAN DO BETTER.
YOU KNOW THE GAME. YOU THINK YOU'RE READY?
ANYTIME **YOU'RE** READY.
TURN **OFF** THE BOOTS WHEN WE'RE HALF WAY DOWN. WE'LL FREE FALL!
YES! WHOEVER GETS THERE FIRST GETS THE **FRUIT!**

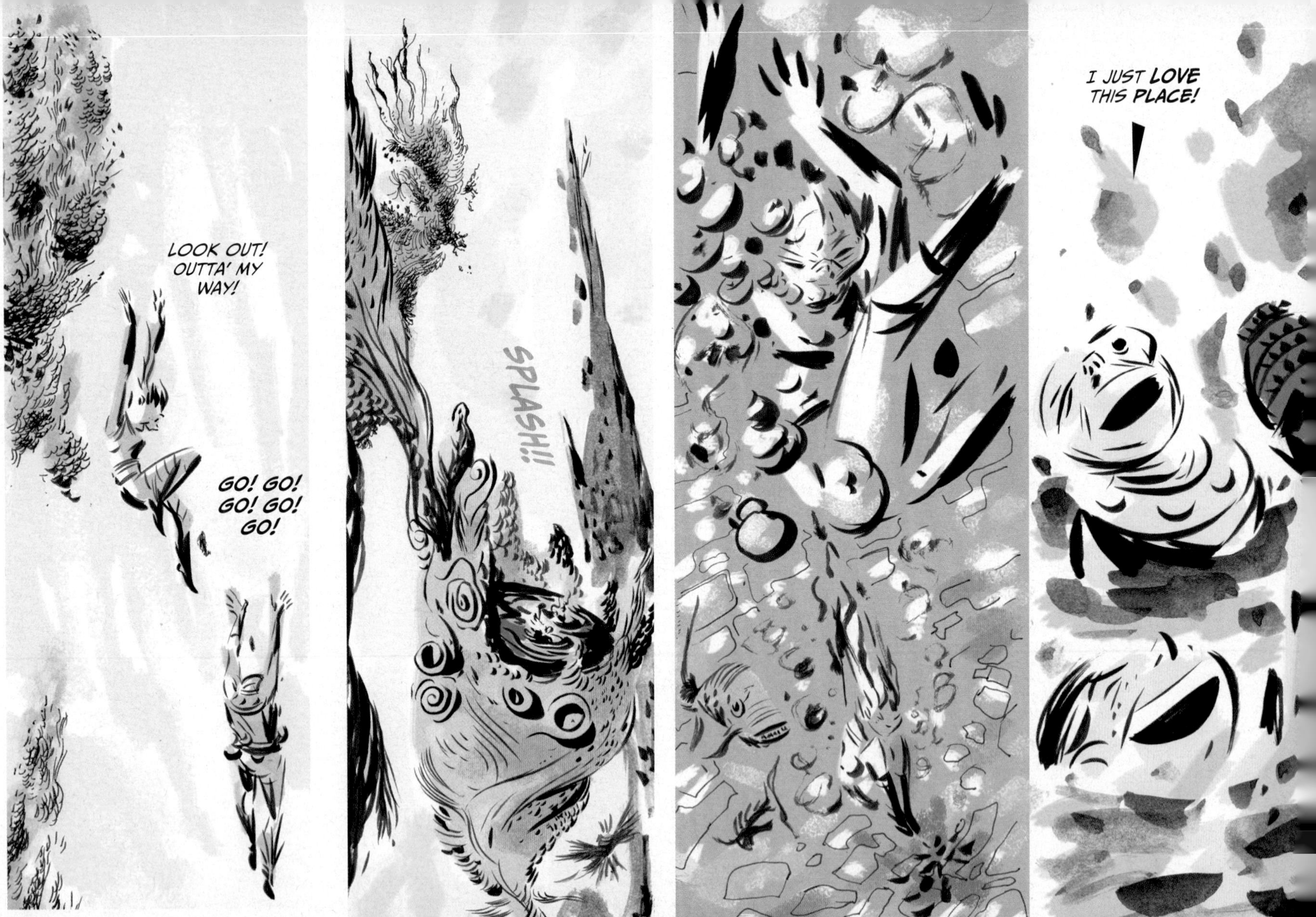
LOOK OUT! OUTTA' MY WAY!
GO! GO! GO! GO! GO!
SPLASH!!
I JUST **LOVE** THIS **PLACE!**

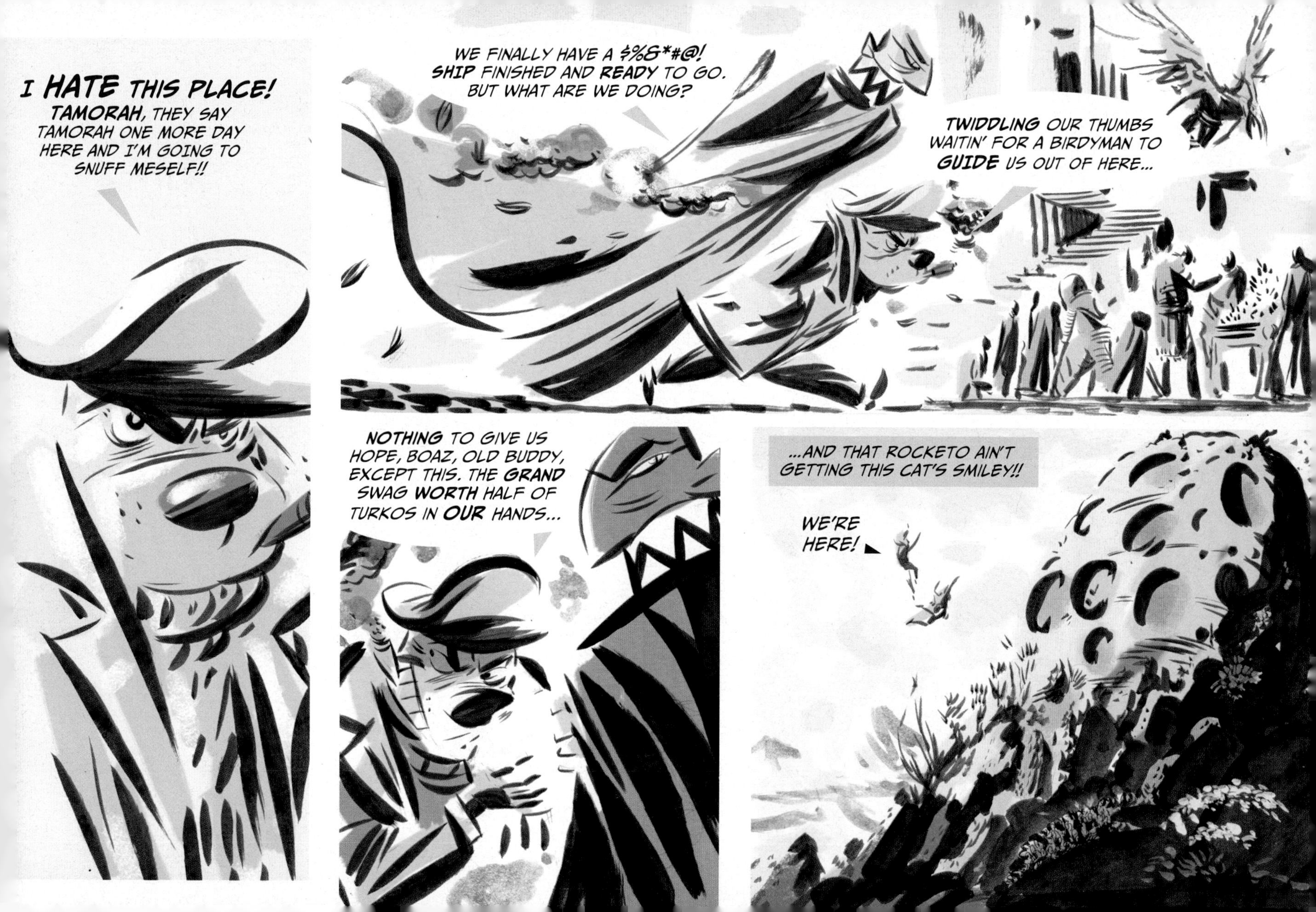
I HATE THIS PLACE! TAMORAH, THEY SAY TAMORAH ONE MORE DAY HERE AND I'M GOING TO SNUFF MESELF!!
WE FINALLY HAVE A $%&*#@! SHIP FINISHED AND READY TO GO. BUT WHAT ARE WE DOING?
TWIDDLING OUR THUMBS WAITIN' FOR A BIRDYMAN TO GUIDE US OUT OF HERE...
NOTHING TO GIVE US HOPE, BOAZ, OLD BUDDY, EXCEPT THIS. THE GRAND SWAG WORTH HALF OF TURKOS IN OUR HANDS...
...AND THAT ROCKETO AIN'T GETTING THIS CAT'S SMILEY!!
WE'RE HERE!

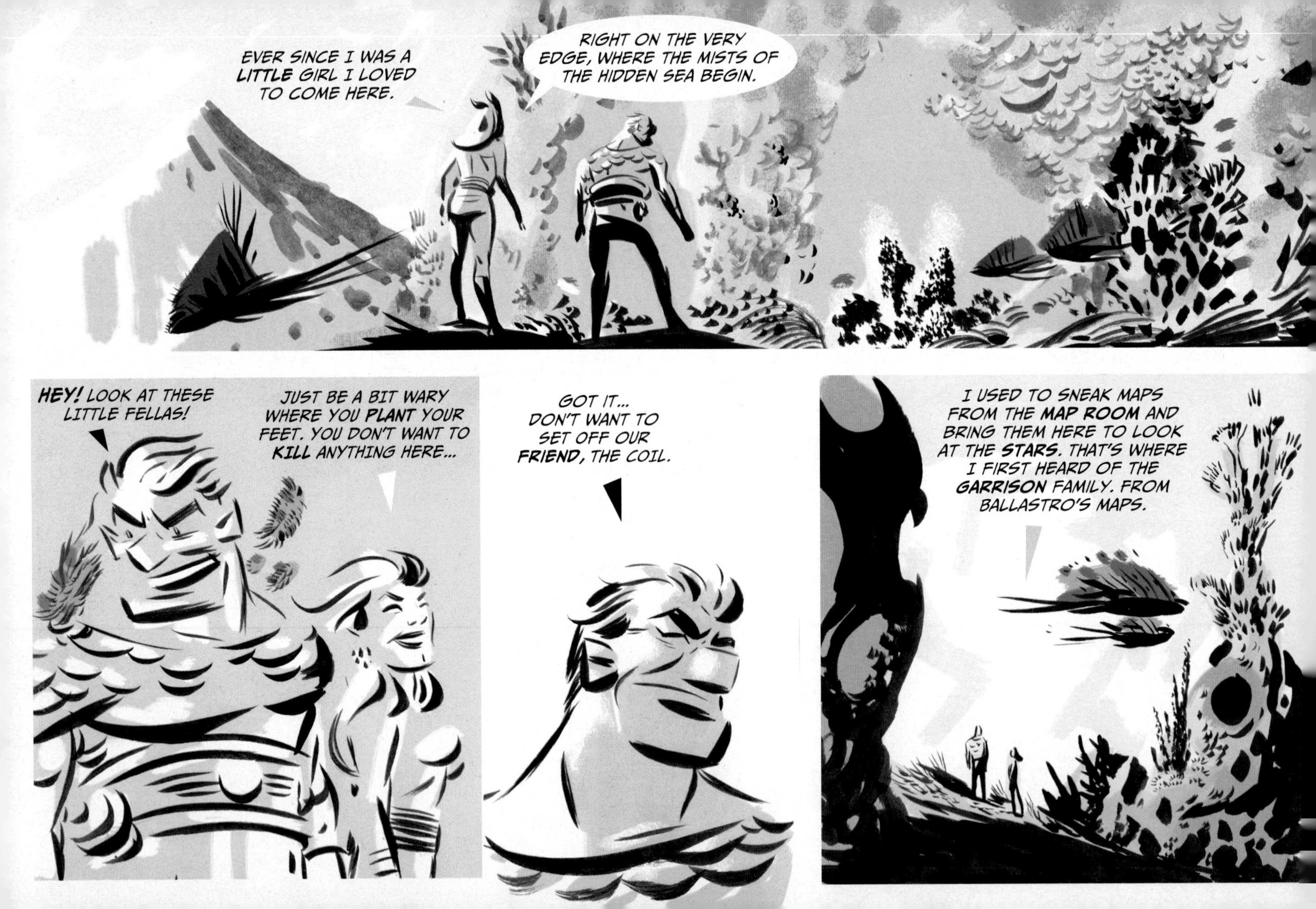
EVER SINCE I WAS A LITTLE GIRL I LOVED TO COME HERE.
RIGHT ON THE VERY EDGE, WHERE THE MISTS OF THE HIDDEN SEA BEGIN.
HEY! LOOK AT THESE LITTLE FELLAS!
JUST BE A BIT WARY WHERE YOU PLANT YOUR FEET. YOU DON'T WANT TO KILL ANYTHING HERE...
GOT IT... DON'T WANT TO SET OFF OUR FRIEND, THE COIL.
I USED TO SNEAK MAPS FROM THE MAP ROOM AND BRING THEM HERE TO LOOK AT THE STARS. THAT'S WHERE I FIRST HEARD OF THE GARRISON FAMILY. FROM BALLASTRO'S MAPS.

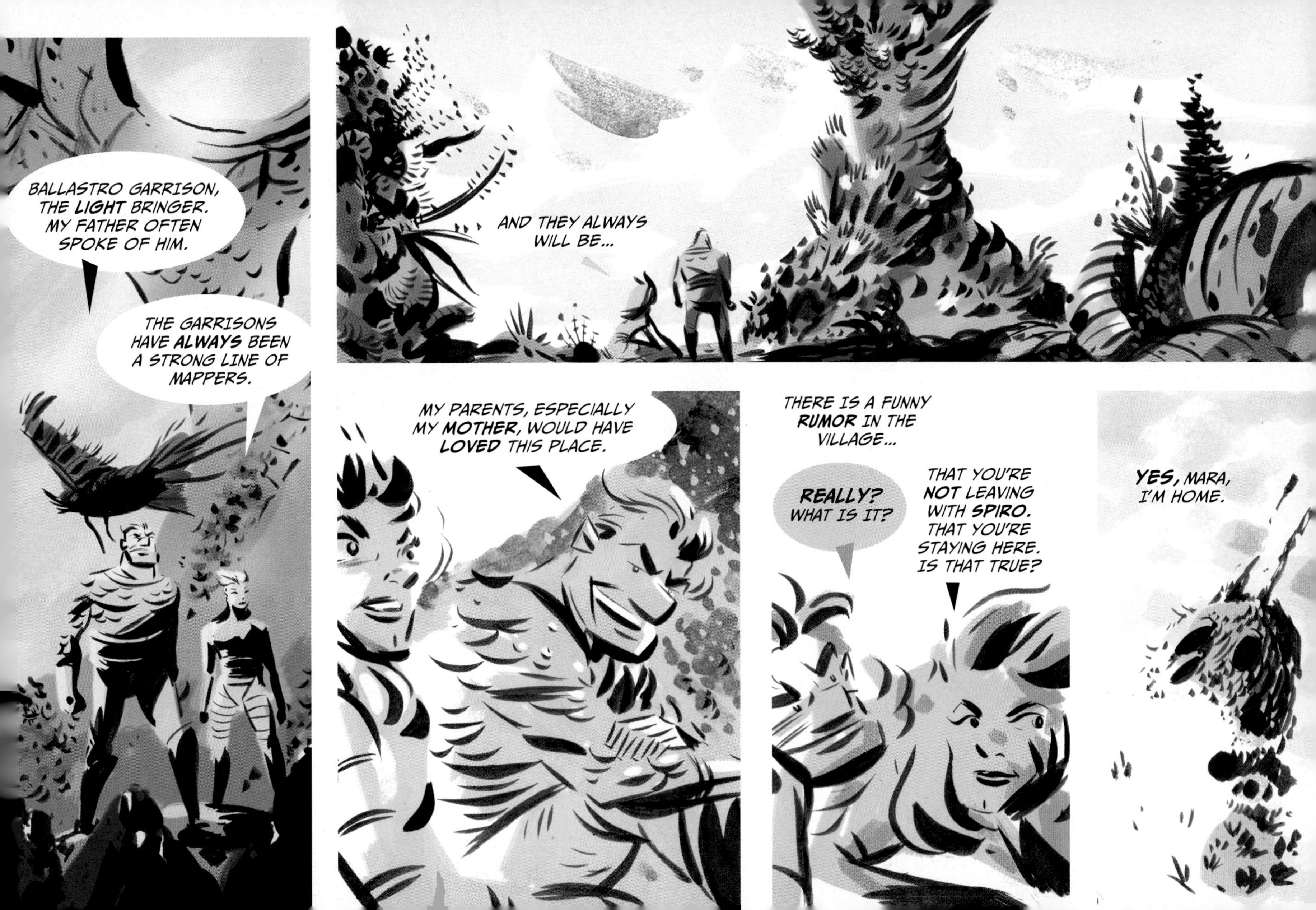
BALLASTRO GARRISON, THE LIGHT BRINGER. MY FATHER OFTEN SPOKE OF HIM.
THE GARRISONS HAVE ALWAYS BEEN A STRONG LINE OF MAPPERS.
AND THEY ALWAYS WILL BE...
MY PARENTS, ESPECIALLY MY MOTHER, WOULD HAVE LOVED THIS PLACE.
THERE IS A FUNNY RUMOR IN THE VILLAGE...
REALLY? WHAT IS IT?
THAT YOU'RE NOT LEAVING WITH SPIRO. THAT YOU'RE STAYING HERE. IS THAT TRUE?
YES, MARA, I'M HOME.

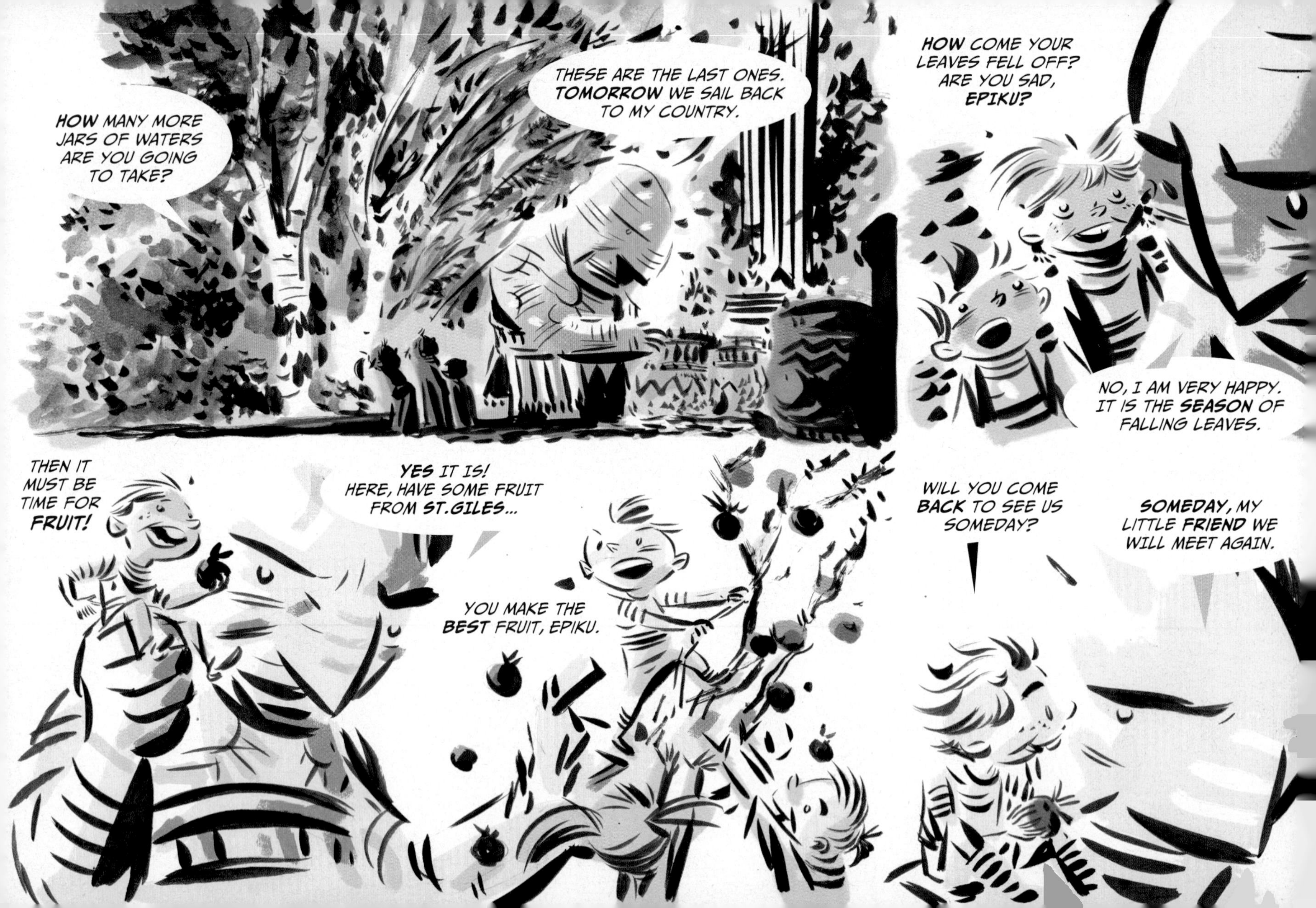
HOW MANY MORE JARS OF WATERS ARE YOU GOING TO TAKE?
THESE ARE THE LAST ONES. TOMORROW WE SAIL BACK TO MY COUNTRY.
HOW COME YOUR LEAVES FELL OFF? ARE YOU SAD, EPIKU?
NO, I AM VERY HAPPY. IT IS THE SEASON OF FALLING LEAVES.
THEN IT MUST BE TIME FOR FRUIT!
YES IT IS! HERE, HAVE SOME FRUIT FROM ST.GILES...
YOU MAKE THE BEST FRUIT, EPIKU.
WILL YOU COME BACK TO SEE US SOMEDAY?
SOMEDAY, MY LITTLE FRIEND WE WILL MEET AGAIN.

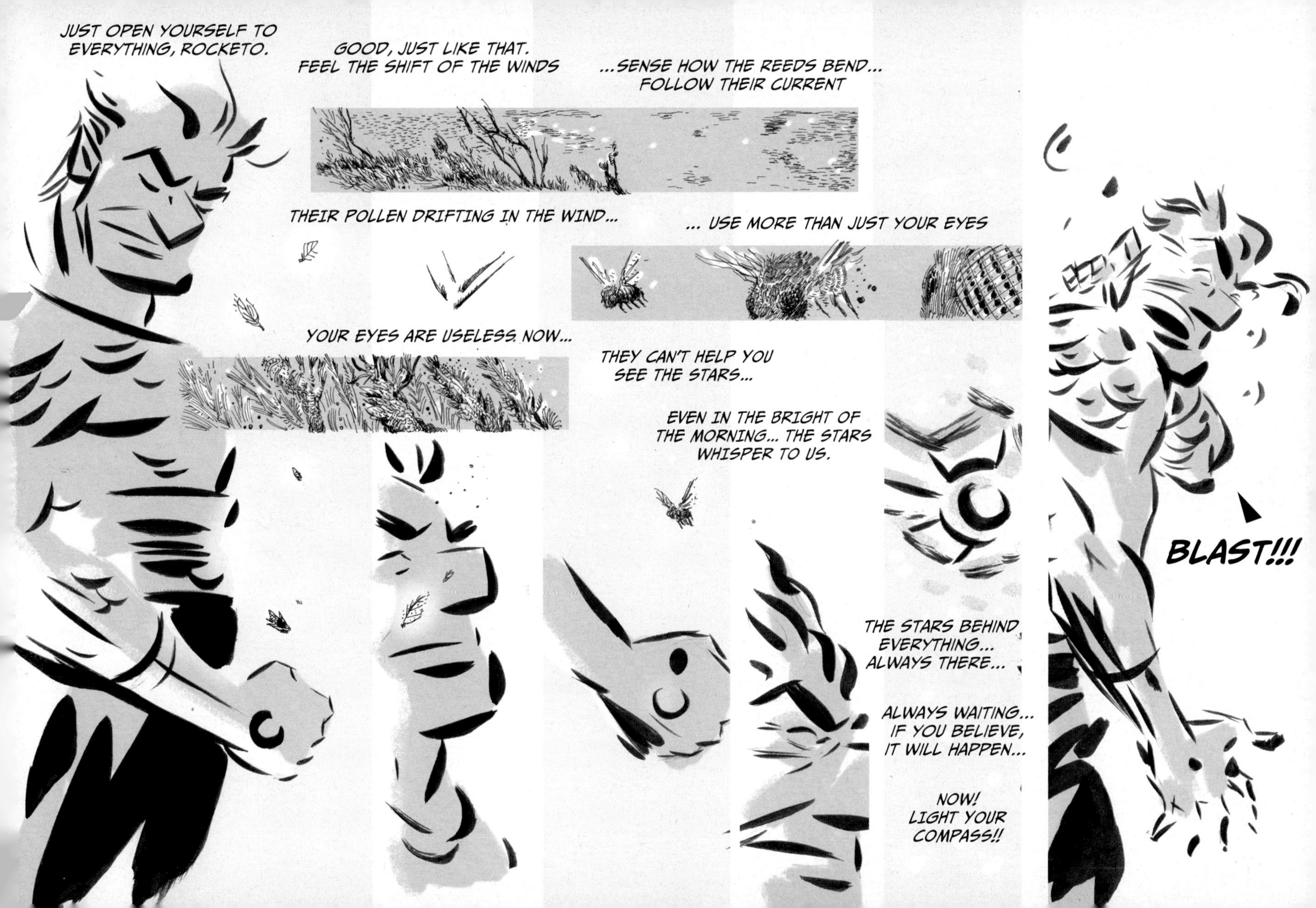

JUST OPEN YOURSELF TO EVERYTHING, ROCKETO.
GOOD, JUST LIKE THAT. FEEL THE SHIFT OF THE WINDS
...SENSE HOW THE REEDS BEND... FOLLOW THEIR CURRENT
THEIR POLLEN DRIFTING IN THE WIND...
... USE MORE THAN JUST YOUR EYES
YOUR EYES ARE USELESS NOW...
THEY CAN'T HELP YOU SEE THE STARS...
EVEN IN THE BRIGHT OF THE MORNING... THE STARS WHISPER TO US.
THE STARS BEHIND EVERYTHING... ALWAYS THERE...
ALWAYS WAITING... IF YOU BELIEVE, IT WILL HAPPEN...
NOW! LIGHT YOUR COMPASS!!
BLAST!!!

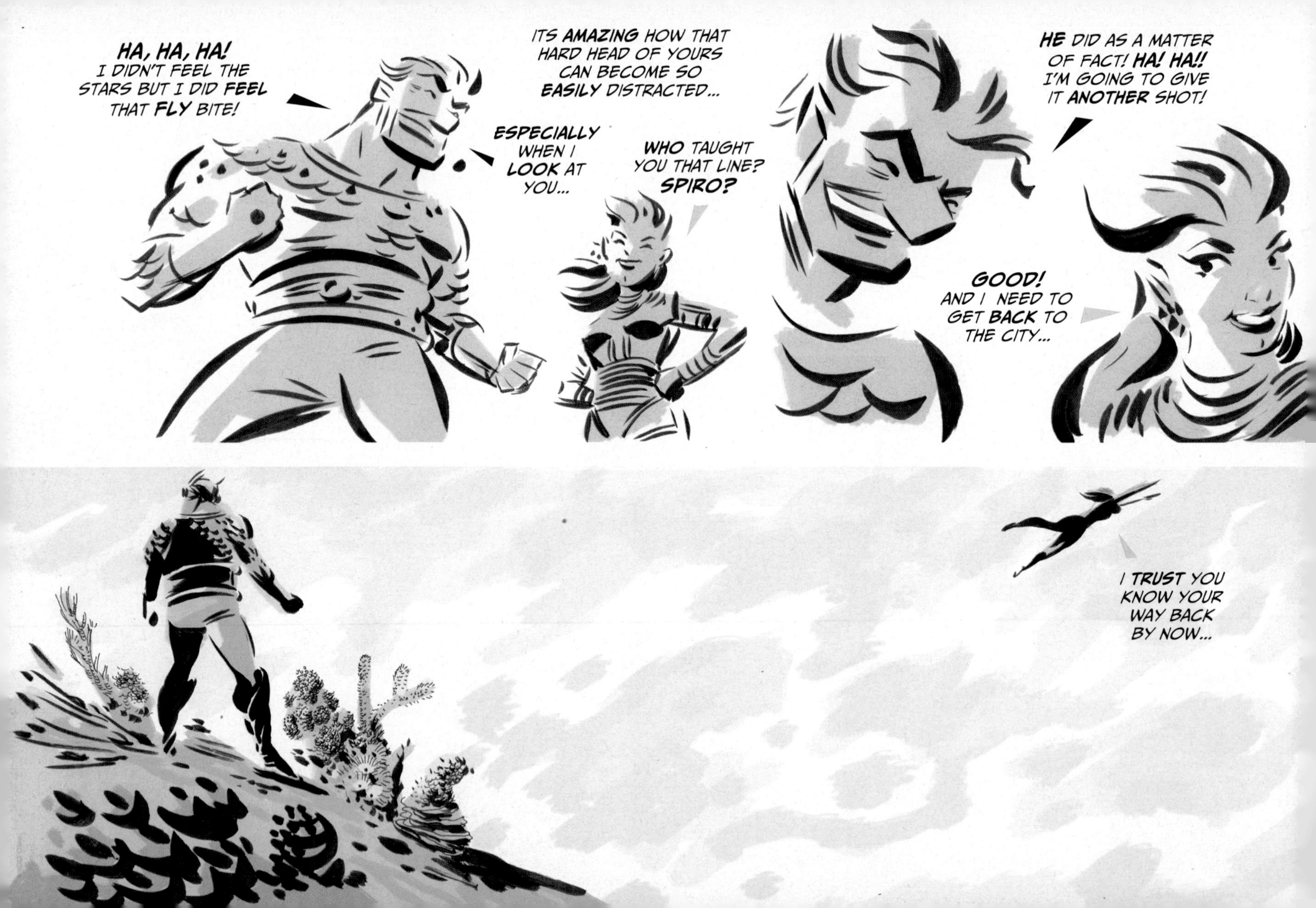
HA, HA, HA! I DIDN'T FEEL THE STARS BUT I DID FEEL THAT FLY BITE!
ITS AMAZING HOW THAT HARD HEAD OF YOURS CAN BECOME SO EASILY DISTRACTED...
ESPECIALLY WHEN I LOOK AT YOU...
WHO TAUGHT YOU THAT LINE? SPIRO?
HE DID AS A MATTER OF FACT! HA! HA!! I'M GOING TO GIVE IT ANOTHER SHOT!
GOOD! AND I NEED TO GET BACK TO THE CITY...
I TRUST YOU KNOW YOUR WAY BACK BY NOW...

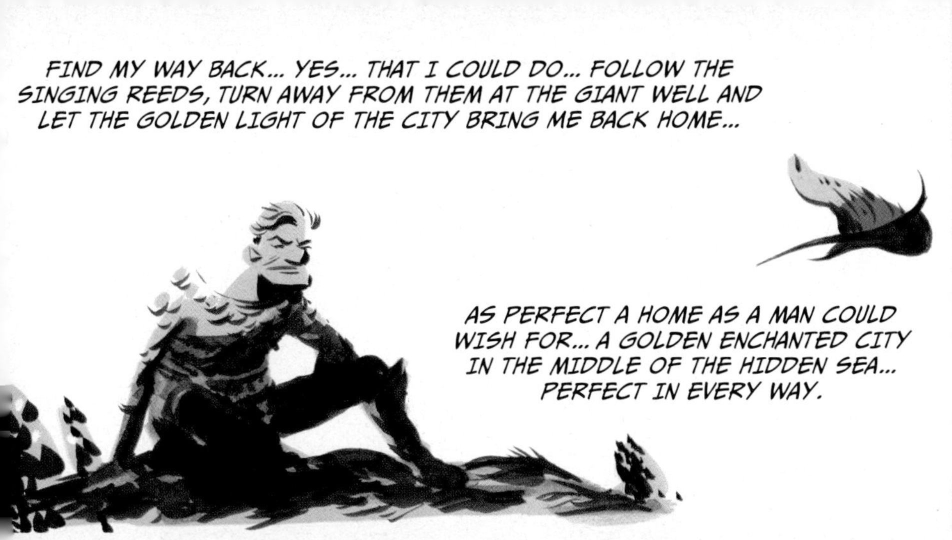
FIND MY WAY BACK... YES... THAT I COULD DO... FOLLOW THE SINGING REEDS, TURN AWAY FROM THEM AT THE GIANT WELL AND LET THE GOLDEN LIGHT OF THE CITY BRING ME BACK HOME...
AS PERFECT A HOME AS A MAN COULD WISH FOR... A GOLDEN ENCHANTED CITY IN THE MIDDLE OF THE HIDDEN SEA... PERFECT IN EVERY WAY.

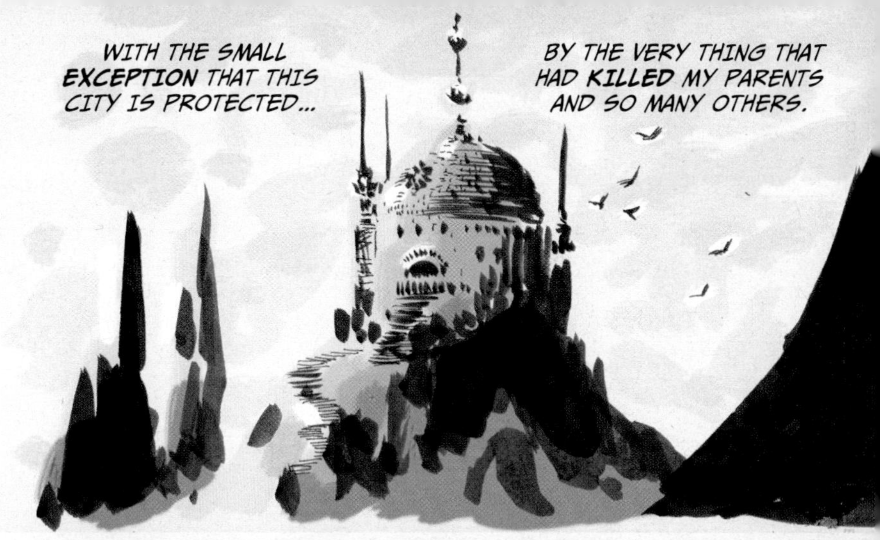
WITH THE SMALL **EXCEPTION** THAT THIS CITY IS PROTECTED...
BY THE VERY THING THAT HAD **KILLED** MY PARENTS AND SO MANY OTHERS.

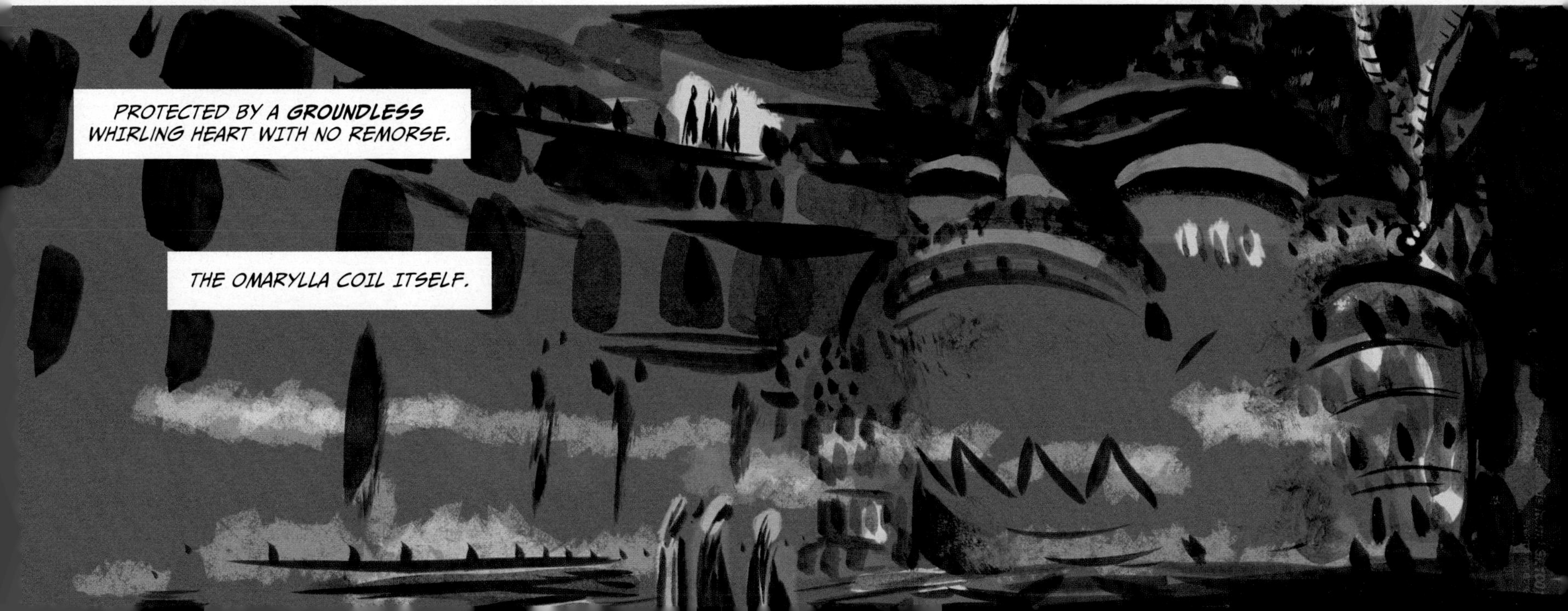
PROTECTED BY A **GROUNDLESS** WHIRLING HEART WITH NO REMORSE.
THE OMARYLLA COIL ITSELF.

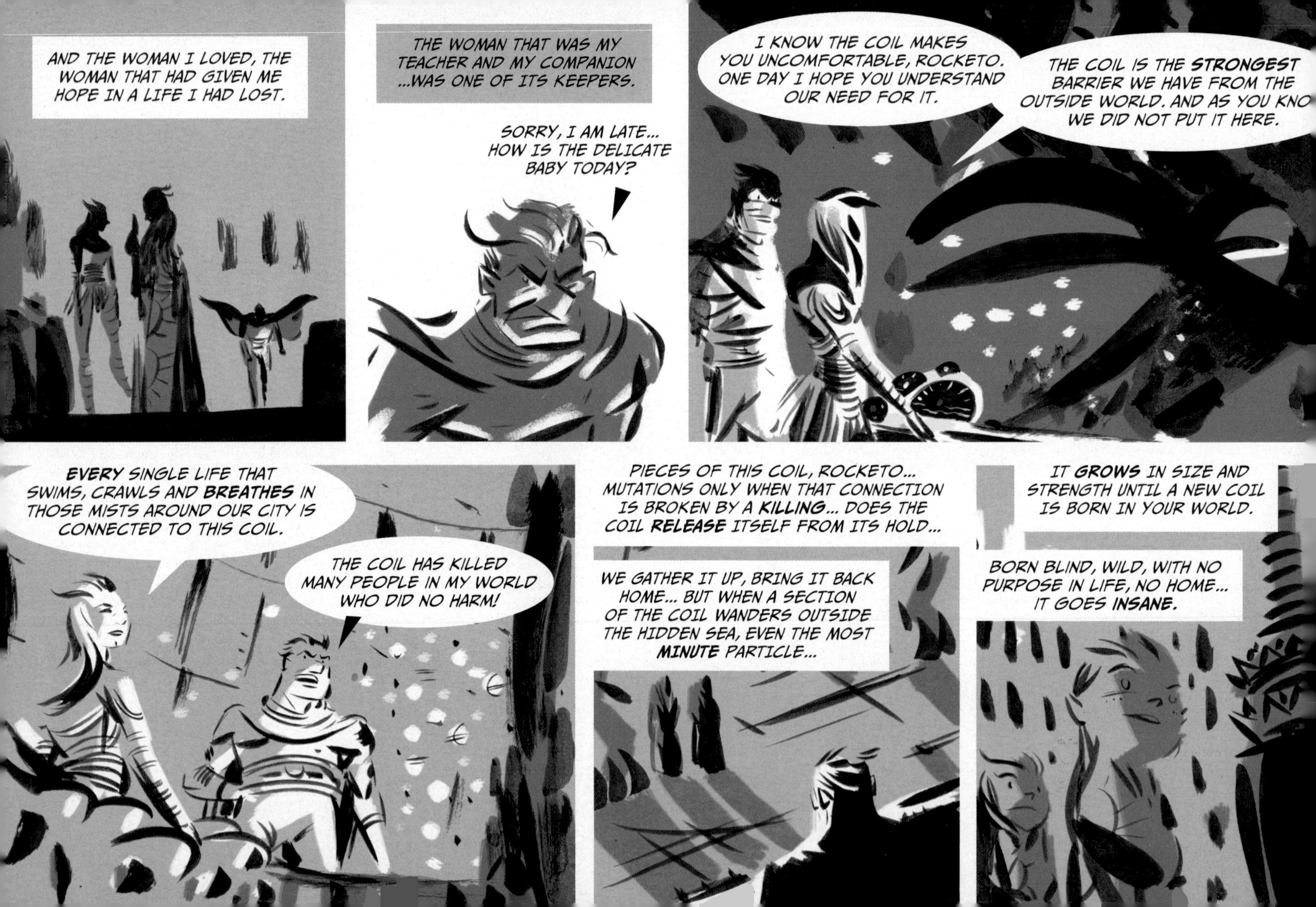
AND THE WOMAN I LOVED, THE WOMAN THAT HAD GIVEN ME HOPE IN A LIFE I HAD LOST.
THE WOMAN THAT WAS MY TEACHER AND MY COMPANION ...WAS ONE OF ITS KEEPERS.
SORRY, I AM LATE... HOW IS THE DELICATE BABY TODAY?
I KNOW THE COIL MAKES YOU UNCOMFORTABLE, ROCKETO. ONE DAY I HOPE YOU UNDERSTAND OUR NEED FOR IT.
THE COIL IS THE **STRONGEST** BARRIER WE HAVE FROM THE OUTSIDE WORLD. AND AS YOU KNO WE DID NOT PUT IT HERE.
EVERY SINGLE LIFE THAT SWIMS, CRAWLS AND **BREATHES** IN THOSE MISTS AROUND OUR CITY IS CONNECTED TO THIS COIL.
THE COIL HAS KILLED MANY PEOPLE IN MY WORLD WHO DID NO HARM!
PIECES OF THIS COIL, ROCKETO... MUTATIONS ONLY WHEN THAT CONNECTION IS BROKEN BY A **KILLING**... DOES THE COIL **RELEASE** ITSELF FROM ITS HOLD...
WE GATHER IT UP, BRING IT BACK HOME... BUT WHEN A SECTION OF THE COIL WANDERS OUTSIDE THE HIDDEN SEA, EVEN THE MOST **MINUTE** PARTICLE...
IT **GROWS** IN SIZE AND STRENGTH UNTIL A NEW COIL IS BORN IN YOUR WORLD.
BORN BLIND, WILD, WITH NO PURPOSE IN LIFE, NO HOME... IT GOES **INSANE**.

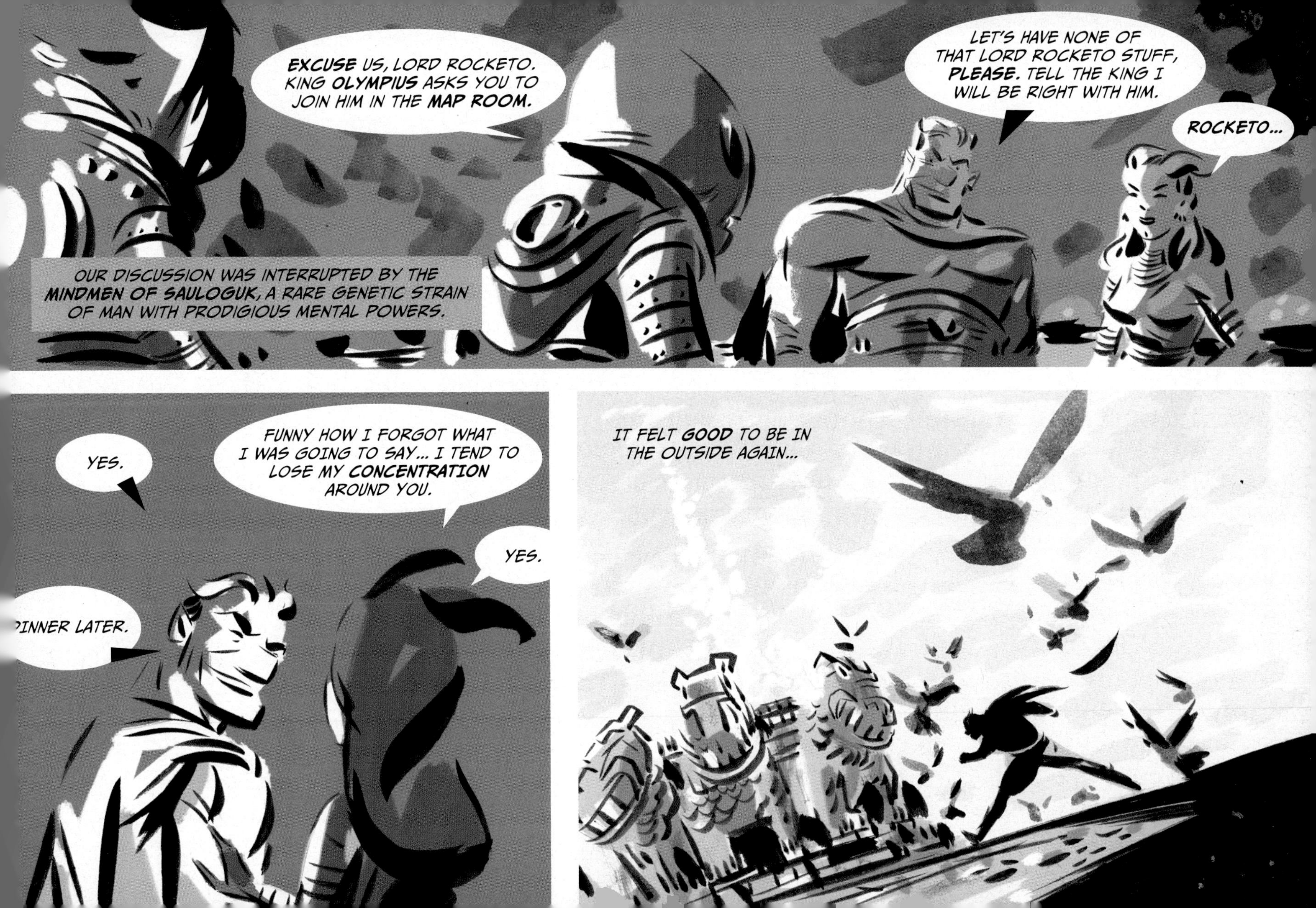
OUR DISCUSSION WAS INTERRUPTED BY THE **MINDMEN OF SAULOGUK**, A RARE GENETIC STRAIN OF MAN WITH PRODIGIOUS MENTAL POWERS.
EXCUSE US, LORD ROCKETO. KING **OLYMPIUS** ASKS YOU TO JOIN HIM IN THE **MAP ROOM.**
LET'S HAVE NONE OF THAT LORD ROCKETO STUFF, **PLEASE**. TELL THE KING I WILL BE RIGHT WITH HIM.
ROCKETO...
YES.
FUNNY HOW I FORGOT WHAT I WAS GOING TO SAY... I TEND TO LOSE MY **CONCENTRATION** AROUND YOU.
YES.
DINNER LATER.
IT FELT **GOOD** TO BE IN THE OUTSIDE AGAIN...

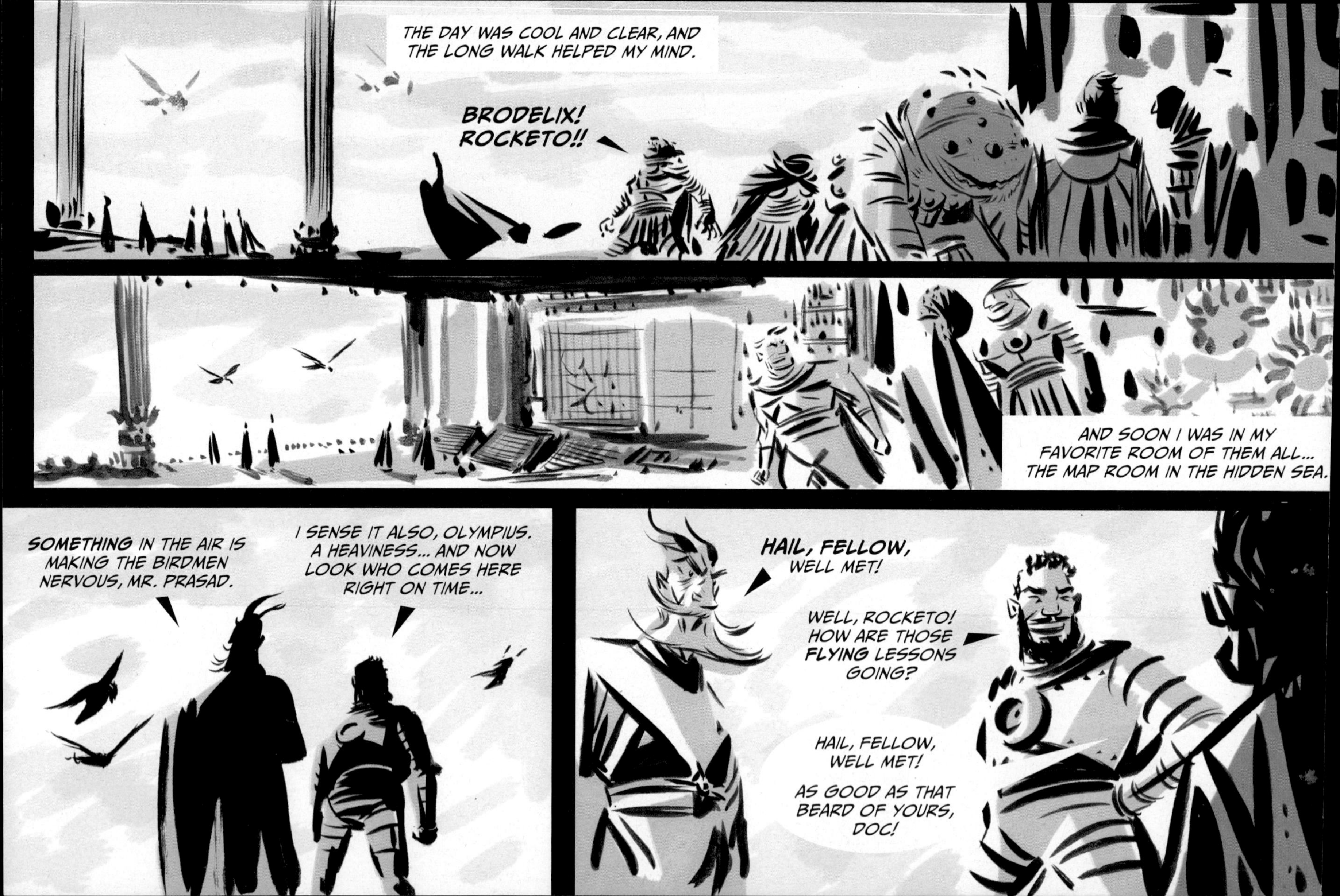
THE DAY WAS COOL AND CLEAR, AND THE LONG WALK HELPED MY MIND.
BRODELIX! ROCKETO!!
AND SOON I WAS IN MY FAVORITE ROOM OF THEM ALL... THE MAP ROOM IN THE HIDDEN SEA.
SOMETHING IN THE AIR IS MAKING THE BIRDMEN NERVOUS, MR. PRASAD.
I SENSE IT ALSO, OLYMPIUS. A HEAVINESS... AND NOW LOOK WHO COMES HERE RIGHT ON TIME...
HAIL, FELLOW, WELL MET!
WELL, ROCKETO! HOW ARE THOSE FLYING LESSONS GOING?
HAIL, FELLOW, WELL MET!
AS GOOD AS THAT BEARD OF YOURS, DOC!

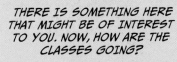

THERE IS SOMETHING HERE THAT MIGHT BE OF INTEREST TO YOU. NOW, HOW ARE THE CLASSES GOING?

ALMOST CRACKED MY SKULL. THE FLIES GOT THE BETTER PIECES OF ME... OTHERWISE... IT'S GOOD.

DEATH'S CRUEL BITE CAN AWAKEN DELIGHT IN THE MOST BORING OF NIGHTS...

HERE, ROCKETO! AN EXPLORATION TEAM TO THE SEA OF DERELICTS FOUND THIS OLD MAP IN ONE OF THE HULKS.

IT'S A GARRISON MAP JUDGING FROM THE STRONG, GRACEFUL GENETIC WORK ON IT.

I LOVE THE FEEL OF THE OLD MAPS... HOW THEY COME ALIVE UNDER THE SLIGHTEST TOUCH..

HAVE YOU FOUND SOMEONE THAT CAN OPEN THIS YET, OLYMPIUS?

YES, HE IS ON HIS WAY HERE... I THOUGHT YOU WOULD LIKE TO BE HERE WHEN WE OPEN IT.

THANK YOU.

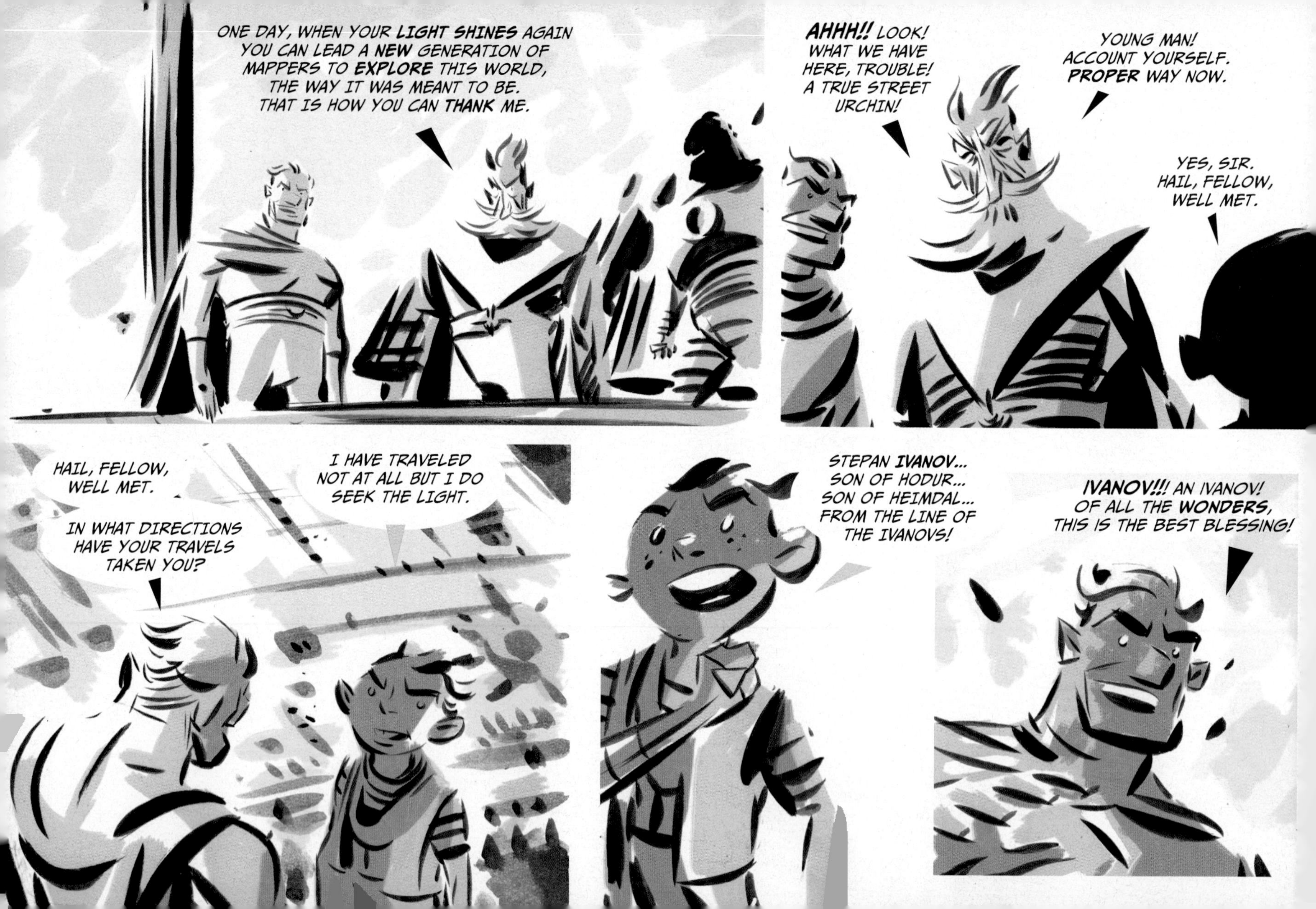
ONE DAY, WHEN YOUR LIGHT SHINES AGAIN YOU CAN LEAD A NEW GENERATION OF MAPPERS TO EXPLORE THIS WORLD, THE WAY IT WAS MEANT TO BE. THAT IS HOW YOU CAN THANK ME.
AHHH!! LOOK! WHAT WE HAVE HERE, TROUBLE! A TRUE STREET URCHIN!
YOUNG MAN! ACCOUNT YOURSELF. PROPER WAY NOW.
YES, SIR. HAIL, FELLOW, WELL MET.
HAIL, FELLOW, WELL MET.
IN WHAT DIRECTIONS HAVE YOUR TRAVELS TAKEN YOU?
I HAVE TRAVELED NOT AT ALL BUT I DO SEEK THE LIGHT.
STEPAN IVANOV... SON OF HODUR... SON OF HEIMDAL... FROM THE LINE OF THE IVANOVS!
IVANOV!!! AN IVANOV! OF ALL THE WONDERS, THIS IS THE BEST BLESSING!

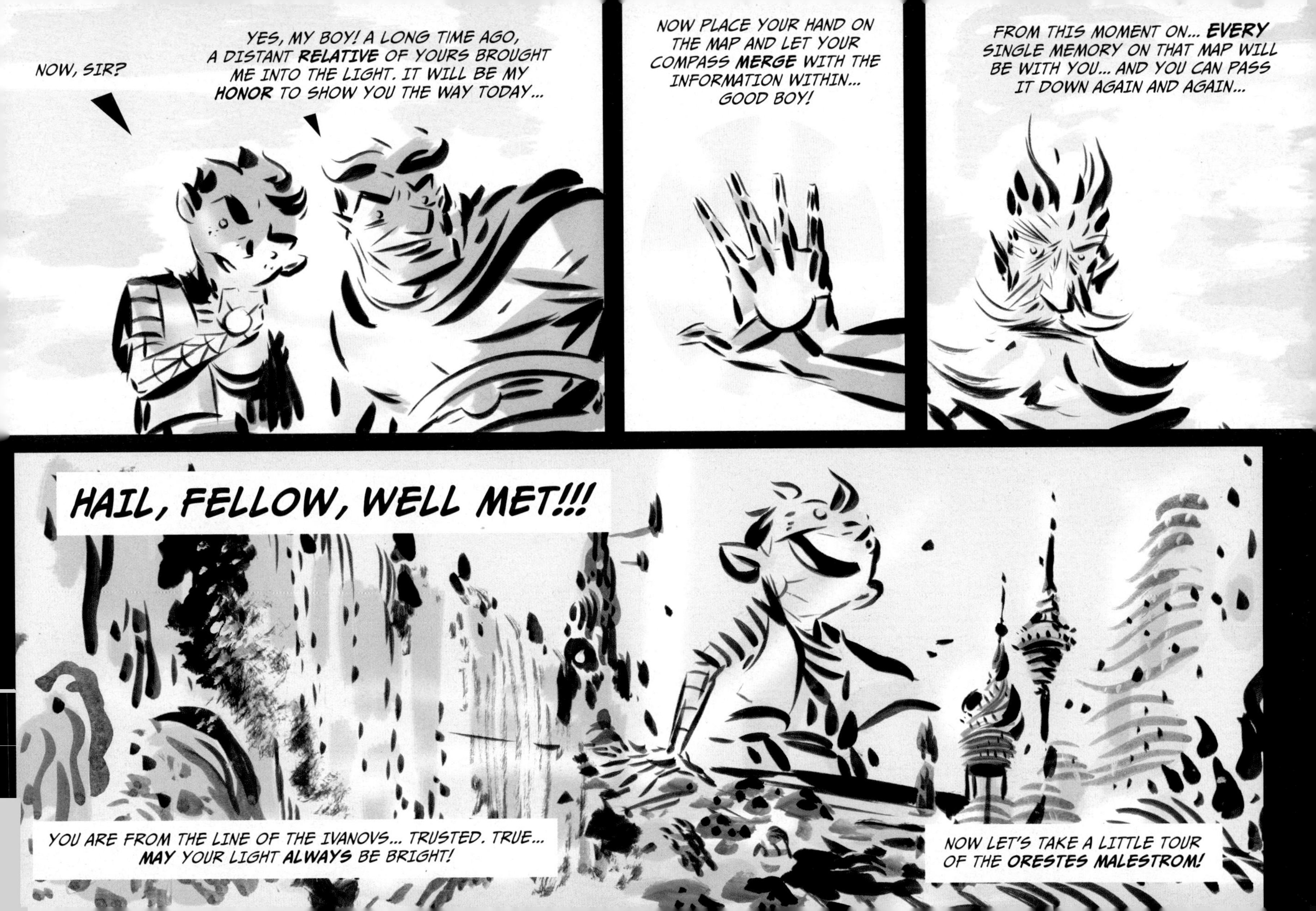
NOW, SIR?
YES, MY BOY! A LONG TIME AGO, A DISTANT RELATIVE OF YOURS BROUGHT ME INTO THE LIGHT. IT WILL BE MY HONOR TO SHOW YOU THE WAY TODAY...
NOW PLACE YOUR HAND ON THE MAP AND LET YOUR COMPASS MERGE WITH THE INFORMATION WITHIN... GOOD BOY!
FROM THIS MOMENT ON... EVERY SINGLE MEMORY ON THAT MAP WILL BE WITH YOU... AND YOU CAN PASS IT DOWN AGAIN AND AGAIN...
HAIL, FELLOW, WELL MET!!!
YOU ARE FROM THE LINE OF THE IVANOVS... TRUSTED. TRUE... MAY YOUR LIGHT ALWAYS BE BRIGHT!
NOW LET'S TAKE A LITTLE TOUR OF THE ORESTES MALESTROM!

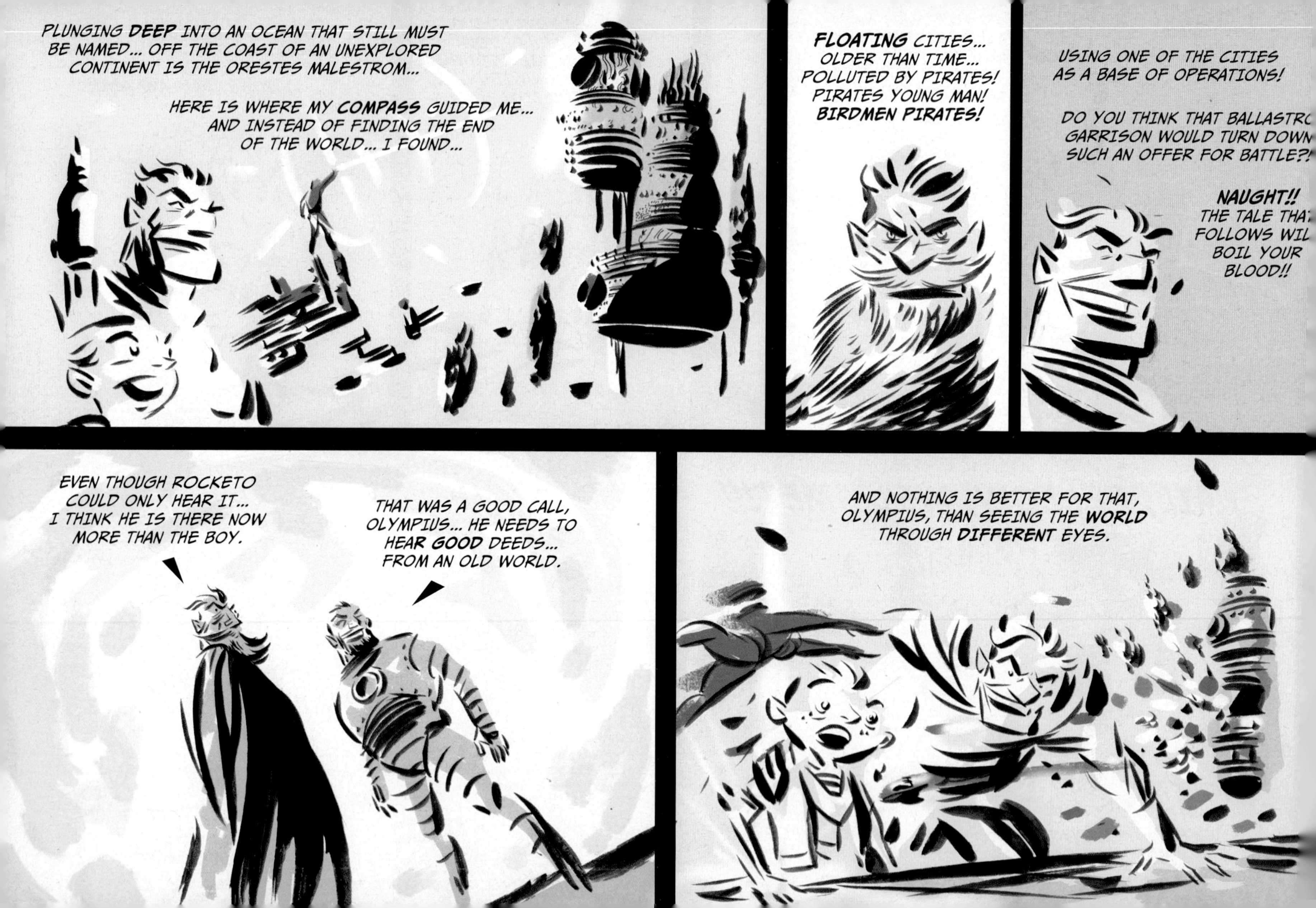
PLUNGING DEEP INTO AN OCEAN THAT STILL MUST BE NAMED... OFF THE COAST OF AN UNEXPLORED CONTINENT IS THE ORESTES MALESTROM...
HERE IS WHERE MY COMPASS GUIDED ME... AND INSTEAD OF FINDING THE END OF THE WORLD... I FOUND...
FLOATING CITIES... OLDER THAN TIME... POLLUTED BY PIRATES! PIRATES YOUNG MAN! BIRDMEN PIRATES!
USING ONE OF THE CITIES AS A BASE OF OPERATIONS!
DO YOU THINK THAT BALLASTRO GARRISON WOULD TURN DOWN SUCH AN OFFER FOR BATTLE?!
NAUGHT!! THE TALE THAT FOLLOWS WILL BOIL YOUR BLOOD!!
EVEN THOUGH ROCKETO COULD ONLY HEAR IT... I THINK HE IS THERE NOW MORE THAN THE BOY.
THAT WAS A GOOD CALL, OLYMPIUS... HE NEEDS TO HEAR GOOD DEEDS... FROM AN OLD WORLD.
AND NOTHING IS BETTER FOR THAT, OLYMPIUS, THAN SEEING THE WORLD THROUGH DIFFERENT EYES.

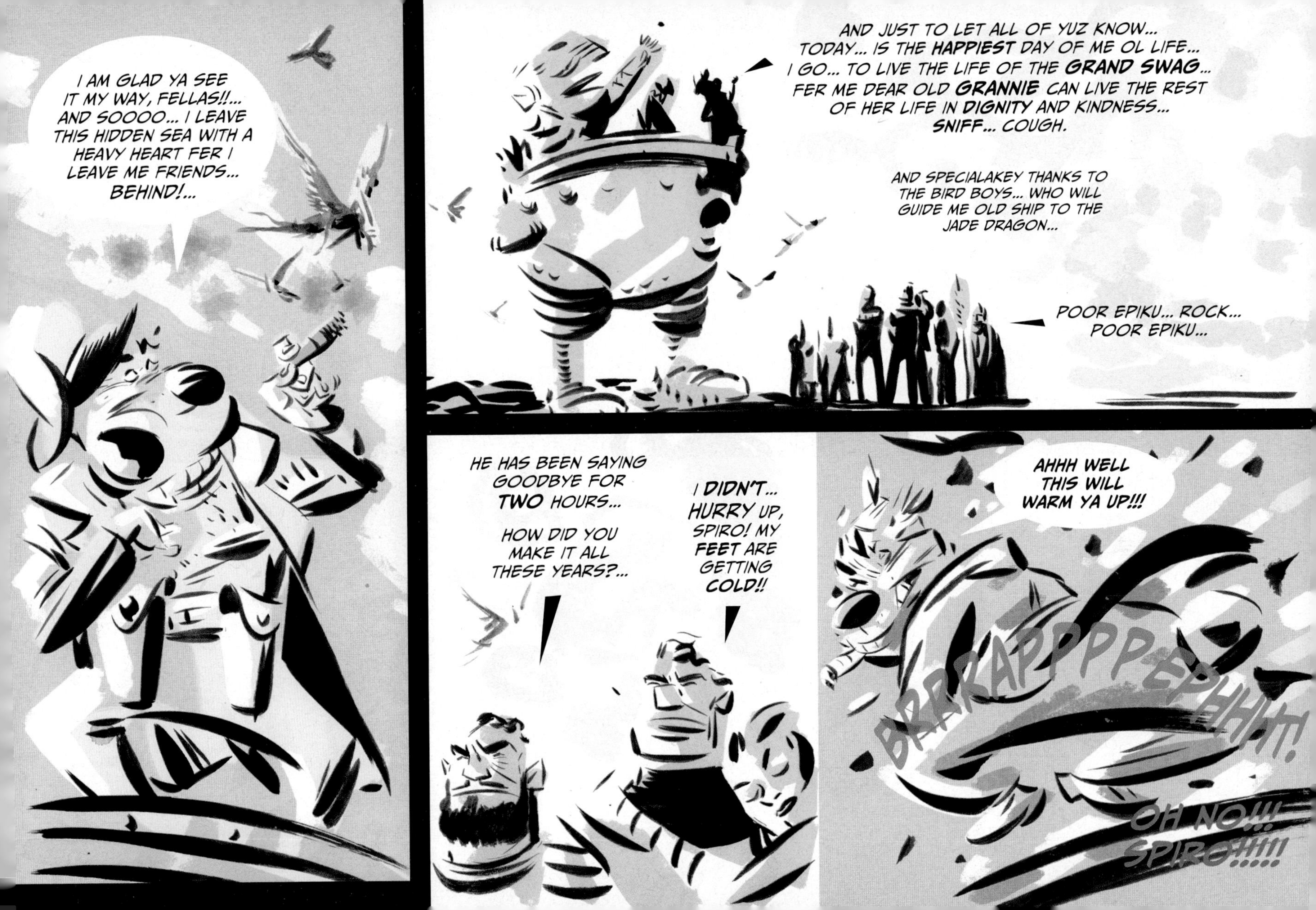
I AM GLAD YA SEE IT MY WAY, FELLAS!!... AND SOOOO... I LEAVE THIS HIDDEN SEA WITH A HEAVY HEART FER I LEAVE ME FRIENDS... BEHIND!...
AND JUST TO LET ALL OF YUZ KNOW... TODAY... IS THE HAPPIEST DAY OF ME OL LIFE... I GO... TO LIVE THE LIFE OF THE GRAND SWAG... FER ME DEAR OLD GRANNIE CAN LIVE THE REST OF HER LIFE IN DIGNITY AND KINDNESS... SNIFF... COUGH.
AND SPECIALAKEY THANKS TO THE BIRD BOYS... WHO WILL GUIDE ME OLD SHIP TO THE JADE DRAGON...
POOR EPIKU... ROCK... POOR EPIKU...
HE HAS BEEN SAYING GOODBYE FOR TWO HOURS...
HOW DID YOU MAKE IT ALL THESE YEARS?...
I DIDN'T... HURRY UP, SPIRO! MY FEET ARE GETTING COLD!!
AHHH WELL THIS WILL WARM YA UP!!!
BRRRAPPPPPEPHHH!
OH NO!!! SPIRO!!!!!

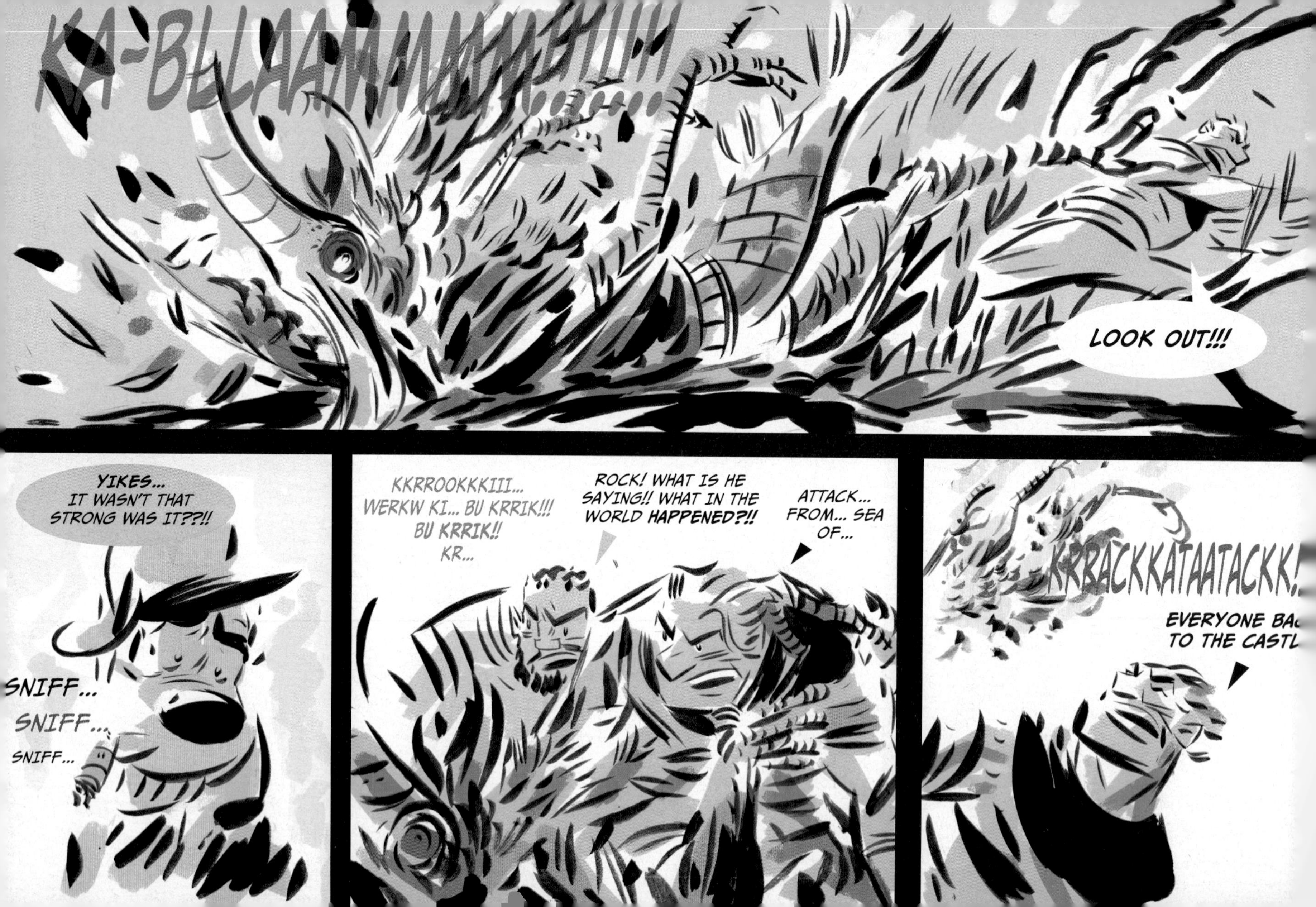
KA-BLLAAMMMMHHH...
LOOK OUT!!!
YIKES... IT WASN'T THAT STRONG WAS IT??!!
SNIFF...
SNIFF...
SNIFF...
KKRROOKKKIII... WERKW KI... BU KRRIK!!! BU KRRIK!! KR...
ROCK! WHAT IS HE SAYING!! WHAT IN THE WORLD HAPPENED?!!
ATTACK... FROM... SEA OF...
KRRACKKATAATACKK!
EVERYONE BA
TO THE CASTL

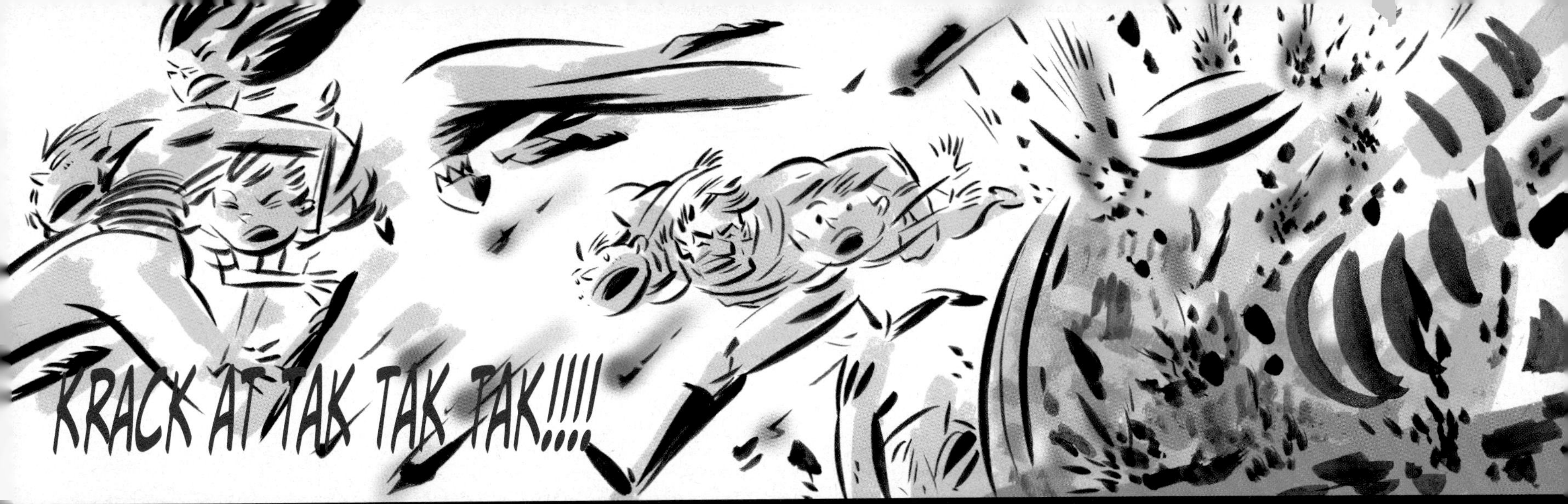
KRACK AT TAK TAK TAK!!!!

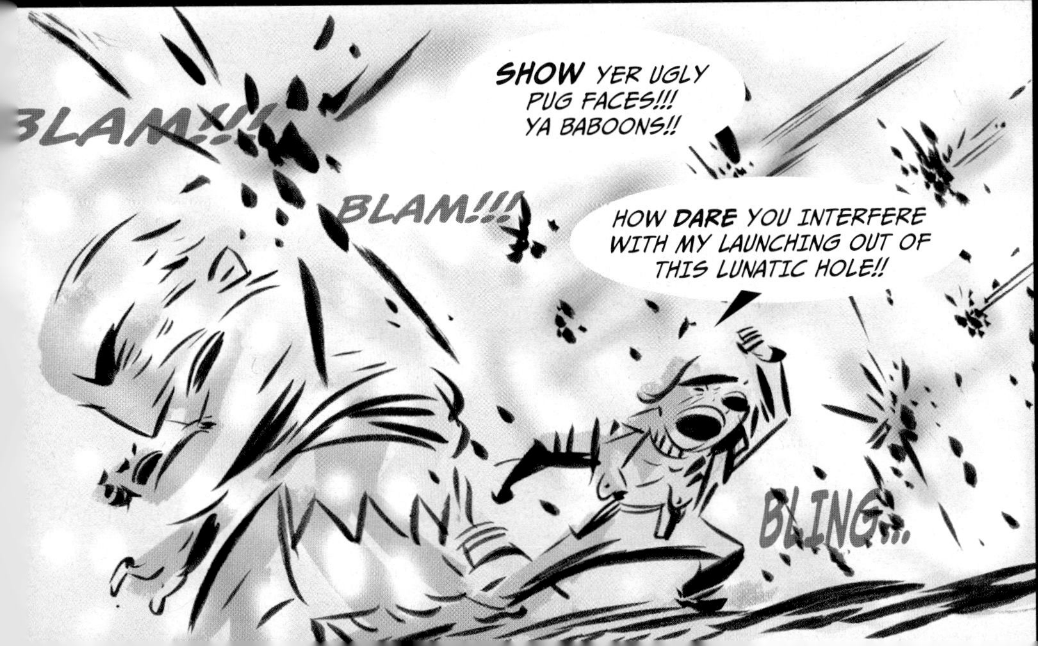
BLAM!!!
SHOW YER UGLY PUG FACES!!! YA BABOONS!!
BLAM!!!
HOW DARE YOU INTERFERE WITH MY LAUNCHING OUT OF THIS LUNATIC HOLE!!
BLING...

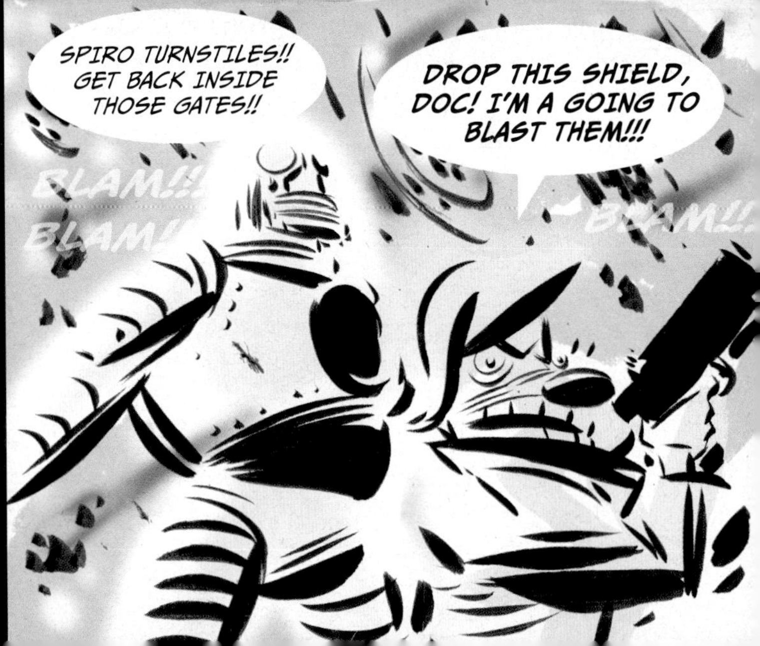
SPIRO TURNSTILES!! GET BACK INSIDE THOSE GATES!!
DROP THIS SHIELD, DOC! I'M A GOING TO BLAST THEM!!!
BLAM!!!
BLAM!!
BLAM!!

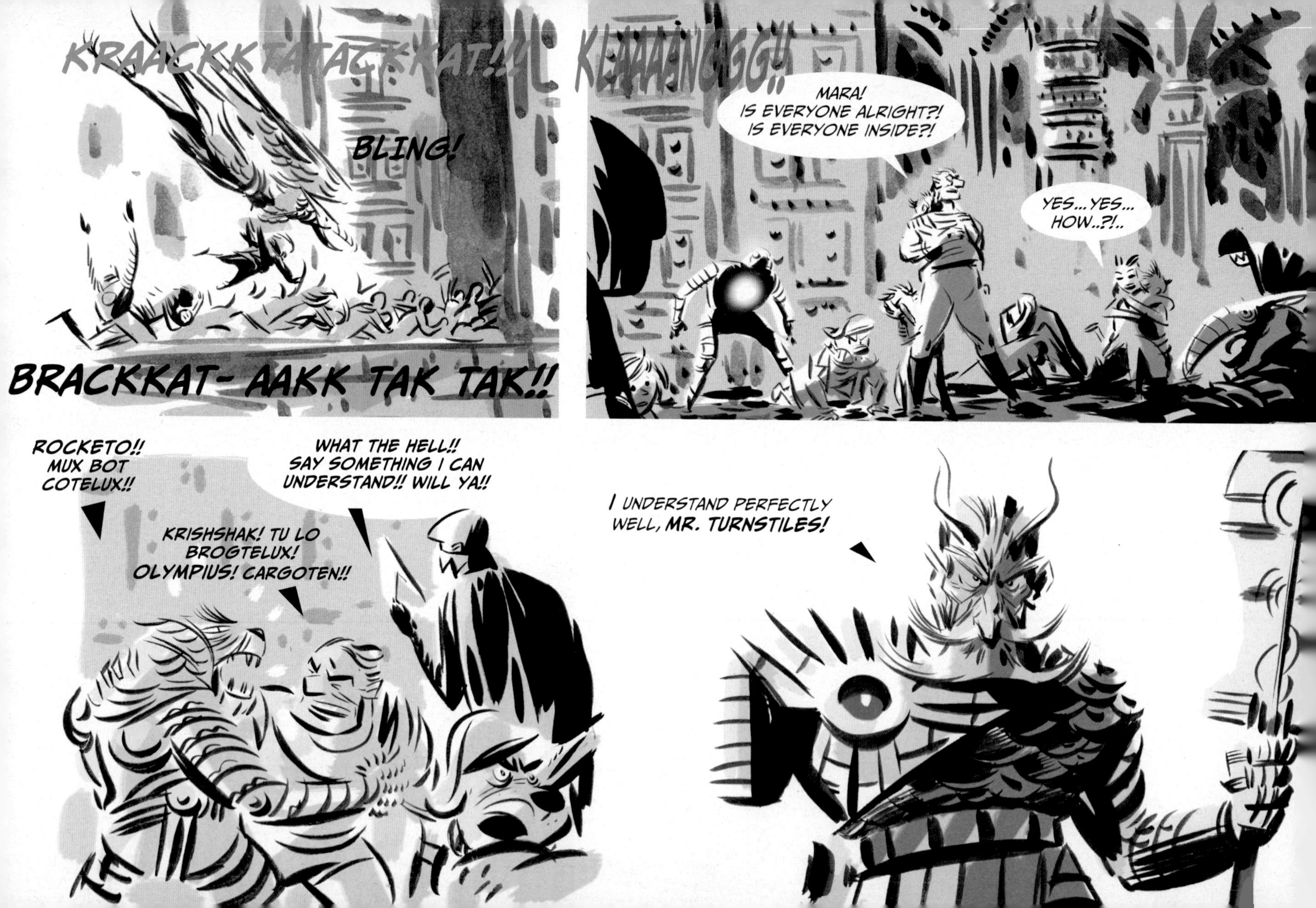

KRAACKKTATACKKAT!!!
BLING!
BRACKKAT- AAKK TAK TAK!!
KLAAAANGGG!!
MARA!
IS EVERYONE ALRIGHT?!
IS EVERYONE INSIDE?!
YES...YES...
HOW..?!..
ROCKETO!!
MUX BOT
COTELUX!!
KRISHSHAK! TU LO
BROGTELUX!
OLYMPIUS! CARGOTEN!!
WHAT THE HELL!!
SAY SOMETHING I CAN
UNDERSTAND!! WILL YA!!
I UNDERSTAND PERFECTLY
WELL, MR. TURNSTILES!

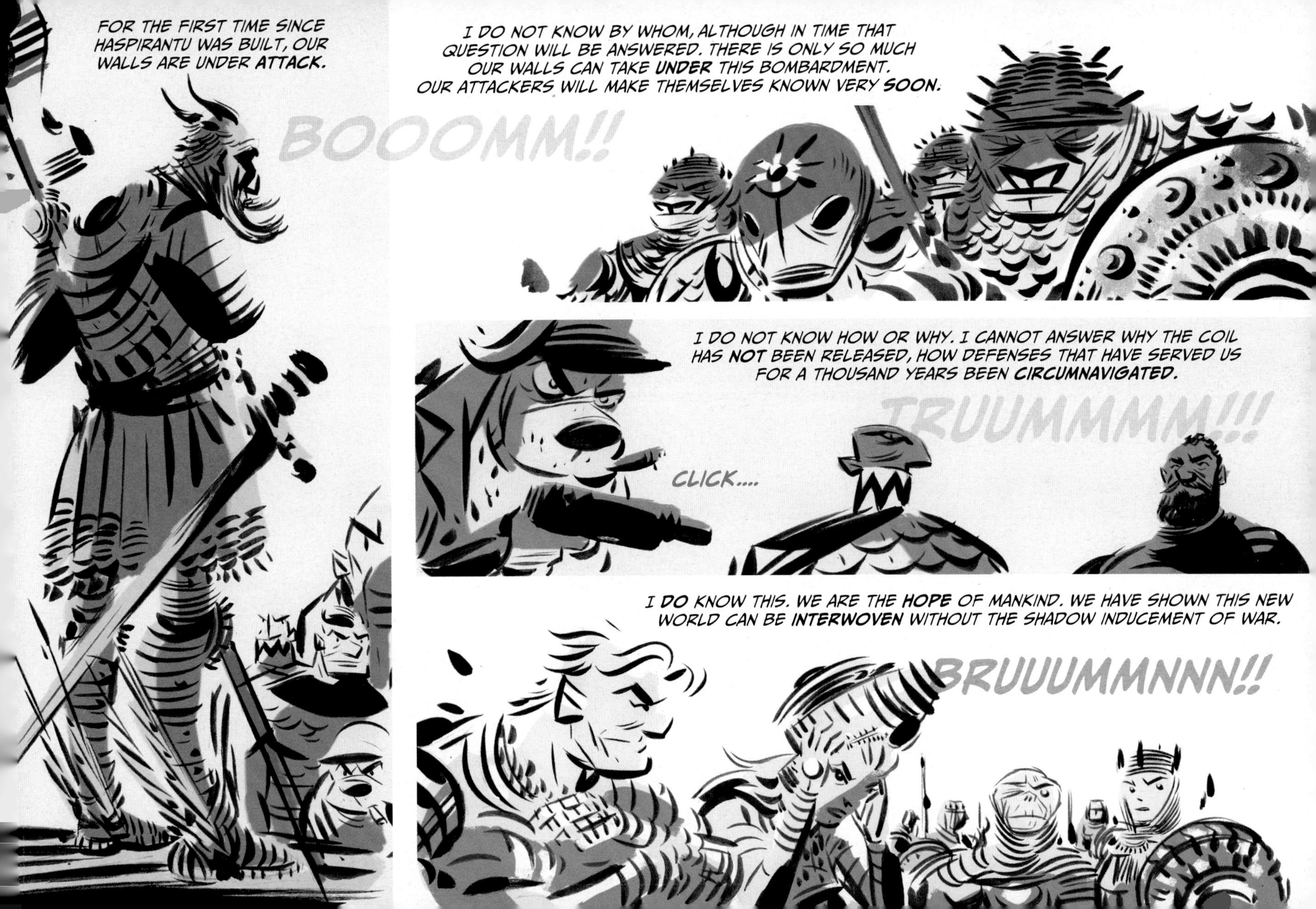

FOR THE FIRST TIME SINCE HASPIRANTU WAS BUILT, OUR WALLS ARE UNDER ATTACK.
BOOOMM!!
I DO NOT KNOW BY WHOM, ALTHOUGH IN TIME THAT QUESTION WILL BE ANSWERED. THERE IS ONLY SO MUCH OUR WALLS CAN TAKE UNDER THIS BOMBARDMENT. OUR ATTACKERS WILL MAKE THEMSELVES KNOWN VERY SOON.
I DO NOT KNOW HOW OR WHY. I CANNOT ANSWER WHY THE COIL HAS NOT BEEN RELEASED, HOW DEFENSES THAT HAVE SERVED US FOR A THOUSAND YEARS BEEN CIRCUMNAVIGATED.
TRUUMMMM!!
CLICK....
I DO KNOW THIS. WE ARE THE HOPE OF MANKIND. WE HAVE SHOWN THIS NEW WORLD CAN BE INTERWOVEN WITHOUT THE SHADOW INDUCEMENT OF WAR.
BRUUUMMNNN!!

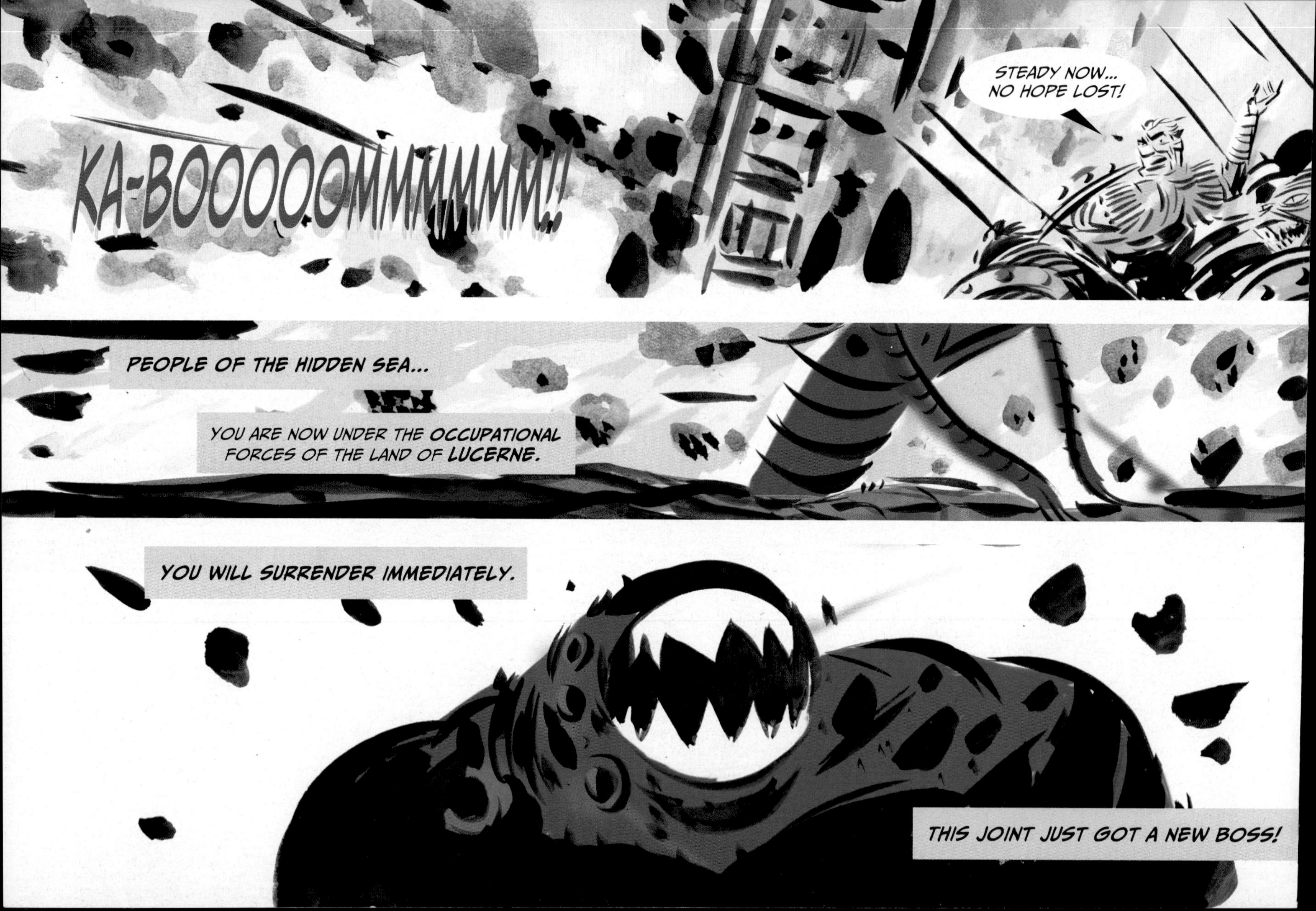
KA-BOOOOOMMMMMM!!
STEADY NOW... NO HOPE LOST!
PEOPLE OF THE HIDDEN SEA...
YOU ARE NOW UNDER THE OCCUPATIONAL FORCES OF THE LAND OF LUCERNE.
YOU WILL SURRENDER IMMEDIATELY.
THIS JOINT JUST GOT A NEW BOSS!

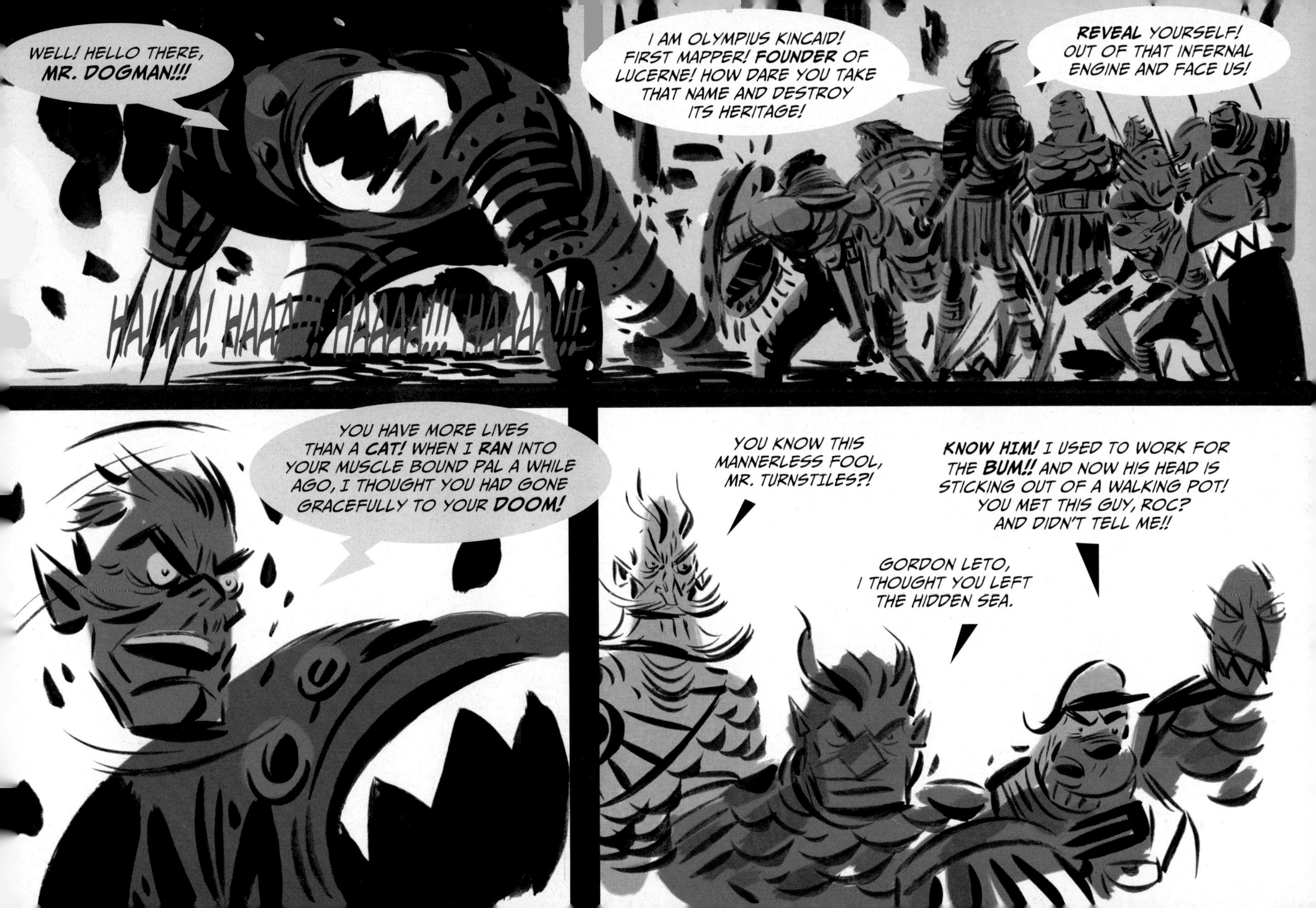
WELL! HELLO THERE, MR. DOGMAN!!!
HA! HA! HAAA...! HAAAA!!! HAAAA!!!
I AM OLYMPIUS KINCAID! FIRST MAPPER! FOUNDER OF LUCERNE! HOW DARE YOU TAKE THAT NAME AND DESTROY ITS HERITAGE!
REVEAL YOURSELF! OUT OF THAT INFERNAL ENGINE AND FACE US!
YOU HAVE MORE LIVES THAN A CAT! WHEN I RAN INTO YOUR MUSCLE BOUND PAL A WHILE AGO, I THOUGHT YOU HAD GONE GRACEFULLY TO YOUR DOOM!
YOU KNOW THIS MANNERLESS FOOL, MR. TURNSTILES?!
KNOW HIM! I USED TO WORK FOR THE BUM!! AND NOW HIS HEAD IS STICKING OUT OF A WALKING POT! YOU MET THIS GUY, ROC? AND DIDN'T TELL ME!!
GORDON LETO, I THOUGHT YOU LEFT THE HIDDEN SEA.

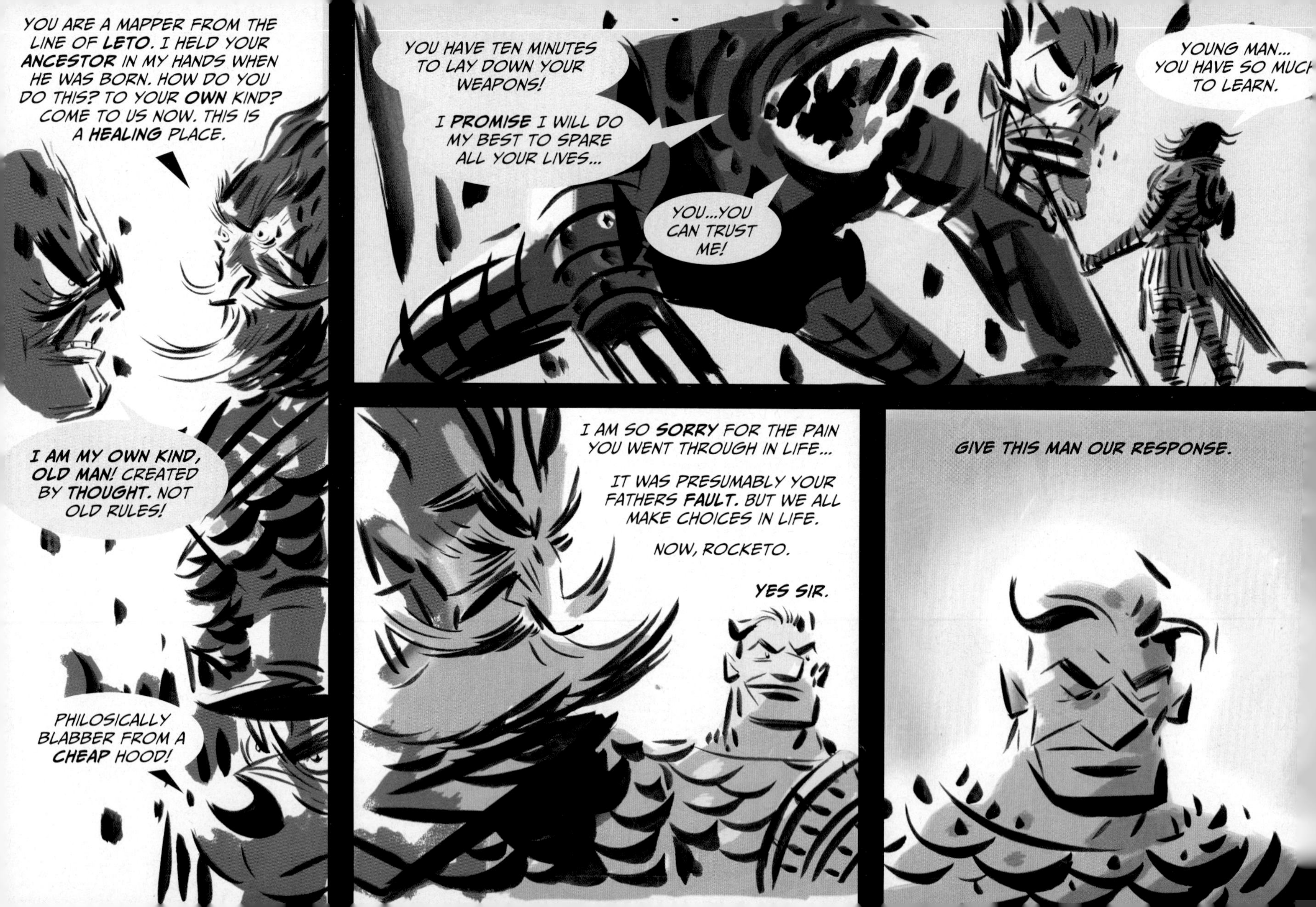
YOU ARE A MAPPER FROM THE LINE OF LETO. I HELD YOUR ANCESTOR IN MY HANDS WHEN HE WAS BORN. HOW DO YOU DO THIS? TO YOUR OWN KIND? COME TO US NOW. THIS IS A HEALING PLACE.
I AM MY OWN KIND, OLD MAN! CREATED BY THOUGHT. NOT OLD RULES!
PHILOSICALLY BLABBER FROM A CHEAP HOOD!
YOU HAVE TEN MINUTES TO LAY DOWN YOUR WEAPONS!
I PROMISE I WILL DO MY BEST TO SPARE ALL YOUR LIVES...
YOU...YOU CAN TRUST ME!
YOUNG MAN... YOU HAVE SO MUCH TO LEARN.
I AM SO SORRY FOR THE PAIN YOU WENT THROUGH IN LIFE...
IT WAS PRESUMABLY YOUR FATHERS FAULT. BUT WE ALL MAKE CHOICES IN LIFE.
NOW, ROCKETO.
YES SIR.
GIVE THIS MAN OUR RESPONSE.

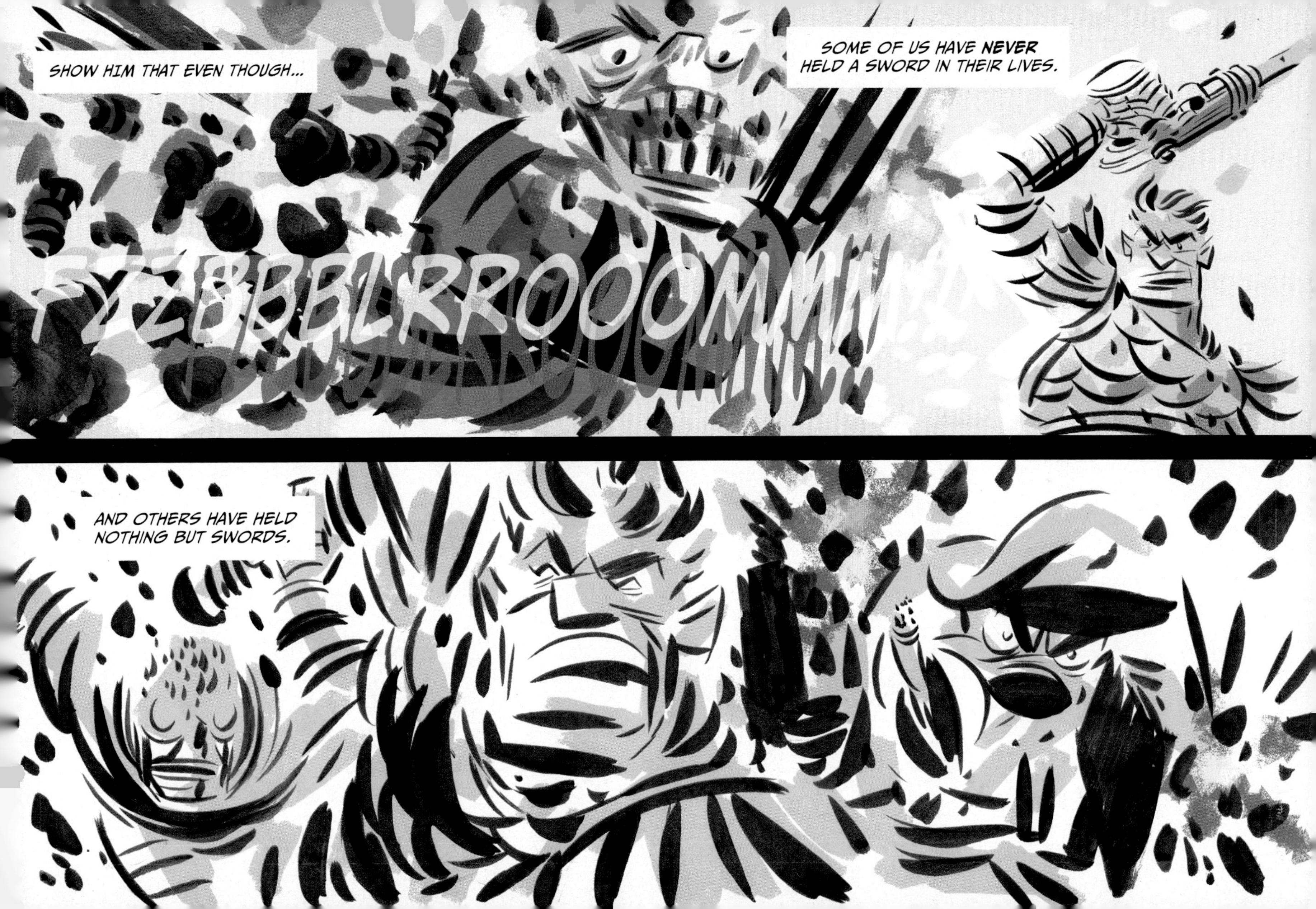
SHOW HIM THAT EVEN THOUGH...
SOME OF US HAVE **NEVER** HELD A SWORD IN THEIR LIVES.
FZZBBBLRROOOMM!!
AND OTHERS HAVE HELD NOTHING BUT SWORDS.

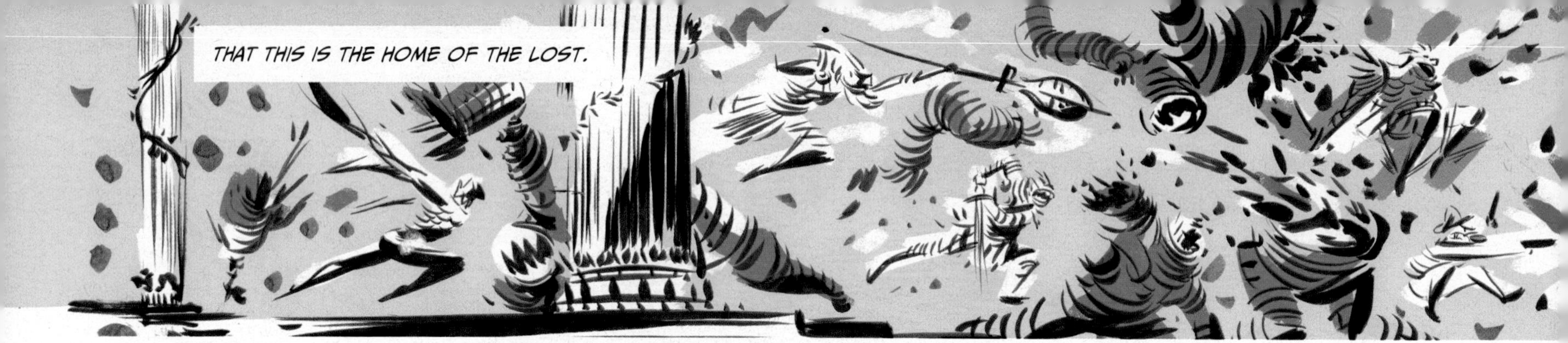
THAT THIS IS THE HOME OF THE LOST.

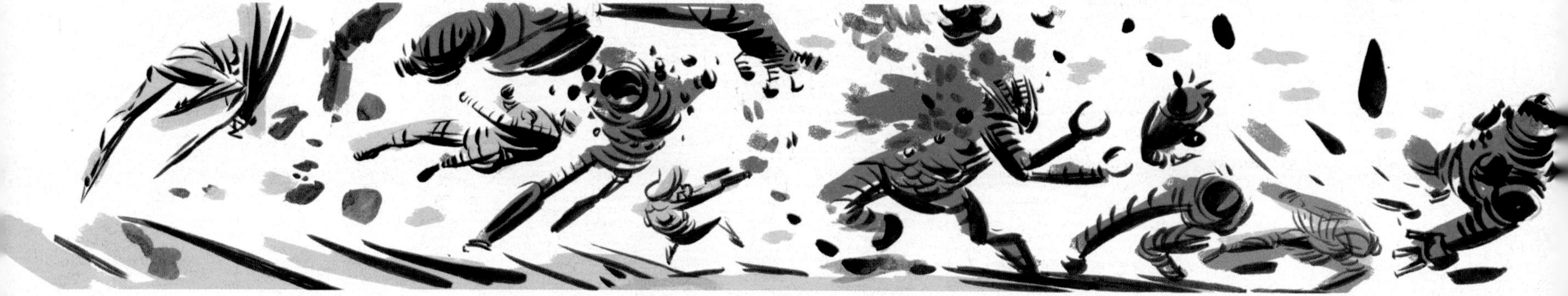

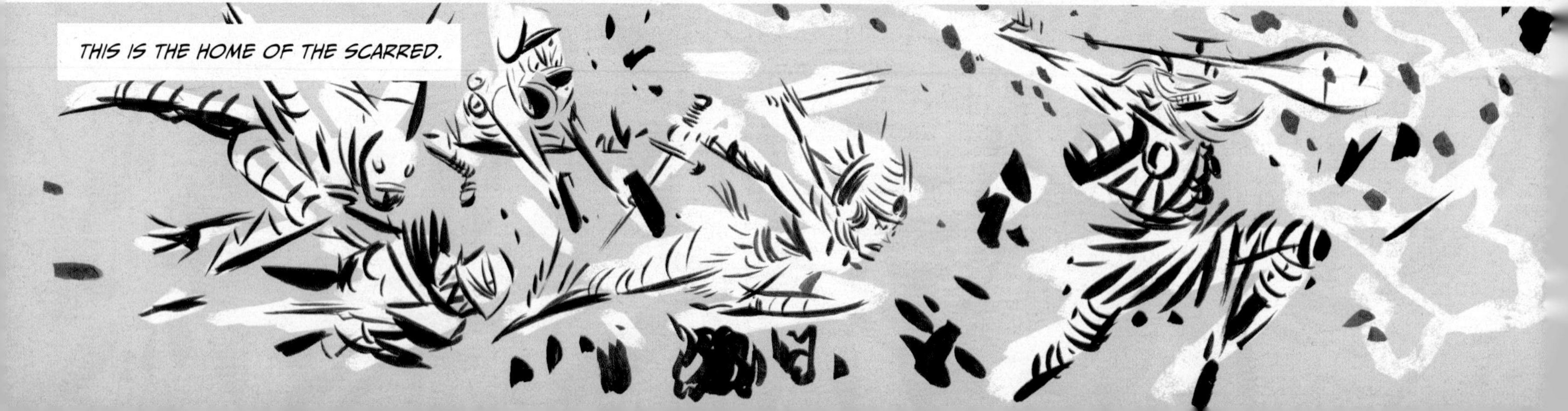
THIS IS THE HOME OF THE SCARRED.

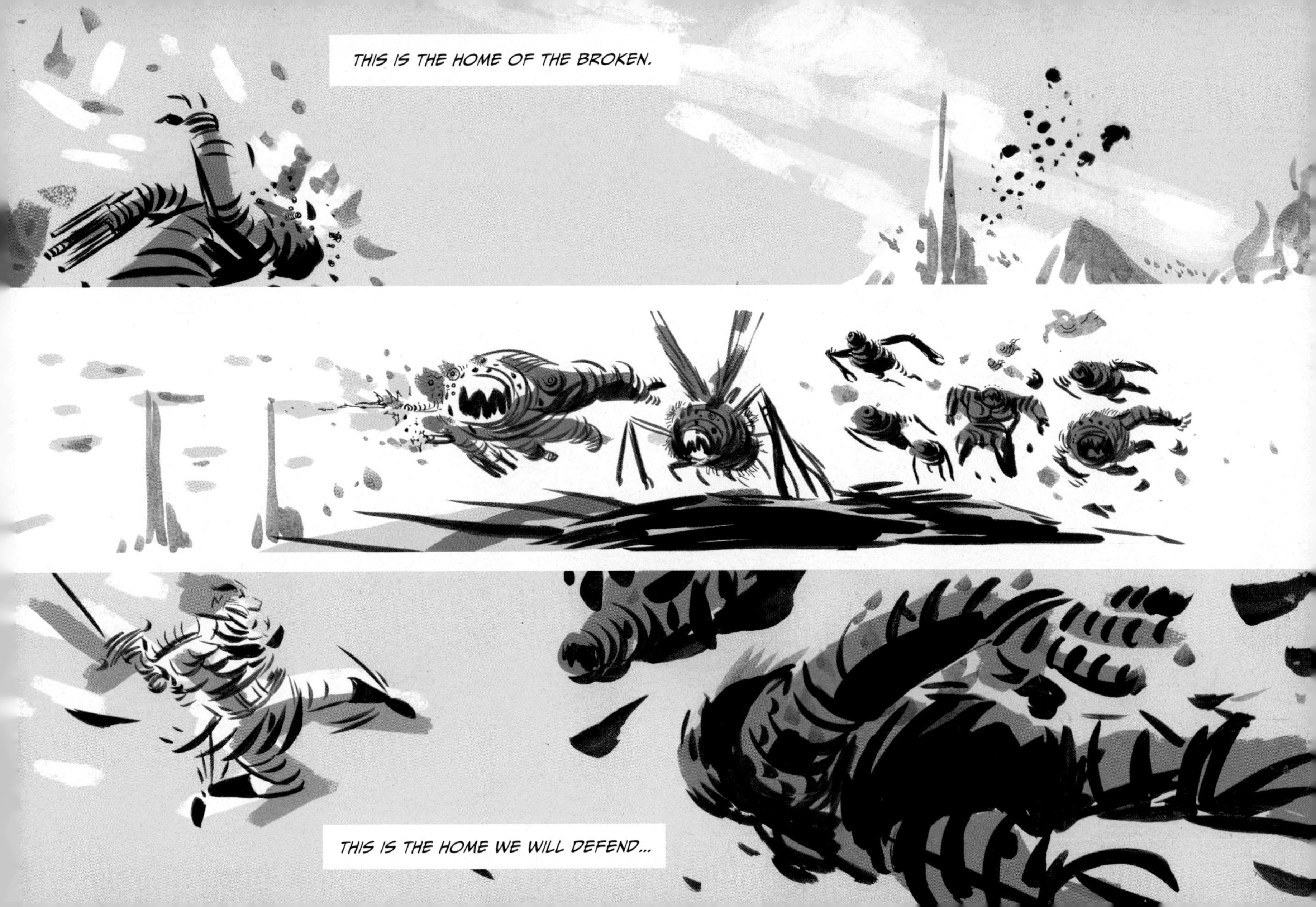
THIS IS THE HOME OF THE BROKEN.
THIS IS THE HOME WE WILL DEFEND...

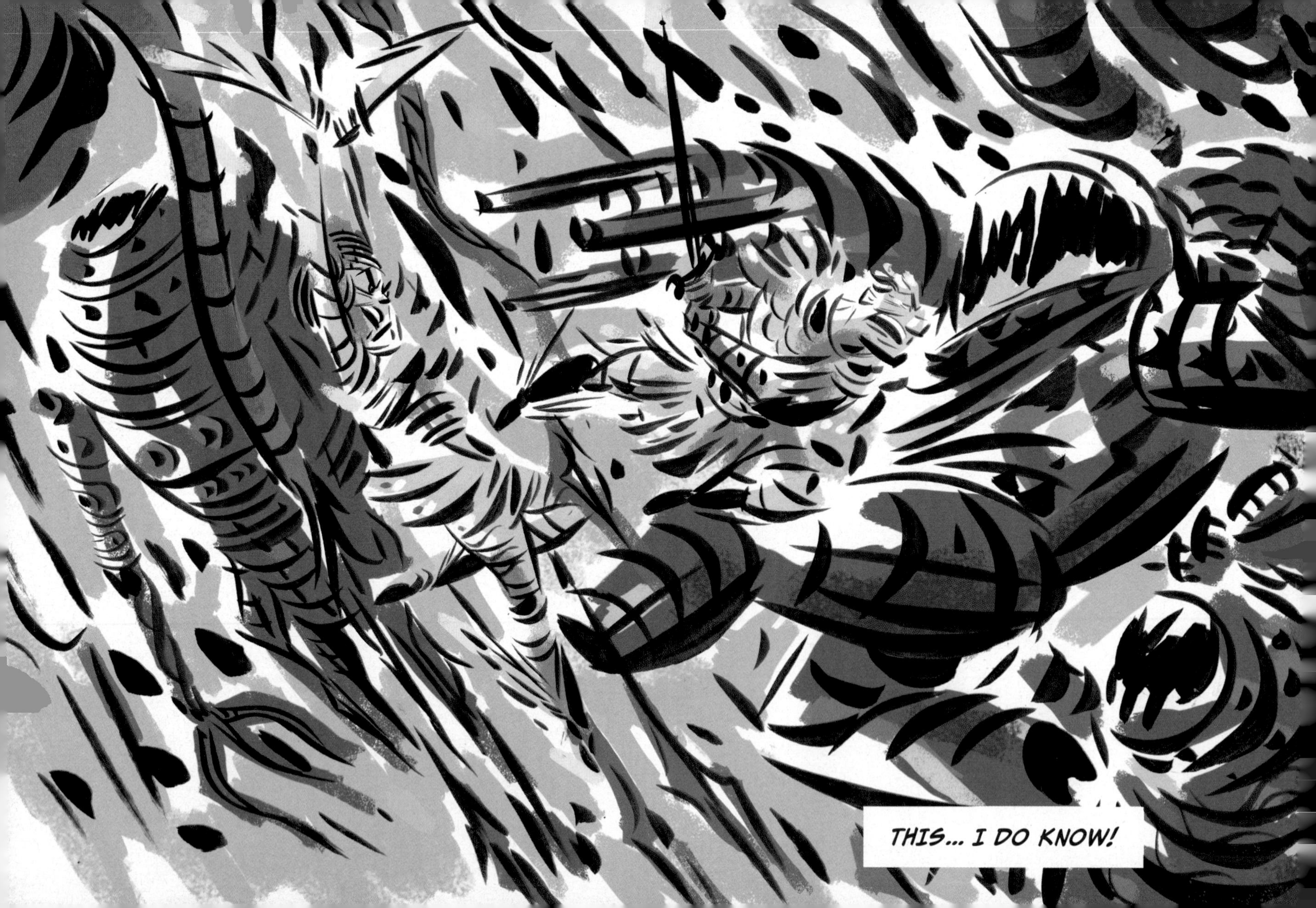
THIS... I DO KNOW!

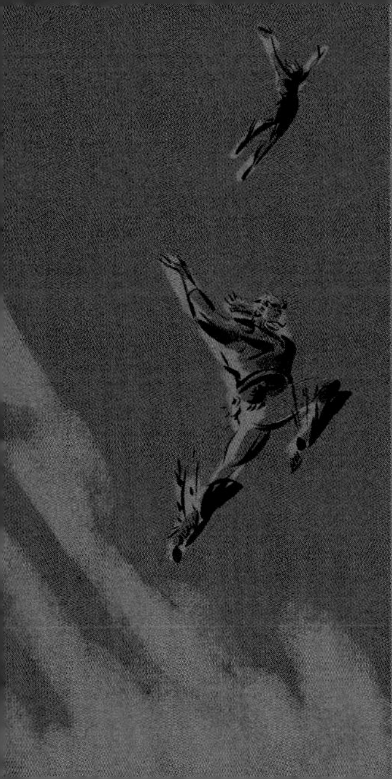

ROCKETO

10

CONQUESTS

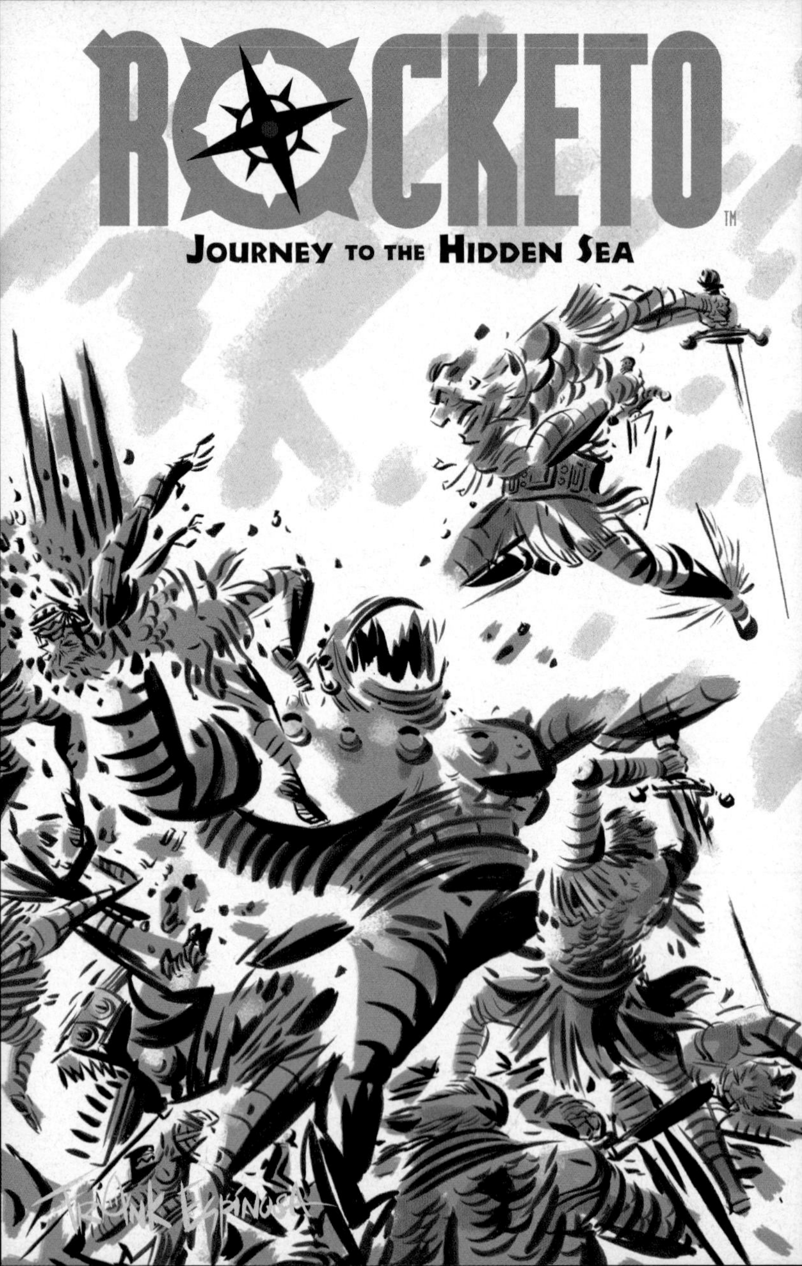
ROCKETO™
JOURNEY TO THE HIDDEN SEA

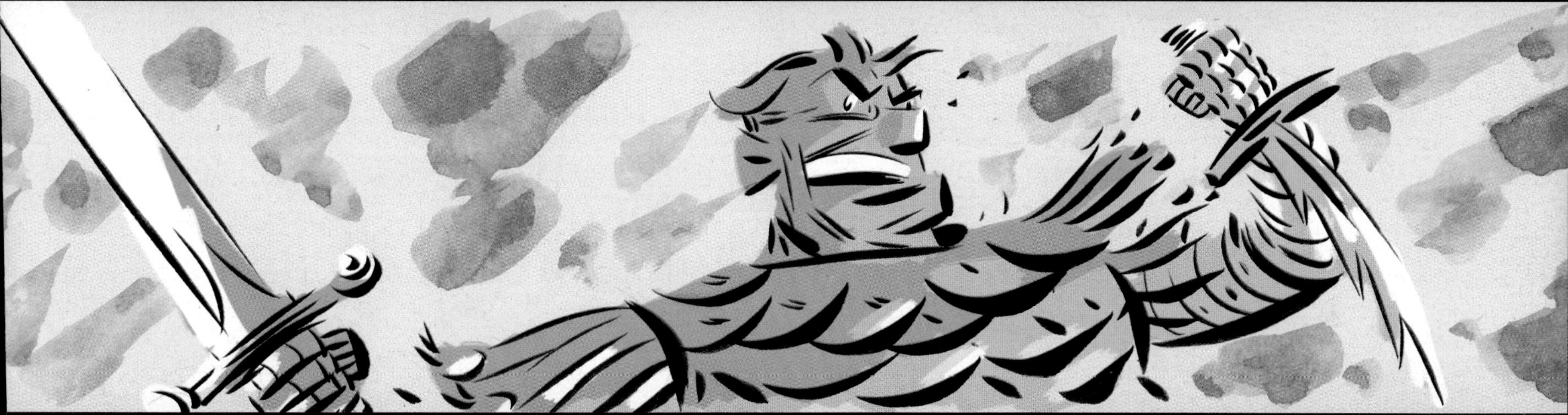

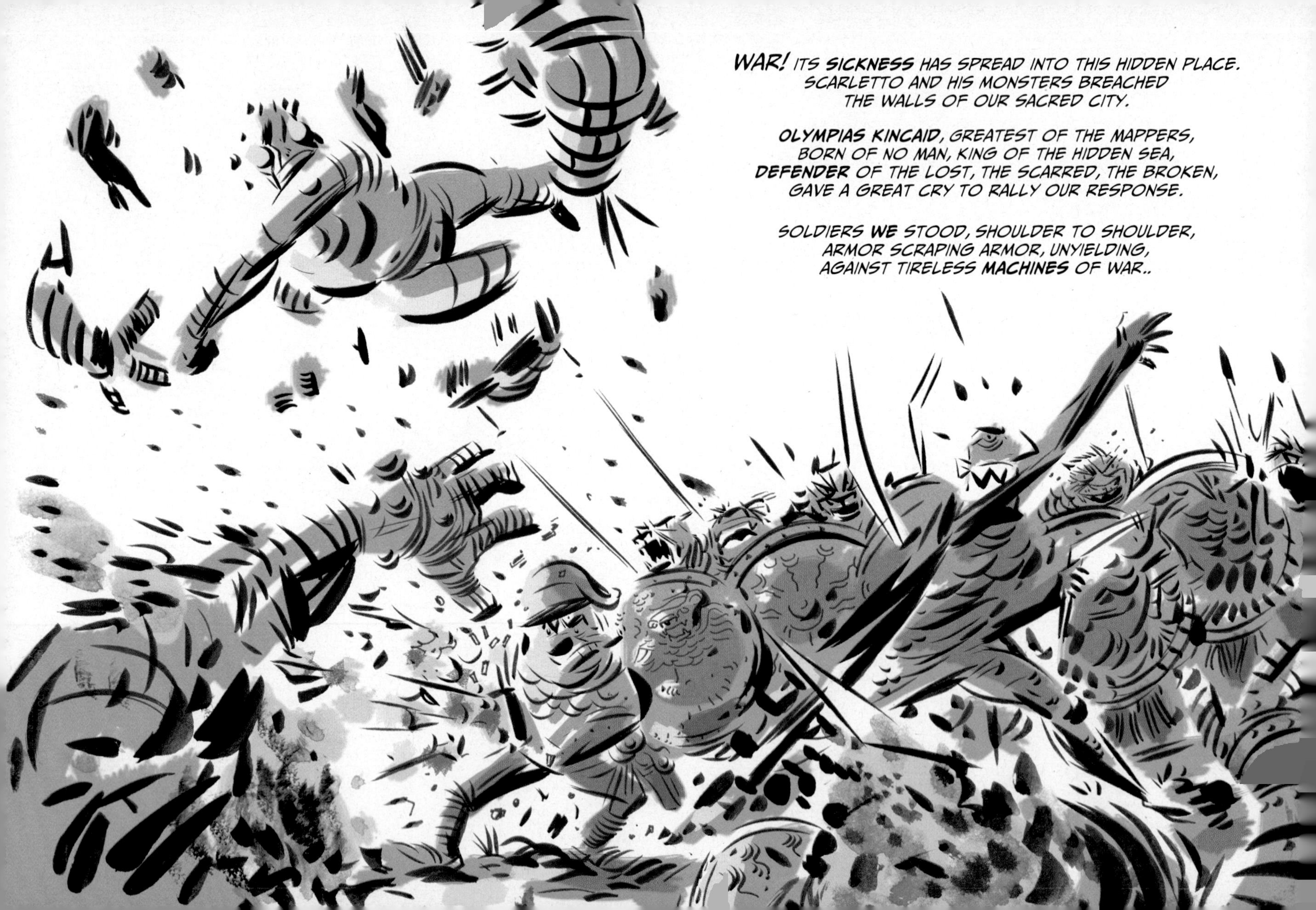
WAR! ITS SICKNESS HAS SPREAD INTO THIS HIDDEN PLACE. SCARLETTO AND HIS MONSTERS BREACHED THE WALLS OF OUR SACRED CITY.
OLYMPIAS KINCAID, GREATEST OF THE MAPPERS, BORN OF NO MAN, KING OF THE HIDDEN SEA, DEFENDER OF THE LOST, THE SCARRED, THE BROKEN, GAVE A GREAT CRY TO RALLY OUR RESPONSE.
SOLDIERS WE STOOD, SHOULDER TO SHOULDER, ARMOR SCRAPING ARMOR, UNYIELDING, AGAINST TIRELESS MACHINES OF WAR..

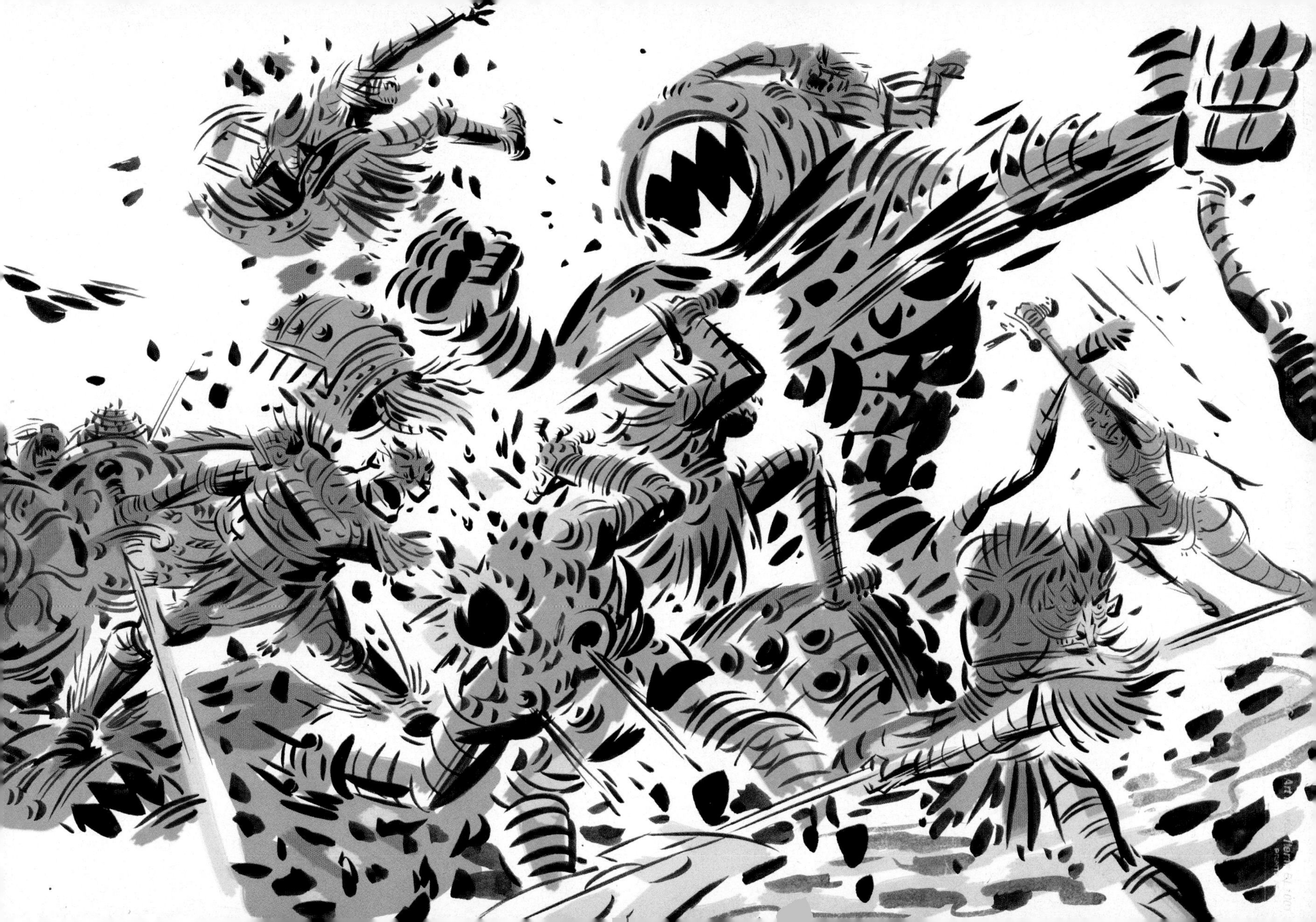

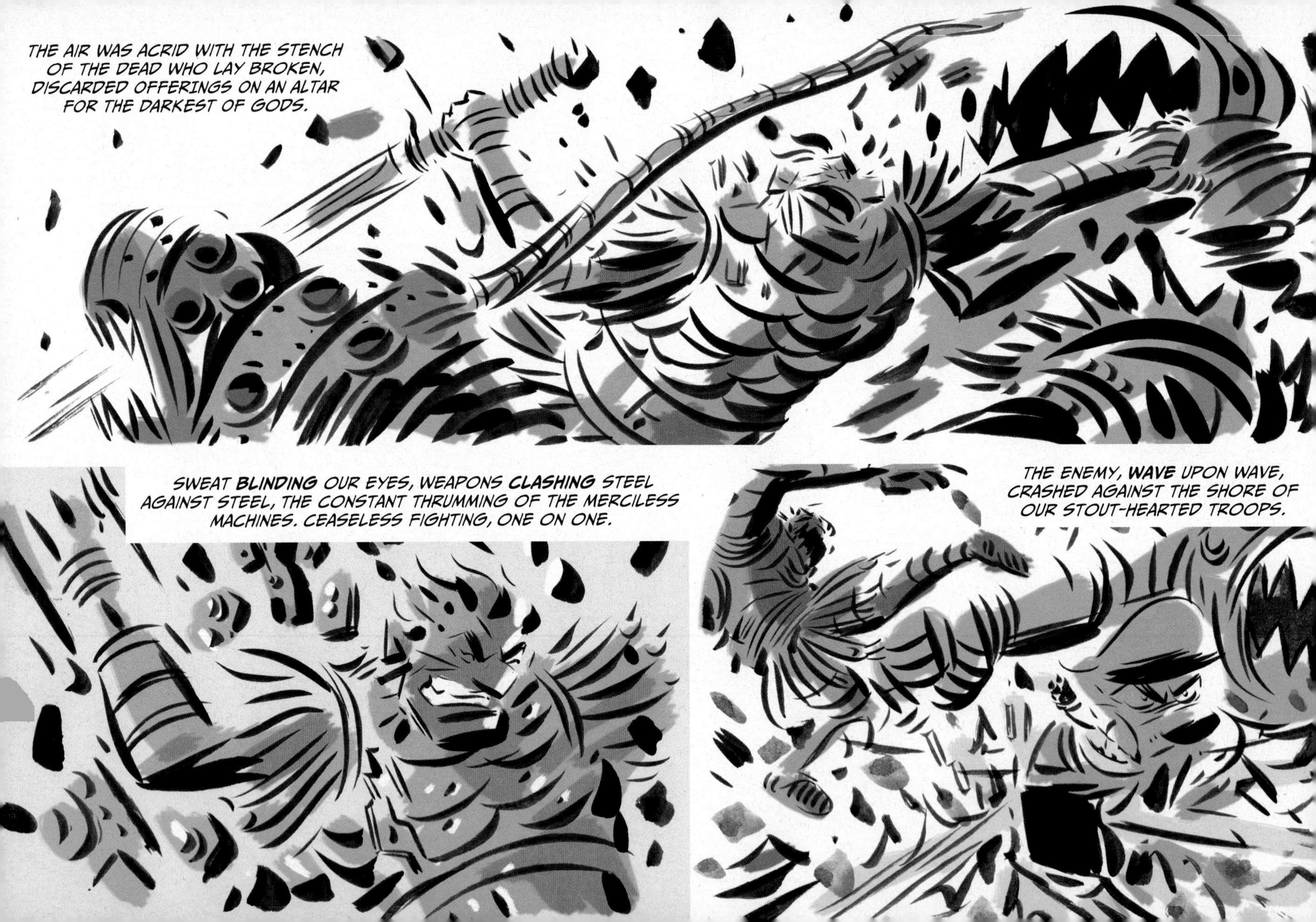
THE AIR WAS ACRID WITH THE STENCH OF THE DEAD WHO LAY BROKEN, DISCARDED OFFERINGS ON AN ALTAR FOR THE DARKEST OF GODS.
SWEAT **BLINDING** OUR EYES, WEAPONS **CLASHING** STEEL AGAINST STEEL, THE CONSTANT THRUMMING OF THE MERCILESS MACHINES. CEASELESS FIGHTING, ONE ON ONE.
THE ENEMY, **WAVE** UPON WAVE, CRASHED AGAINST THE SHORE OF OUR STOUT-HEARTED TROOPS.

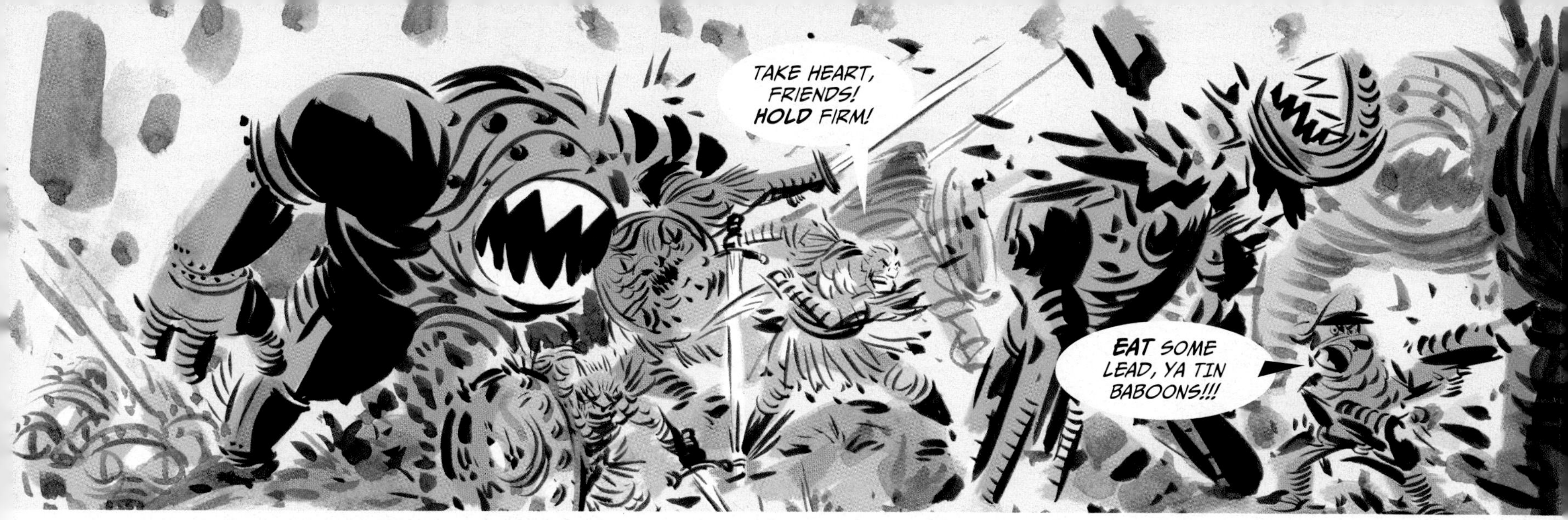
TAKE HEART, FRIENDS! HOLD FIRM!
EAT SOME LEAD, YA TIN BABOONS!!!

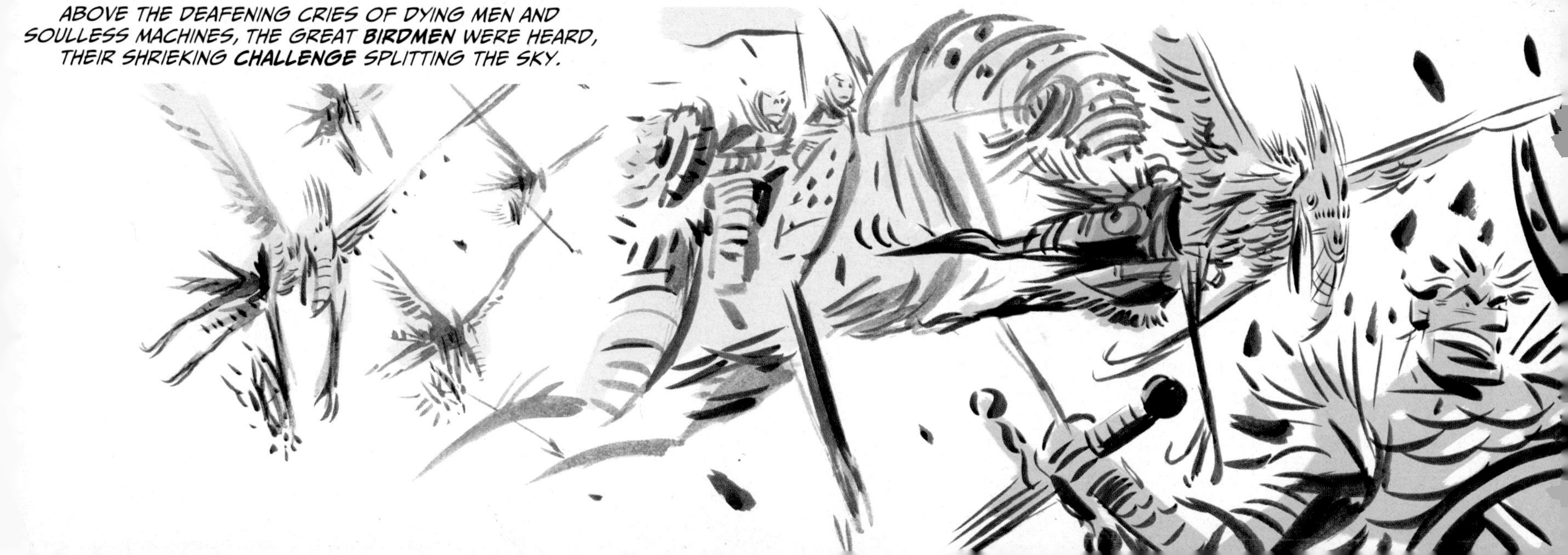
ABOVE THE DEAFENING CRIES OF DYING MEN AND SOULLESS MACHINES, THE GREAT BIRDMEN WERE HEARD, THEIR SHRIEKING CHALLENGE SPLITTING THE SKY.

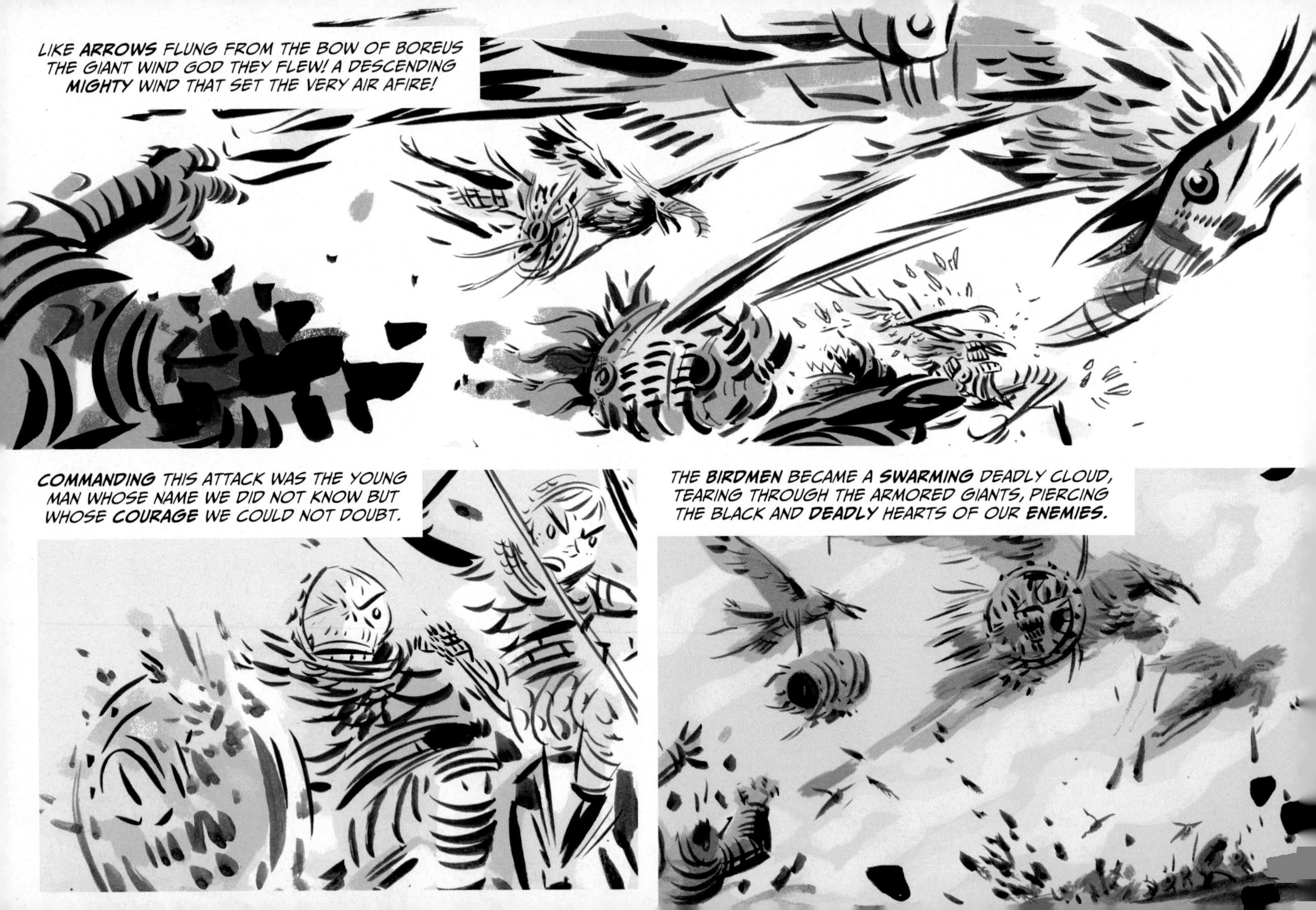
LIKE ARROWS FLUNG FROM THE BOW OF BOREUS THE GIANT WIND GOD THEY FLEW! A DESCENDING MIGHTY WIND THAT SET THE VERY AIR AFIRE!
COMMANDING THIS ATTACK WAS THE YOUNG MAN WHOSE NAME WE DID NOT KNOW BUT WHOSE COURAGE WE COULD NOT DOUBT.
THE BIRDMEN BECAME A SWARMING DEADLY CLOUD, TEARING THROUGH THE ARMORED GIANTS, PIERCING THE BLACK AND DEADLY HEARTS OF OUR ENEMIES.

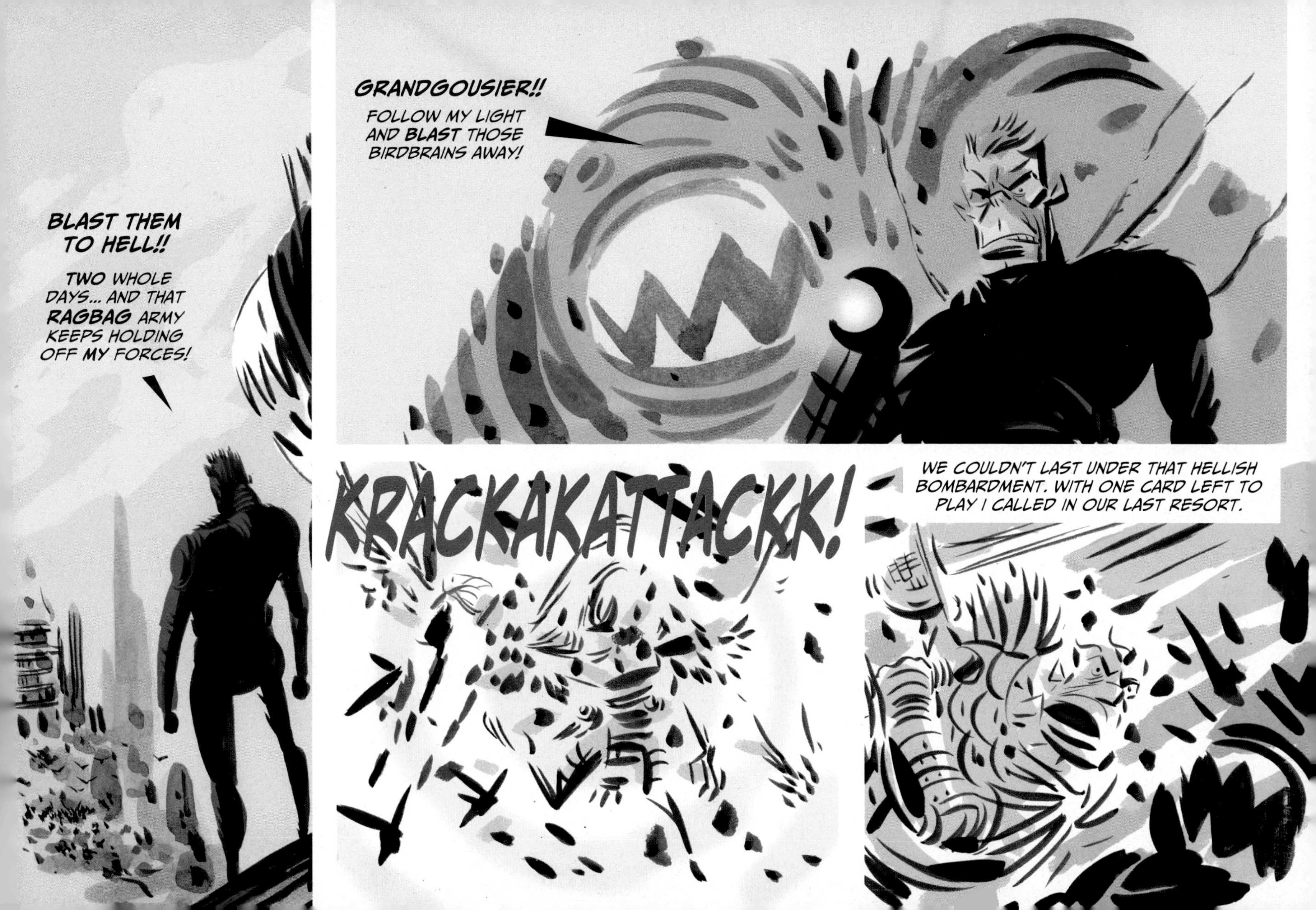
BLAST THEM TO HELL!!
TWO WHOLE DAYS... AND THAT RAGBAG ARMY KEEPS HOLDING OFF MY FORCES!
GRANDGOUSIER!!
FOLLOW MY LIGHT AND BLAST THOSE BIRDBRAINS AWAY!
KRACKAKATTACKK!
WE COULDN'T LAST UNDER THAT HELLISH BOMBARDMENT. WITH ONE CARD LEFT TO PLAY I CALLED IN OUR LAST RESORT.

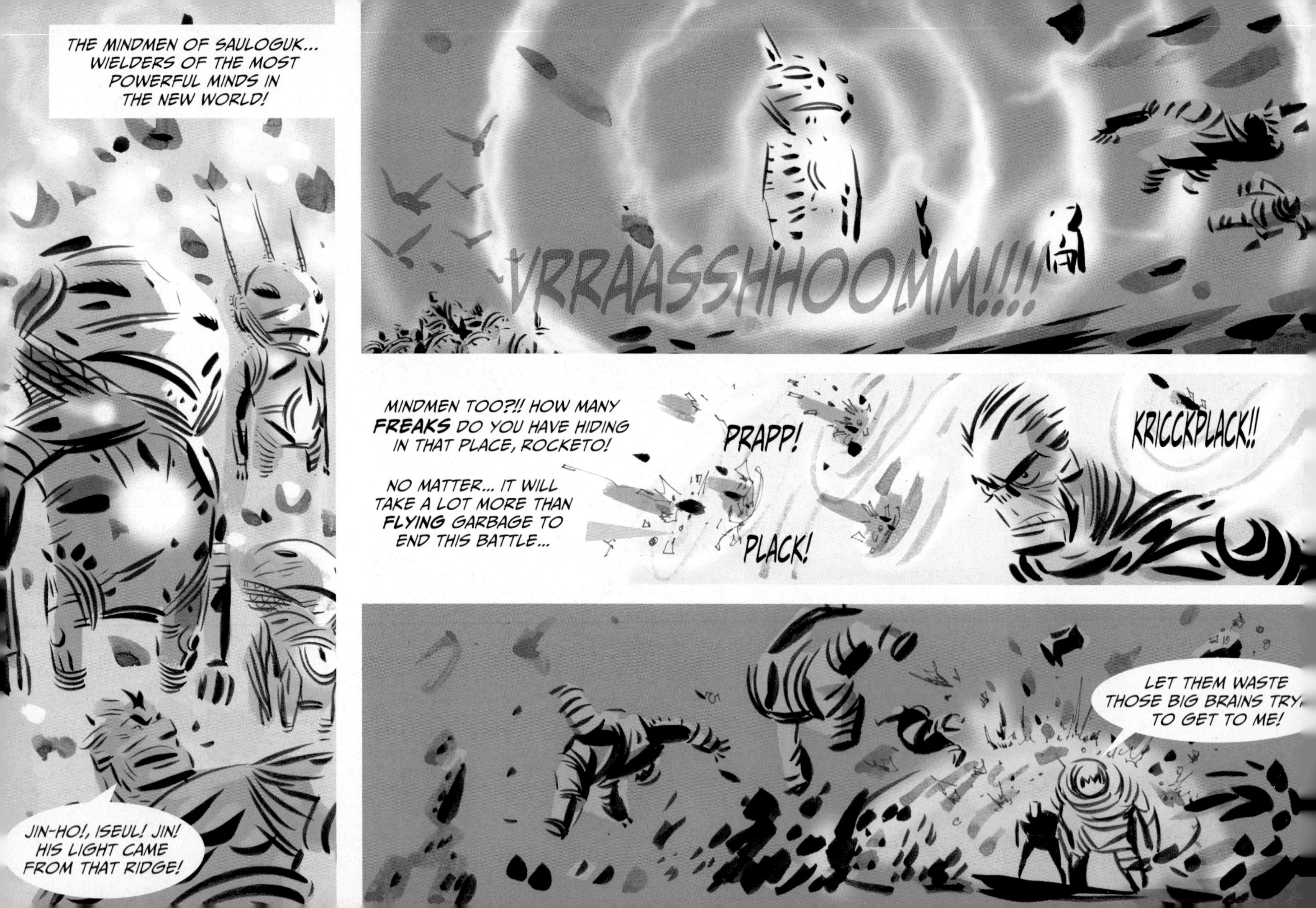

THE MINDMEN OF SAULOGUK... WIELDERS OF THE MOST POWERFUL MINDS IN THE NEW WORLD!
JIN-HO!, ISEUL! JIN! HIS LIGHT CAME FROM THAT RIDGE!
VRRAASSHHOOMM!!!!
MINDMEN TOO?!! HOW MANY FREAKS DO YOU HAVE HIDING IN THAT PLACE, ROCKETO!
NO MATTER... IT WILL TAKE A LOT MORE THAN FLYING GARBAGE TO END THIS BATTLE...
PRAPP!
PLACK!
KRICCKPLACK!!
LET THEM WASTE THOSE BIG BRAINS TRY TO GET TO ME!

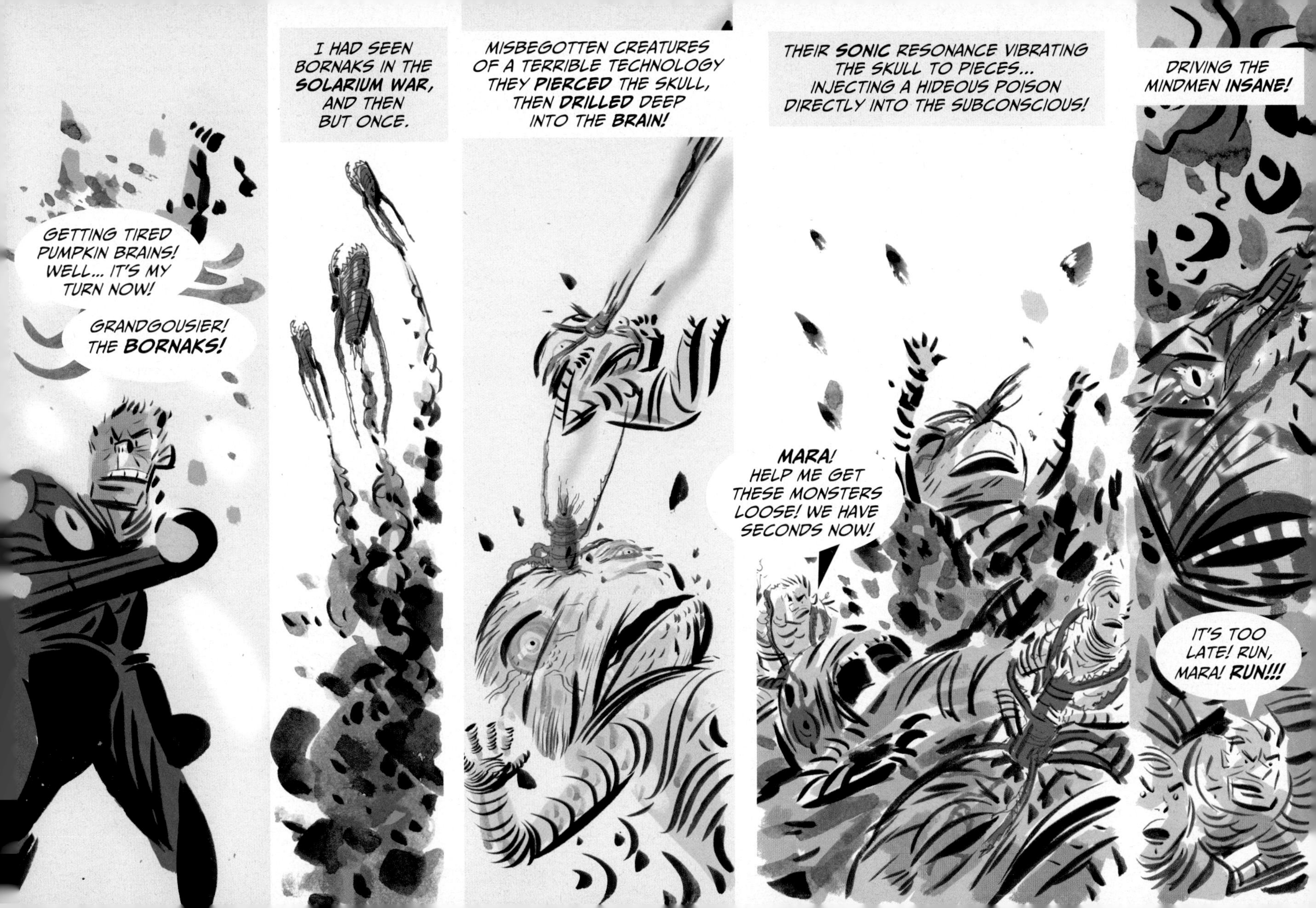
GETTING TIRED PUMPKIN BRAINS! WELL... IT'S MY TURN NOW!
GRANDGOUSIER! THE BORNAKS!
I HAD SEEN BORNAKS IN THE SOLARIUM WAR, AND THEN BUT ONCE.
MISBEGOTTEN CREATURES OF A TERRIBLE TECHNOLOGY THEY PIERCED THE SKULL, THEN DRILLED DEEP INTO THE BRAIN!
THEIR SONIC RESONANCE VIBRATING THE SKULL TO PIECES... INJECTING A HIDEOUS POISON DIRECTLY INTO THE SUBCONSCIOUS!
MARA! HELP ME GET THESE MONSTERS LOOSE! WE HAVE SECONDS NOW!
DRIVING THE MINDMEN INSANE!
IT'S TOO LATE! RUN, MARA! RUN!!!

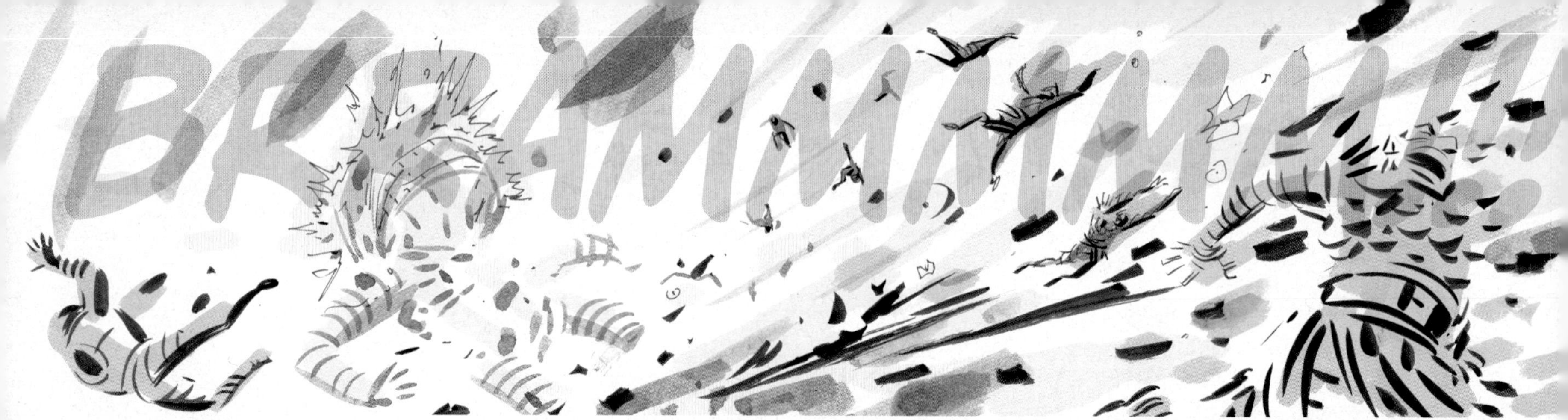
BRAMMMMM!!

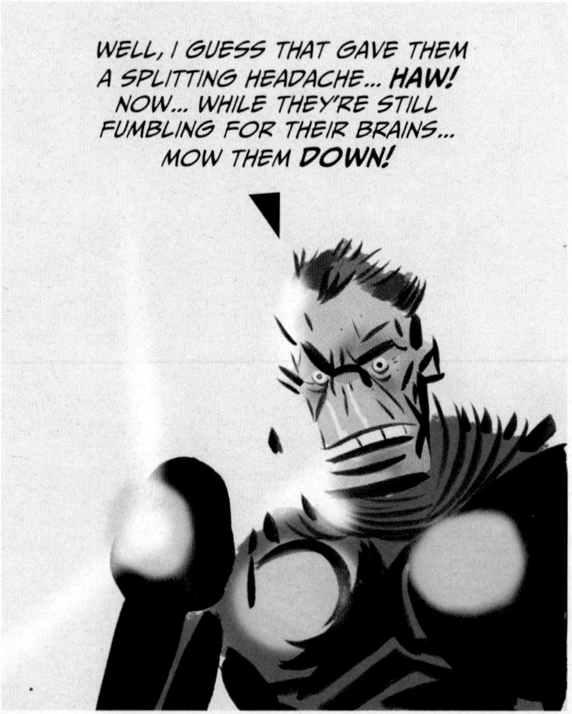
WELL, I GUESS THAT GAVE THEM A SPLITTING HEADACHE... HAW! NOW... WHILE THEY'RE STILL FUMBLING FOR THEIR BRAINS... MOW THEM DOWN!

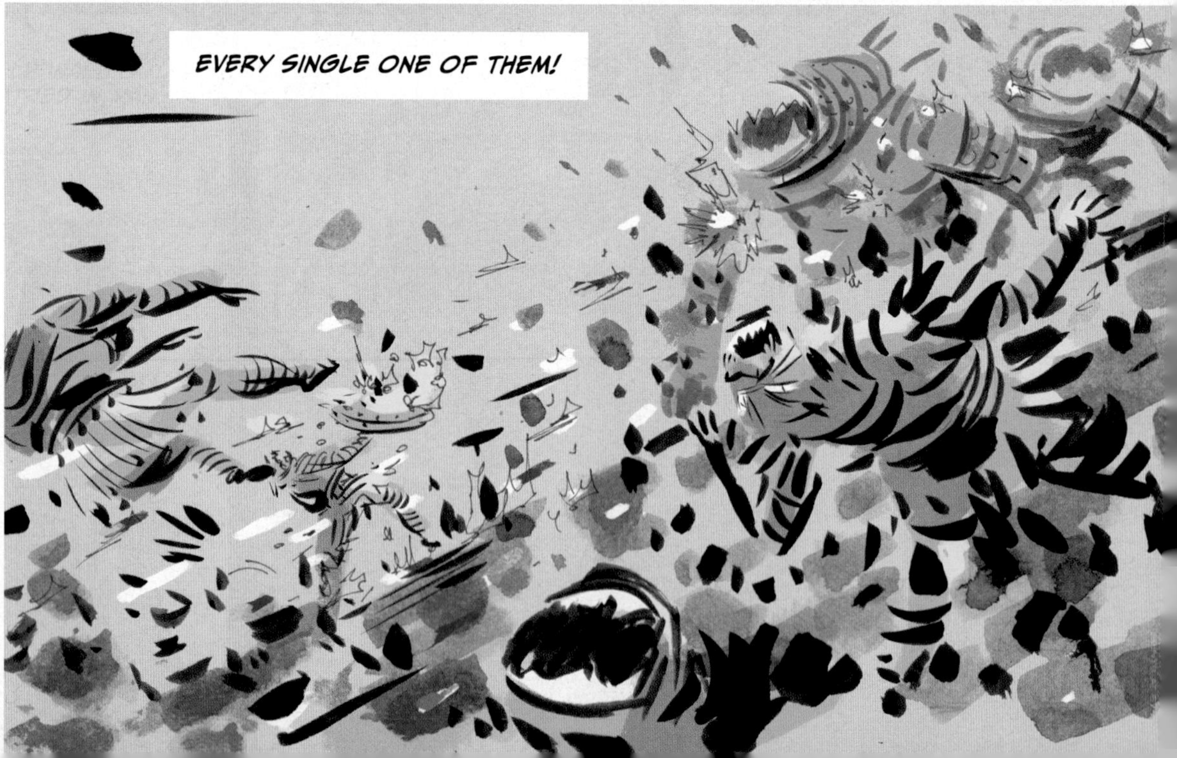
EVERY SINGLE ONE OF THEM!

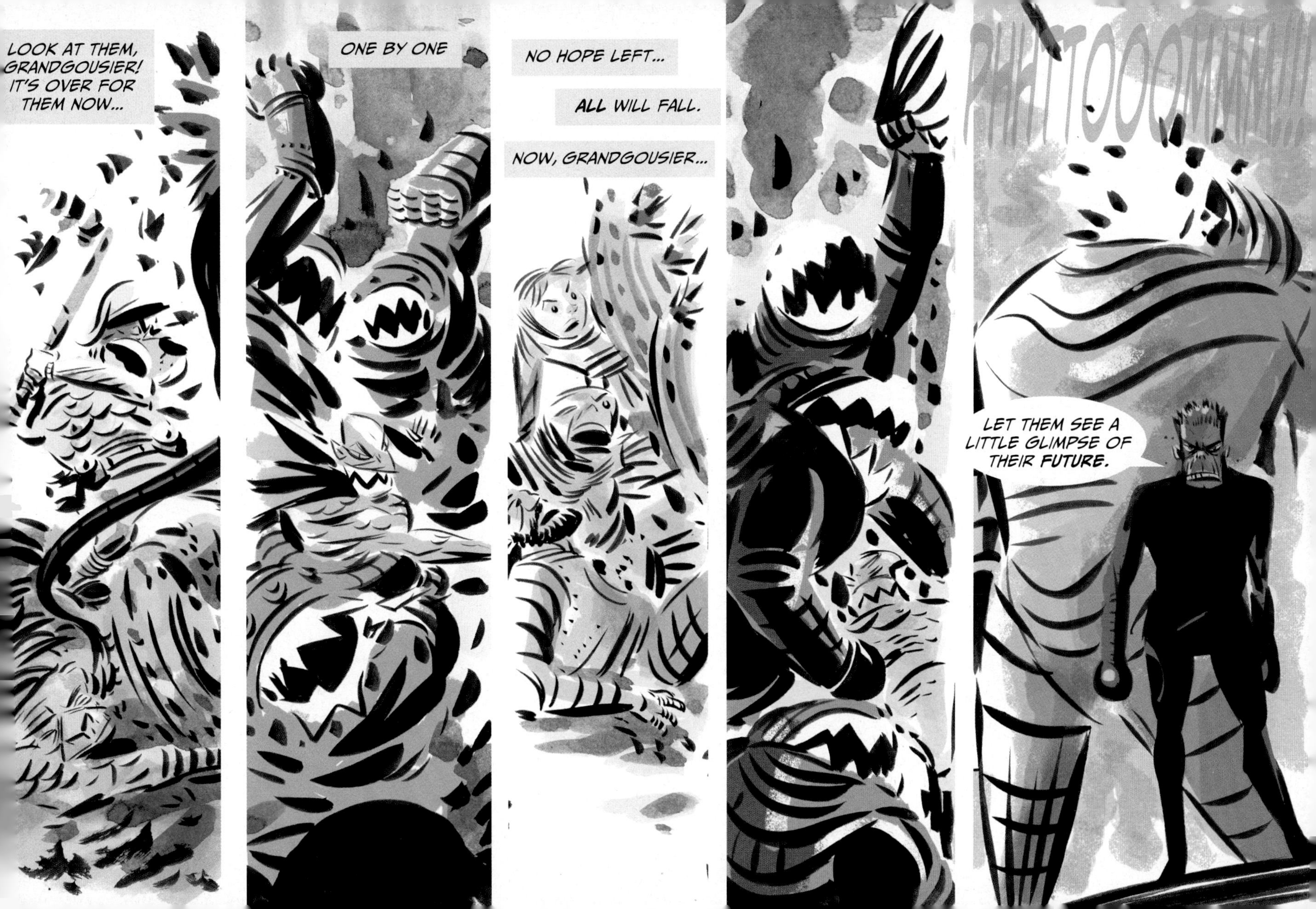
LOOK AT THEM, GRANDGOUSIER! IT'S OVER FOR THEM NOW...
ONE BY ONE
NO HOPE LEFT...
ALL WILL FALL.
NOW, GRANDGOUSIER...
PHHTTOOOMMM!!!
LET THEM SEE A LITTLE GLIMPSE OF THEIR FUTURE.

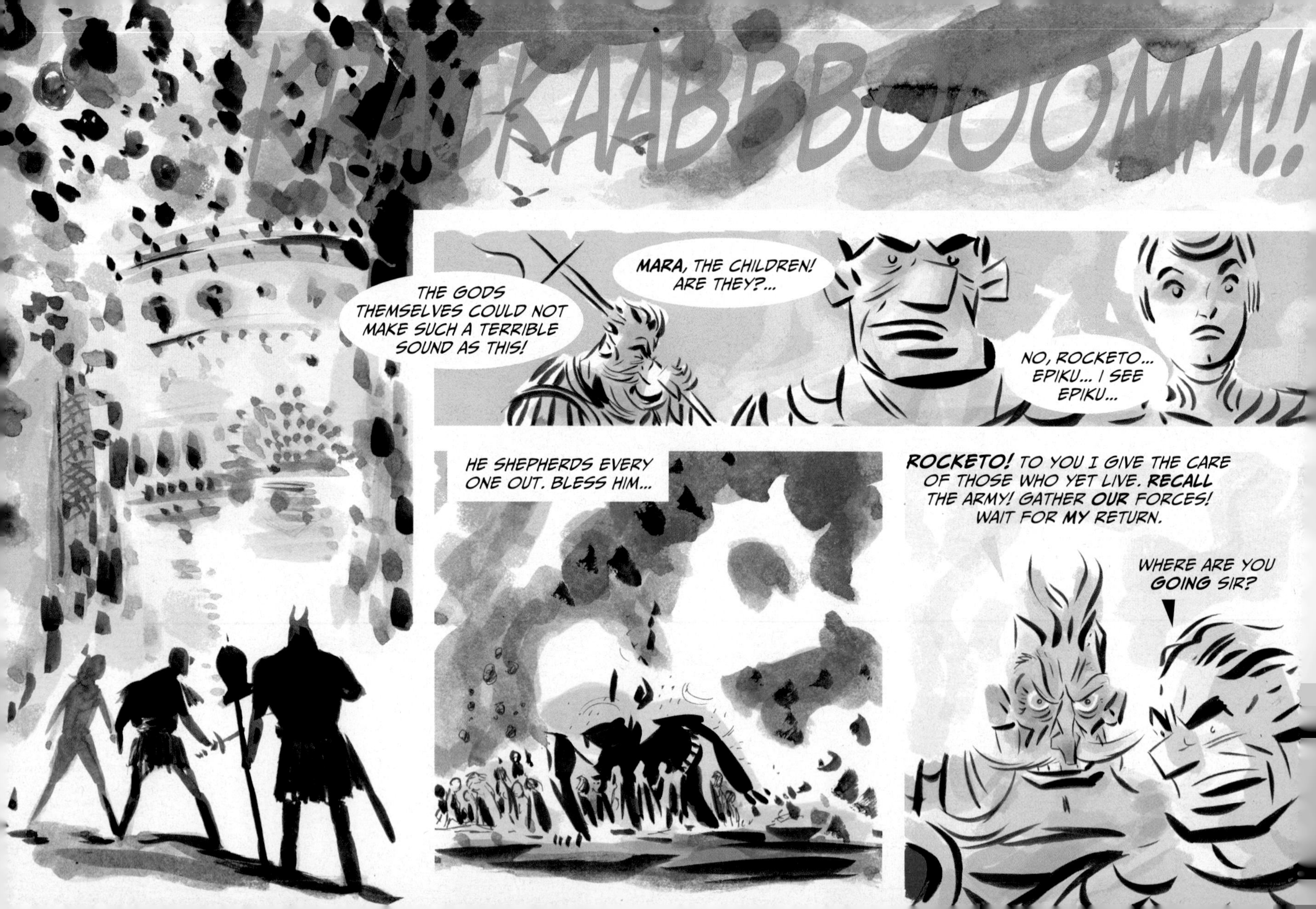
KRAKKAABBBOOOMM!!
MARA, THE CHILDREN! ARE THEY?...
THE GODS THEMSELVES COULD NOT MAKE SUCH A TERRIBLE SOUND AS THIS!
NO, ROCKETO... EPIKU... I SEE EPIKU...
HE SHEPHERDS EVERY ONE OUT. BLESS HIM...
ROCKETO! TO YOU I GIVE THE CARE OF THOSE WHO YET LIVE. RECALL THE ARMY! GATHER OUR FORCES! WAIT FOR MY RETURN.
WHERE ARE YOU GOING SIR?

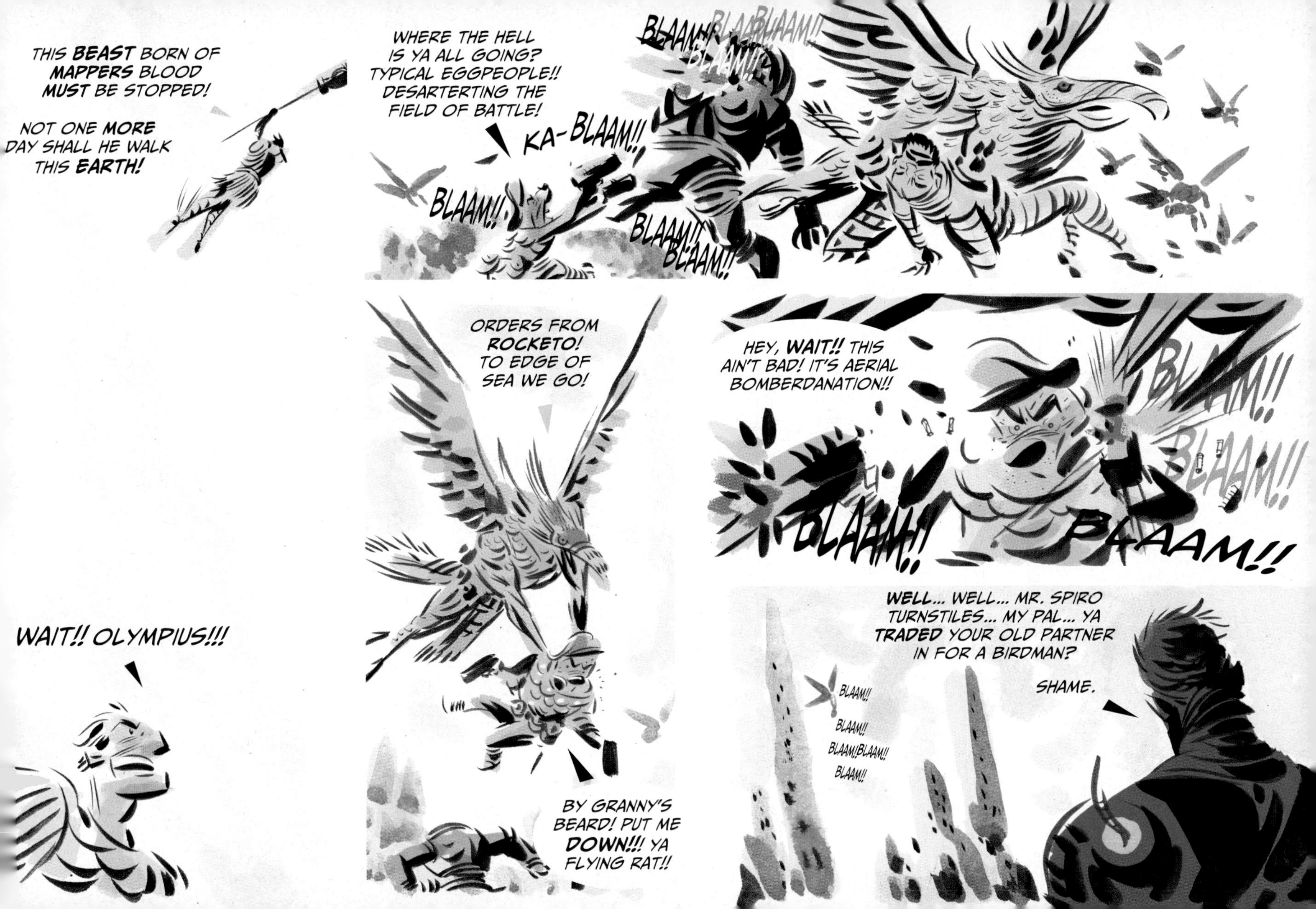
THIS BEAST BORN OF MAPPERS BLOOD MUST BE STOPPED!
NOT ONE MORE DAY SHALL HE WALK THIS EARTH!
WHERE THE HELL IS YA ALL GOING? TYPICAL EGGPEOPLE!! DESARTERTING THE FIELD OF BATTLE!
KA-BLAAM!!
BLAAM!!
BLAAM!! BLAAM!!
WAIT!! OLYMPIUS!!!
ORDERS FROM ROCKETO! TO EDGE OF SEA WE GO!
BY GRANNY'S BEARD! PUT ME DOWN!!! YA FLYING RAT!!
HEY, WAIT!! THIS AIN'T BAD! IT'S AERIAL BOMBERDANATION!!
BLAAM!!
BLAAM!!
BLAAM!!
BLAAM!!
WELL... WELL... MR. SPIRO TURNSTILES... MY PAL... YA TRADED YOUR OLD PARTNER IN FOR A BIRDMAN?
SHAME.
BLAAM!!
BLAAM!!
BLAAM!BLAAM!!
BLAAM!!

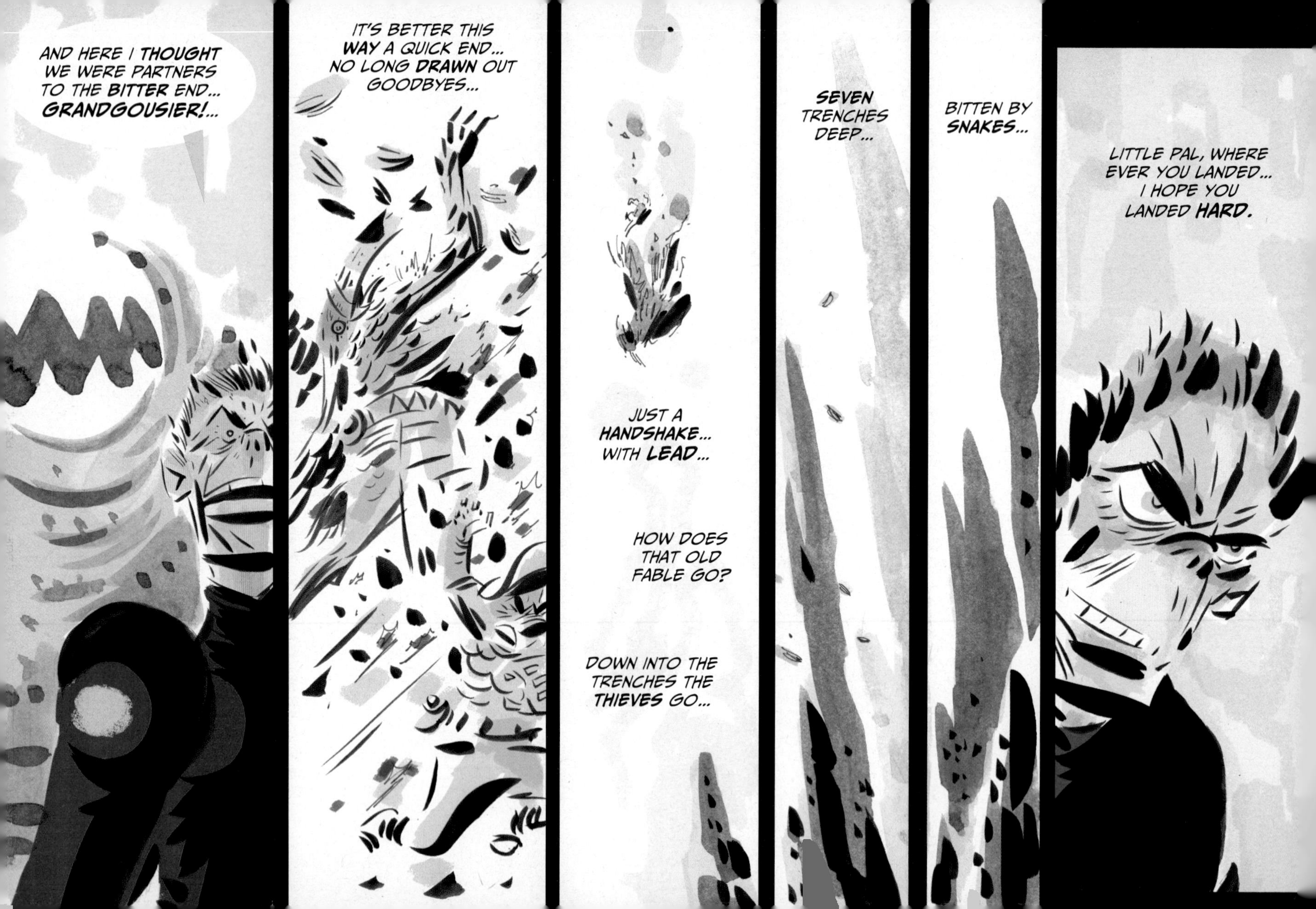
AND HERE I THOUGHT WE WERE PARTNERS TO THE BITTER END... GRANDGOUSIER!...
IT'S BETTER THIS WAY A QUICK END... NO LONG DRAWN OUT GOODBYES...
JUST A HANDSHAKE... WITH LEAD...
HOW DOES THAT OLD FABLE GO?
DOWN INTO THE TRENCHES THE THIEVES GO...
SEVEN TRENCHES DEEP...
BITTEN BY SNAKES...
LITTLE PAL, WHERE EVER YOU LANDED... I HOPE YOU LANDED HARD.

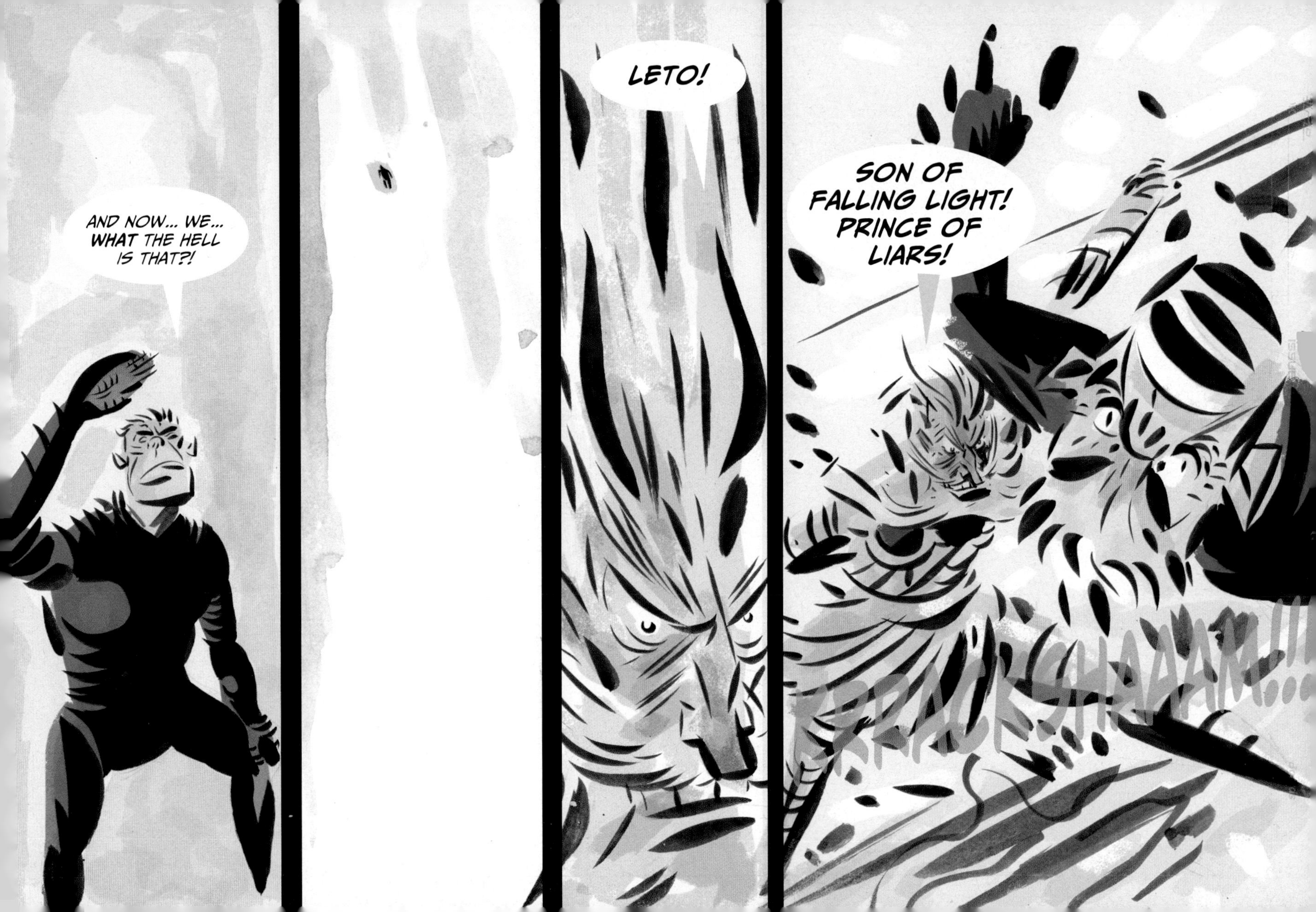
AND NOW... WE... WHAT THE HELL IS THAT?!
LETO!
SON OF FALLING LIGHT! PRINCE OF LIARS!
KRRACKSHAAAM!!!

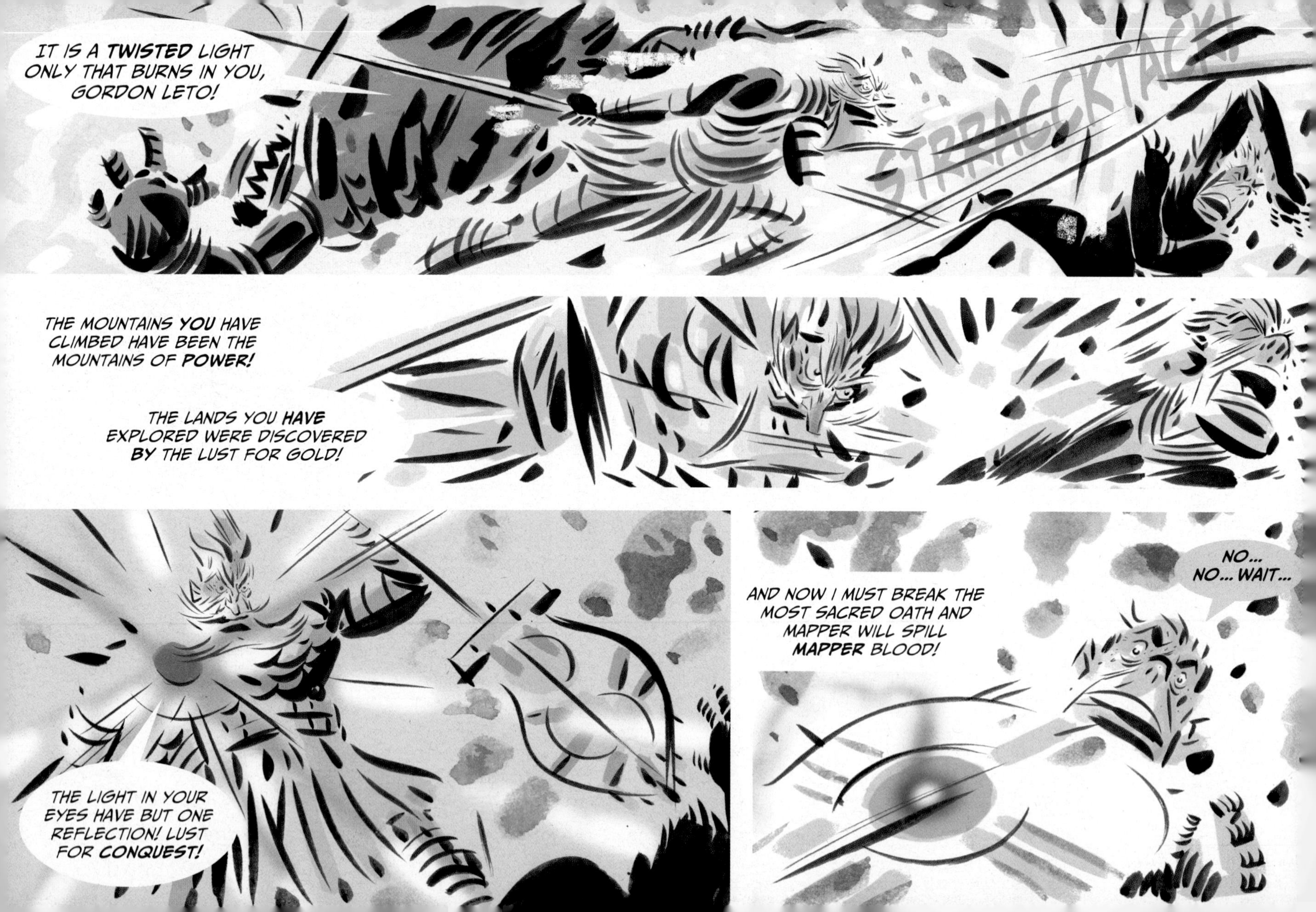

IT IS A TWISTED LIGHT ONLY THAT BURNS IN YOU, GORDON LETO!
STRRACCKTACK!
THE MOUNTAINS YOU HAVE CLIMBED HAVE BEEN THE MOUNTAINS OF POWER!
THE LANDS YOU HAVE EXPLORED WERE DISCOVERED BY THE LUST FOR GOLD!
THE LIGHT IN YOUR EYES HAVE BUT ONE REFLECTION! LUST FOR CONQUEST!
AND NOW I MUST BREAK THE MOST SACRED OATH AND MAPPER WILL SPILL MAPPER BLOOD!
NO... NO... WAIT...

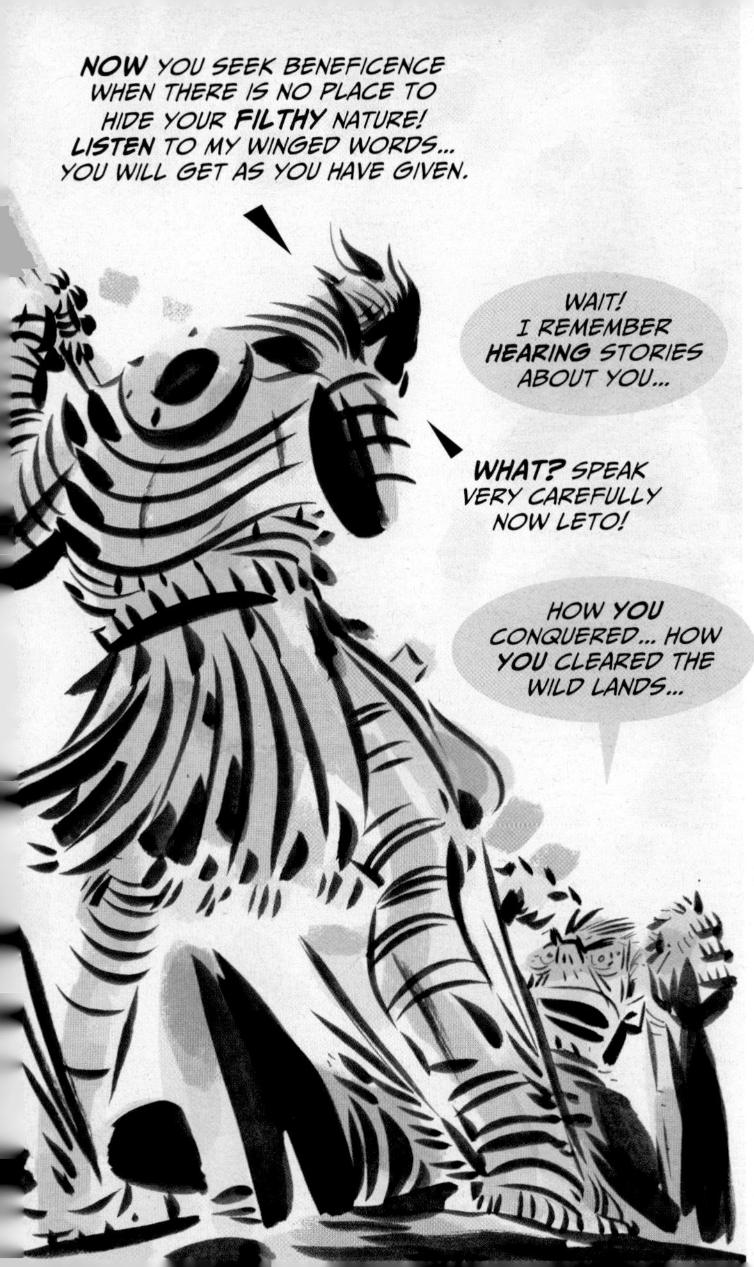
NOW YOU SEEK BENEFICENCE WHEN THERE IS NO PLACE TO HIDE YOUR FILTHY NATURE! LISTEN TO MY WINGED WORDS... YOU WILL GET AS YOU HAVE GIVEN.
WAIT! I REMEMBER HEARING STORIES ABOUT YOU...
WHAT? SPEAK VERY CAREFULLY NOW LETO!
HOW YOU CONQUERED... HOW YOU CLEARED THE WILD LANDS...

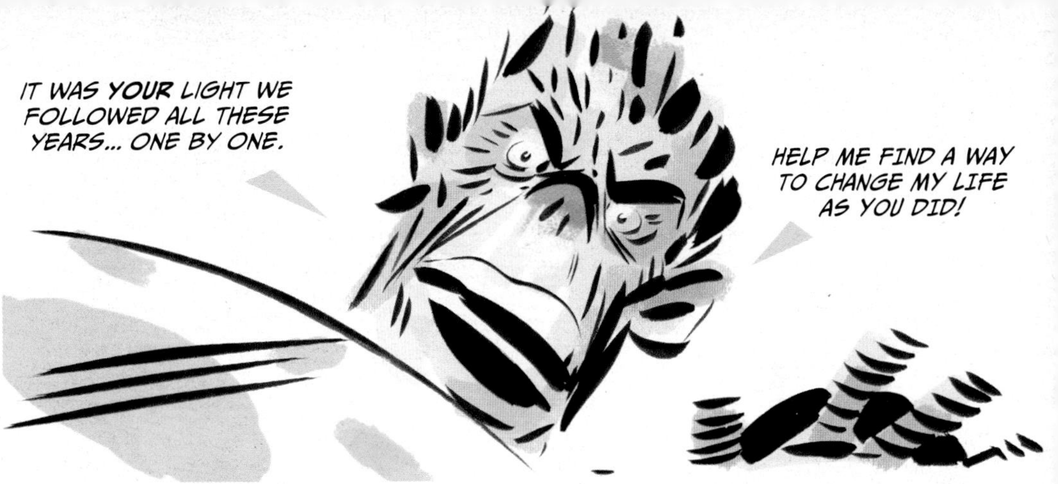
IT WAS YOUR LIGHT WE FOLLOWED ALL THESE YEARS... ONE BY ONE.
HELP ME FIND A WAY TO CHANGE MY LIFE AS YOU DID!

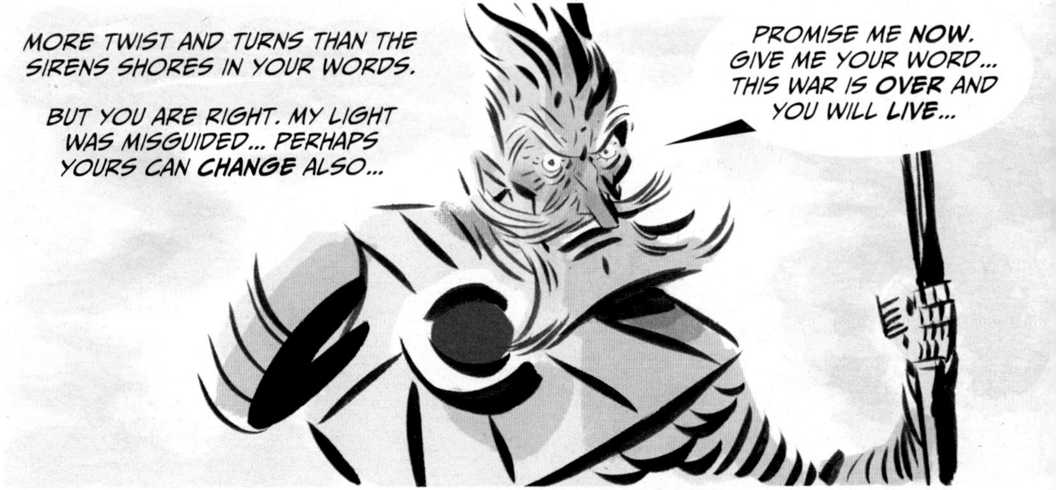
MORE TWIST AND TURNS THAN THE SIRENS SHORES IN YOUR WORDS.
BUT YOU ARE RIGHT. MY LIGHT WAS MISGUIDED... PERHAPS YOURS CAN CHANGE ALSO...
PROMISE ME NOW. GIVE ME YOUR WORD... THIS WAR IS OVER AND YOU WILL LIVE...

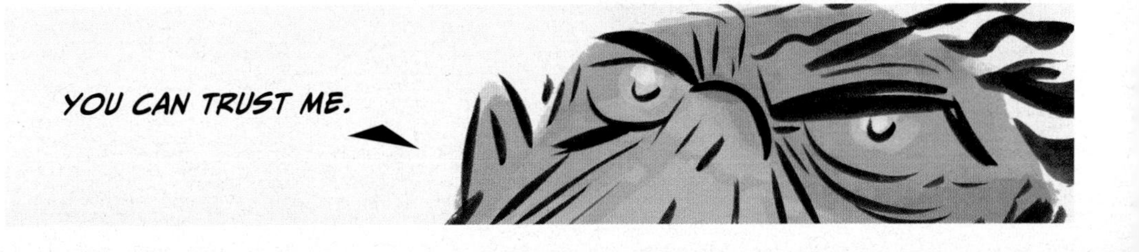
YOU CAN TRUST ME.

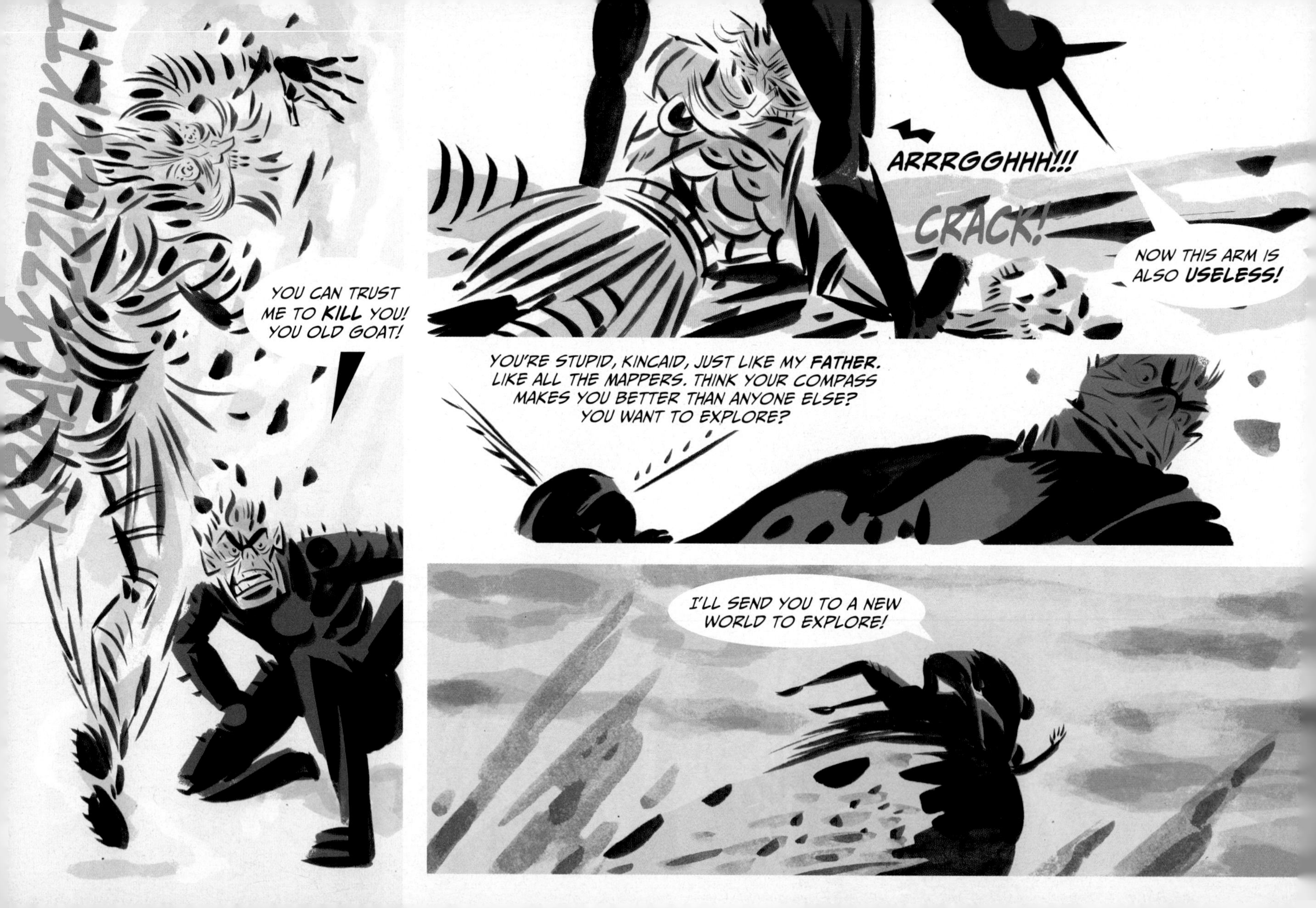
YOU CAN TRUST ME TO KILL YOU! YOU OLD GOAT!
ARRRGGHHH!!!
CRACK!
NOW THIS ARM IS ALSO USELESS!
YOU'RE STUPID, KINCAID, JUST LIKE MY FATHER. LIKE ALL THE MAPPERS. THINK YOUR COMPASS MAKES YOU BETTER THAN ANYONE ELSE? YOU WANT TO EXPLORE?
I'LL SEND YOU TO A NEW WORLD TO EXPLORE!

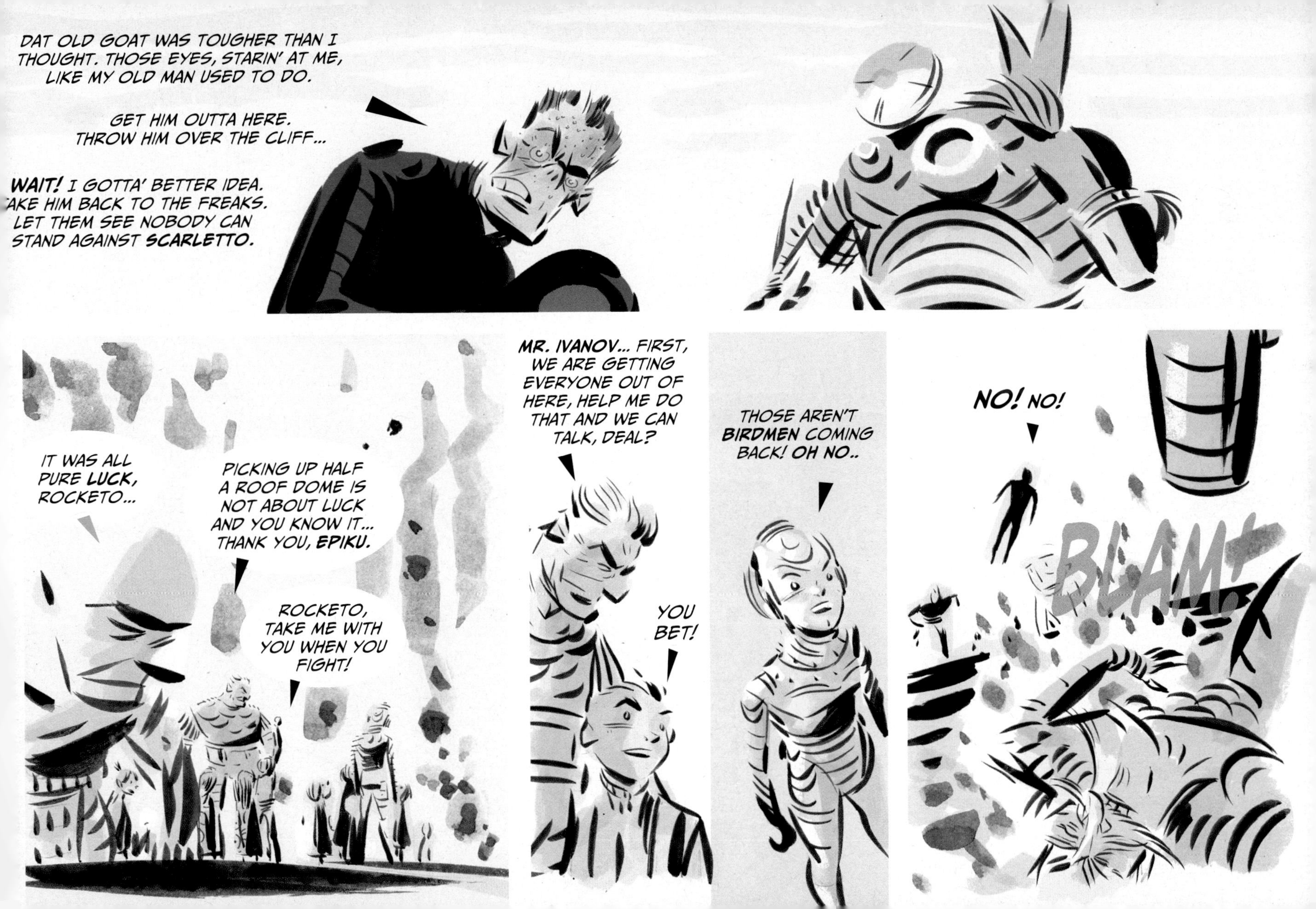
DAT OLD GOAT WAS TOUGHER THAN I THOUGHT. THOSE EYES, STARIN' AT ME, LIKE MY OLD MAN USED TO DO.
GET HIM OUTTA HERE. THROW HIM OVER THE CLIFF...
WAIT! I GOTTA' BETTER IDEA. AKE HIM BACK TO THE FREAKS. LET THEM SEE NOBODY CAN STAND AGAINST SCARLETTO.
IT WAS ALL PURE LUCK, ROCKETO...
PICKING UP HALF A ROOF DOME IS NOT ABOUT LUCK AND YOU KNOW IT... THANK YOU, EPIKU.
ROCKETO, TAKE ME WITH YOU WHEN YOU FIGHT!
MR. IVANOV... FIRST, WE ARE GETTING EVERYONE OUT OF HERE, HELP ME DO THAT AND WE CAN TALK, DEAL?
YOU BET!
THOSE AREN'T BIRDMEN COMING BACK! OH NO..
NO! NO!
BLAM!

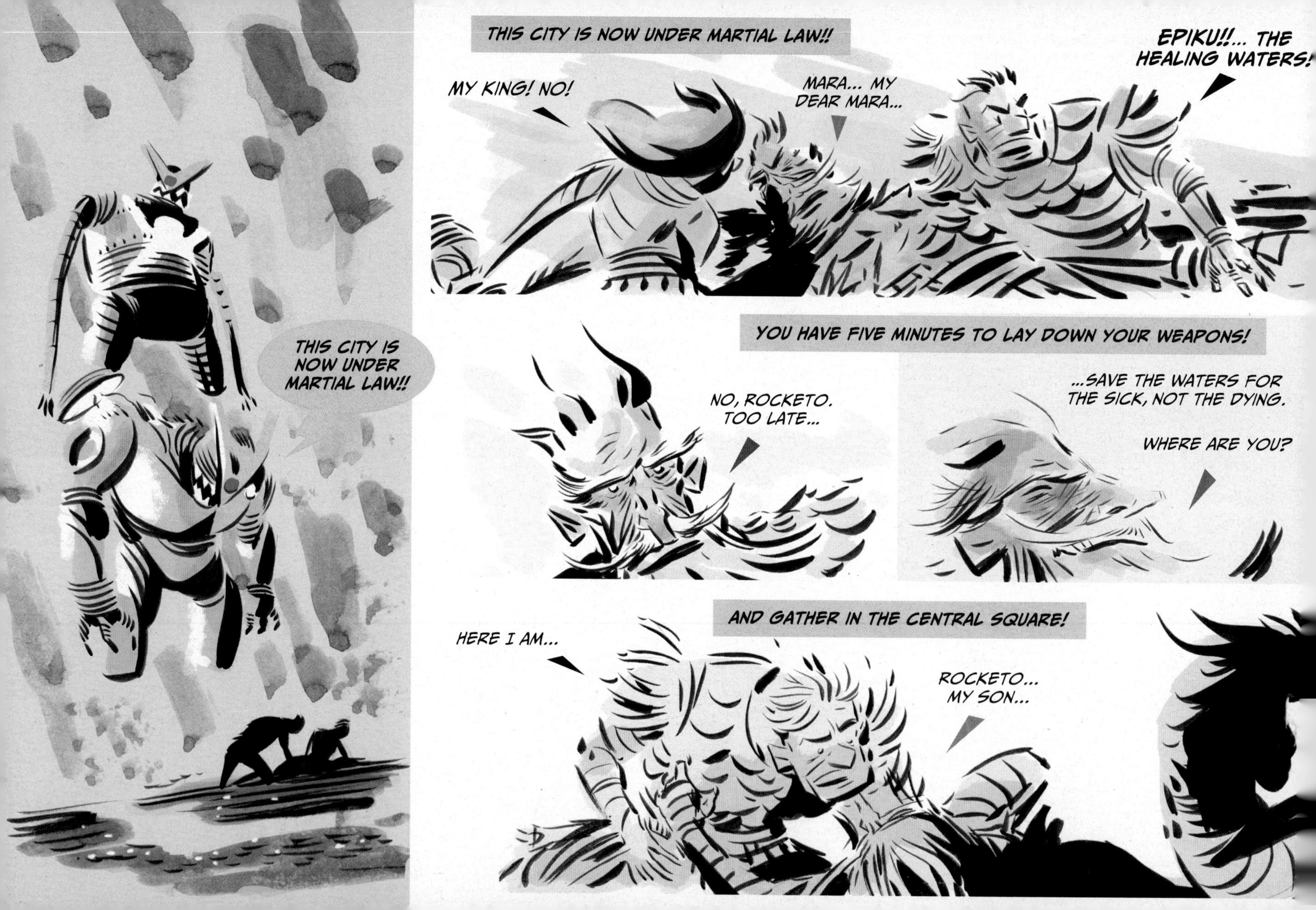
THIS CITY IS NOW UNDER MARTIAL LAW!!
THIS CITY IS NOW UNDER MARTIAL LAW!!
MY KING! NO!
MARA... MY DEAR MARA...
EPIKU!!... THE HEALING WATERS!
YOU HAVE FIVE MINUTES TO LAY DOWN YOUR WEAPONS!
NO, ROCKETO. TOO LATE...
...SAVE THE WATERS FOR THE SICK, NOT THE DYING.
WHERE ARE YOU?
AND GATHER IN THE CENTRAL SQUARE!
HERE I AM...
ROCKETO... MY SON...

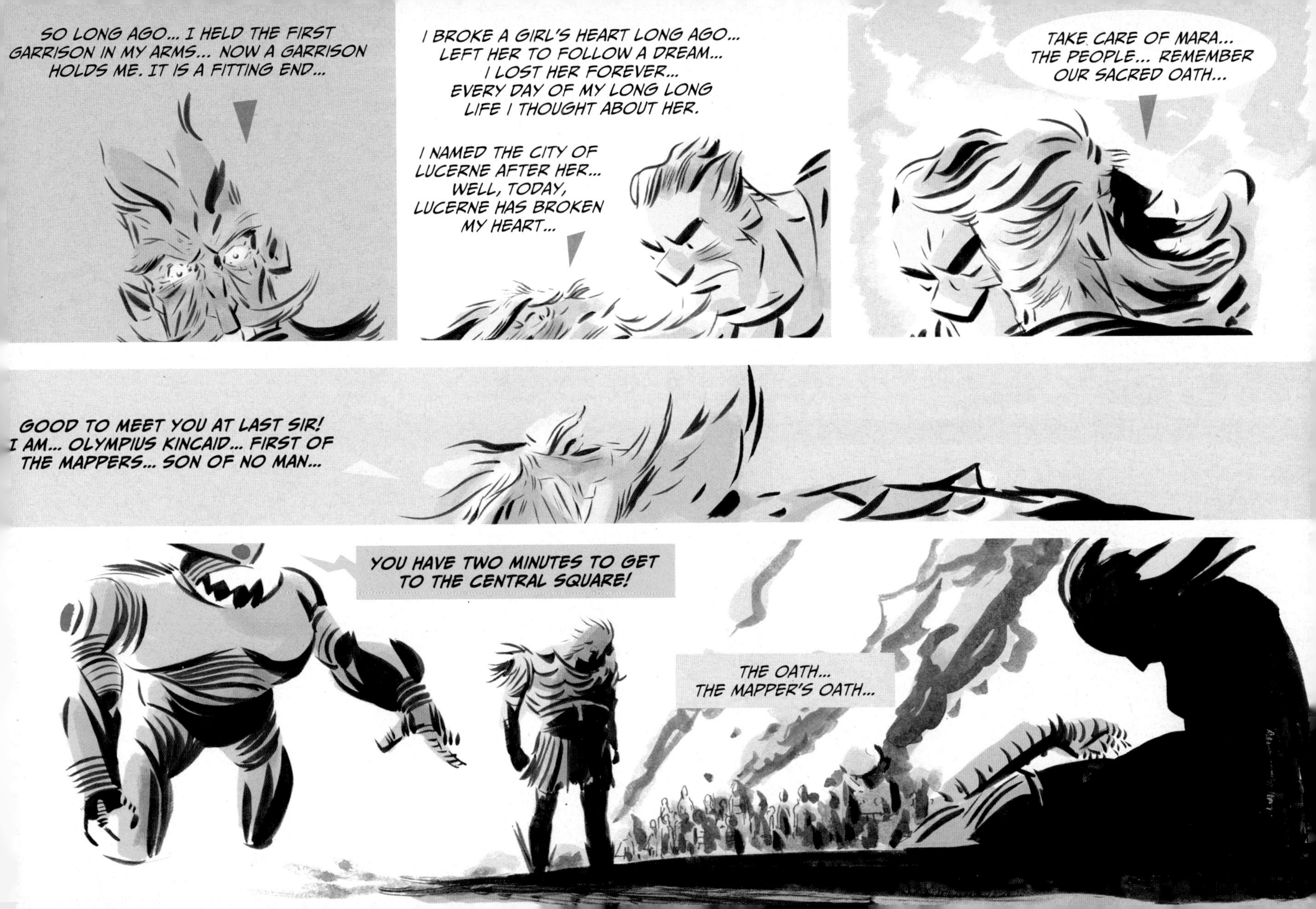
SO LONG AGO... I HELD THE FIRST GARRISON IN MY ARMS... NOW A GARRISON HOLDS ME. IT IS A FITTING END...
I BROKE A GIRL'S HEART LONG AGO... LEFT HER TO FOLLOW A DREAM... I LOST HER FOREVER... EVERY DAY OF MY LONG LONG LIFE I THOUGHT ABOUT HER.
I NAMED THE CITY OF LUCERNE AFTER HER... WELL, TODAY, LUCERNE HAS BROKEN MY HEART...
TAKE CARE OF MARA... THE PEOPLE... REMEMBER OUR SACRED OATH...
GOOD TO MEET YOU AT LAST SIR! I AM... OLYMPIUS KINCAID... FIRST OF THE MAPPERS... SON OF NO MAN...
YOU HAVE TWO MINUTES TO GET TO THE CENTRAL SQUARE!
THE OATH... THE MAPPER'S OATH...

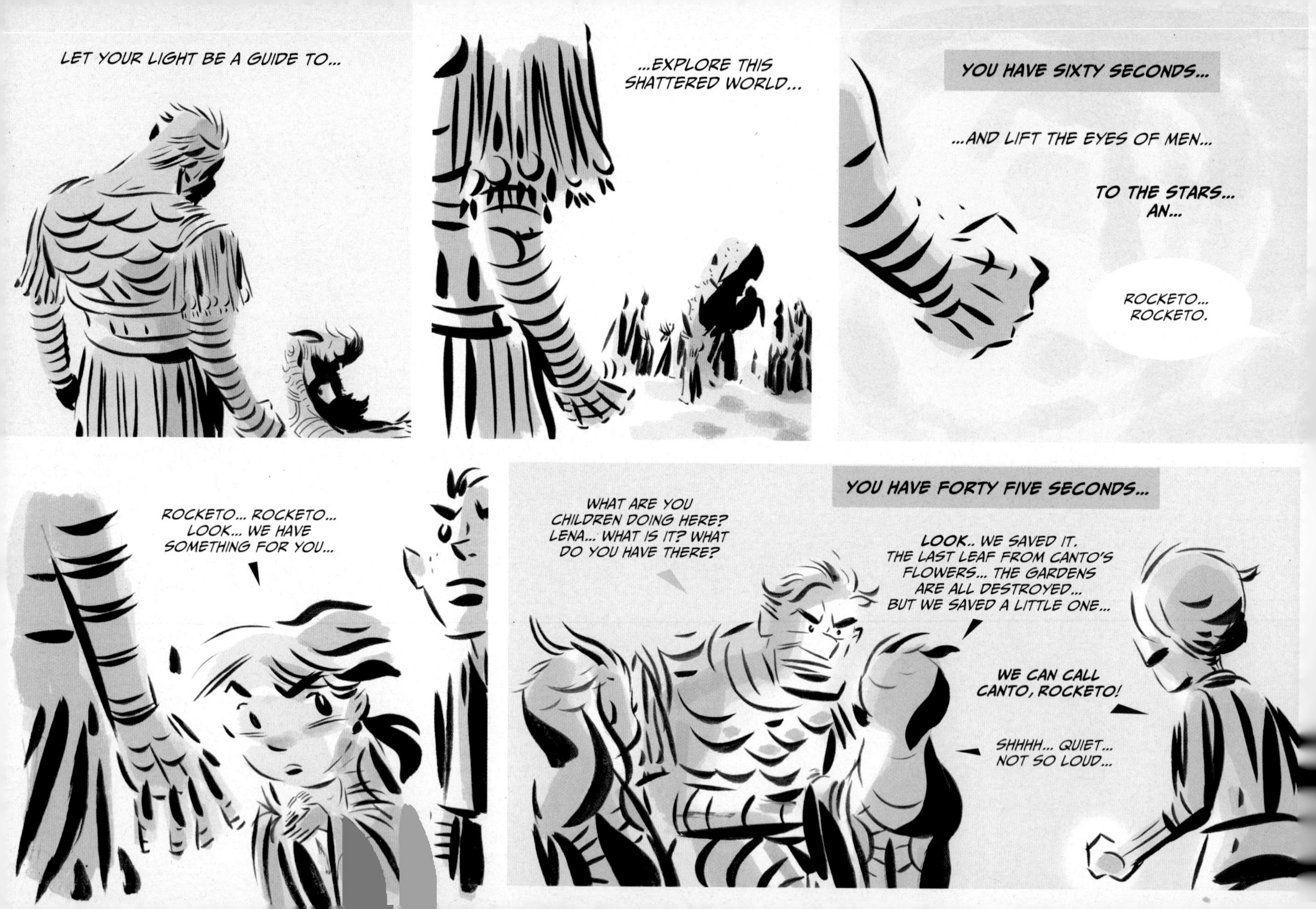
LET YOUR LIGHT BE A GUIDE TO...
...EXPLORE THIS SHATTERED WORLD...
YOU HAVE SIXTY SECONDS...
...AND LIFT THE EYES OF MEN...
TO THE STARS... AN...
ROCKETO... ROCKETO.
ROCKETO... ROCKETO... LOOK... WE HAVE SOMETHING FOR YOU...
YOU HAVE FORTY FIVE SECONDS...
WHAT ARE YOU CHILDREN DOING HERE? LENA... WHAT IS IT? WHAT DO YOU HAVE THERE?
LOOK.. WE SAVED IT. THE LAST LEAF FROM CANTO'S FLOWERS... THE GARDENS ARE ALL DESTROYED... BUT WE SAVED A LITTLE ONE...
WE CAN CALL CANTO, ROCKETO!
SHHHH... QUIET... NOT SO LOUD...

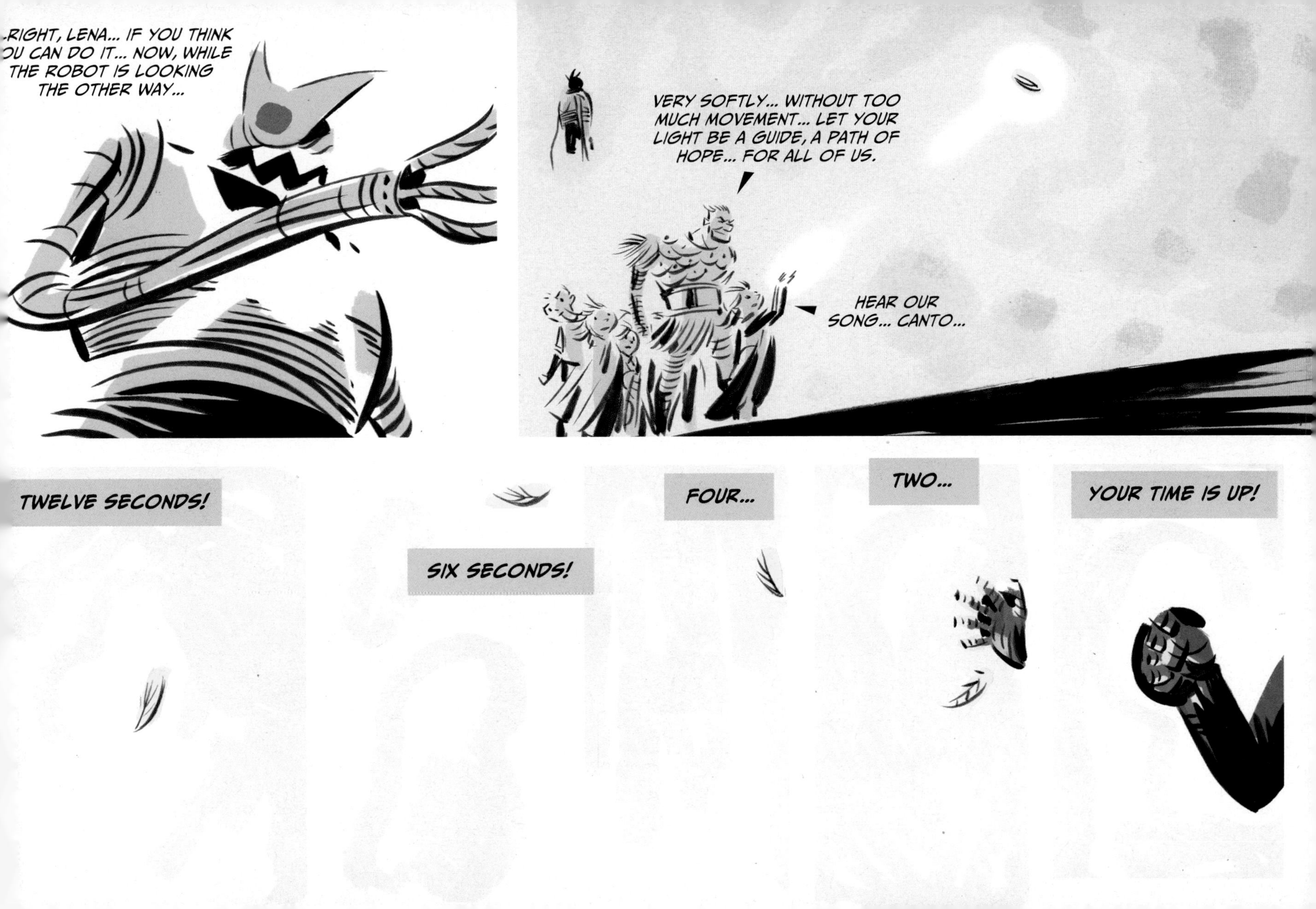
-RIGHT, LENA... IF YOU THINK
OU CAN DO IT... NOW, WHILE THE ROBOT IS LOOKING THE OTHER WAY...
VERY SOFTLY... WITHOUT TOO MUCH MOVEMENT... LET YOUR LIGHT BE A GUIDE, A PATH OF HOPE... FOR ALL OF US.
HEAR OUR SONG... CANTO...
TWELVE SECONDS!
SIX SECONDS!
FOUR...
TWO...
YOUR TIME IS UP!

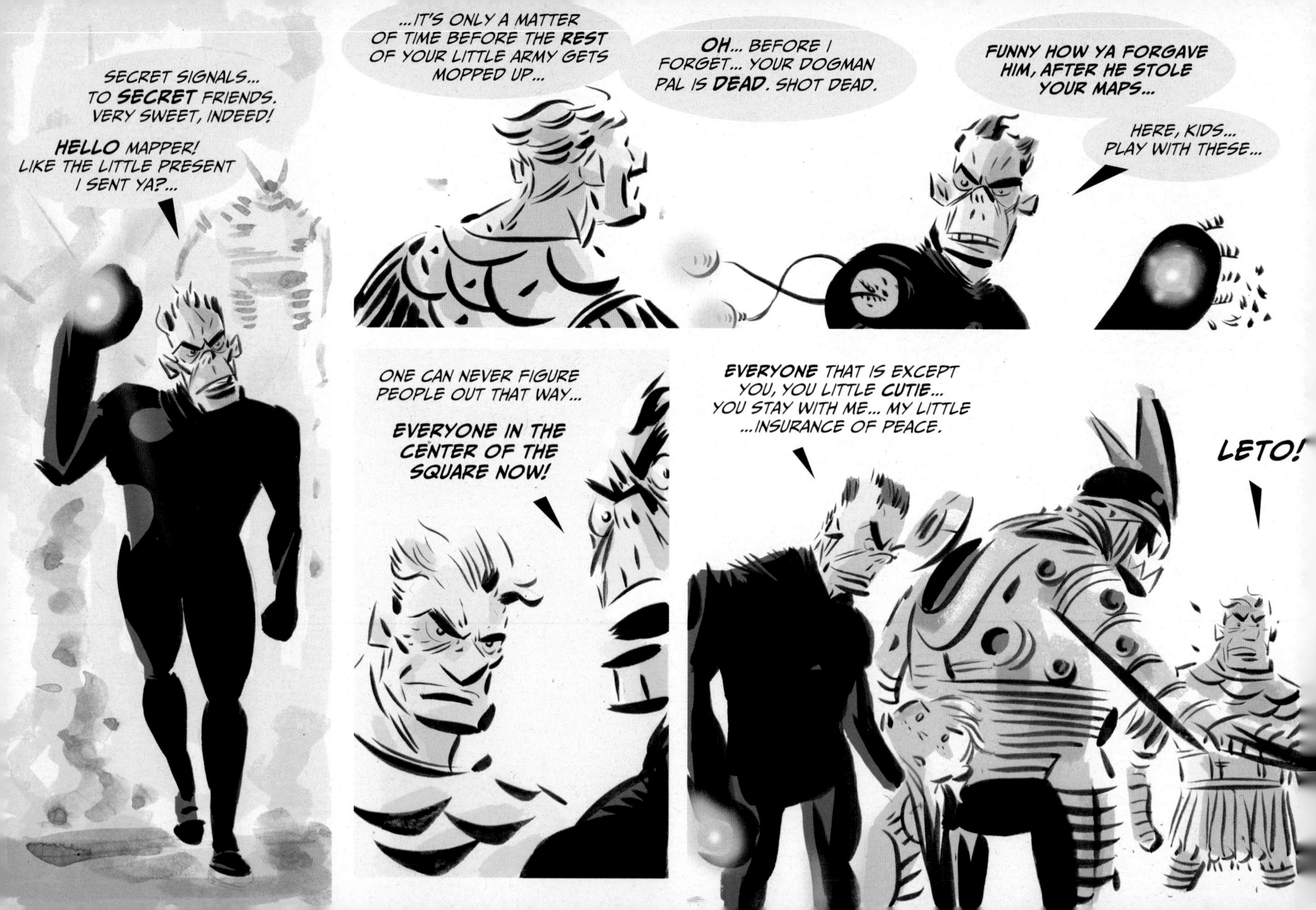
SECRET SIGNALS... TO SECRET FRIENDS. VERY SWEET, INDEED!
HELLO MAPPER! LIKE THE LITTLE PRESENT I SENT YA?...
...IT'S ONLY A MATTER OF TIME BEFORE THE REST OF YOUR LITTLE ARMY GETS MOPPED UP...
OH... BEFORE I FORGET... YOUR DOGMAN PAL IS DEAD. SHOT DEAD.
FUNNY HOW YA FORGAVE HIM, AFTER HE STOLE YOUR MAPS...
HERE, KIDS... PLAY WITH THESE...
ONE CAN NEVER FIGURE PEOPLE OUT THAT WAY...
EVERYONE IN THE CENTER OF THE SQUARE NOW!
EVERYONE THAT IS EXCEPT YOU, YOU LITTLE CUTIE... YOU STAY WITH ME... MY LITTLE ...INSURANCE OF PEACE.
LETO!

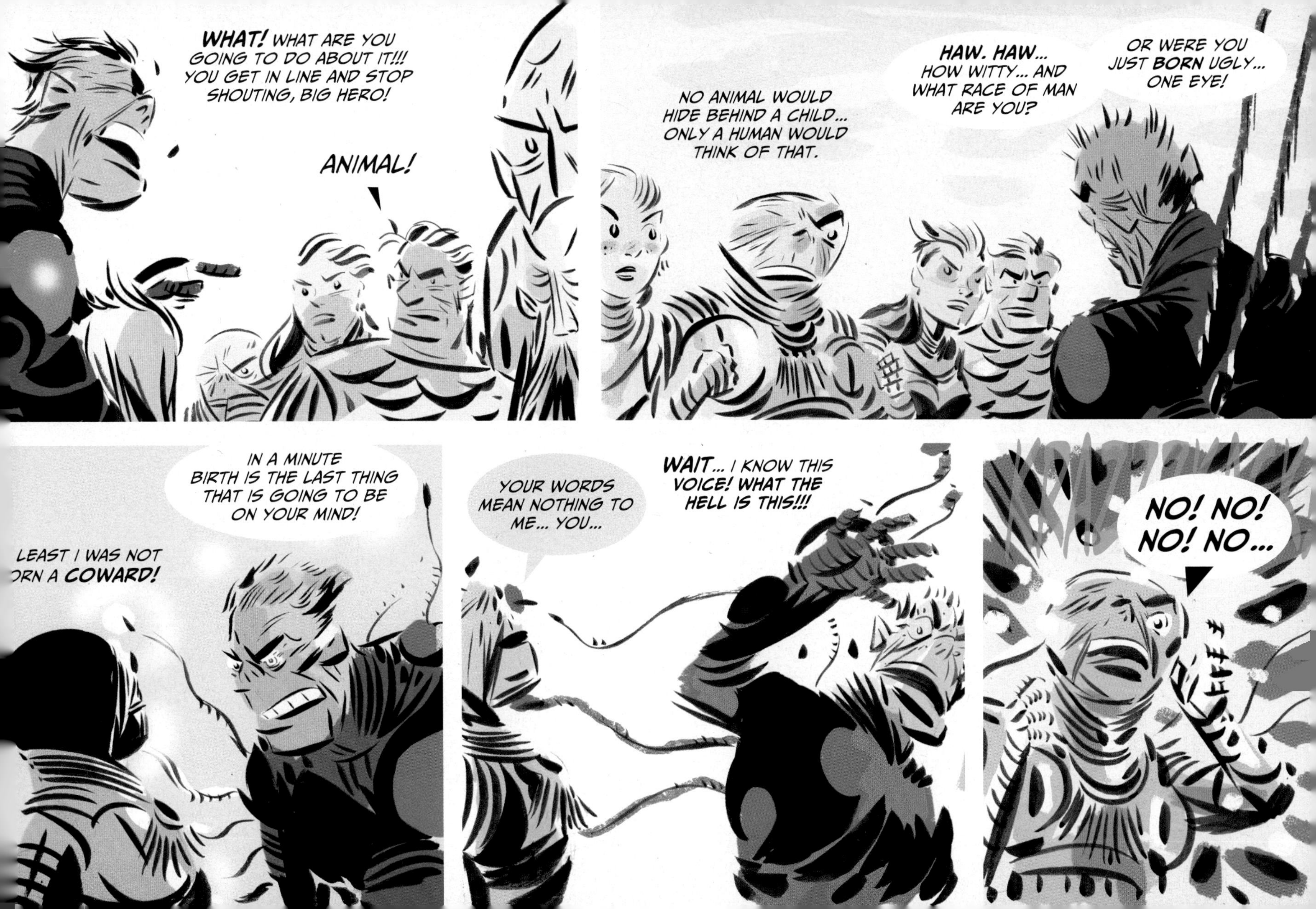
WHAT! WHAT ARE YOU GOING TO DO ABOUT IT!!! YOU GET IN LINE AND STOP SHOUTING, BIG HERO!
ANIMAL!
NO ANIMAL WOULD HIDE BEHIND A CHILD... ONLY A HUMAN WOULD THINK OF THAT.
HAW. HAW... HOW WITTY... AND WHAT RACE OF MAN ARE YOU?
OR WERE YOU JUST BORN UGLY... ONE EYE!
LEAST I WAS NOT
ORN A COWARD!
IN A MINUTE BIRTH IS THE LAST THING THAT IS GOING TO BE ON YOUR MIND!
YOUR WORDS MEAN NOTHING TO ME... YOU...
WAIT... I KNOW THIS VOICE! WHAT THE HELL IS THIS!!!
NO! NO! NO! NO...

HAW! HAW!
WHAT A TRICK THIS IS!!!
HAW! HAW!

YOU KNOW WHO THIS MAN IS?

KNOW HIM! HELL, I'M **WEARING** HIS SKIN! **HAW!**

I CAN'T BELIEVE YOU SURVIVED... FEELS LIKE AGES AGO. HOW CAN YOU EVEN BEAR TO **LOOK** AT YOURSELF? PEOPLE, YOU BEEN TAKEN IN... THIS HERE IS A YOUNG **SNAKE**...

IF IT WOULD NOT BE ME STANDING HERE IT WOULD BE HIM... AND HE MIGHT NOT BE AS KIND...

I GUESS INTRODUCTIO ARE IN ORDER HERE..

THE MIGHTY **PRINCE AVITUS**, FOLKS. FOURTH IN THE LINE TO THRONE OF LUCERNE. LEADER OF **THE GOLDEN MISSION** AND MY ONE-TIME ALLY.

WHICH SIDE ARE YOU ON NOW, PRINCE? SPEAK UP! YOU ALWAYS HAD THE BIGGEST MOUTH ON TWO CONTINENTS.

BUT NOTHING'S CHANGED... YOU'RE STILL **GROVELING**...

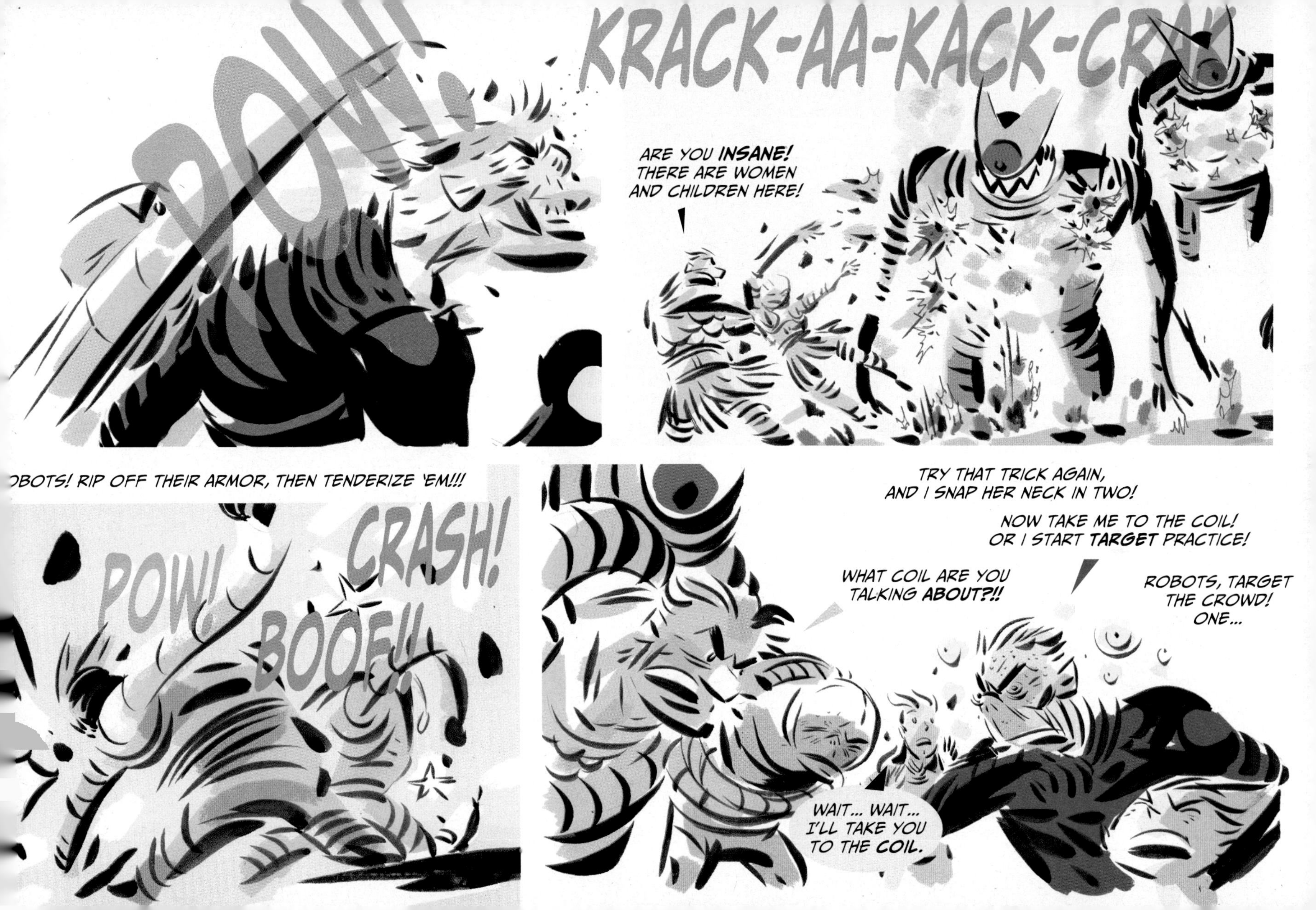
POW!
KRACK-AA-KACK-CRA
ARE YOU **INSANE!** THERE ARE WOMEN AND CHILDREN HERE!
OBOTS! RIP OFF THEIR ARMOR, THEN TENDERIZE 'EM!!!
POW!
CRASH!
BOOF!!
TRY THAT TRICK AGAIN, AND I SNAP HER NECK IN TWO!
NOW TAKE ME TO THE COIL! OR I START **TARGET** PRACTICE!
WHAT COIL ARE YOU TALKING **ABOUT?!!**
ROBOTS, TARGET THE CROWD! ONE...
WAIT... WAIT... I'LL TAKE YOU TO THE **COIL.**

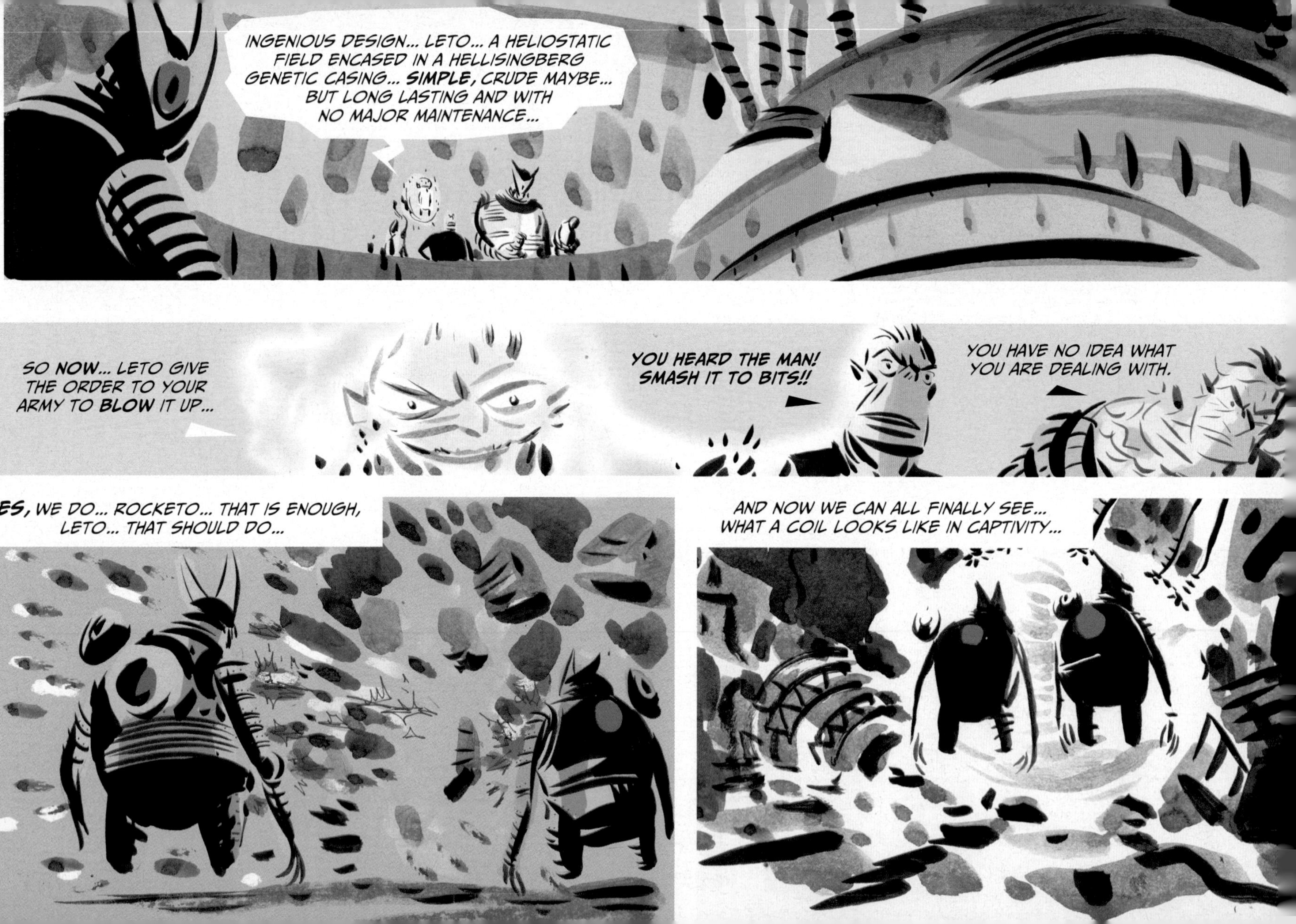
INGENIOUS DESIGN... LETO... A HELIOSTATIC FIELD ENCASED IN A HELLISINGBERG GENETIC CASING... SIMPLE, CRUDE MAYBE... BUT LONG LASTING AND WITH NO MAJOR MAINTENANCE...
SO NOW... LETO GIVE THE ORDER TO YOUR ARMY TO BLOW IT UP...
YOU HEARD THE MAN! SMASH IT TO BITS!!
YOU HAVE NO IDEA WHAT YOU ARE DEALING WITH.
YES, WE DO... ROCKETO... THAT IS ENOUGH, LETO... THAT SHOULD DO...
AND NOW WE CAN ALL FINALLY SEE... WHAT A COIL LOOKS LIKE IN CAPTIVITY...

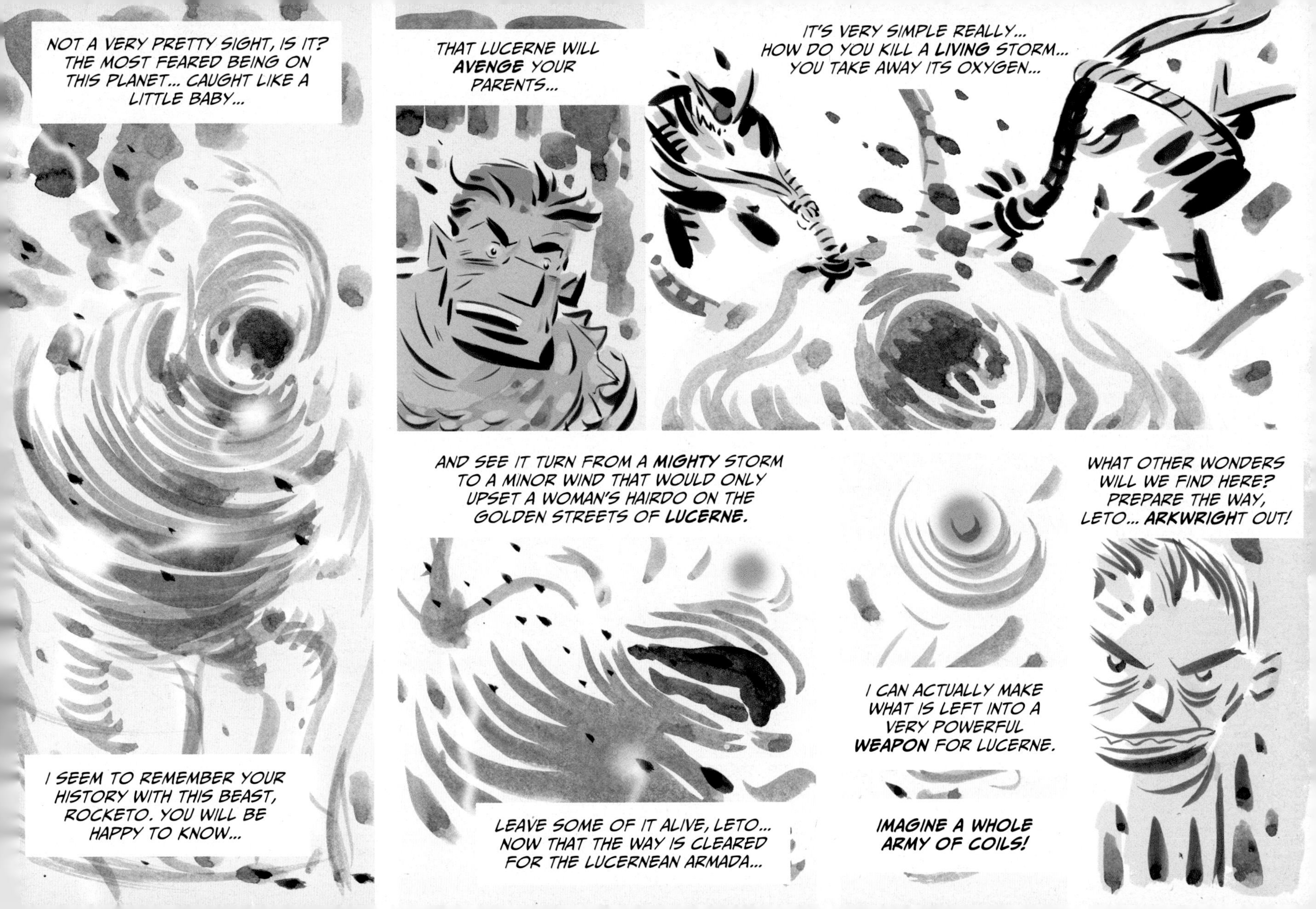
NOT A VERY PRETTY SIGHT, IS IT? THE MOST FEARED BEING ON THIS PLANET... CAUGHT LIKE A LITTLE BABY...
I SEEM TO REMEMBER YOUR HISTORY WITH THIS BEAST, ROCKETO. YOU WILL BE HAPPY TO KNOW...
THAT LUCERNE WILL AVENGE YOUR PARENTS...
IT'S VERY SIMPLE REALLY... HOW DO YOU KILL A LIVING STORM... YOU TAKE AWAY ITS OXYGEN...
AND SEE IT TURN FROM A MIGHTY STORM TO A MINOR WIND THAT WOULD ONLY UPSET A WOMAN'S HAIRDO ON THE GOLDEN STREETS OF LUCERNE.
LEAVE SOME OF IT ALIVE, LETO... NOW THAT THE WAY IS CLEARED FOR THE LUCERNEAN ARMADA...
I CAN ACTUALLY MAKE WHAT IS LEFT INTO A VERY POWERFUL WEAPON FOR LUCERNE.
IMAGINE A WHOLE ARMY OF COILS!
WHAT OTHER WONDERS WILL WE FIND HERE? PREPARE THE WAY, LETO... ARKWRIGHT OUT!

GRAB HIM TIGHT! WE WANT HIM IN ONE PIECE WHEN THE NAVY FINDS HIM!

LETO! DON'T BE AN IDIOT! ARKWRIGHT IS USING YOU.

WHAT MAKES YOU THINK I AIN'T USING HIM TOO?!!

BUT YOU DO NOT NEED TO WORRY ABOUT THAT...

NO... YOU AND THE PRINCE HAVE MORE URGENT THINGS TO WORRY ABOUT...

THOSE MARKER BUOYS SE OUT A NICE LITTLE SIGNAL THAT WILL GUIDE THE RES OF THE ARMADA HERE...

WELL. THAT ENDS THAT... NOW FOR YOUR BOYFRIEND AND THE PRINCE.

YOU'RE A MAPPER RIGHT! SO YOU BOTH GET TO GUIDE THE BIG BOYS IN...

HAW! HAW! HAW! I JUST HEARD FROM ARKWRIGHT YOU PULLED A SIMILAR STUNT LIKE THIS AT DARGOPEL...

IN FACT THOSE MARKER BUOYS WERE MADE POSSIBLE BY YOUR GENES!

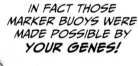

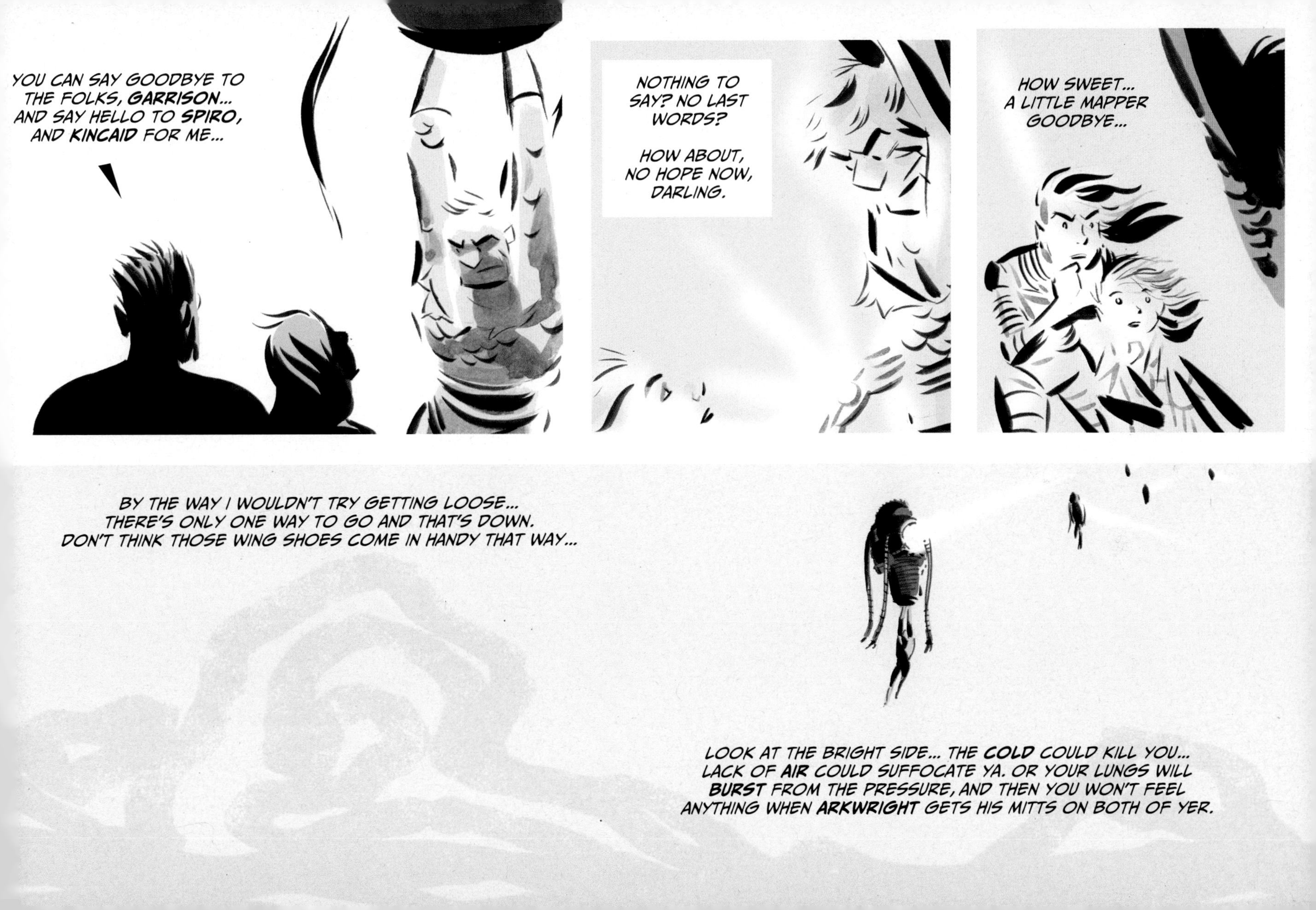
YOU CAN SAY GOODBYE TO THE FOLKS, GARRISON... AND SAY HELLO TO SPIRO, AND KINCAID FOR ME...
NOTHING TO SAY? NO LAST WORDS?
HOW ABOUT, NO HOPE NOW, DARLING.
HOW SWEET... A LITTLE MAPPER GOODBYE...
BY THE WAY I WOULDN'T TRY GETTING LOOSE... THERE'S ONLY ONE WAY TO GO AND THAT'S DOWN. DON'T THINK THOSE WING SHOES COME IN HANDY THAT WAY...
LOOK AT THE BRIGHT SIDE... THE COLD COULD KILL YOU... LACK OF AIR COULD SUFFOCATE YA. OR YOUR LUNGS WILL BURST FROM THE PRESSURE, AND THEN YOU WON'T FEEL ANYTHING WHEN ARKWRIGHT GETS HIS MITTS ON BOTH OF YER.

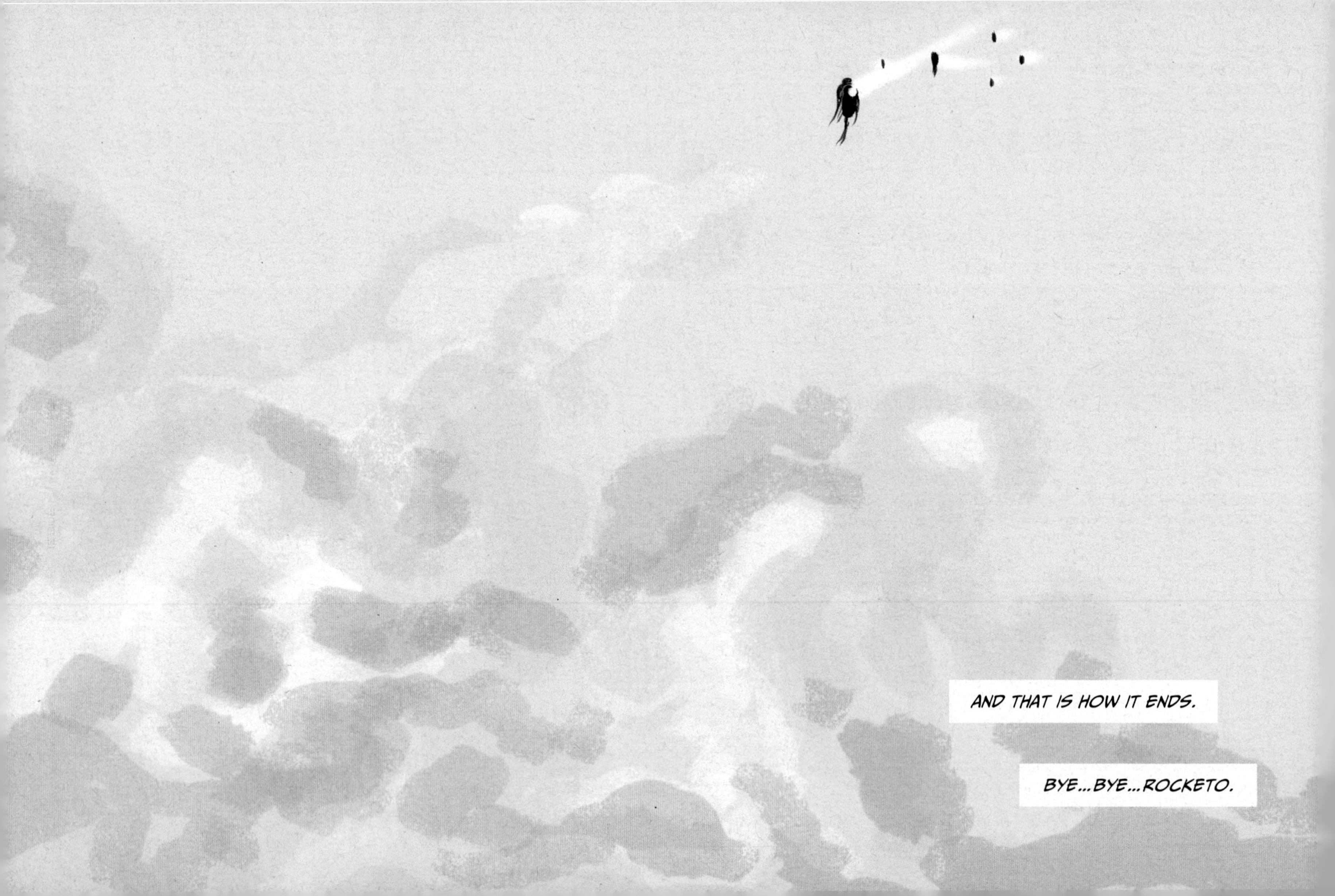
AND THAT IS HOW IT ENDS.
BYE...BYE...ROCKETO.

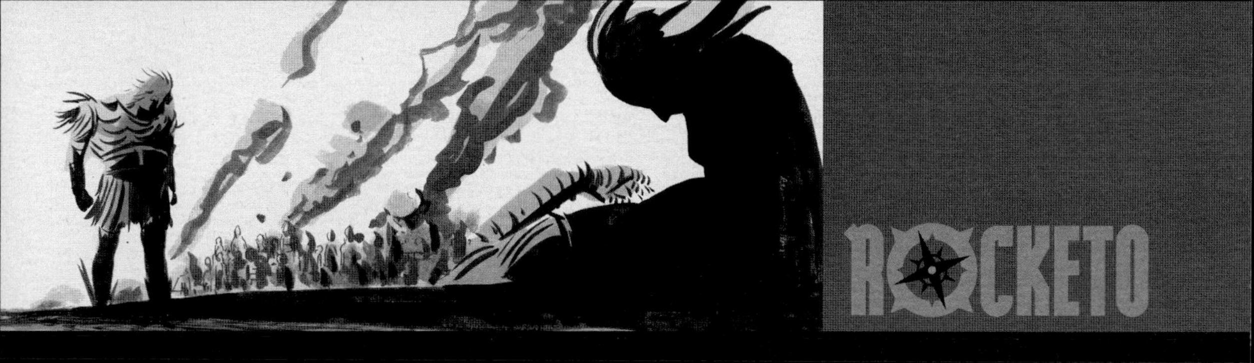

ROCKETO

11

ILLUMINATIONS

ROCKETO
TM
JOURNEY TO THE HIDDEN SEA
FRANK ESPINOSA

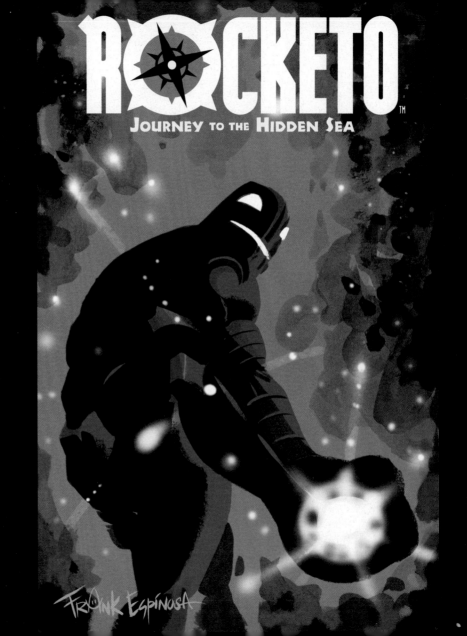

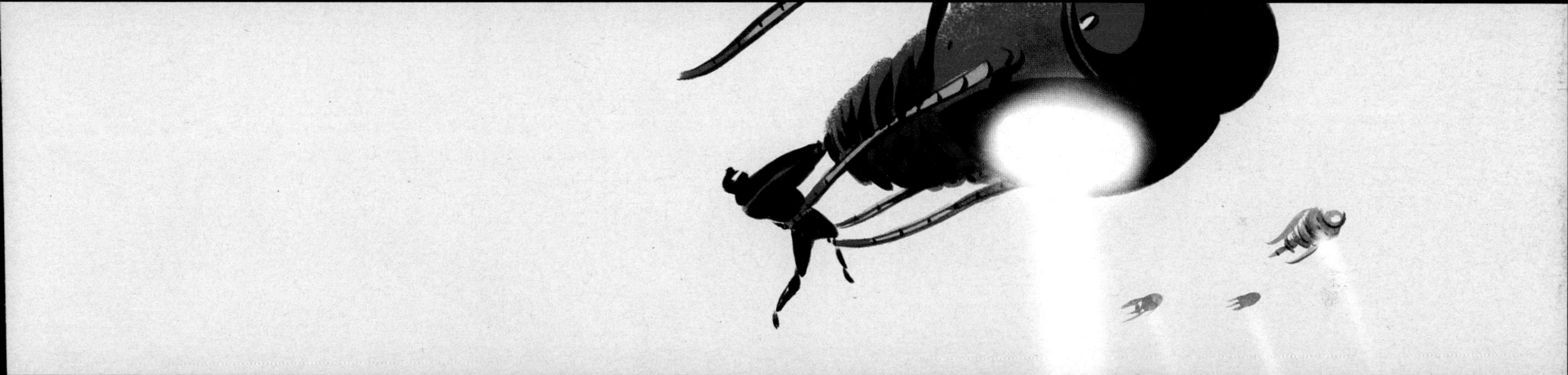

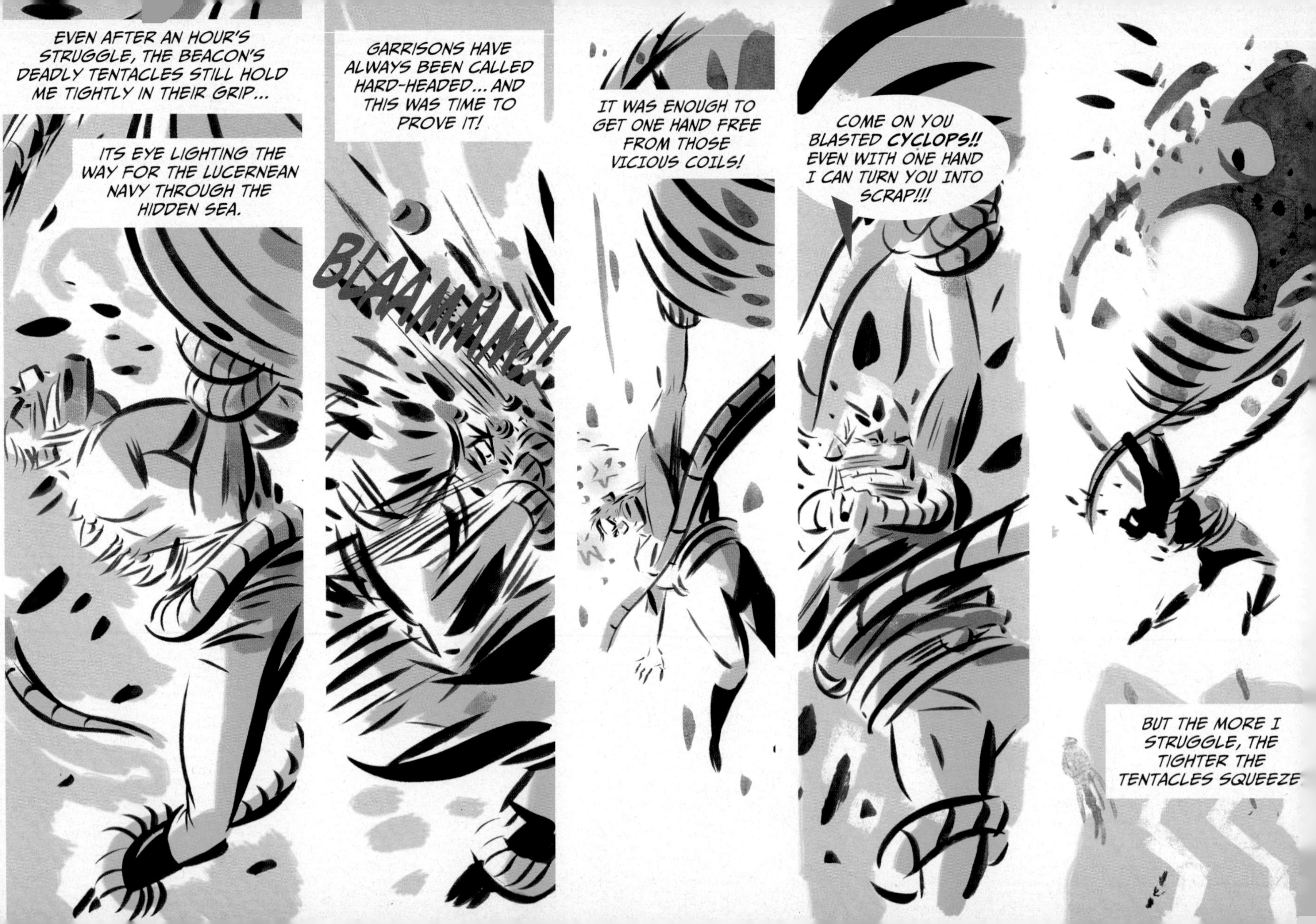
EVEN AFTER AN HOUR'S STRUGGLE, THE BEACON'S DEADLY TENTACLES STILL HOLD ME TIGHTLY IN THEIR GRIP...
ITS EYE LIGHTING THE WAY FOR THE LUCERNEAN NAVY THROUGH THE HIDDEN SEA.
GARRISONS HAVE ALWAYS BEEN CALLED HARD-HEADED... AND THIS WAS TIME TO PROVE IT!
BLAAMMMM!!
IT WAS ENOUGH TO GET ONE HAND FREE FROM THOSE VICIOUS COILS!
COME ON YOU BLASTED **CYCLOPS!!** EVEN WITH ONE HAND I CAN TURN YOU INTO SCRAP!!!
BUT THE MORE I STRUGGLE, THE TIGHTER THE TENTACLES SQUEEZE

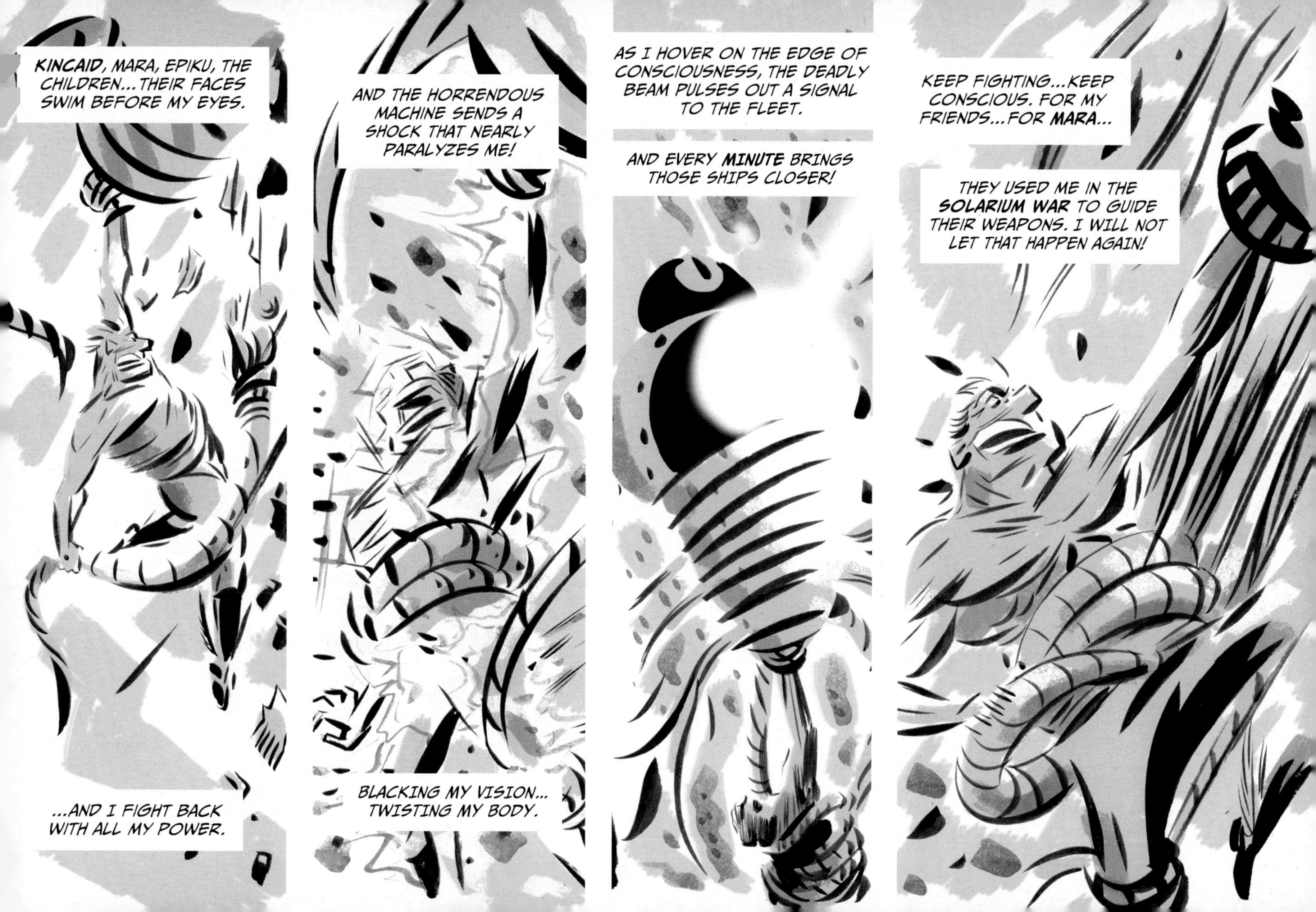
KINCAID, MARA, EPIKU, THE CHILDREN...THEIR FACES SWIM BEFORE MY EYES.
...AND I FIGHT BACK WITH ALL MY POWER.
AND THE HORRENDOUS MACHINE SENDS A SHOCK THAT NEARLY PARALYZES ME!
BLACKING MY VISION... TWISTING MY BODY.
AS I HOVER ON THE EDGE OF CONSCIOUSNESS, THE DEADLY BEAM PULSES OUT A SIGNAL TO THE FLEET.
AND EVERY MINUTE BRINGS THOSE SHIPS CLOSER!
KEEP FIGHTING...KEEP CONSCIOUS. FOR MY FRIENDS...FOR MARA...
THEY USED ME IN THE SOLARIUM WAR TO GUIDE THEIR WEAPONS. I WILL NOT LET THAT HAPPEN AGAIN!

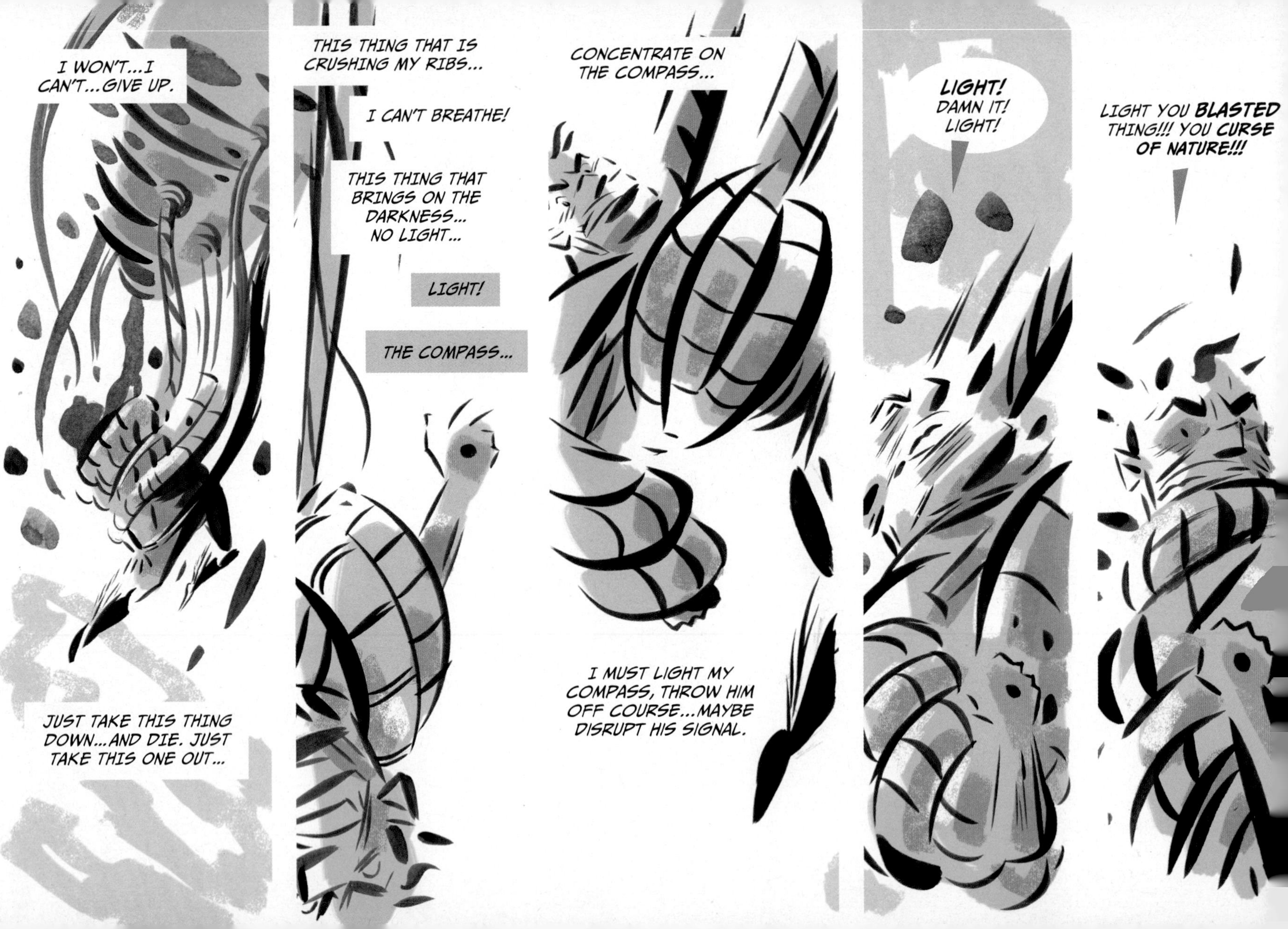
I WON'T...I CAN'T...GIVE UP.
JUST TAKE THIS THING DOWN...AND DIE. JUST TAKE THIS ONE OUT...
THIS THING THAT IS CRUSHING MY RIBS...
I CAN'T BREATHE!
THIS THING THAT BRINGS ON THE DARKNESS... NO LIGHT...
LIGHT!
THE COMPASS...
CONCENTRATE ON THE COMPASS...
I MUST LIGHT MY COMPASS, THROW HIM OFF COURSE...MAYBE DISRUPT HIS SIGNAL.
LIGHT! DAMN IT! LIGHT!
LIGHT YOU BLASTED THING!!! YOU CURSE OF NATURE!!!

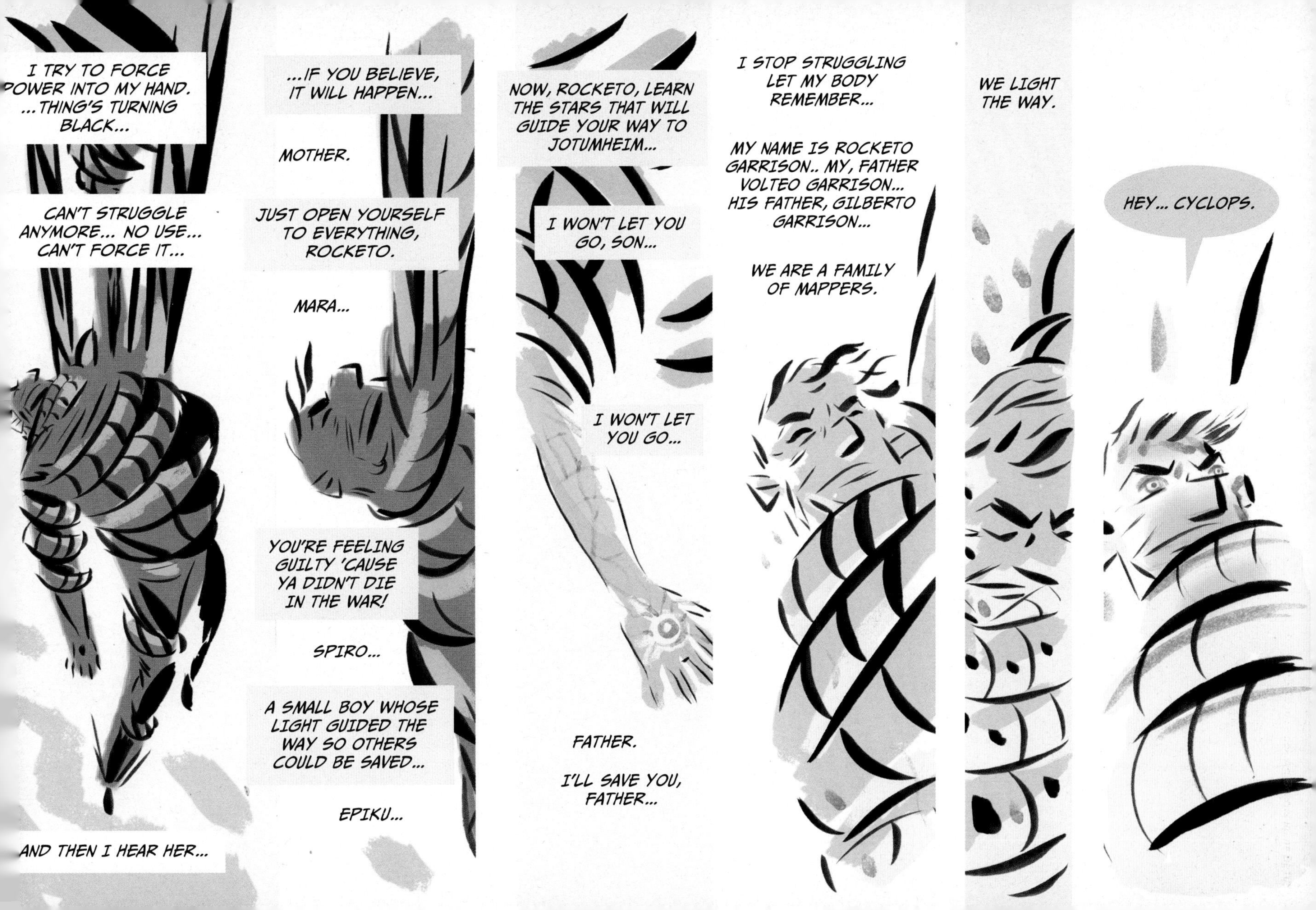
I TRY TO FORCE POWER INTO MY HAND. ...THING'S TURNING BLACK...
CAN'T STRUGGLE ANYMORE... NO USE... CAN'T FORCE IT...
AND THEN I HEAR HER...
...IF YOU BELIEVE, IT WILL HAPPEN...
MOTHER.
JUST OPEN YOURSELF TO EVERYTHING, ROCKETO.
MARA...
YOU'RE FEELING GUILTY 'CAUSE YA DIDN'T DIE IN THE WAR!
SPIRO...
A SMALL BOY WHOSE LIGHT GUIDED THE WAY SO OTHERS COULD BE SAVED...
EPIKU...
NOW, ROCKETO, LEARN THE STARS THAT WILL GUIDE YOUR WAY TO JOTUMHEIM...
I WON'T LET YOU GO, SON...
I WON'T LET YOU GO...
FATHER.
I'LL SAVE YOU, FATHER...
I STOP STRUGGLING LET MY BODY REMEMBER...
MY NAME IS ROCKETO GARRISON.. MY, FATHER VOLTEO GARRISON... HIS FATHER, GILBERTO GARRISON...
WE ARE A FAMILY OF MAPPERS.
WE LIGHT THE WAY.
HEY... CYCLOPS.

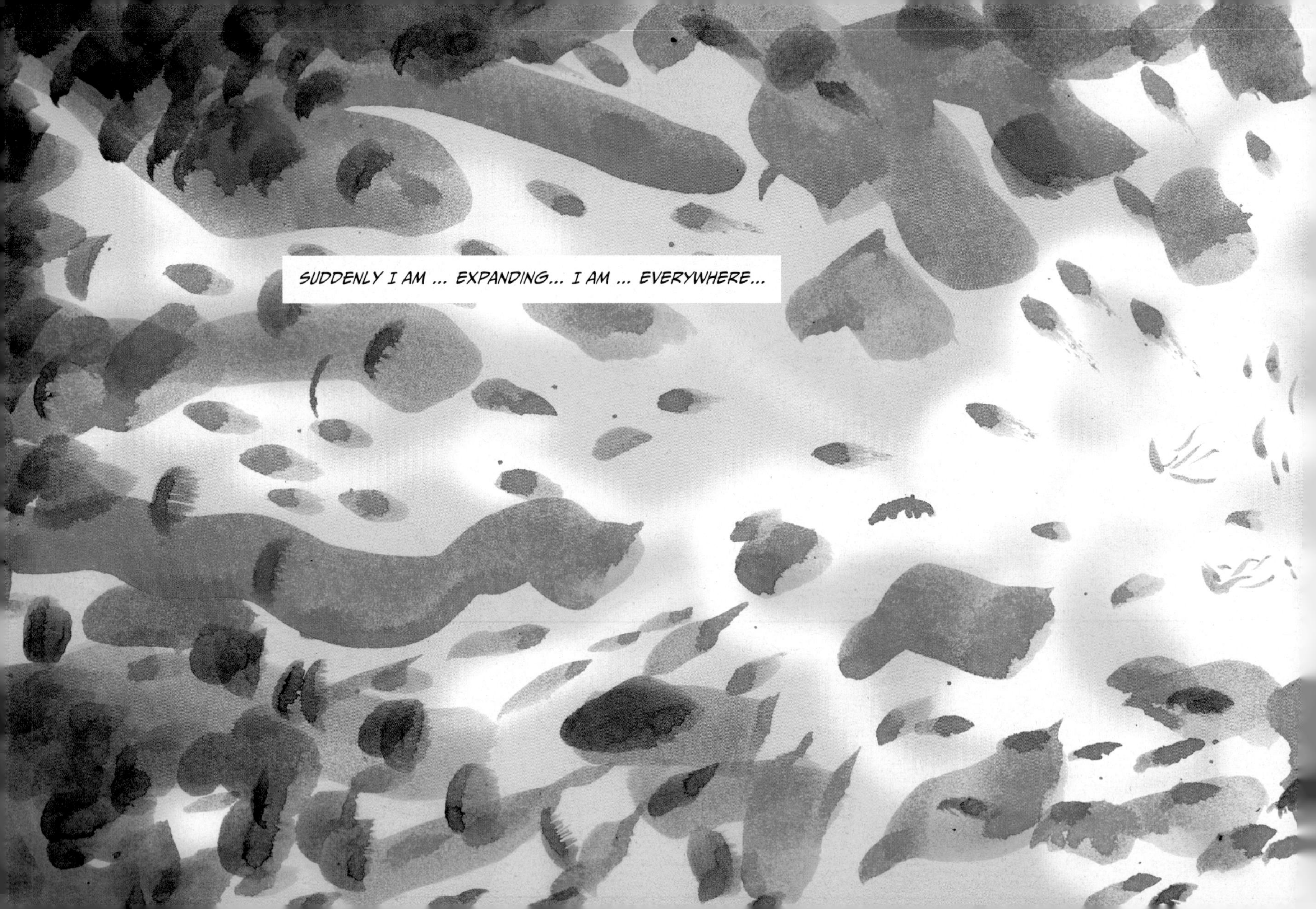
SUDDENLY I AM ... EXPANDING... I AM ... EVERYWHERE...

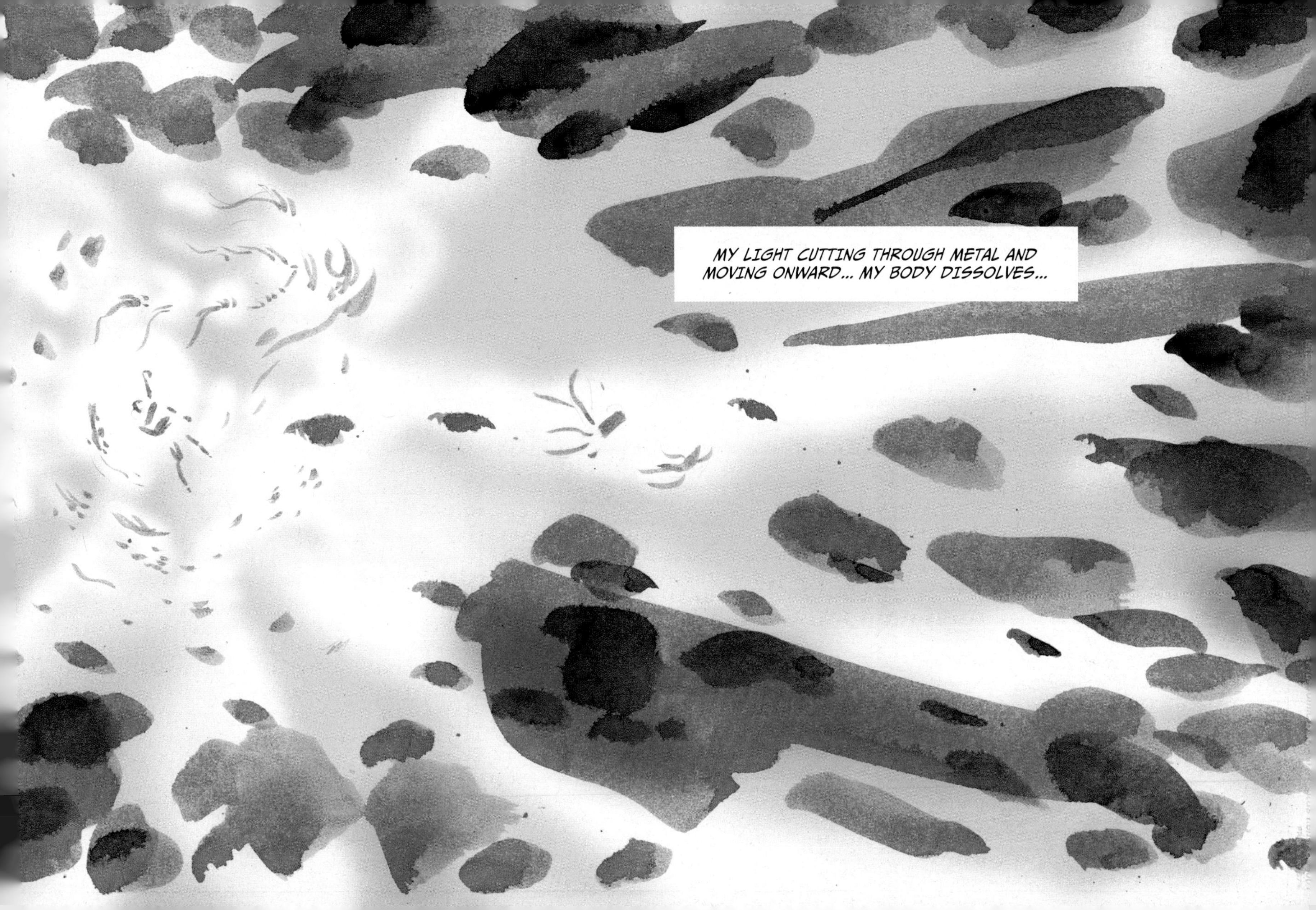
MY LIGHT CUTTING THROUGH METAL AND
MOVING ONWARD... MY BODY DISSOLVES...

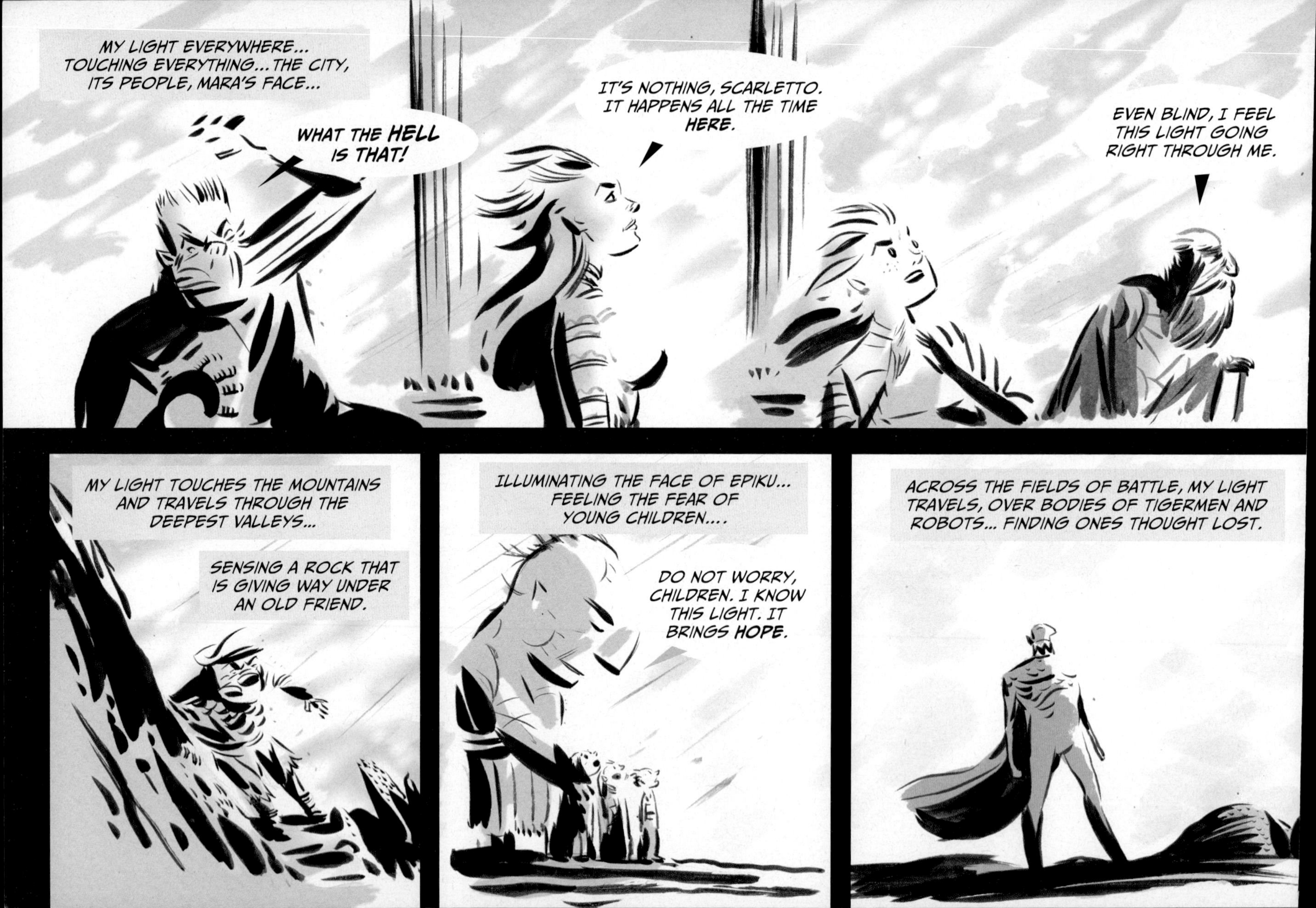
MY LIGHT EVERYWHERE... TOUCHING EVERYTHING... THE CITY, ITS PEOPLE, MARA'S FACE...
WHAT THE HELL IS THAT!
IT'S NOTHING, SCARLETTO. IT HAPPENS ALL THE TIME HERE.
EVEN BLIND, I FEEL THIS LIGHT GOING RIGHT THROUGH ME.
MY LIGHT TOUCHES THE MOUNTAINS AND TRAVELS THROUGH THE DEEPEST VALLEYS...
SENSING A ROCK THAT IS GIVING WAY UNDER AN OLD FRIEND.
ILLUMINATING THE FACE OF EPIKU... FEELING THE FEAR OF YOUNG CHILDREN....
DO NOT WORRY, CHILDREN. I KNOW THIS LIGHT. IT BRINGS HOPE.
ACROSS THE FIELDS OF BATTLE, MY LIGHT TRAVELS, OVER BODIES OF TIGERMEN AND ROBOTS... FINDING ONES THOUGHT LOST.

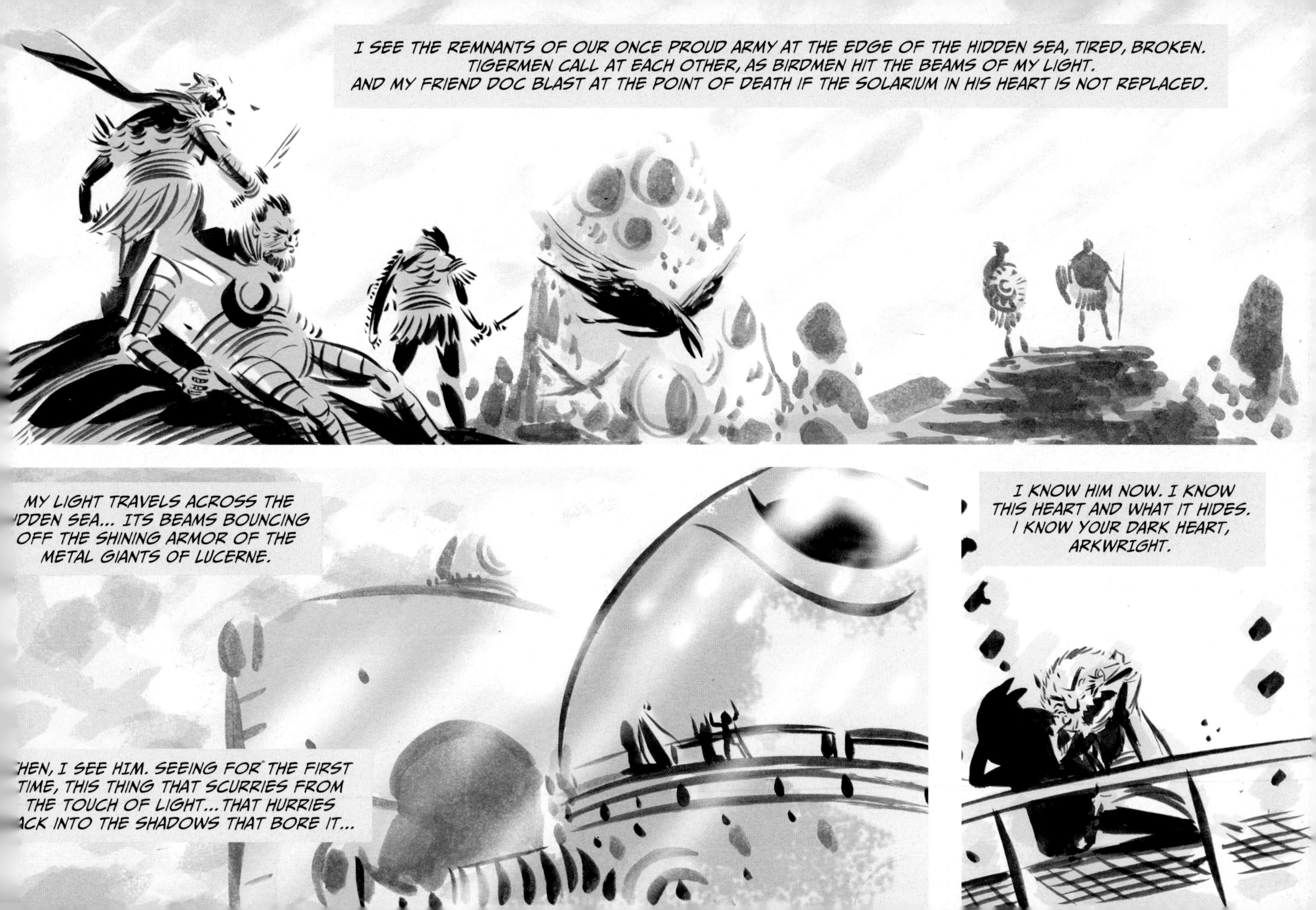
I SEE THE REMNANTS OF OUR ONCE PROUD ARMY AT THE EDGE OF THE HIDDEN SEA, TIRED, BROKEN. TIGERMEN CALL AT EACH OTHER, AS BIRDMEN HIT THE BEAMS OF MY LIGHT. AND MY FRIEND DOC BLAST AT THE POINT OF DEATH IF THE SOLARIUM IN HIS HEART IS NOT REPLACED.
MY LIGHT TRAVELS ACROSS THE IDDEN SEA... ITS BEAMS BOUNCING OFF THE SHINING ARMOR OF THE METAL GIANTS OF LUCERNE.
HEN, I SEE HIM. SEEING FOR THE FIRST TIME, THIS THING THAT SCURRIES FROM THE TOUCH OF LIGHT...THAT HURRIES ACK INTO THE SHADOWS THAT BORE IT...
I KNOW HIM NOW. I KNOW THIS HEART AND WHAT IT HIDES. I KNOW YOUR DARK HEART, ARKWRIGHT.

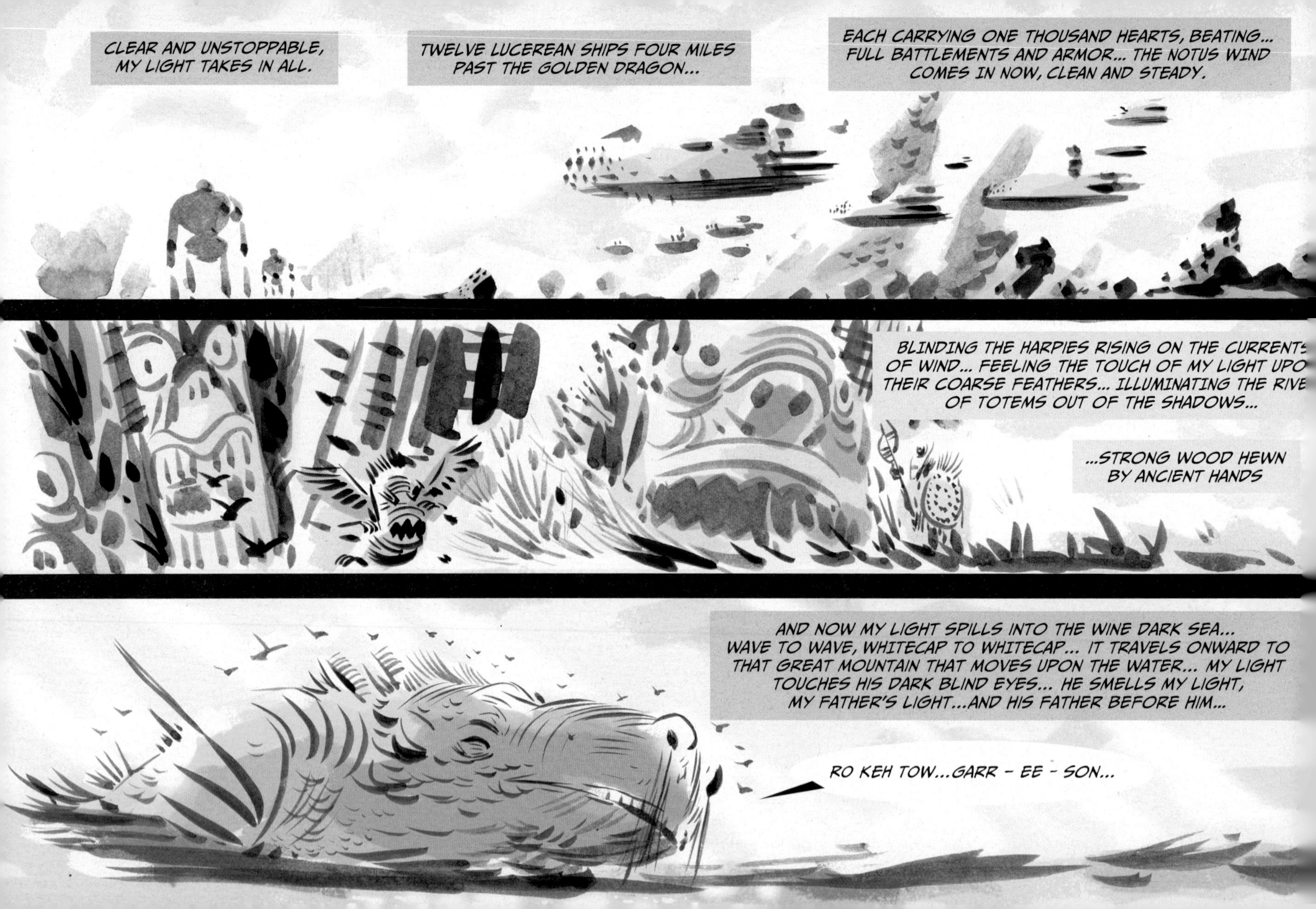
CLEAR AND UNSTOPPABLE, MY LIGHT TAKES IN ALL.
TWELVE LUCEREAN SHIPS FOUR MILES PAST THE GOLDEN DRAGON...
EACH CARRYING ONE THOUSAND HEARTS, BEATING... FULL BATTLEMENTS AND ARMOR... THE NOTUS WIND COMES IN NOW, CLEAN AND STEADY.
BLINDING THE HARPIES RISING ON THE CURRENTS OF WIND... FEELING THE TOUCH OF MY LIGHT UPO THEIR COARSE FEATHERS... ILLUMINATING THE RIVE OF TOTEMS OUT OF THE SHADOWS...
...STRONG WOOD HEWN BY ANCIENT HANDS
AND NOW MY LIGHT SPILLS INTO THE WINE DARK SEA... WAVE TO WAVE, WHITECAP TO WHITECAP... IT TRAVELS ONWARD TO THAT GREAT MOUNTAIN THAT MOVES UPON THE WATER... MY LIGHT TOUCHES HIS DARK BLIND EYES... HE SMELLS MY LIGHT, MY FATHER'S LIGHT...AND HIS FATHER BEFORE HIM...
RO KEH TOW...GARR - EE - SON...

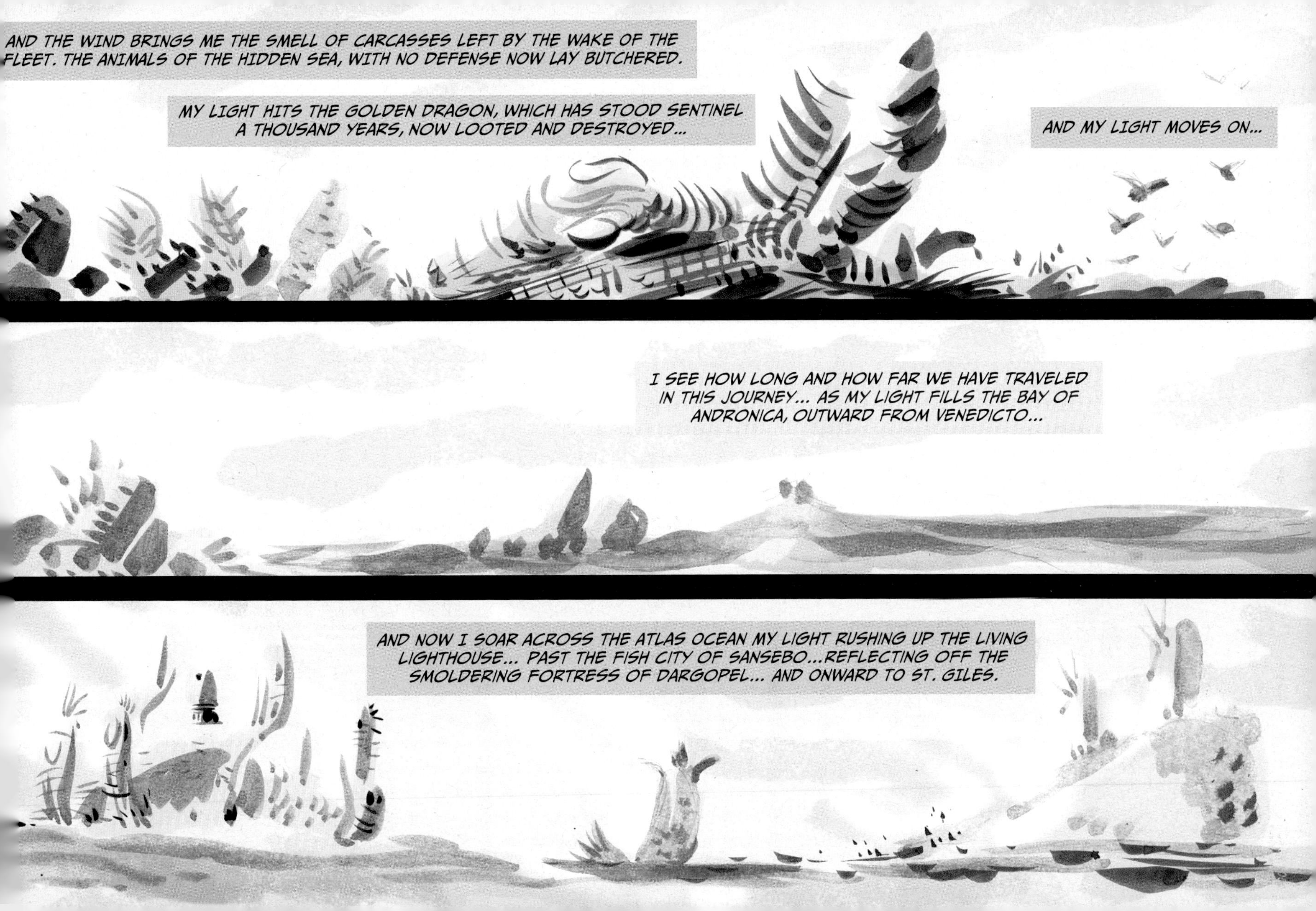

AND THE WIND BRINGS ME THE SMELL OF CARCASSES LEFT BY THE WAKE OF THE FLEET. THE ANIMALS OF THE HIDDEN SEA, WITH NO DEFENSE NOW LAY BUTCHERED.
MY LIGHT HITS THE GOLDEN DRAGON, WHICH HAS STOOD SENTINEL A THOUSAND YEARS, NOW LOOTED AND DESTROYED...
AND MY LIGHT MOVES ON...
I SEE HOW LONG AND HOW FAR WE HAVE TRAVELED IN THIS JOURNEY... AS MY LIGHT FILLS THE BAY OF ANDRONICA, OUTWARD FROM VENEDICTO...
AND NOW I SOAR ACROSS THE ATLAS OCEAN MY LIGHT RUSHING UP THE LIVING LIGHTHOUSE... PAST THE FISH CITY OF SANSEBO...REFLECTING OFF THE SMOLDERING FORTRESS OF DARGOPEL... AND ONWARD TO ST. GILES.

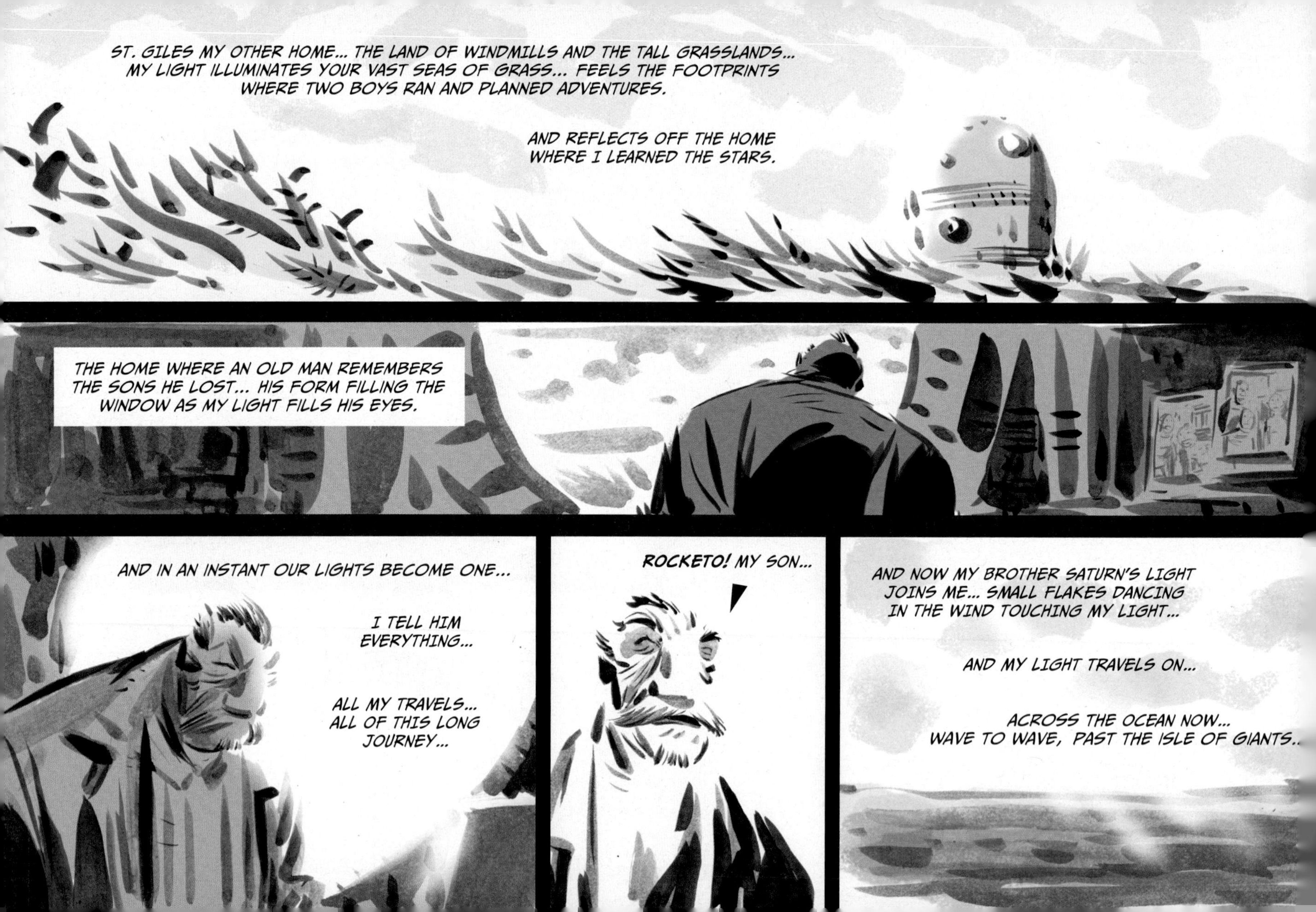
ST. GILES MY OTHER HOME... THE LAND OF WINDMILLS AND THE TALL GRASSLANDS... MY LIGHT ILLUMINATES YOUR VAST SEAS OF GRASS... FEELS THE FOOTPRINTS WHERE TWO BOYS RAN AND PLANNED ADVENTURES.
AND REFLECTS OFF THE HOME WHERE I LEARNED THE STARS.
THE HOME WHERE AN OLD MAN REMEMBERS THE SONS HE LOST... HIS FORM FILLING THE WINDOW AS MY LIGHT FILLS HIS EYES.
AND IN AN INSTANT OUR LIGHTS BECOME ONE...
I TELL HIM EVERYTHING...
ALL MY TRAVELS... ALL OF THIS LONG JOURNEY...
ROCKETO! MY SON...
AND NOW MY BROTHER SATURN'S LIGHT JOINS ME... SMALL FLAKES DANCING IN THE WIND TOUCHING MY LIGHT...
AND MY LIGHT TRAVELS ON...
ACROSS THE OCEAN NOW... WAVE TO WAVE, PAST THE ISLE OF GIANTS...

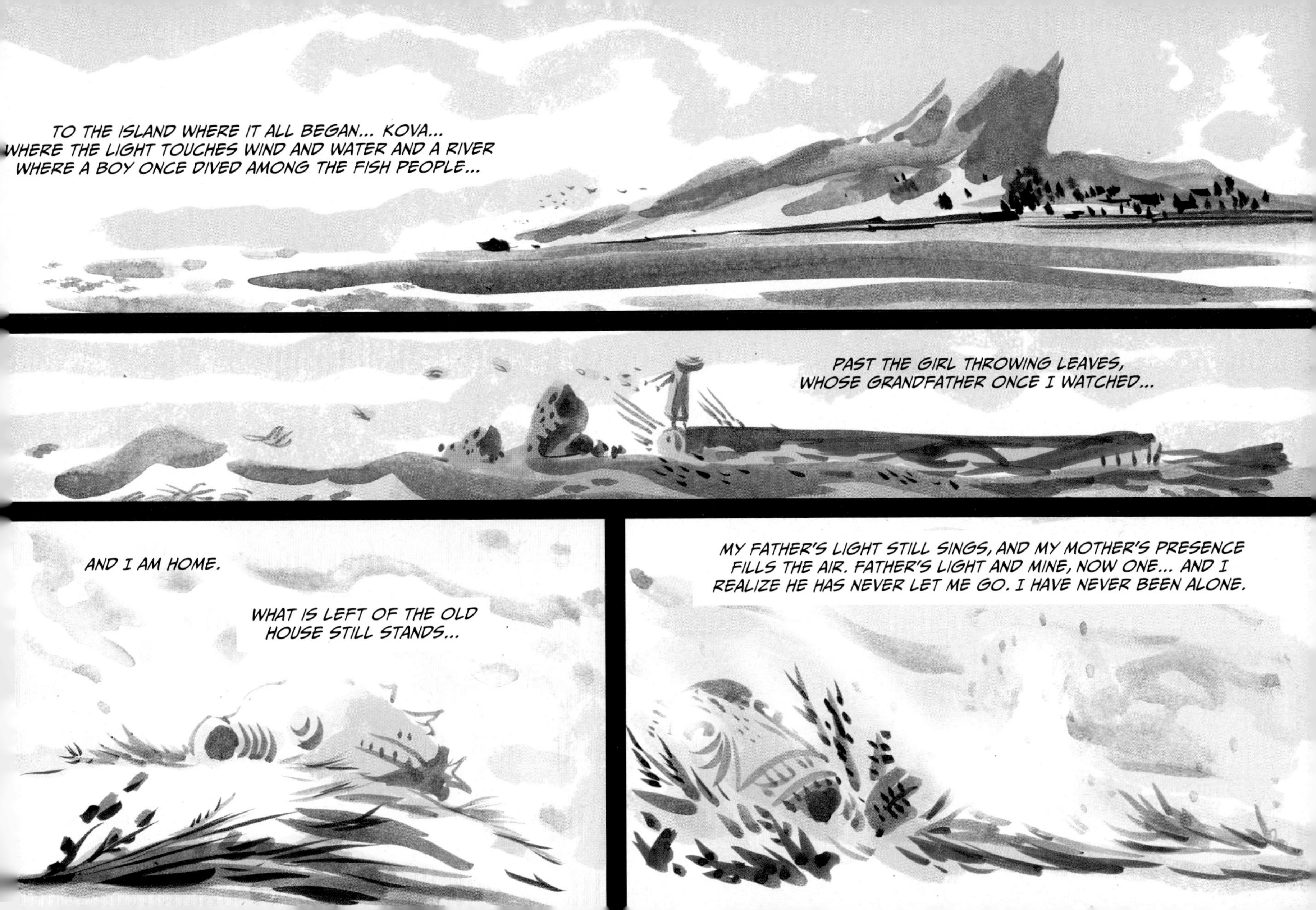
TO THE ISLAND WHERE IT ALL BEGAN... KOVA... WHERE THE LIGHT TOUCHES WIND AND WATER AND A RIVER WHERE A BOY ONCE DIVED AMONG THE FISH PEOPLE...
PAST THE GIRL THROWING LEAVES, WHOSE GRANDFATHER ONCE I WATCHED...
AND I AM HOME.
WHAT IS LEFT OF THE OLD HOUSE STILL STANDS...
MY FATHER'S LIGHT STILL SINGS, AND MY MOTHER'S PRESENCE FILLS THE AIR. FATHER'S LIGHT AND MINE, NOW ONE... AND I REALIZE HE HAS NEVER LET ME GO. I HAVE NEVER BEEN ALONE.

MY HEART FILLS WITH ALL THEIR LIGHT, ALL WHO HAVE CROSSED MY PATH.

AND I KNOW WHAT I MUST DO...

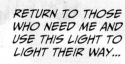

RETURN TO THOSE WHO NEED ME AND USE THIS LIGHT TO LIGHT THEIR WAY...

TWENTY TWO FEET BELOW ME... PRINCE AVITUS FALLS...

FIVE SECONDS HAVE PASSED SINCE MY ILLUMINATION.

I LET THE NOTUS WIND CATCH MY JUMP BOOTS...

EASY, SON! LET THE WIND DO ALL THE WORK!

WHAATTT!!! ROCKETO!

STAY THERE, PRINCE! I'LL BE RIGHT BACK!!

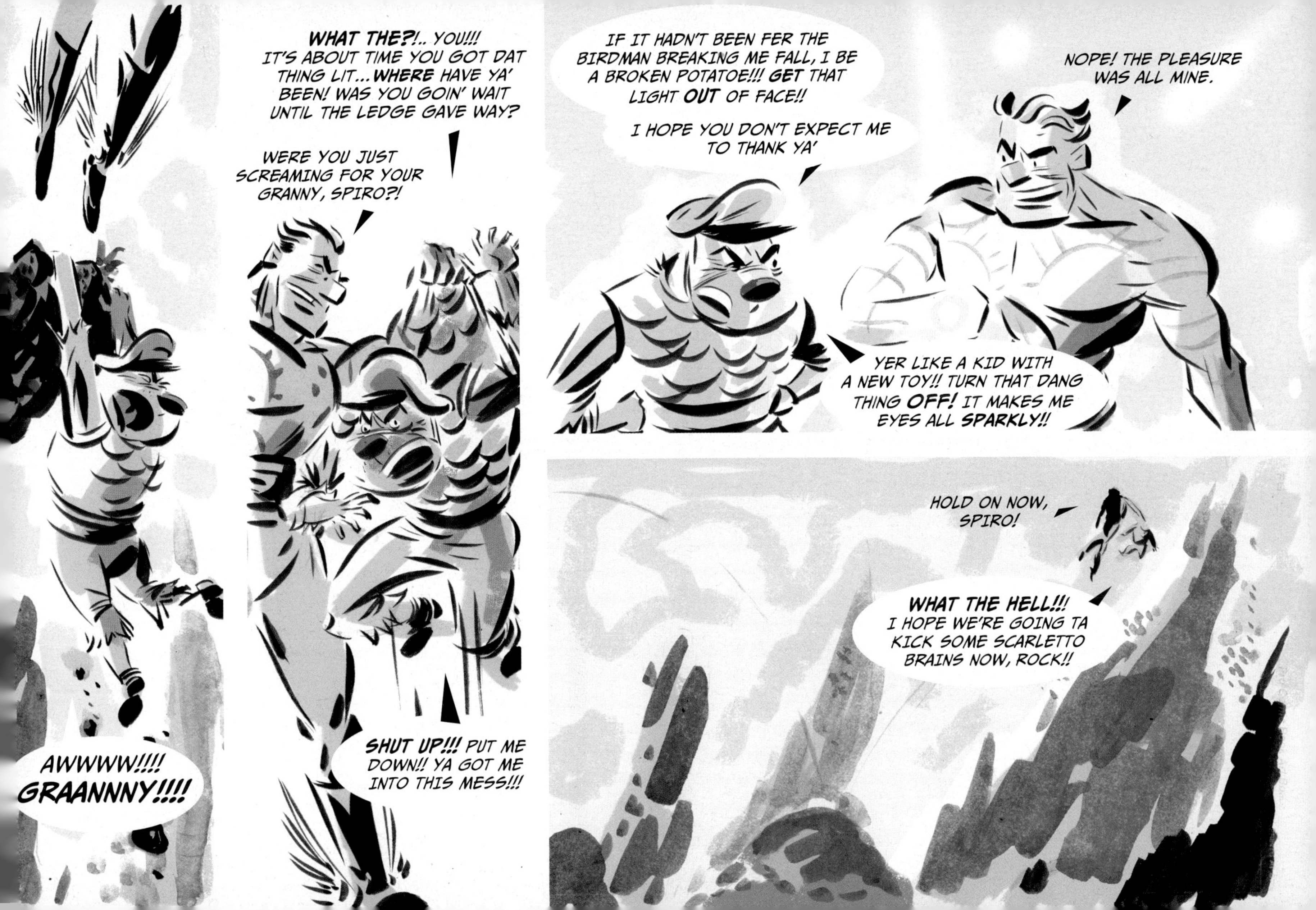
AWWWW!!!! GRAANNY!!!!
WHAT THE?!.. YOU!!! IT'S ABOUT TIME YOU GOT DAT THING LIT... WHERE HAVE YA' BEEN! WAS YOU GOIN' WAIT UNTIL THE LEDGE GAVE WAY?
WERE YOU JUST SCREAMING FOR YOUR GRANNY, SPIRO?!
SHUT UP!!! PUT ME DOWN!! YA GOT ME INTO THIS MESS!!!
IF IT HADN'T BEEN FER THE BIRDMAN BREAKING ME FALL, I BE A BROKEN POTATOE!!! GET THAT LIGHT OUT OF FACE!!
I HOPE YOU DON'T EXPECT ME TO THANK YA'
NOPE! THE PLEASURE WAS ALL MINE.
YER LIKE A KID WITH A NEW TOY!! TURN THAT DANG THING OFF! IT MAKES ME EYES ALL SPARKLY!!
HOLD ON NOW, SPIRO!
WHAT THE HELL!!! I HOPE WE'RE GOING TA KICK SOME SCARLETTO BRAINS NOW, ROCK!!

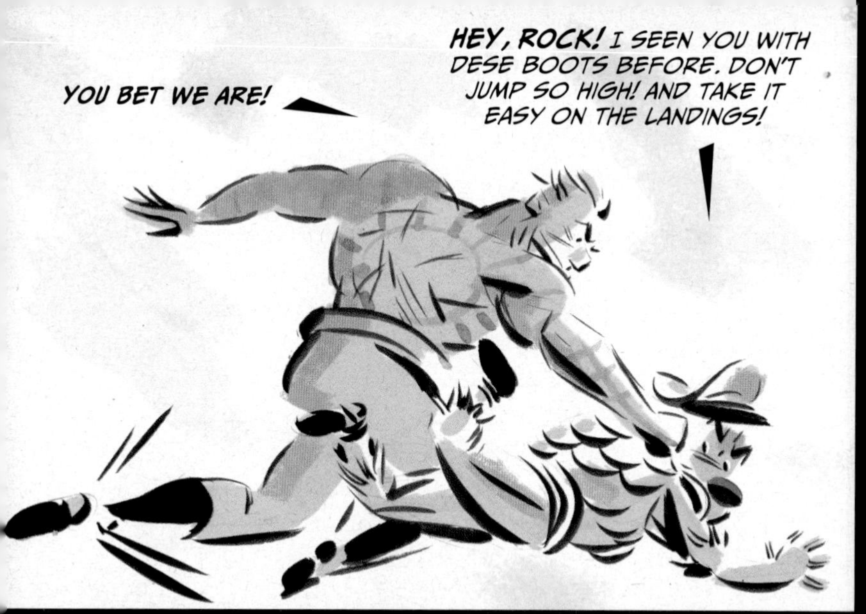
HEY, ROCK! I SEEN YOU WITH DESE BOOTS BEFORE. DON'T JUMP SO HIGH! AND TAKE IT EASY ON THE LANDINGS!
YOU BET WE ARE!

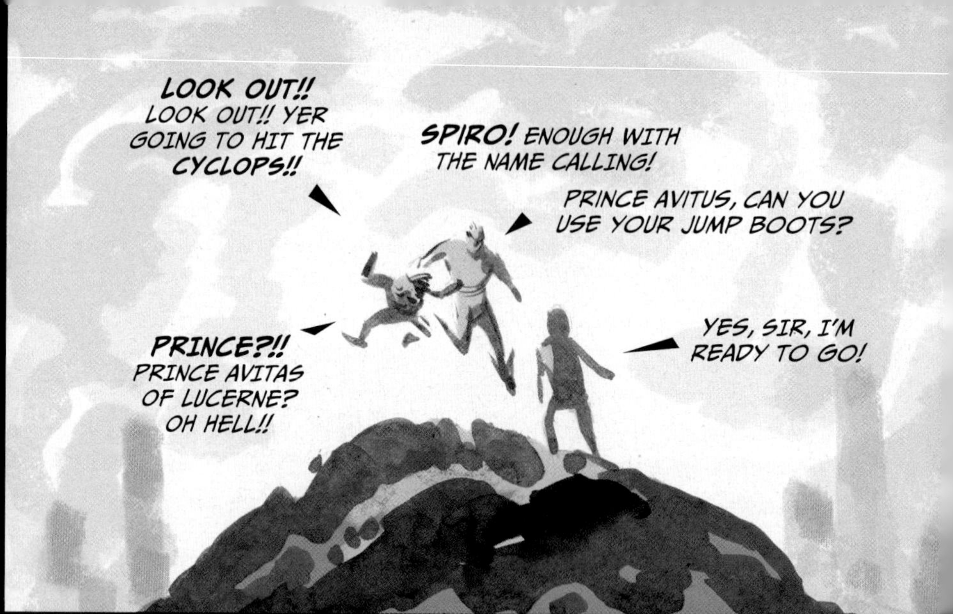
LOOK OUT!! LOOK OUT!! YER GOING TO HIT THE CYCLOPS!!
SPIRO! ENOUGH WITH THE NAME CALLING!
PRINCE AVITUS, CAN YOU USE YOUR JUMP BOOTS?
PRINCE?!! PRINCE AVITAS OF LUCERNE? OH HELL!!
YES, SIR, I'M READY TO GO!

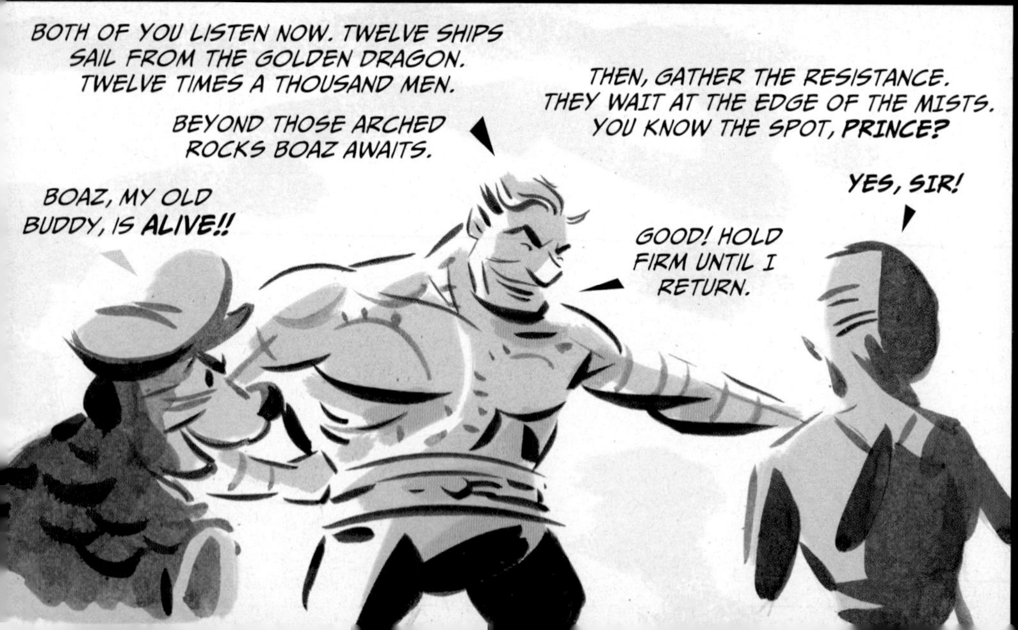
BOTH OF YOU LISTEN NOW. TWELVE SHIPS SAIL FROM THE GOLDEN DRAGON. TWELVE TIMES A THOUSAND MEN.
BEYOND THOSE ARCHED ROCKS BOAZ AWAITS.
THEN, GATHER THE RESISTANCE. THEY WAIT AT THE EDGE OF THE MISTS. YOU KNOW THE SPOT, PRINCE?
BOAZ, MY OLD BUDDY, IS ALIVE!!
YES, SIR!
GOOD! HOLD FIRM UNTIL I RETURN.

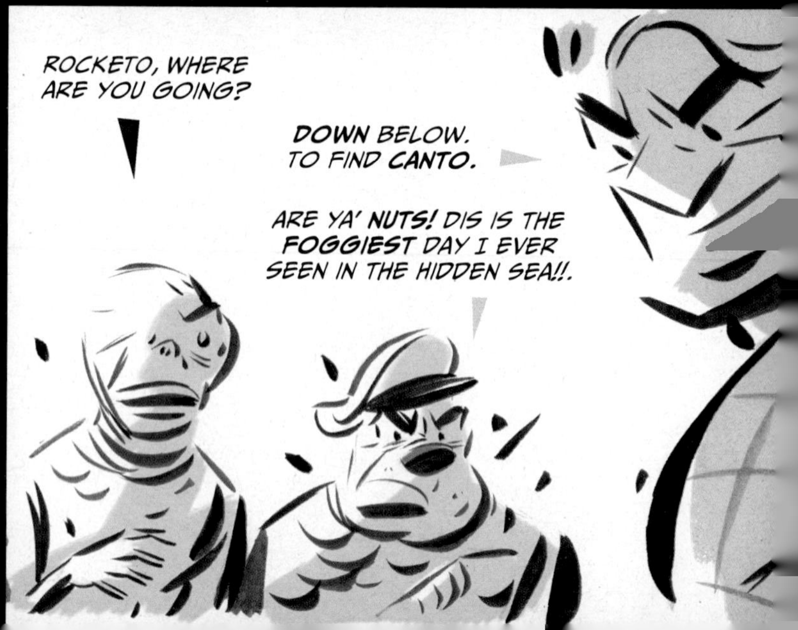
ROCKETO, WHERE ARE YOU GOING?
DOWN BELOW. TO FIND CANTO.
ARE YA' NUTS! DIS IS THE FOGGIEST DAY I EVER SEEN IN THE HIDDEN SEA!!.

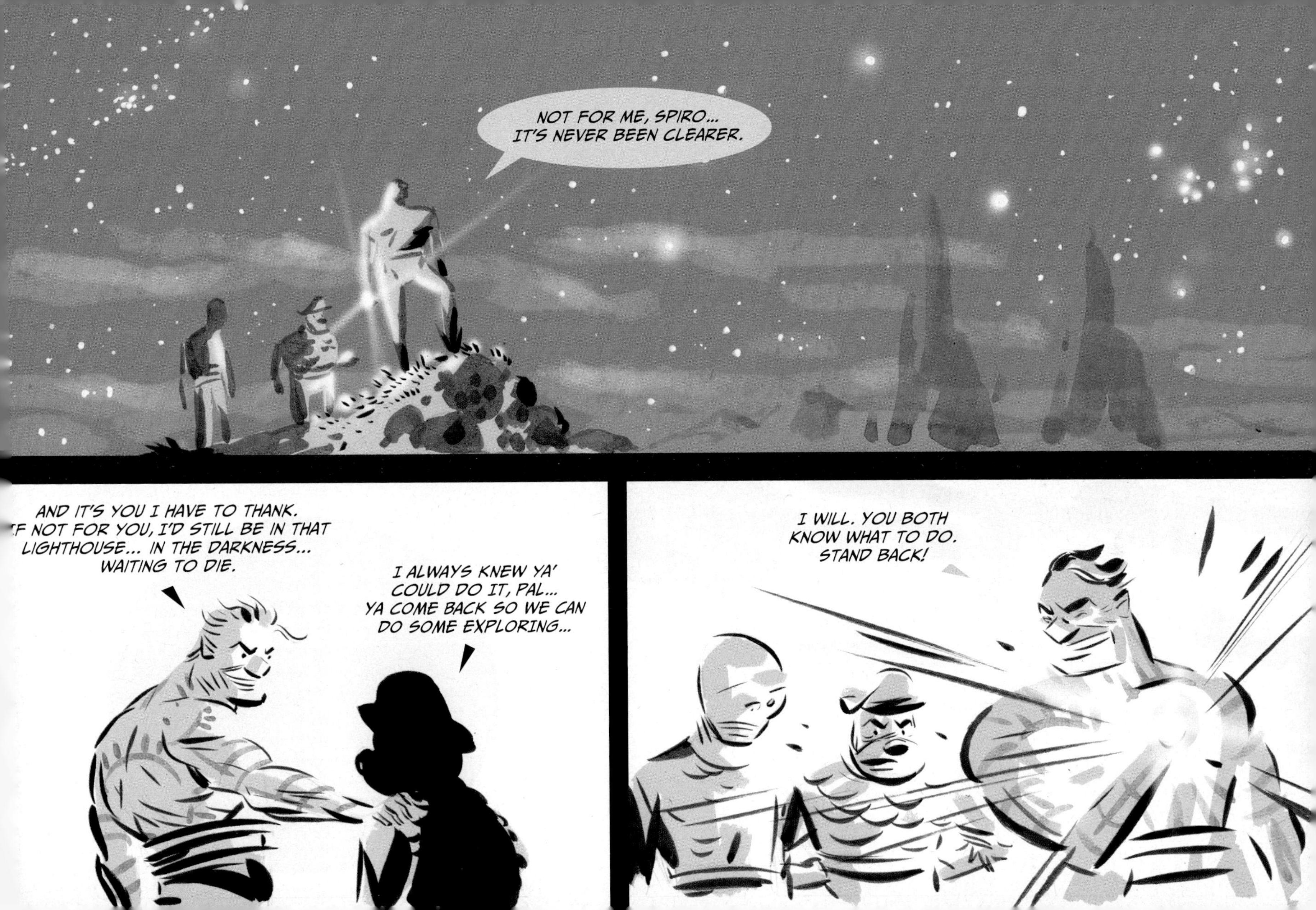
NOT FOR ME, SPIRO... IT'S NEVER BEEN CLEARER.
AND IT'S YOU I HAVE TO THANK. F NOT FOR YOU, I'D STILL BE IN THAT LIGHTHOUSE... IN THE DARKNESS... WAITING TO DIE.
I ALWAYS KNEW YA' COULD DO IT, PAL... YA COME BACK SO WE CAN DO SOME EXPLORING...
I WILL. YOU BOTH KNOW WHAT TO DO. STAND BACK!

OKAY, **PRINCE**, LET'S GET BOAZ AND FIND US SOME TROUBLE!

DOWN INTO THE DARK ABYSS OF THE HIDDEN SEA I DESCEND.

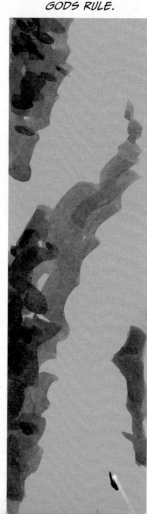

THE UNDERWORLD, WHERE DEATHLESS GODS RULE.

...AND FROM WHICH NONE RETURN.

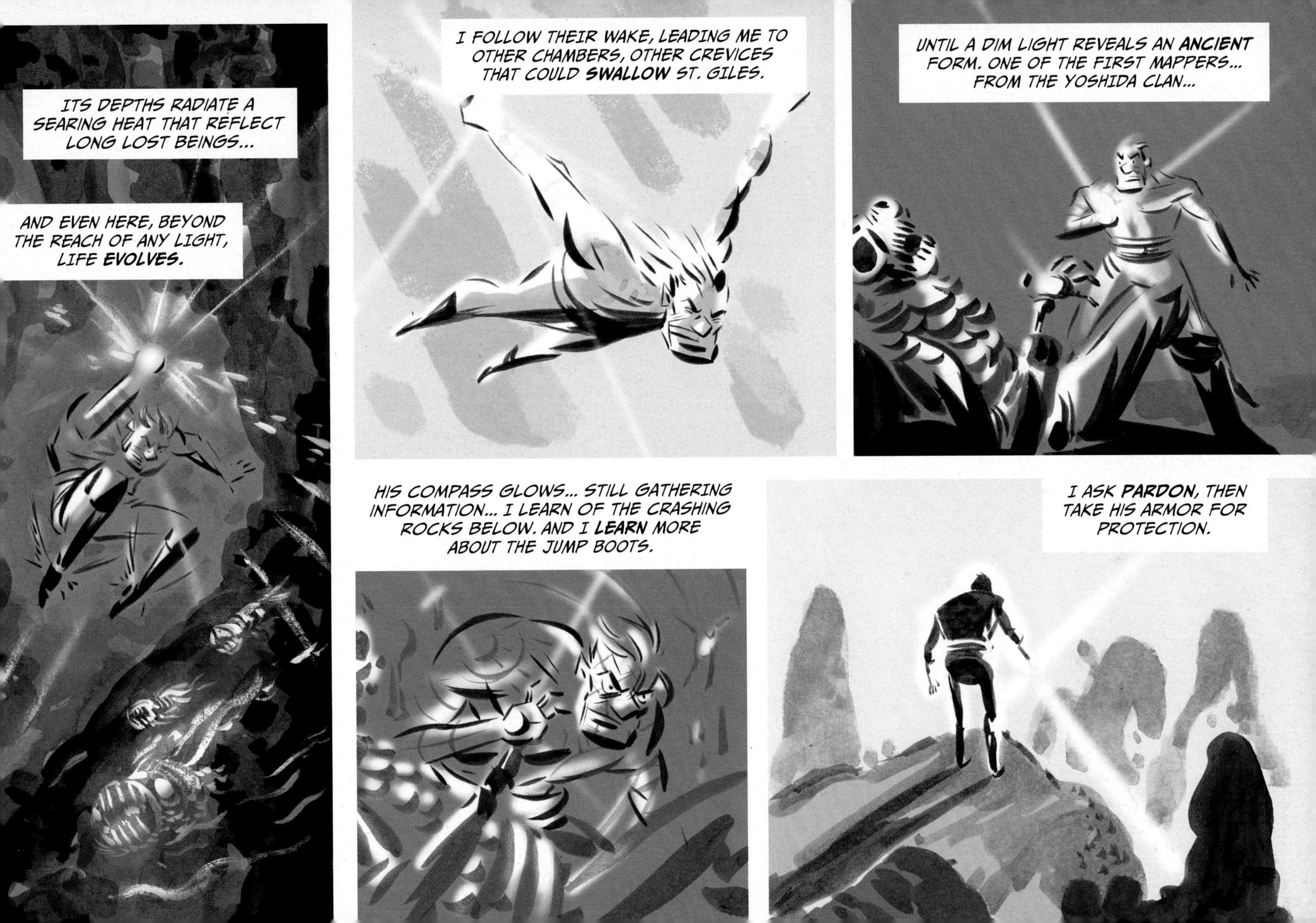
ITS DEPTHS RADIATE A SEARING HEAT THAT REFLECT LONG LOST BEINGS...
AND EVEN HERE, BEYOND THE REACH OF ANY LIGHT, LIFE **EVOLVES.**
I FOLLOW THEIR WAKE, LEADING ME TO OTHER CHAMBERS, OTHER CREVICES THAT COULD **SWALLOW** ST. GILES.
UNTIL A DIM LIGHT REVEALS AN **ANCIENT** FORM. ONE OF THE FIRST MAPPERS... FROM THE YOSHIDA CLAN...
HIS COMPASS GLOWS... STILL GATHERING INFORMATION... I LEARN OF THE CRASHING ROCKS BELOW. AND I **LEARN** MORE ABOUT THE JUMP BOOTS.
I ASK **PARDON,** THEN TAKE HIS ARMOR FOR PROTECTION.

I HAVE TO TIME THE JUMP PERFECTLY. THREE SECONDS BETWEEN CLASHES.

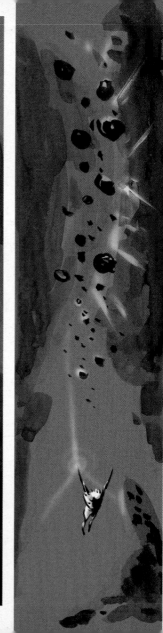

PAST THE CLASHING ROCKS, THE GROUND DISAPPEARS. A GIANT GULF OF MOLTEN MASS UNDULATES **BENEATH**.

MY LIGHT DETECTS AN **OBJECT** SO LARGE THAT IT MUST BE THE PALACE OF CANTO.

AND I SEE MY ONLY **HOPE** OF CROSSING THE INFERNO.

BUT THE JUMP IS TOO STRONG, THE ROCKS TOO **FRAGILE**!

SOLARIUM! PURE SOLARIUM!

A SOFT WIND FROM BELOW COMES IN JUST IN TIME, I TWIST AND LET THE JUMP BOOTS DO THEIR WORK.

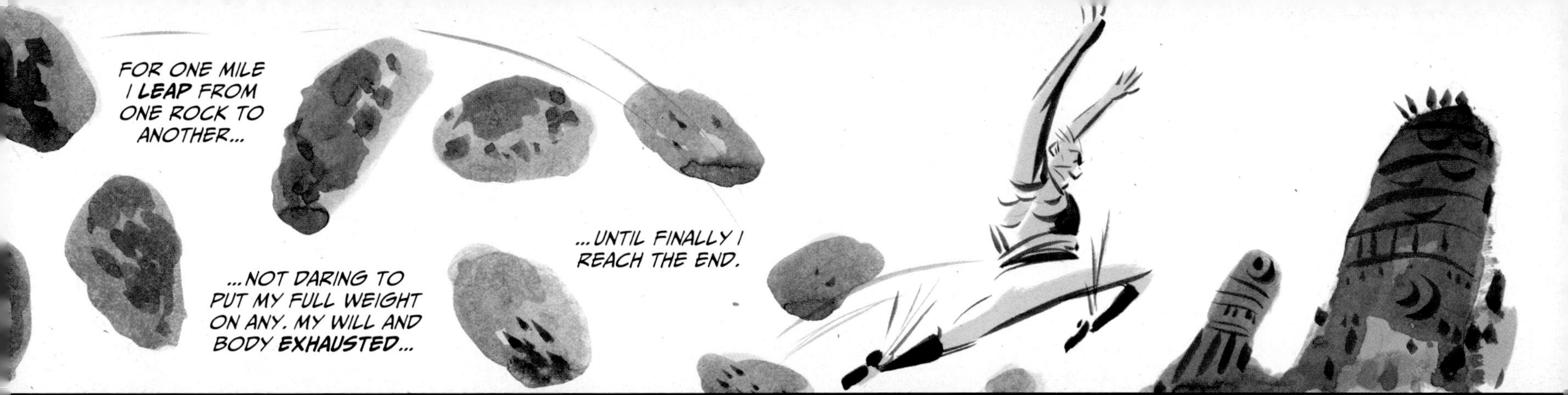
FOR ONE MILE I **LEAP** FROM ONE ROCK TO ANOTHER...
...NOT DARING TO PUT MY FULL WEIGHT ON ANY. MY WILL AND BODY **EXHAUSTED**...
...UNTIL FINALLY I REACH THE END.

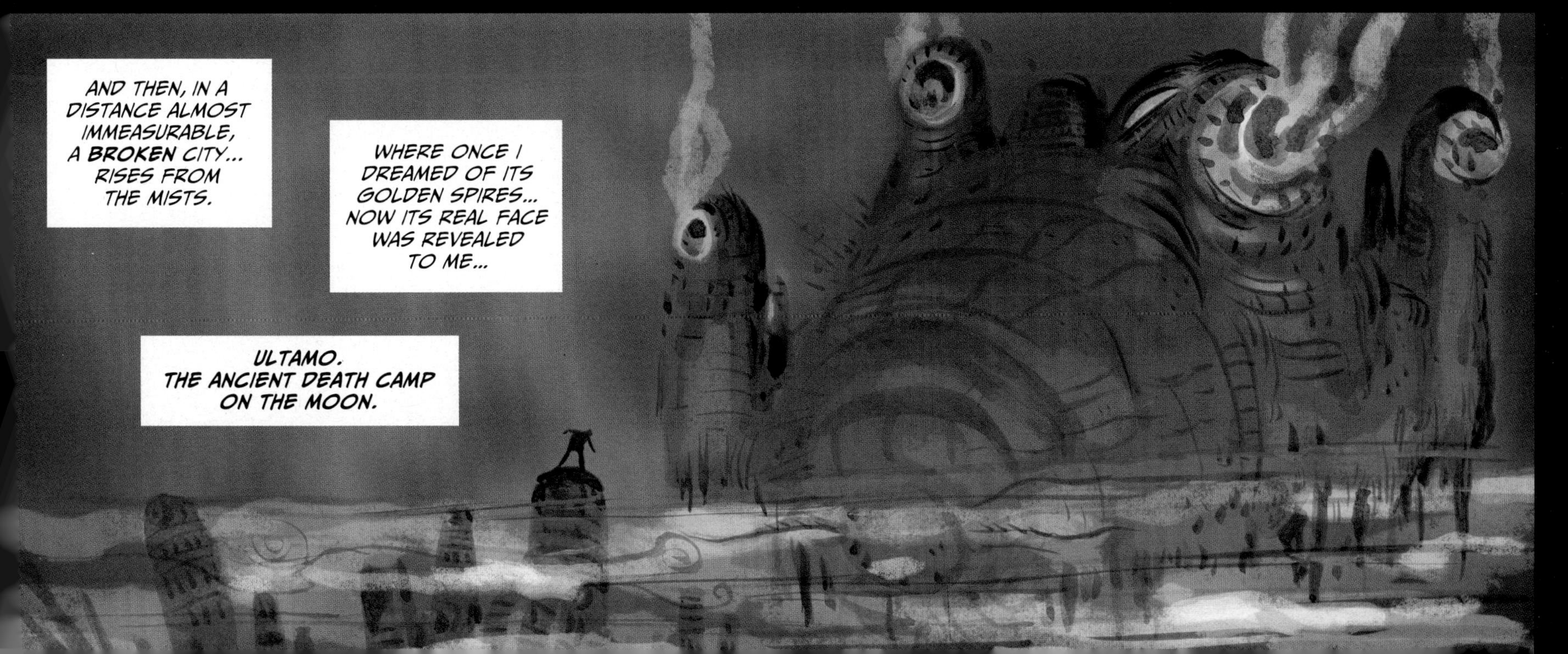
AND THEN, IN A DISTANCE ALMOST IMMEASURABLE, A **BROKEN** CITY... RISES FROM THE MISTS.
WHERE ONCE I DREAMED OF ITS GOLDEN SPIRES... NOW ITS REAL FACE WAS REVEALED TO ME...
ULTAMO. THE ANCIENT DEATH CAMP ON THE MOON.

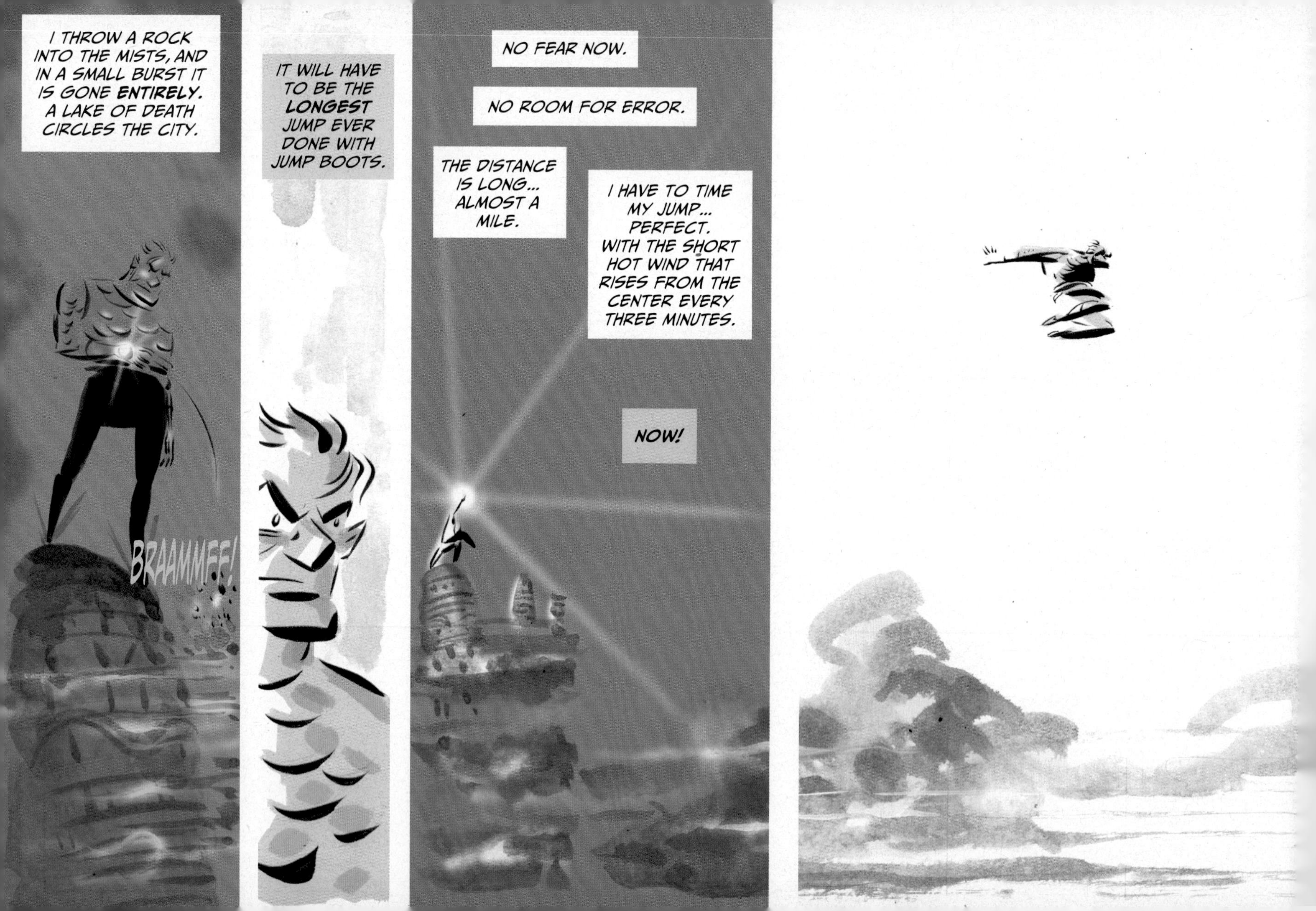
I THROW A ROCK INTO THE MISTS, AND IN A SMALL BURST IT IS GONE **ENTIRELY.** A LAKE OF DEATH CIRCLES THE CITY.
BRAAMMFF!
IT WILL HAVE TO BE THE **LONGEST** JUMP EVER DONE WITH JUMP BOOTS.
NO FEAR NOW.
NO ROOM FOR ERROR.
THE DISTANCE IS LONG... ALMOST A MILE.
I HAVE TO TIME MY JUMP... PERFECT. WITH THE SHORT HOT WIND THAT RISES FROM THE CENTER EVERY THREE MINUTES.
NOW!

KA-BLAAMM!!!

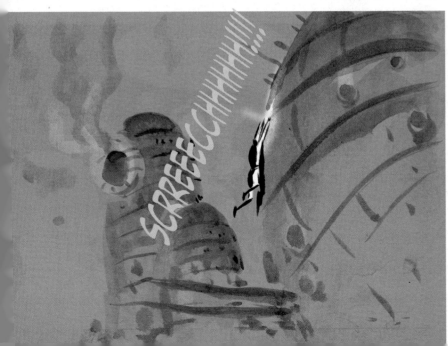

SCREEECCHHHH!!!

KEERASHHHH!!!

WHAT IN THE WORLD?!!...

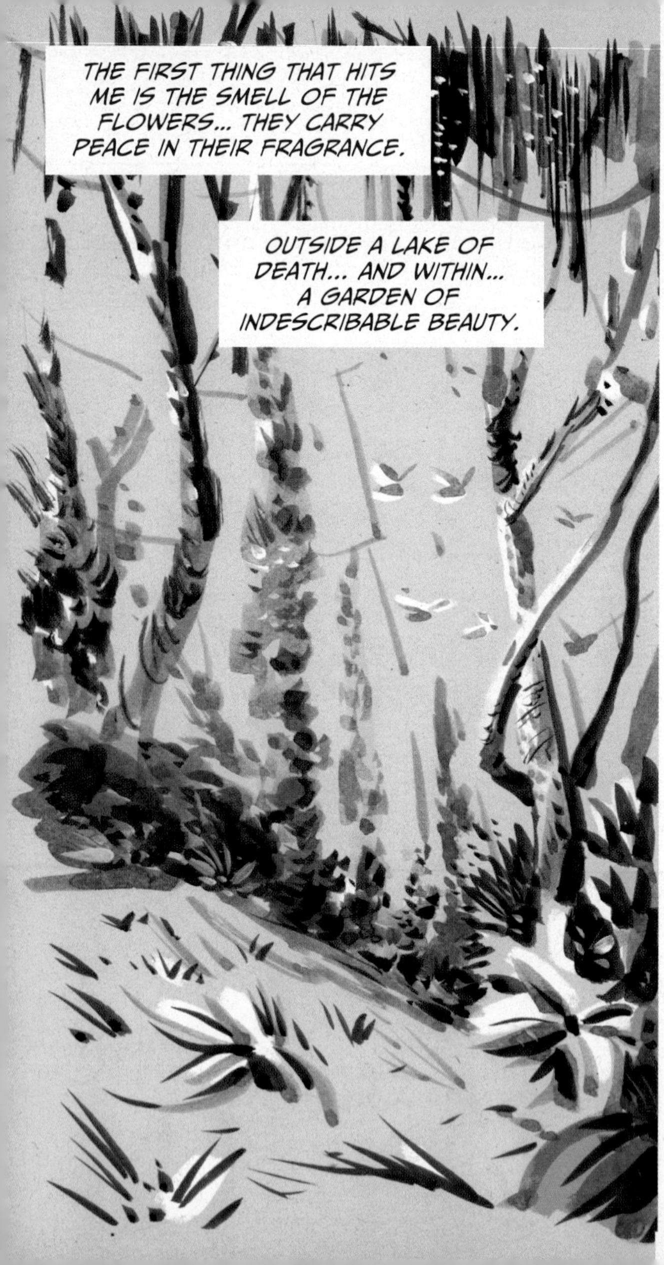
THE FIRST THING THAT HITS ME IS THE SMELL OF THE FLOWERS... THEY CARRY PEACE IN THEIR FRAGRANCE.
OUTSIDE A LAKE OF DEATH... AND WITHIN... A GARDEN OF INDESCRIBABLE BEAUTY.

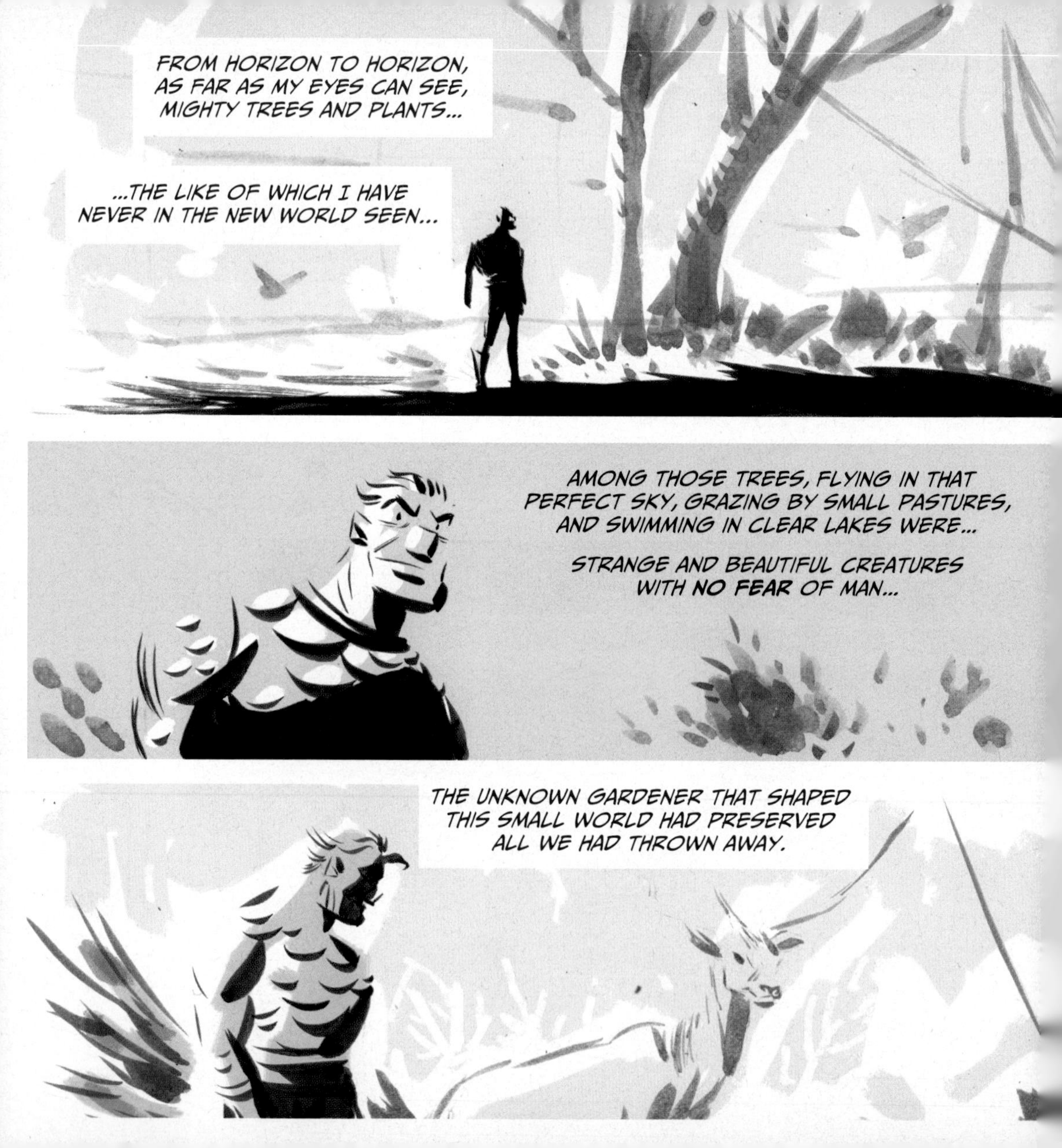
FROM HORIZON TO HORIZON, AS FAR AS MY EYES CAN SEE, MIGHTY TREES AND PLANTS...
...THE LIKE OF WHICH I HAVE NEVER IN THE NEW WORLD SEEN...
AMONG THOSE TREES, FLYING IN THAT PERFECT SKY, GRAZING BY SMALL PASTURES, AND SWIMMING IN CLEAR LAKES WERE...
STRANGE AND BEAUTIFUL CREATURES WITH **NO FEAR** OF MAN...
THE UNKNOWN GARDENER THAT SHAPED THIS SMALL WORLD HAD PRESERVED ALL WE HAD THROWN AWAY.

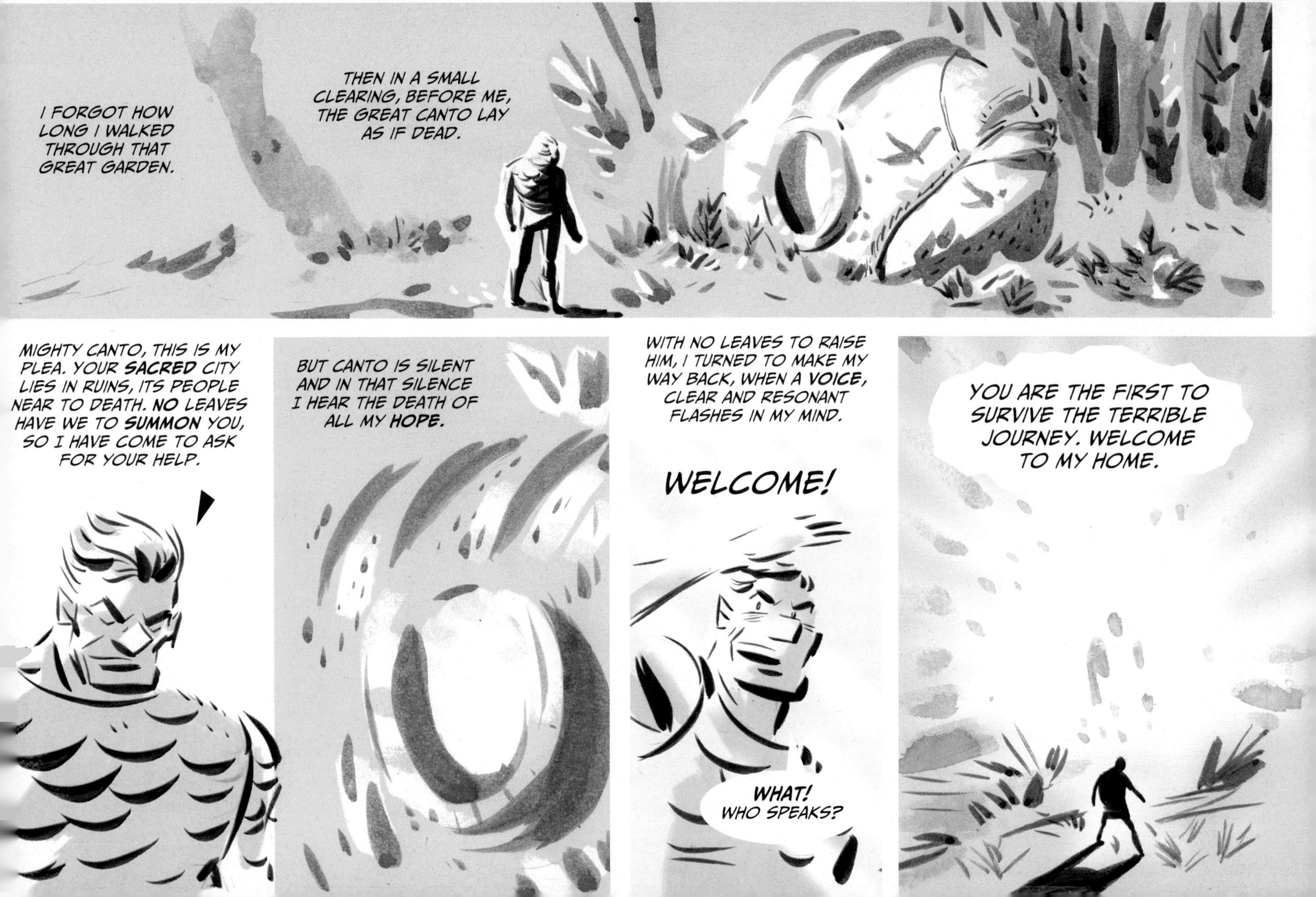
I FORGOT HOW LONG I WALKED THROUGH THAT GREAT GARDEN.
THEN IN A SMALL CLEARING, BEFORE ME, THE GREAT CANTO LAY AS IF DEAD.
MIGHTY CANTO, THIS IS MY PLEA. YOUR SACRED CITY LIES IN RUINS, ITS PEOPLE NEAR TO DEATH. NO LEAVES HAVE WE TO SUMMON YOU, SO I HAVE COME TO ASK FOR YOUR HELP.
BUT CANTO IS SILENT AND IN THAT SILENCE I HEAR THE DEATH OF ALL MY HOPE.
WITH NO LEAVES TO RAISE HIM, I TURNED TO MAKE MY WAY BACK, WHEN A VOICE, CLEAR AND RESONANT FLASHES IN MY MIND.
WELCOME!
WHAT! WHO SPEAKS?
YOU ARE THE FIRST TO SURVIVE THE TERRIBLE JOURNEY. WELCOME TO MY HOME.

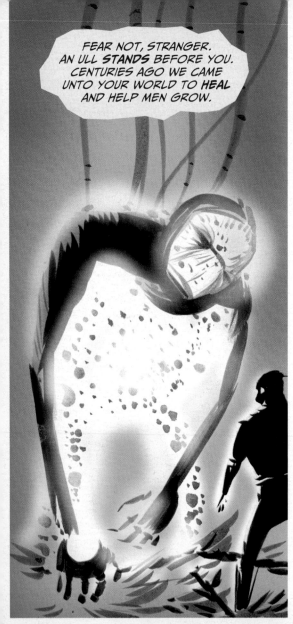

FEAR NOT, STRANGER. AN ULL **STANDS** BEFORE YOU. CENTURIES AGO WE CAME UNTO YOUR WORLD TO **HEAL** AND HELP MEN GROW.

RISE, MY SON. NO NEED TO KNEEL. I AM BUT A **BEING** NOT UNLIKE YOURSELF. LET ME LOOK **WITHIN** YOUR LIGHT.

LET ME SEE THAT SMALL BOY, AND THE STRONG MAN YOU HAVE BECOME... YOUR HISTORY AND YOUR JOURNEY HERE.

YES...

ROCKETO GARRISON...

A **GOOD** MAN YOU ARE, COME FOR CANTO TO SAVE YOUR FRIENDS. BUT CANTO IS NO BEING OF DESTRUCTION. I HAVE NOT WHAT YOU SEEK.

ONLY THE **KNOWLEDGE** OF THE GREAT FLOWER I NOW HOLD. HERE HAVE I WAITED, A PRISONER, YET KEEPING ALIVE ALL THAT IS PURE AND GOOD, IN SAFEKEEPING, UNTIL MEN GROW IN WISDOM.

CAN YOU **SHOW** ME THE FLOWER, MIGHTY FATHER?

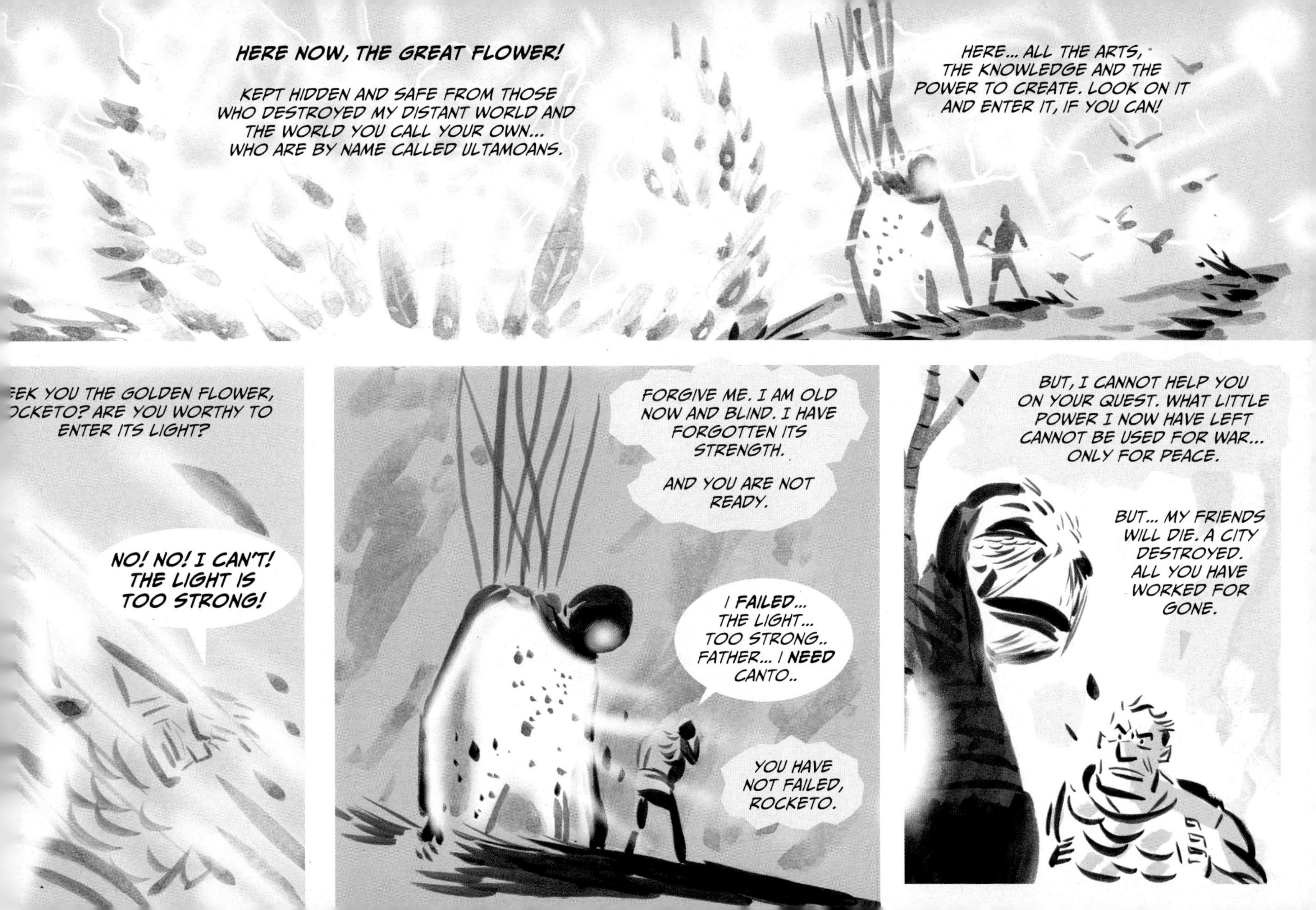
HERE NOW, THE GREAT FLOWER!
KEPT HIDDEN AND SAFE FROM THOSE WHO DESTROYED MY DISTANT WORLD AND THE WORLD YOU CALL YOUR OWN... WHO ARE BY NAME CALLED ULTAMOANS.
HERE... ALL THE ARTS, THE KNOWLEDGE AND THE POWER TO CREATE. LOOK ON IT AND ENTER IT, IF YOU CAN!
EEK YOU THE GOLDEN FLOWER, OCKETO? ARE YOU WORTHY TO ENTER ITS LIGHT?
NO! NO! I CAN'T! THE LIGHT IS TOO STRONG!
FORGIVE ME. I AM OLD NOW AND BLIND. I HAVE FORGOTTEN ITS STRENGTH.
AND YOU ARE NOT READY.
I FAILED... THE LIGHT... TOO STRONG.. FATHER... I NEED CANTO..
YOU HAVE NOT FAILED, ROCKETO.
BUT, I CANNOT HELP YOU ON YOUR QUEST. WHAT LITTLE POWER I NOW HAVE LEFT CANNOT BE USED FOR WAR... ONLY FOR PEACE.
BUT... MY FRIENDS WILL DIE. A CITY DESTROYED. ALL YOU HAVE WORKED FOR GONE.

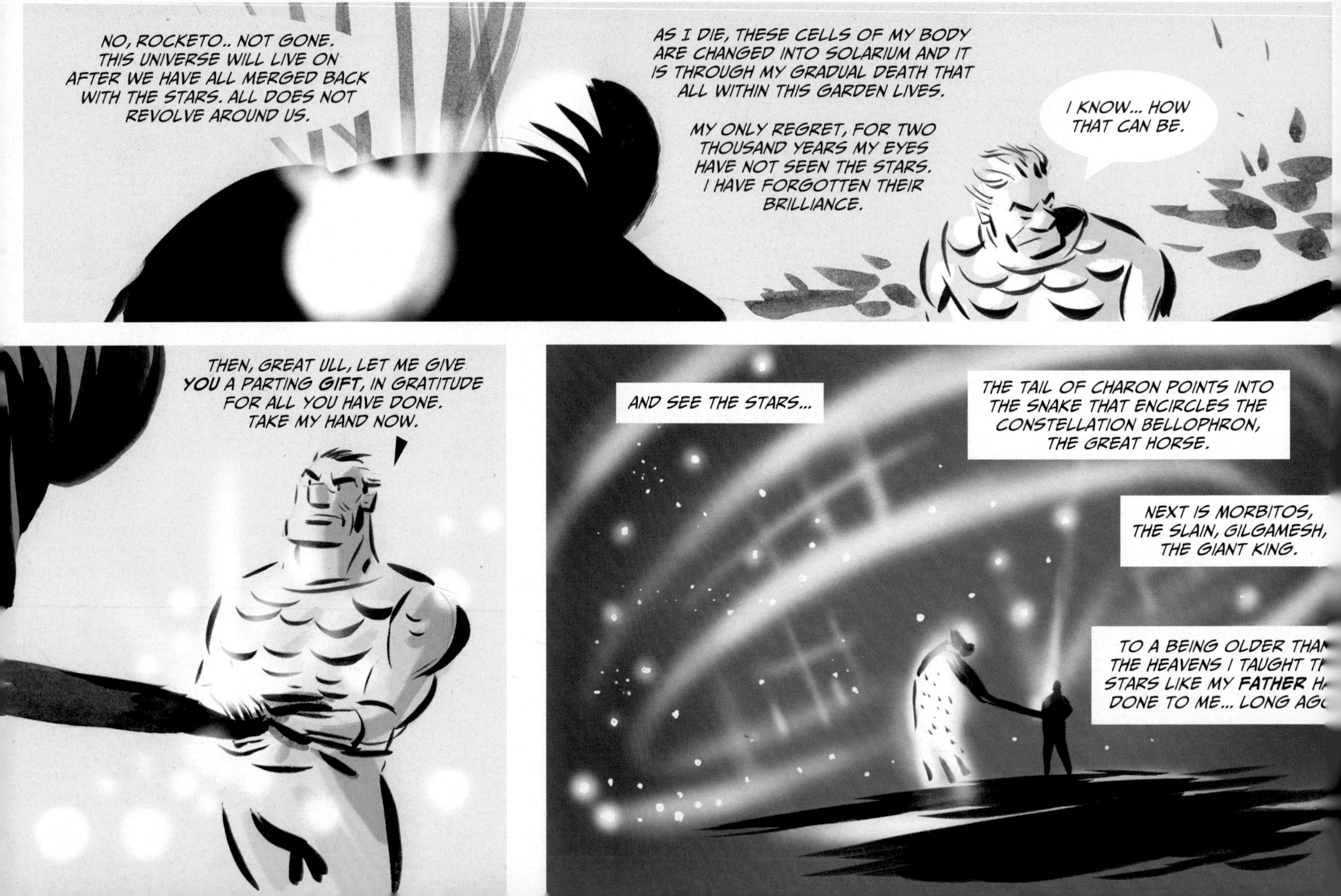
NO, ROCKETO.. NOT GONE. THIS UNIVERSE WILL LIVE ON AFTER WE HAVE ALL MERGED BACK WITH THE STARS. ALL DOES NOT REVOLVE AROUND US.
AS I DIE, THESE CELLS OF MY BODY ARE CHANGED INTO SOLARIUM AND IT IS THROUGH MY GRADUAL DEATH THAT ALL WITHIN THIS GARDEN LIVES.
MY ONLY REGRET, FOR TWO THOUSAND YEARS MY EYES HAVE NOT SEEN THE STARS. I HAVE FORGOTTEN THEIR BRILLIANCE.
I KNOW... HOW THAT CAN BE.
THEN, GREAT ULL, LET ME GIVE **YOU** A PARTING **GIFT**, IN GRATITUDE FOR ALL YOU HAVE DONE. TAKE MY HAND NOW.
AND SEE THE STARS...
THE TAIL OF CHARON POINTS INTO THE SNAKE THAT ENCIRCLES THE CONSTELLATION BELLOPHRON, THE GREAT HORSE.
NEXT IS MORBITOS, THE SLAIN, GILGAMESH, THE GIANT KING.
TO A BEING OLDER THA
THE HEAVENS I TAUGHT T
STARS LIKE MY **FATHER** H
DONE TO ME... LONG AG

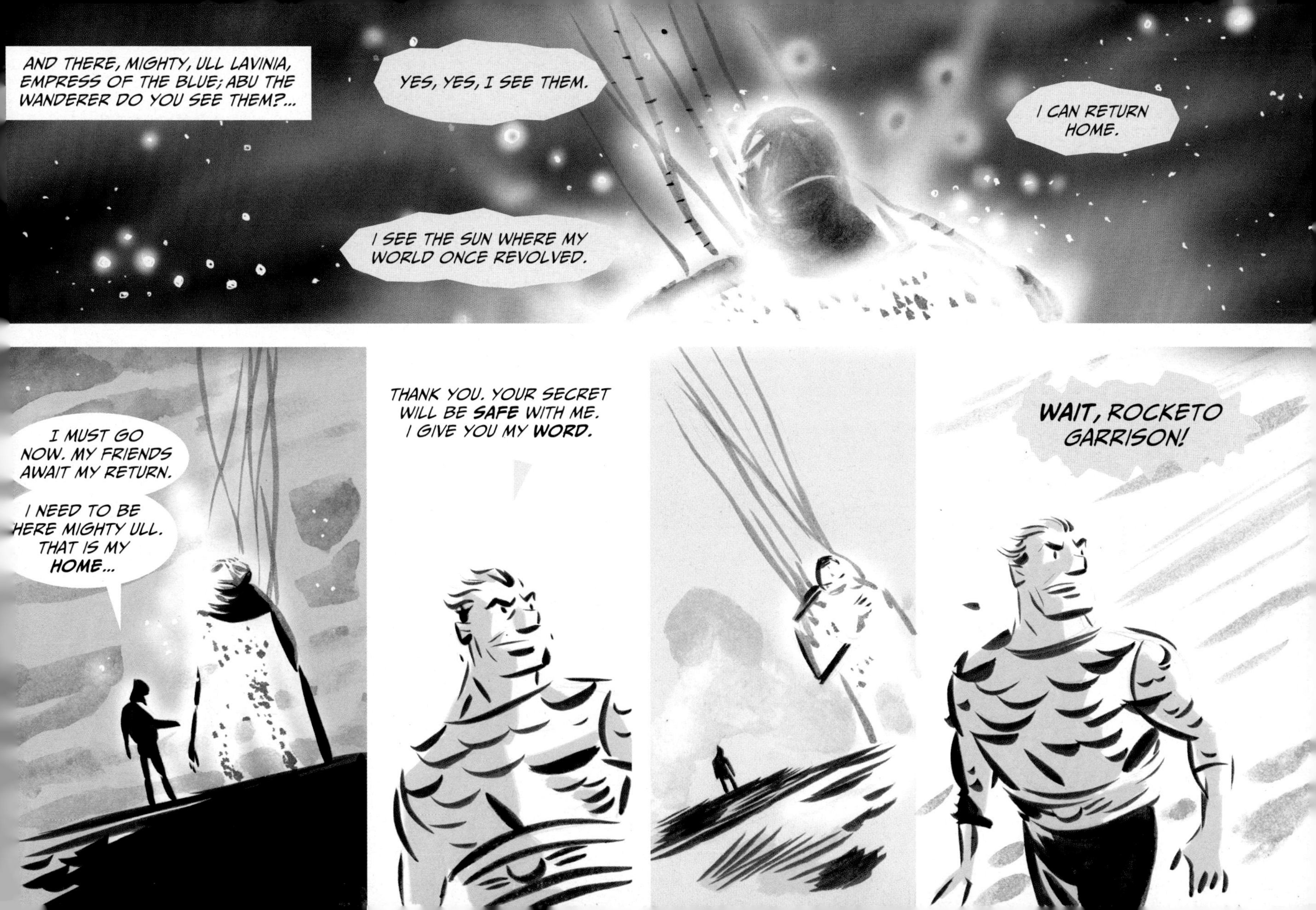
AND THERE, MIGHTY, ULL LAVINIA, EMPRESS OF THE BLUE; ABU THE WANDERER DO YOU SEE THEM?...
YES, YES, I SEE THEM.
I SEE THE SUN WHERE MY WORLD ONCE REVOLVED.
I CAN RETURN HOME.
I MUST GO NOW. MY FRIENDS AWAIT MY RETURN.
I NEED TO BE HERE MIGHTY ULL. THAT IS MY HOME...
THANK YOU. YOUR SECRET WILL BE SAFE WITH ME. I GIVE YOU MY WORD.
WAIT, ROCKETO GARRISON!

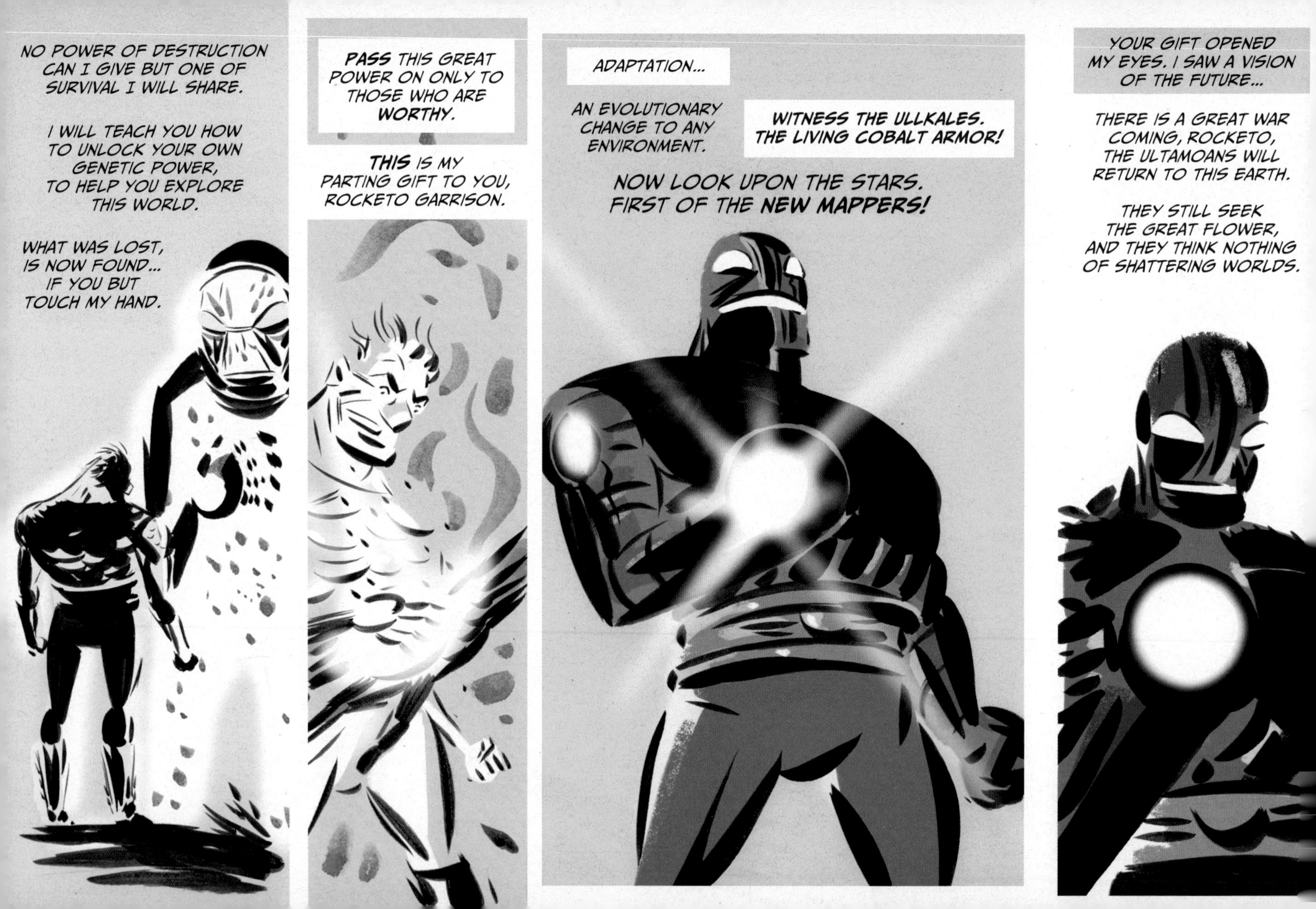
NO POWER OF DESTRUCTION CAN I GIVE BUT ONE OF SURVIVAL I WILL SHARE.
I WILL TEACH YOU HOW TO UNLOCK YOUR OWN GENETIC POWER, TO HELP YOU EXPLORE THIS WORLD.
WHAT WAS LOST, IS NOW FOUND... IF YOU BUT TOUCH MY HAND.
PASS THIS GREAT POWER ON ONLY TO THOSE WHO ARE WORTHY.
THIS IS MY PARTING GIFT TO YOU, ROCKETO GARRISON.
ADAPTATION...
AN EVOLUTIONARY CHANGE TO ANY ENVIRONMENT.
WITNESS THE ULLKALES. THE LIVING COBALT ARMOR!
NOW LOOK UPON THE STARS. FIRST OF THE NEW MAPPERS!
YOUR GIFT OPENED MY EYES. I SAW A VISION OF THE FUTURE...
THERE IS A GREAT WAR COMING, ROCKETO, THE ULTAMOANS WILL RETURN TO THIS EARTH.
THEY STILL SEEK THE GREAT FLOWER, AND THEY THINK NOTHING OF SHATTERING WORLDS.

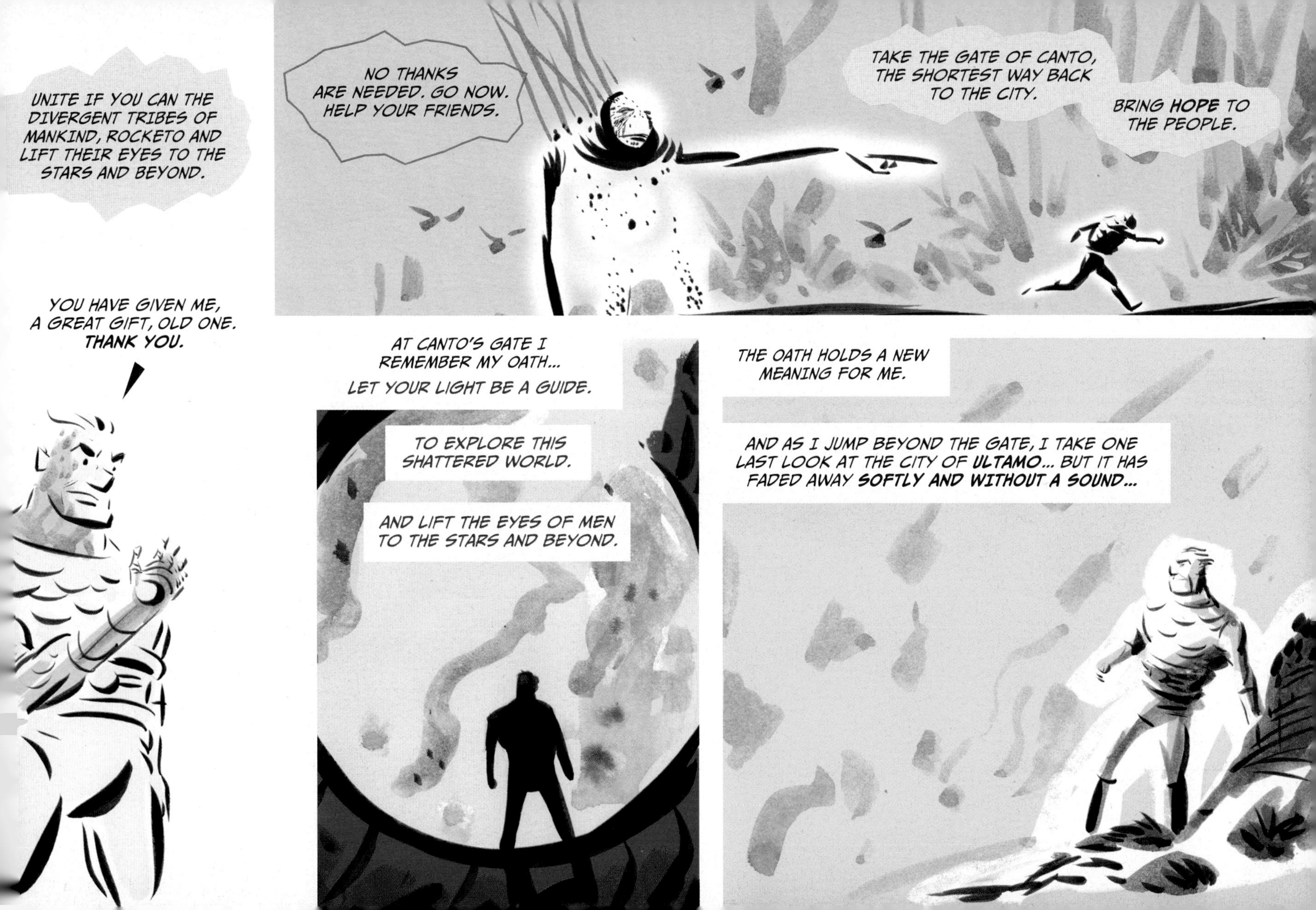
UNITE IF YOU CAN THE DIVERGENT TRIBES OF MANKIND, ROCKETO AND LIFT THEIR EYES TO THE STARS AND BEYOND.
NO THANKS ARE NEEDED. GO NOW. HELP YOUR FRIENDS.
TAKE THE GATE OF CANTO, THE SHORTEST WAY BACK TO THE CITY.
BRING **HOPE** TO THE PEOPLE.
YOU HAVE GIVEN ME, A GREAT GIFT, OLD ONE. **THANK YOU.**
AT CANTO'S GATE I REMEMBER MY OATH...
LET YOUR LIGHT BE A GUIDE.
TO EXPLORE THIS SHATTERED WORLD.
AND LIFT THE EYES OF MEN TO THE STARS AND BEYOND.
THE OATH HOLDS A NEW MEANING FOR ME.
AND AS I JUMP BEYOND THE GATE, I TAKE ONE LAST LOOK AT THE CITY OF **ULTAMO**... BUT IT HAS FADED AWAY **SOFTLY AND WITHOUT A SOUND...**

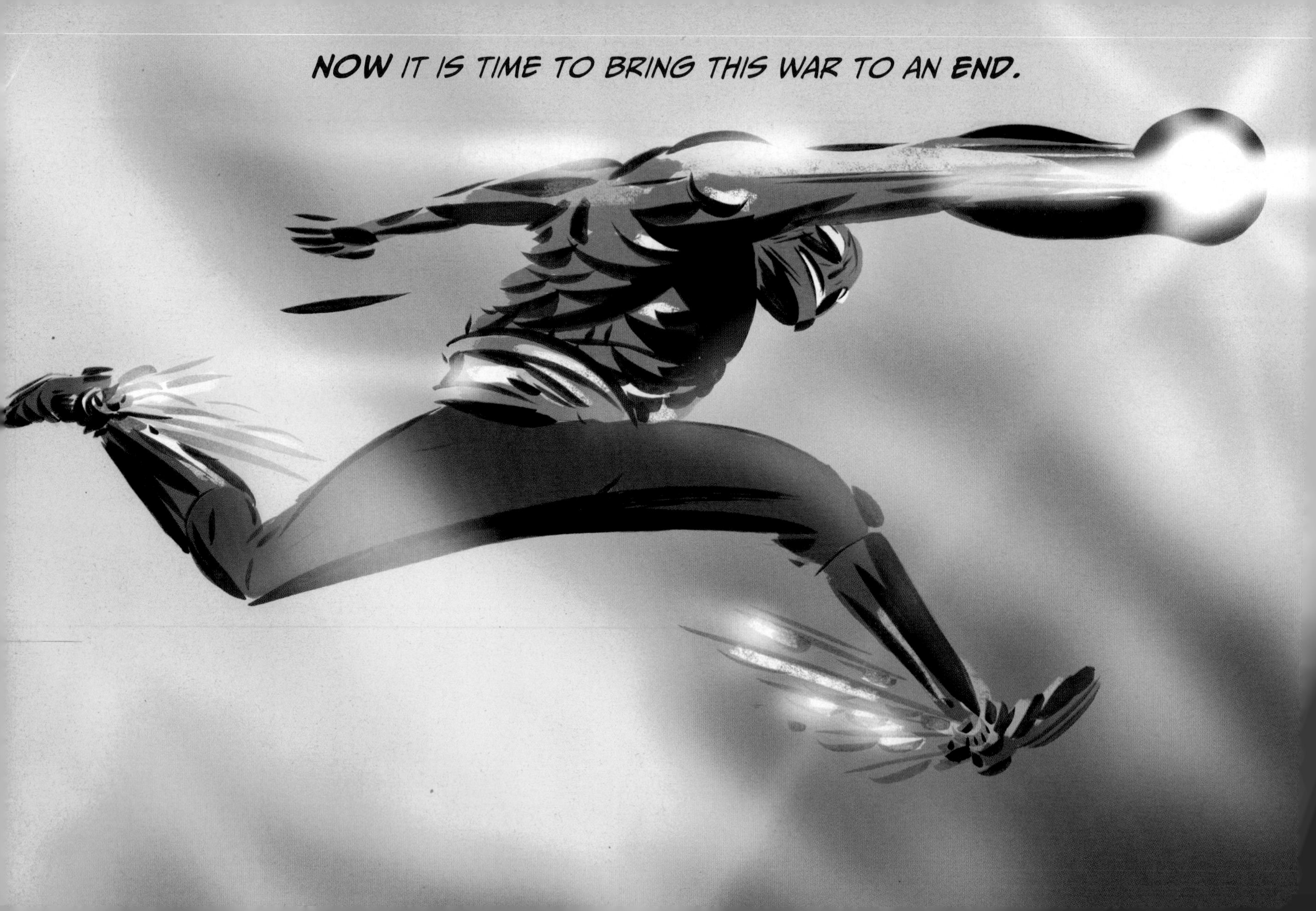
NOW IT IS TIME TO BRING THIS WAR TO AN END.

ROCKETO

12

JOURNEYS

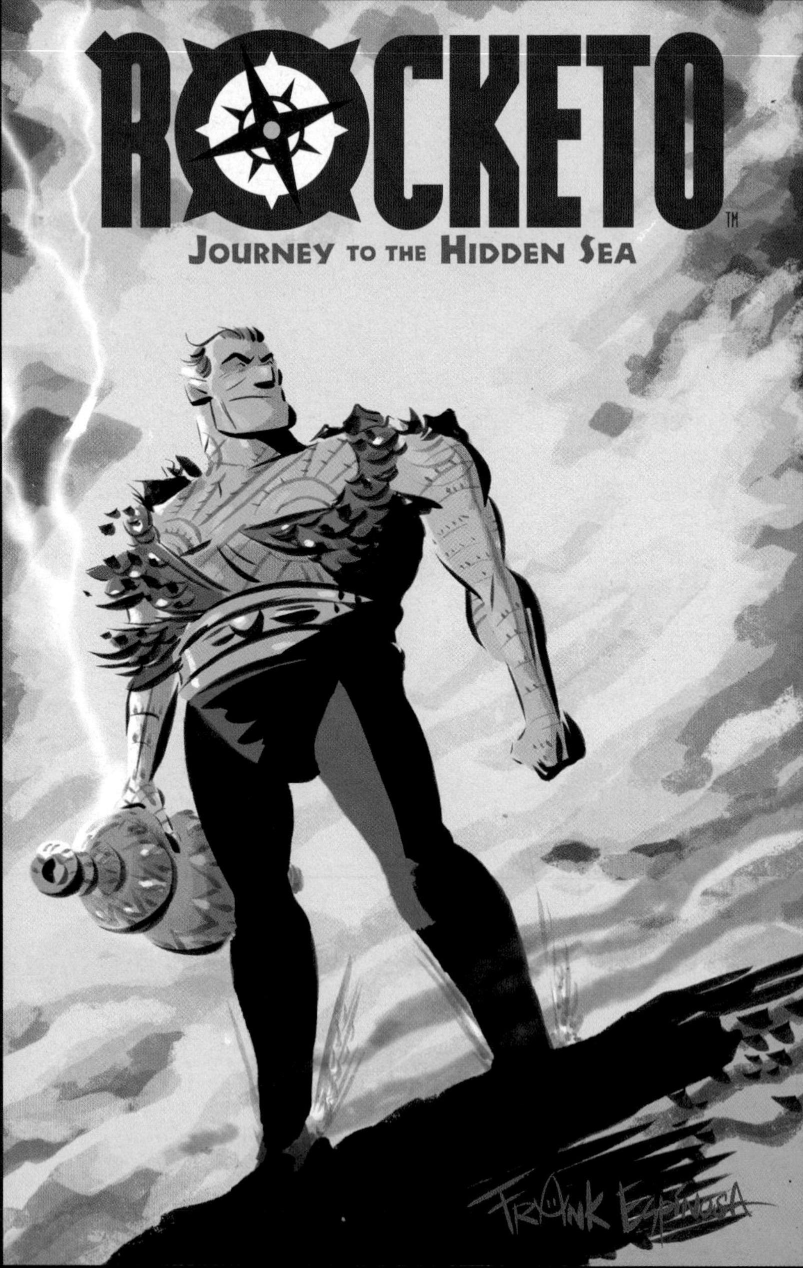
ROCKETO™
JOURNEY TO THE HIDDEN SEA

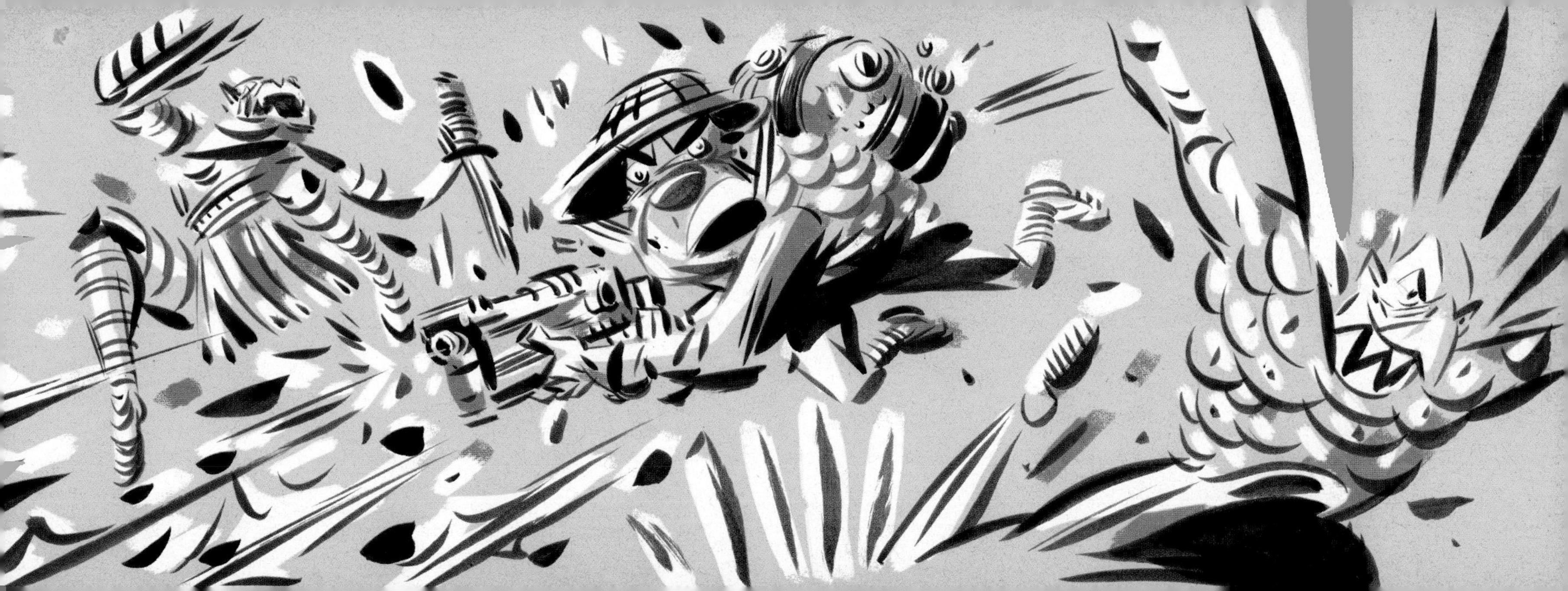

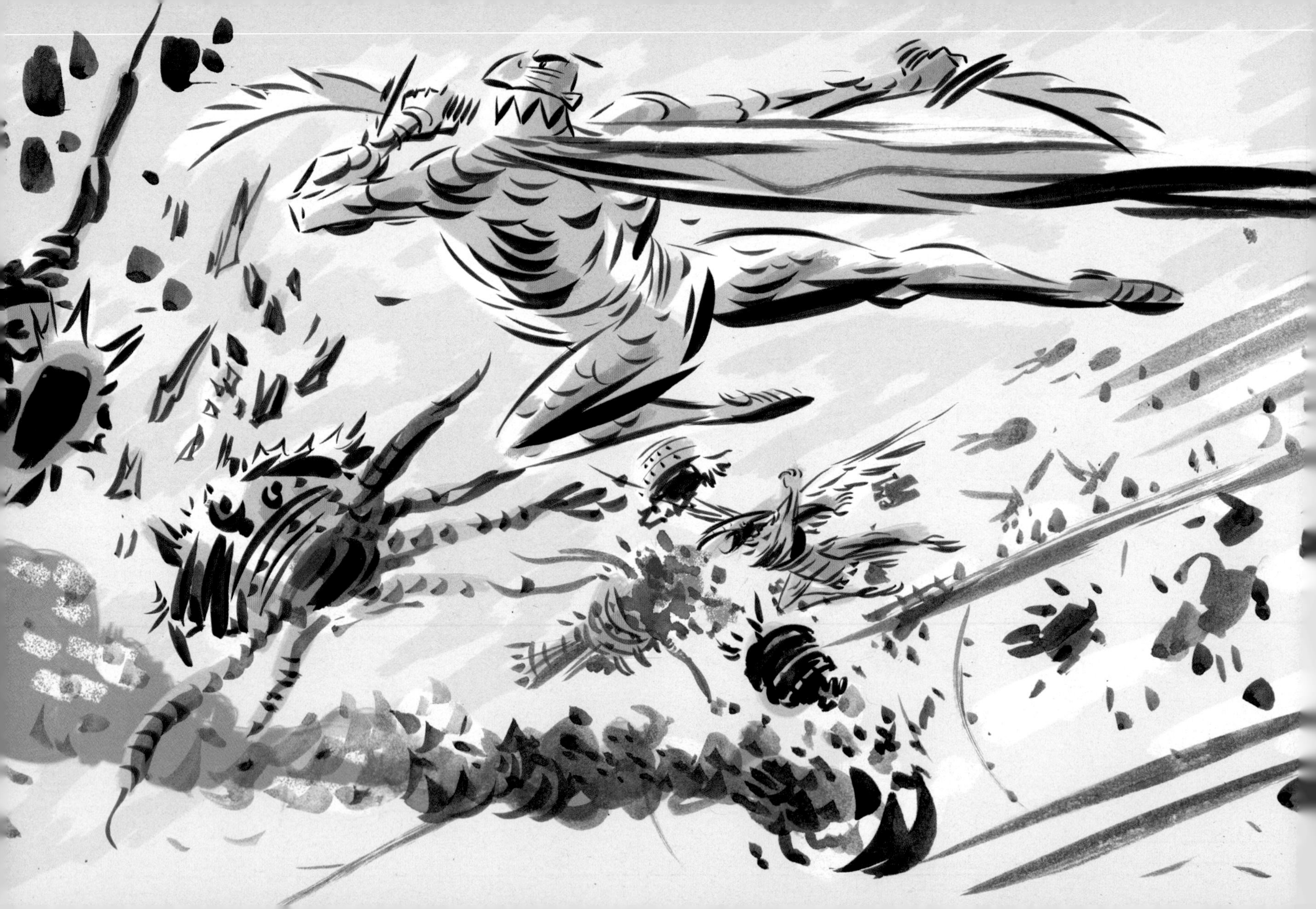

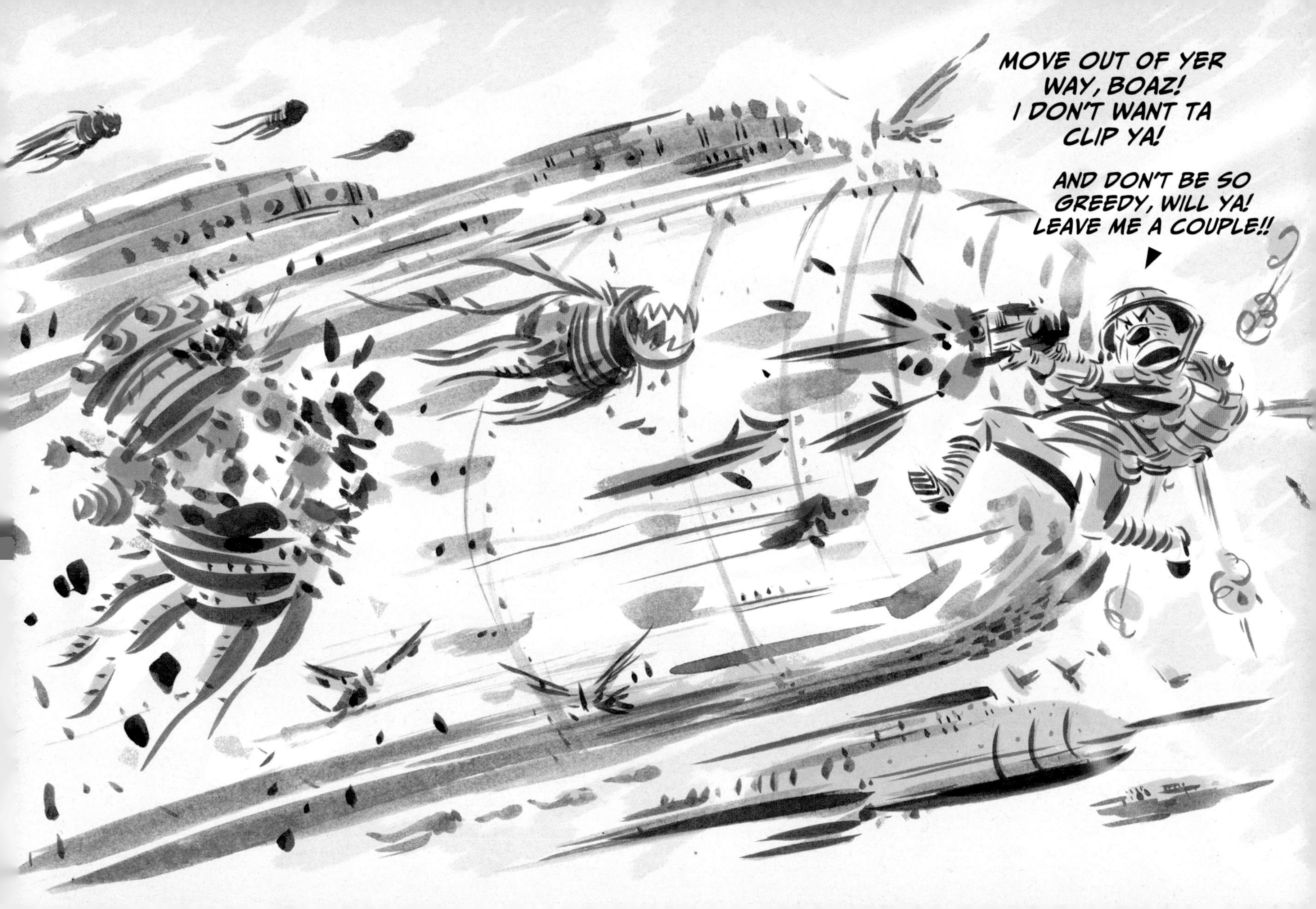
MOVE OUT OF YER WAY, BOAZ! I DON'T WANT TA CLIP YA!
AND DON'T BE SO GREEDY, WILL YA! LEAVE ME A COUPLE!!

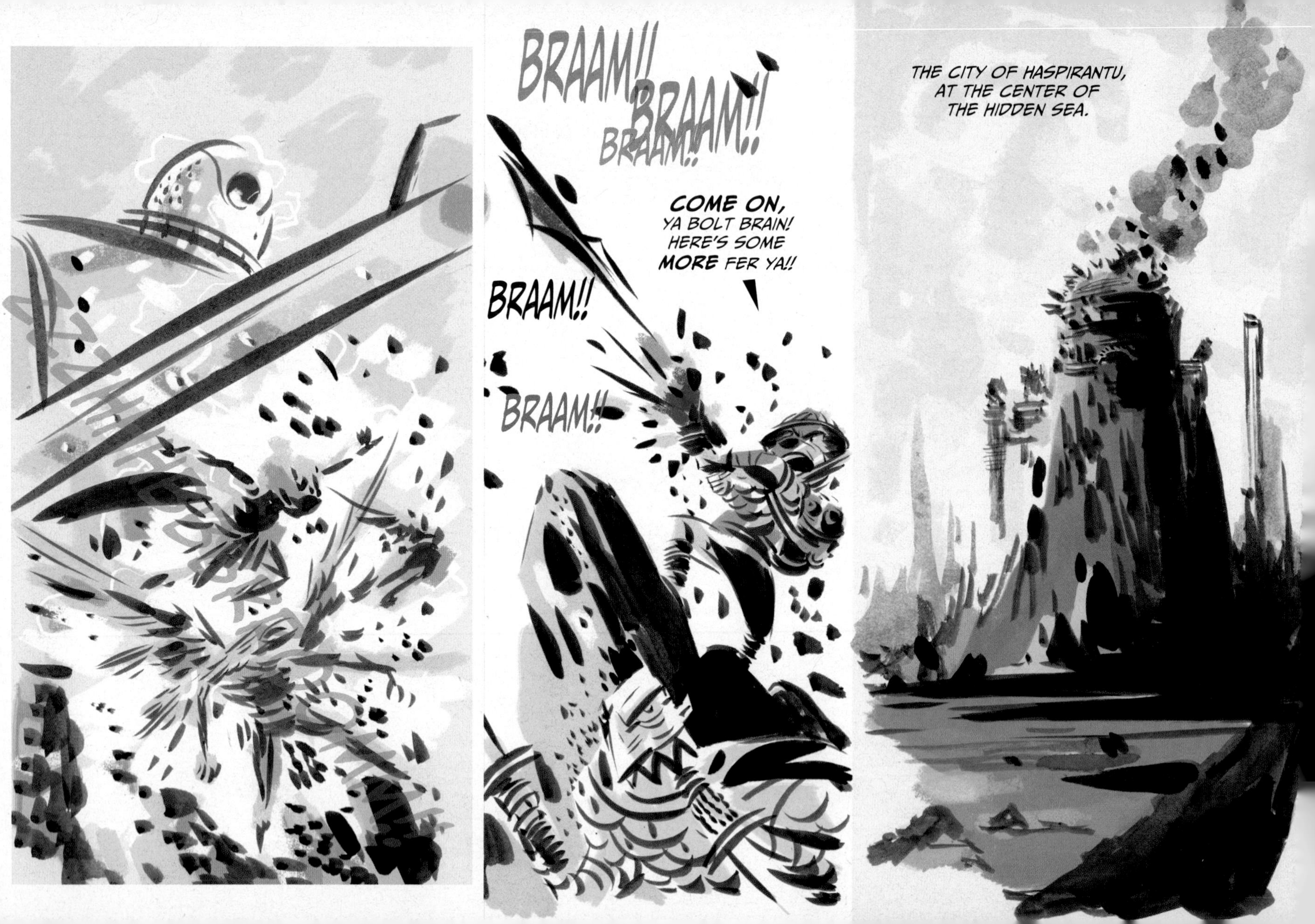

BRAAM!!
BRAAM!!
BRAAM!!
BRAAM!!
BRAAM!!
COME ON, YA BOLT BRAIN! HERE'S SOME MORE FER YA!!
THE CITY OF HASPIRANTU, AT THE CENTER OF THE HIDDEN SEA.

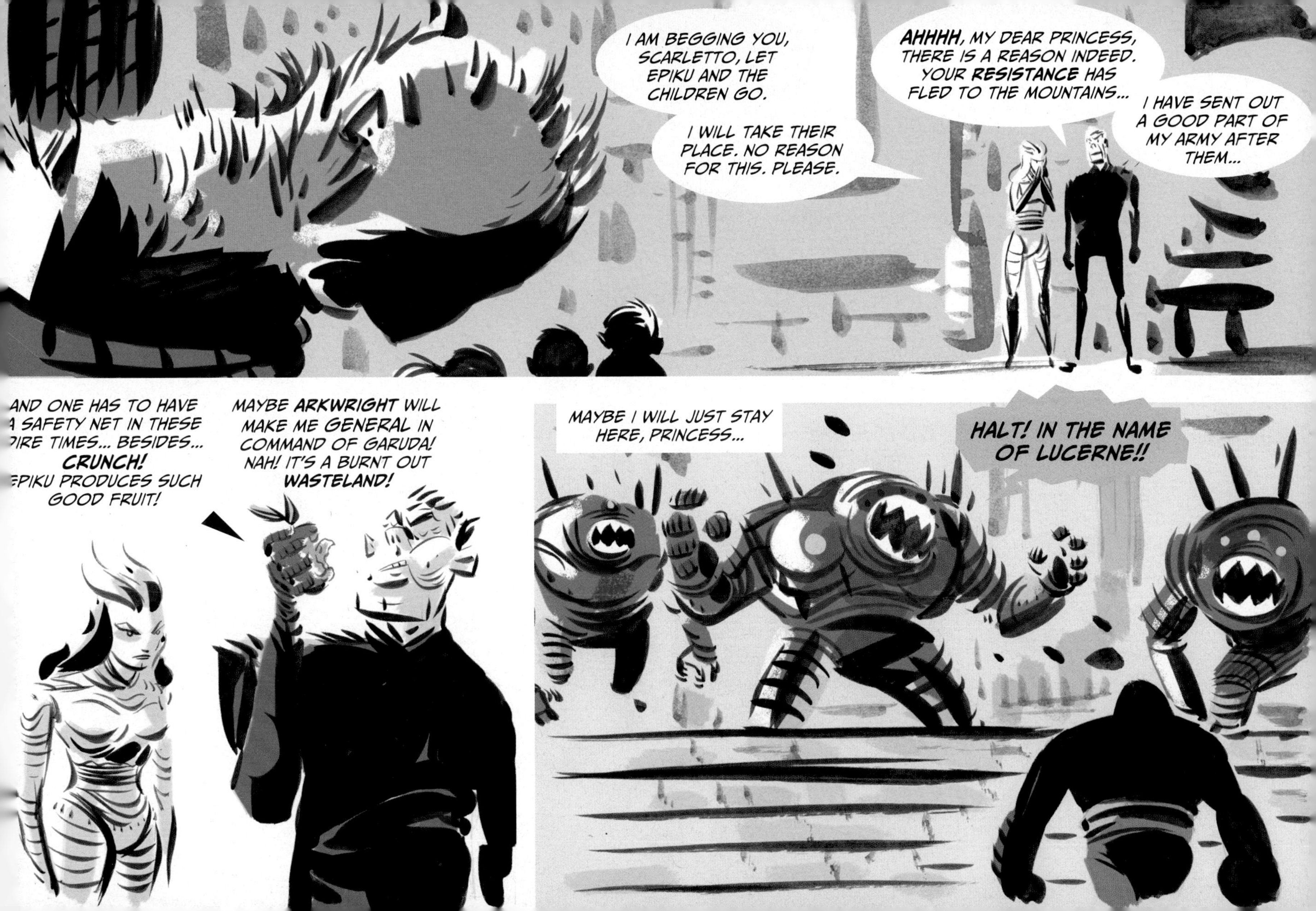

I AM BEGGING YOU, SCARLETTO, LET EPIKU AND THE CHILDREN GO.
I WILL TAKE THEIR PLACE. NO REASON FOR THIS. PLEASE.
AHHHH, MY DEAR PRINCESS, THERE IS A REASON INDEED. YOUR RESISTANCE HAS FLED TO THE MOUNTAINS...
I HAVE SENT OUT A GOOD PART OF MY ARMY AFTER THEM...
AND ONE HAS TO HAVE A SAFETY NET IN THESE DIRE TIMES... BESIDES... CRUNCH! EPIKU PRODUCES SUCH GOOD FRUIT!
MAYBE ARKWRIGHT WILL MAKE ME GENERAL IN COMMAND OF GARUDA! NAH! IT'S A BURNT OUT WASTELAND!
MAYBE I WILL JUST STAY HERE, PRINCESS...
HALT! IN THE NAME OF LUCERNE!!

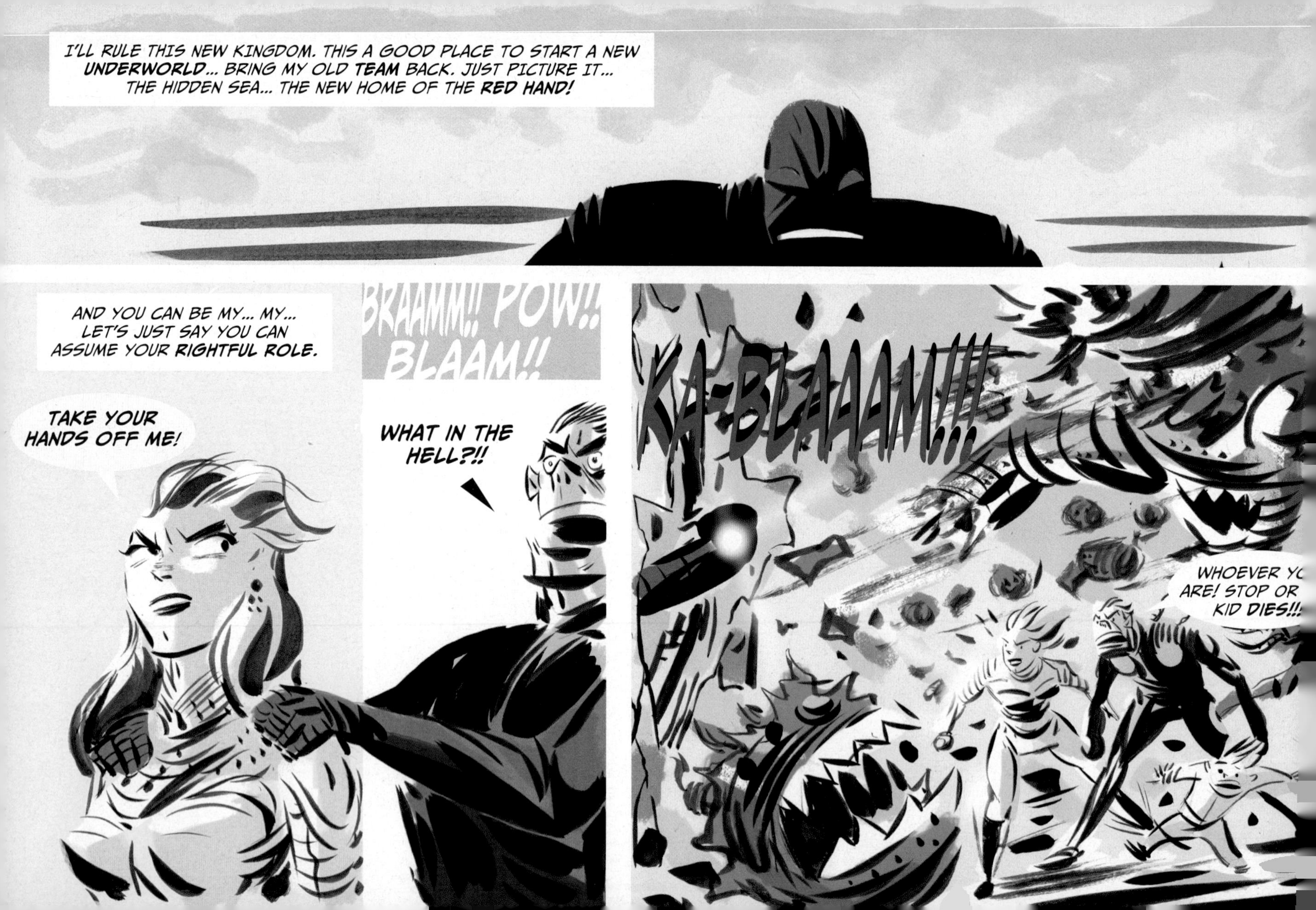
I'LL RULE THIS NEW KINGDOM. THIS A GOOD PLACE TO START A NEW UNDERWORLD... BRING MY OLD TEAM BACK. JUST PICTURE IT... THE HIDDEN SEA... THE NEW HOME OF THE RED HAND!
AND YOU CAN BE MY... MY... LET'S JUST SAY YOU CAN ASSUME YOUR RIGHTFUL ROLE.
TAKE YOUR HANDS OFF ME!
BRAAMM!! POW!! BLAAM!!
WHAT IN THE HELL?!!
KA-BLAAAM!!!
WHOEVER YO ARE! STOP OR KID DIES!!!

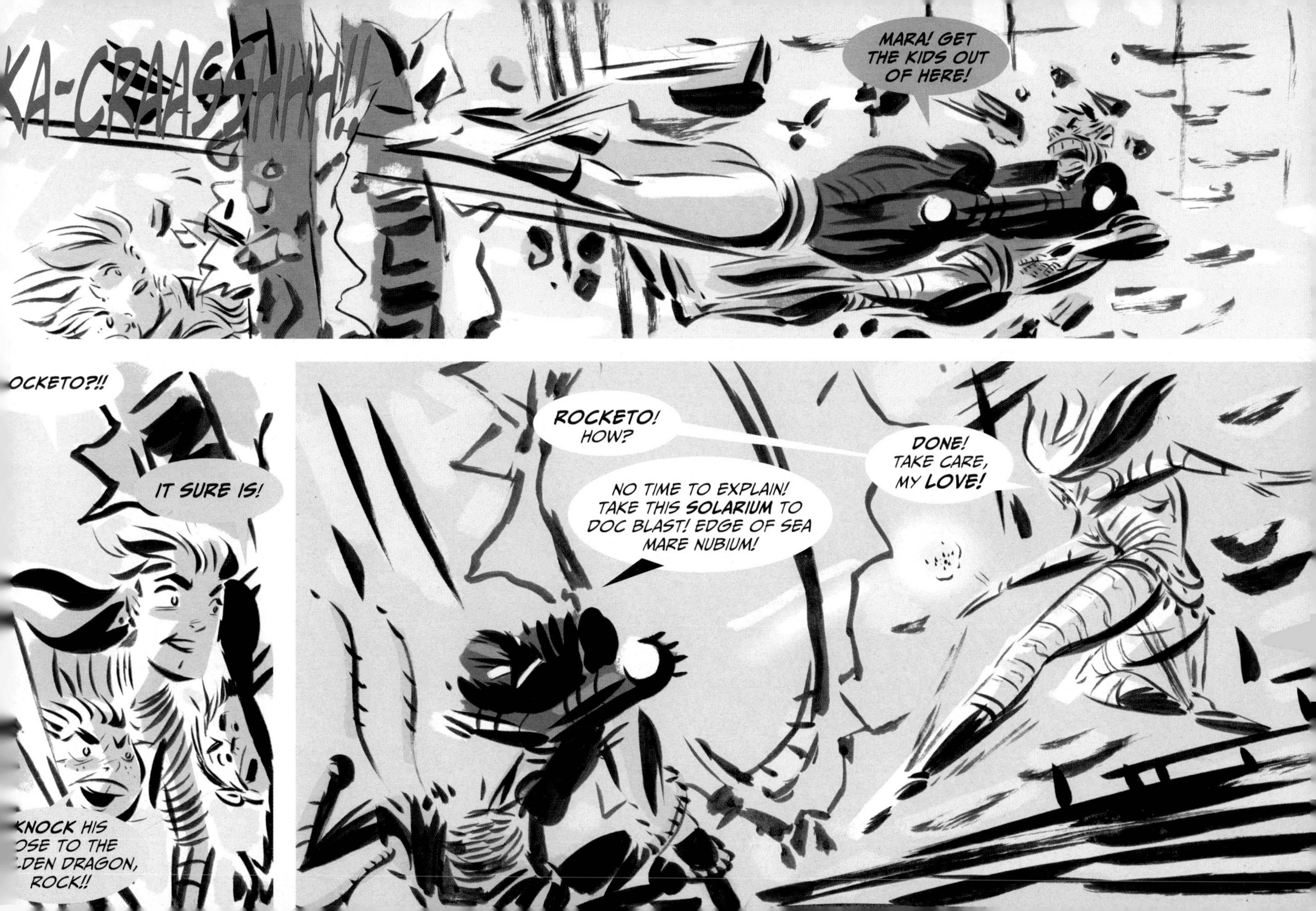
KA-CRAASSHHH!!
MARA! GET THE KIDS OUT OF HERE!
OCKETO?!!
IT SURE IS!
KNOCK HIS
OSE TO THE
-DEN DRAGON,
ROCK!!
ROCKETO! HOW?
NO TIME TO EXPLAIN! TAKE THIS SOLARIUM TO DOC BLAST! EDGE OF SEA MARE NUBIUM!
DONE! TAKE CARE, MY LOVE!

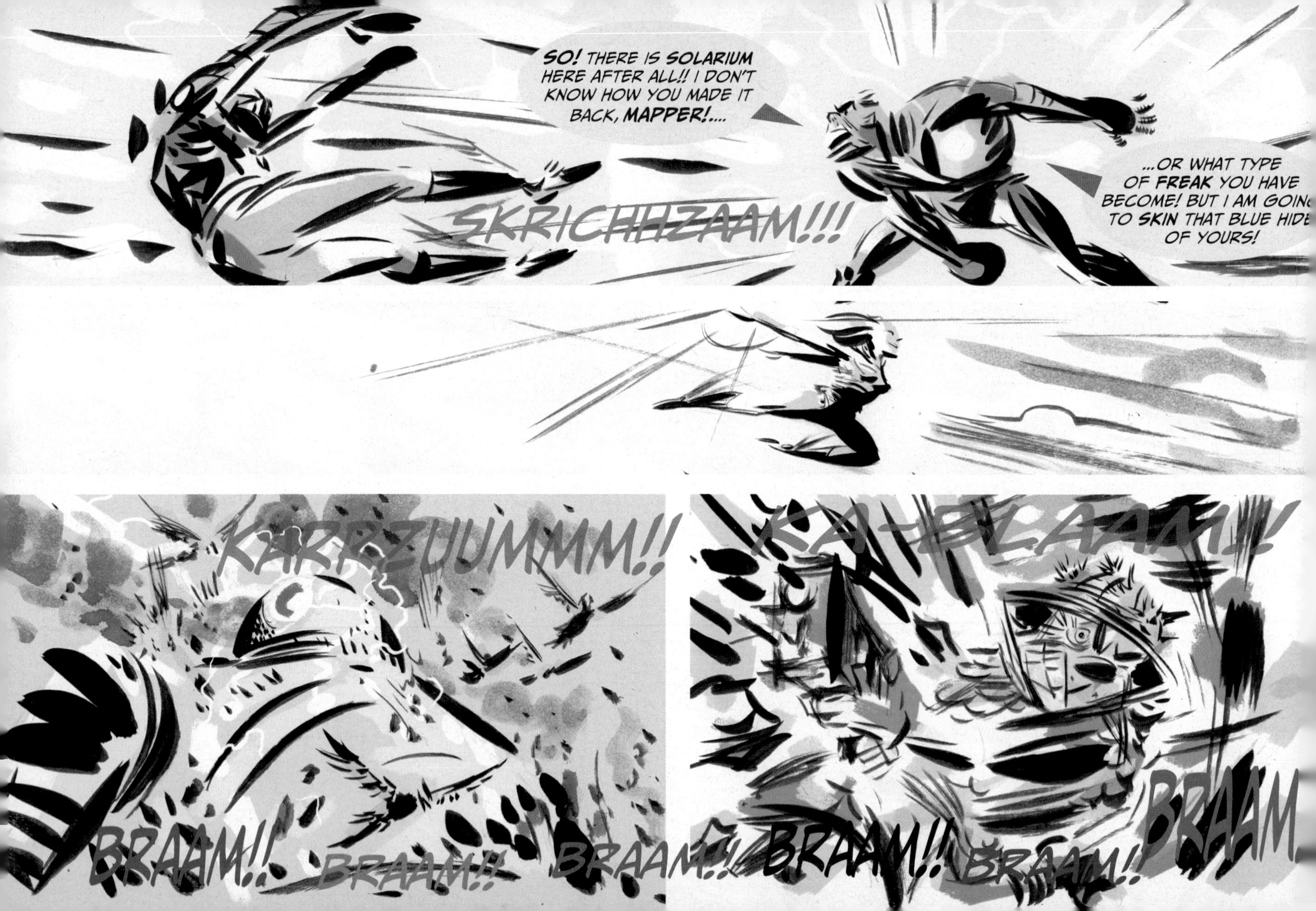

SO! THERE IS SOLARIUM HERE AFTER ALL!! I DON'T KNOW HOW YOU MADE IT BACK, MAPPER!....
SKRICHHZAAM!!!
...OR WHAT TYPE OF FREAK YOU HAVE BECOME! BUT I AM GOIN TO SKIN THAT BLUE HIDE OF YOURS!
KARRZUUMMMM!!
KA-BLAAM!!
BRAAM!!
BRAAM!!
BRAAM!!
BRAAM!!
BRAAM!!
BRAAM

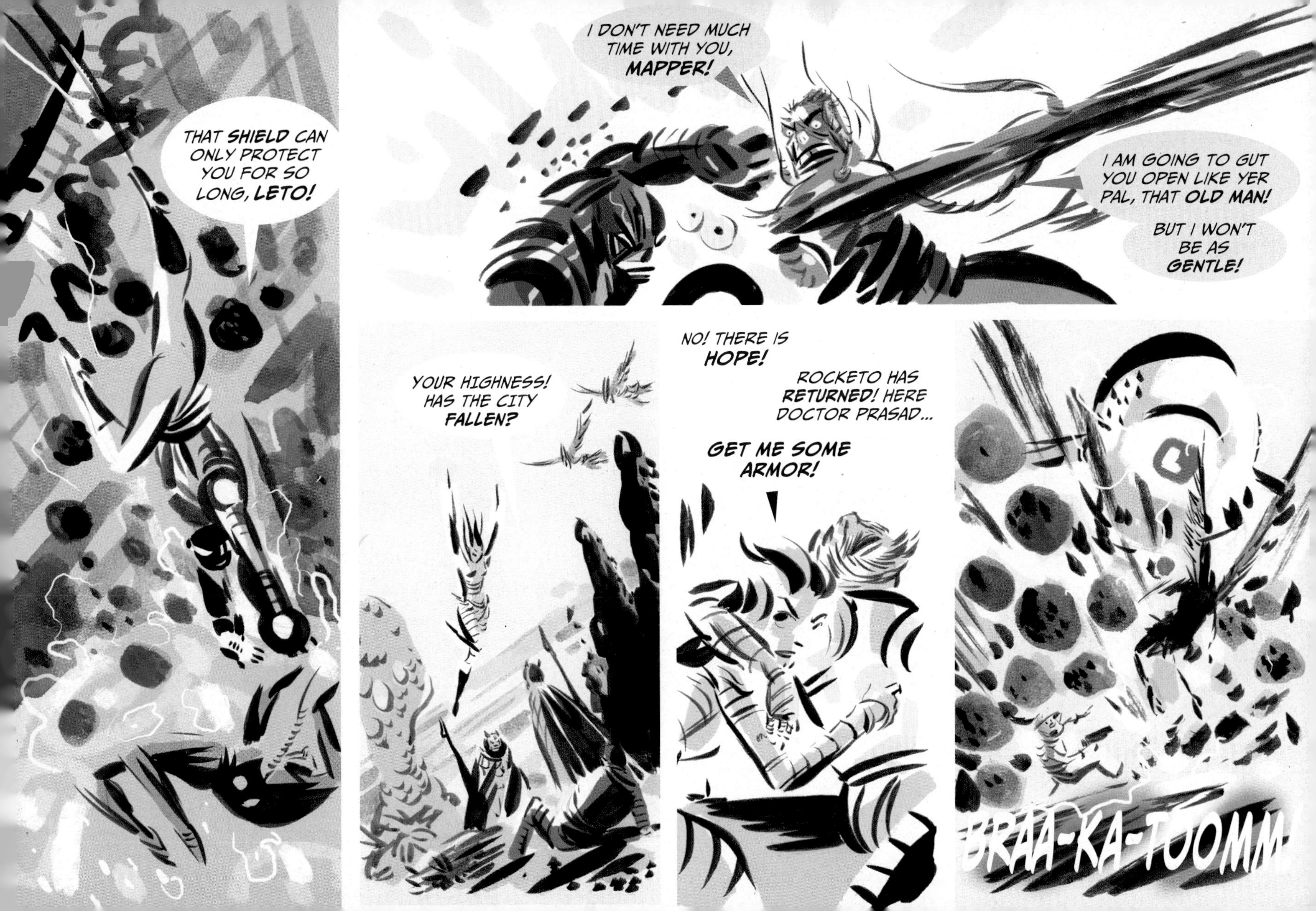
THAT **SHIELD** CAN ONLY PROTECT YOU FOR SO LONG, **LETO!**
I DON'T NEED MUCH TIME WITH YOU, **MAPPER!**
I AM GOING TO GUT YOU OPEN LIKE YER PAL, THAT **OLD MAN!**
BUT I WON'T BE AS **GENTLE!**
YOUR HIGHNESS! HAS THE CITY **FALLEN?**
NO! THERE IS **HOPE!**
ROCKETO HAS **RETURNED!** HERE DOCTOR PRASAD...
GET ME SOME ARMOR!
BRAA-KA-TOOMM

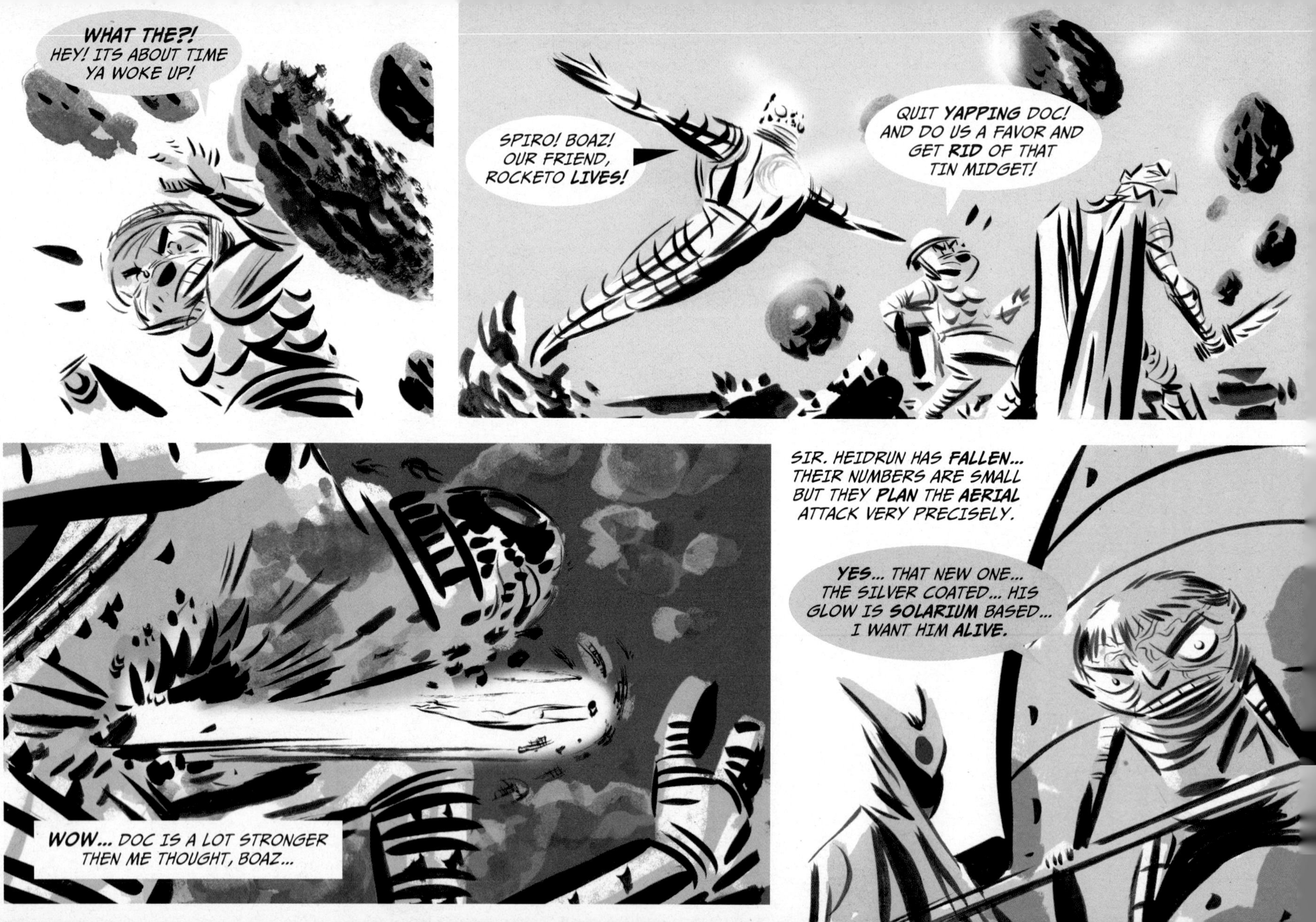
WHAT THE?! HEY! ITS ABOUT TIME YA WOKE UP!
SPIRO! BOAZ! OUR FRIEND, ROCKETO LIVES!
QUIT YAPPING DOC! AND DO US A FAVOR AND GET RID OF THAT TIN MIDGET!
WOW... DOC IS A LOT STRONGER THEN ME THOUGHT, BOAZ...
SIR. HEIDRUN HAS FALLEN... THEIR NUMBERS ARE SMALL BUT THEY PLAN THE AERIAL ATTACK VERY PRECISELY.
YES... THAT NEW ONE... THE SILVER COATED... HIS GLOW IS SOLARIUM BASED... I WANT HIM ALIVE.

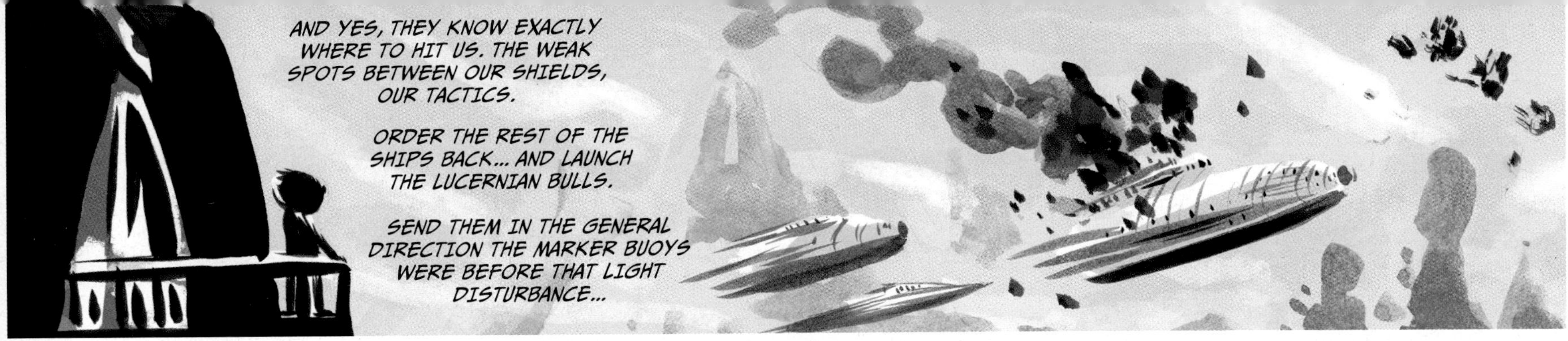
AND YES, THEY KNOW EXACTLY WHERE TO HIT US. THE WEAK SPOTS BETWEEN OUR SHIELDS, OUR TACTICS.
ORDER THE REST OF THE SHIPS BACK... AND LAUNCH THE LUCERNIAN BULLS.
SEND THEM IN THE GENERAL DIRECTION THE MARKER BUOYS WERE BEFORE THAT LIGHT DISTURBANCE...

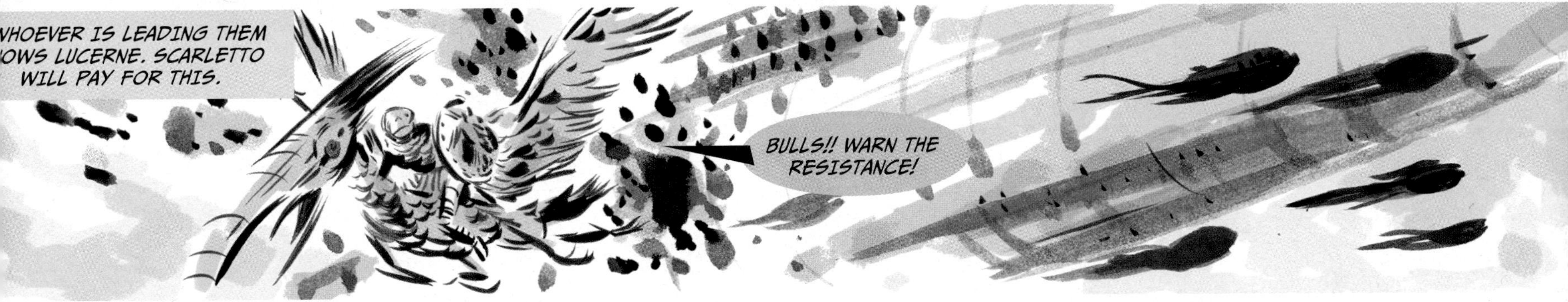
WHOEVER IS LEADING THEM
OWS LUCERNE. SCARLETTO
WILL PAY FOR THIS.
BULLS!! WARN THE RESISTANCE!

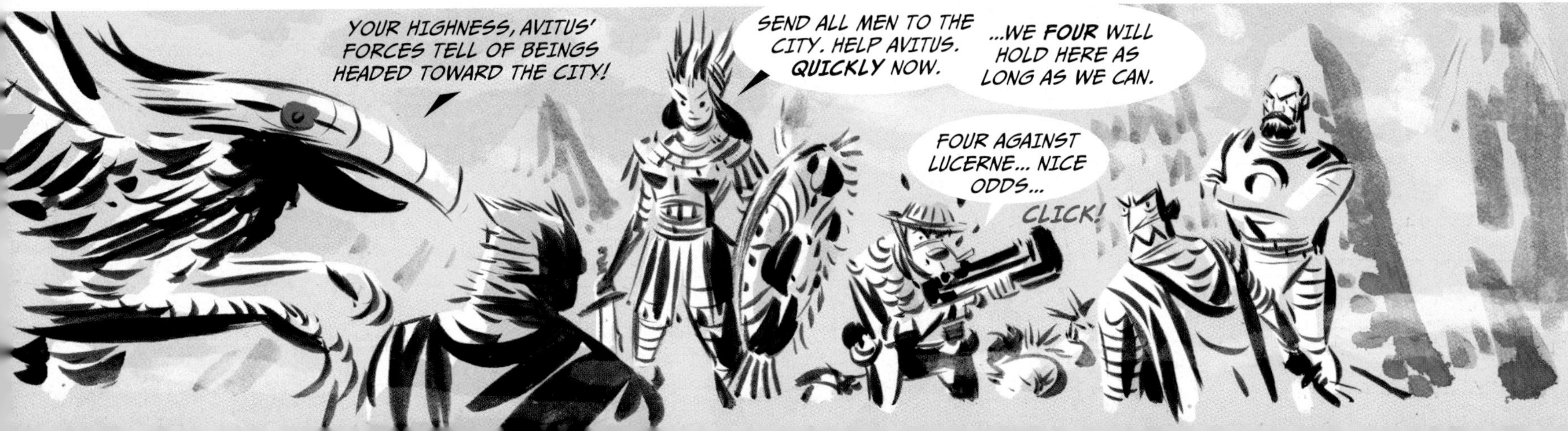
YOUR HIGHNESS, AVITUS' FORCES TELL OF BEINGS HEADED TOWARD THE CITY!
SEND ALL MEN TO THE CITY. HELP AVITUS. QUICKLY NOW.
...WE FOUR WILL HOLD HERE AS LONG AS WE CAN.
FOUR AGAINST LUCERNE... NICE ODDS...
CLICK!

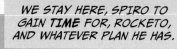
WE STAY HERE, SPIRO TO GAIN **TIME** FOR, ROCKETO, AND WHATEVER PLAN HE HAS.

LET US HOPE ROCK HAS A **PLAN**, YER HOLINESS...

... AND NOT LETTING HIS **HARD HEAD** GET IN THE WAY.

BLAAMMM!!

YOU FORGET, MAPPER, HOW QUICKLY I **ADAPT** ALSO!

FROM RODENT TO SWINE, LETO!

FUNNY, GARRISON! YER WHOLE LINE ENDS NOW! I'M GOING TO BURN YER BONES OUT OF THAT BLUE SKIN!

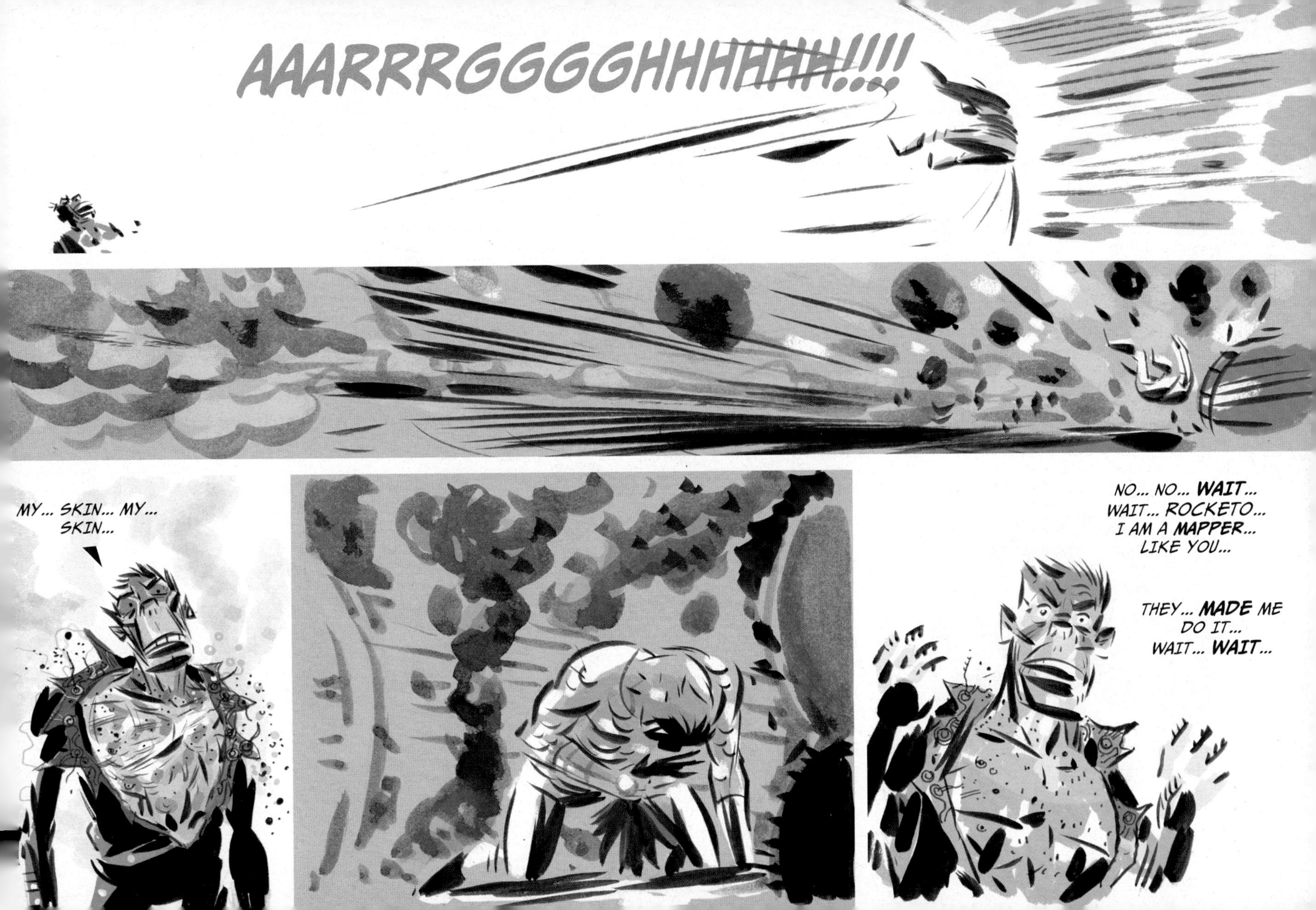
AAARRRGGGGHHHHHH!!!!
MY... SKIN... MY... SKIN...
NO... NO... **WAIT**... WAIT... ROCKETO... I AM A **MAPPER**... LIKE YOU...
THEY... **MADE** ME DO IT... WAIT... **WAIT**...

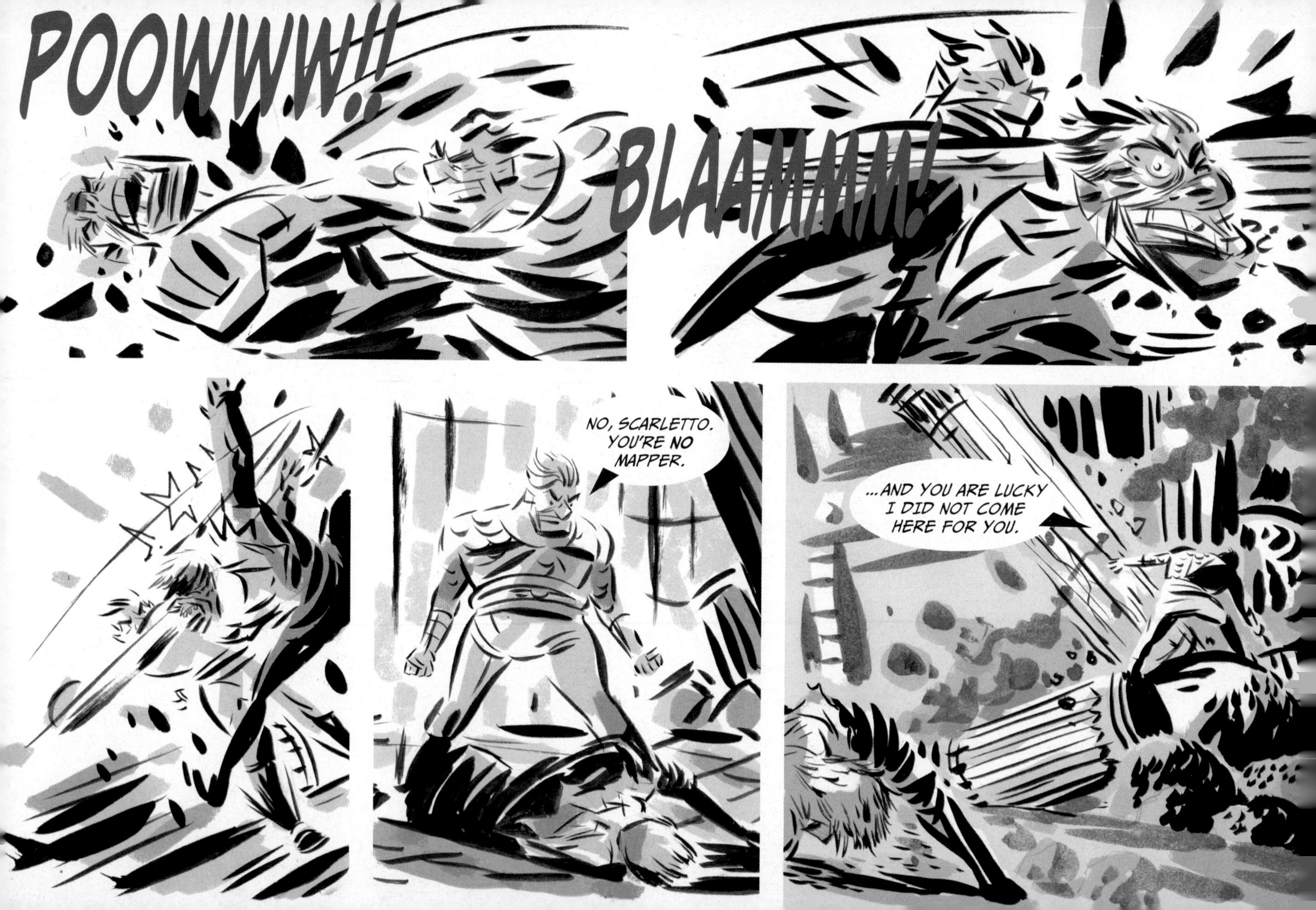
POOWWW!!
BLAAMMM!
NO, SCARLETTO. YOU'RE NO MAPPER.
...AND YOU ARE LUCKY I DID NOT COME HERE FOR YOU.

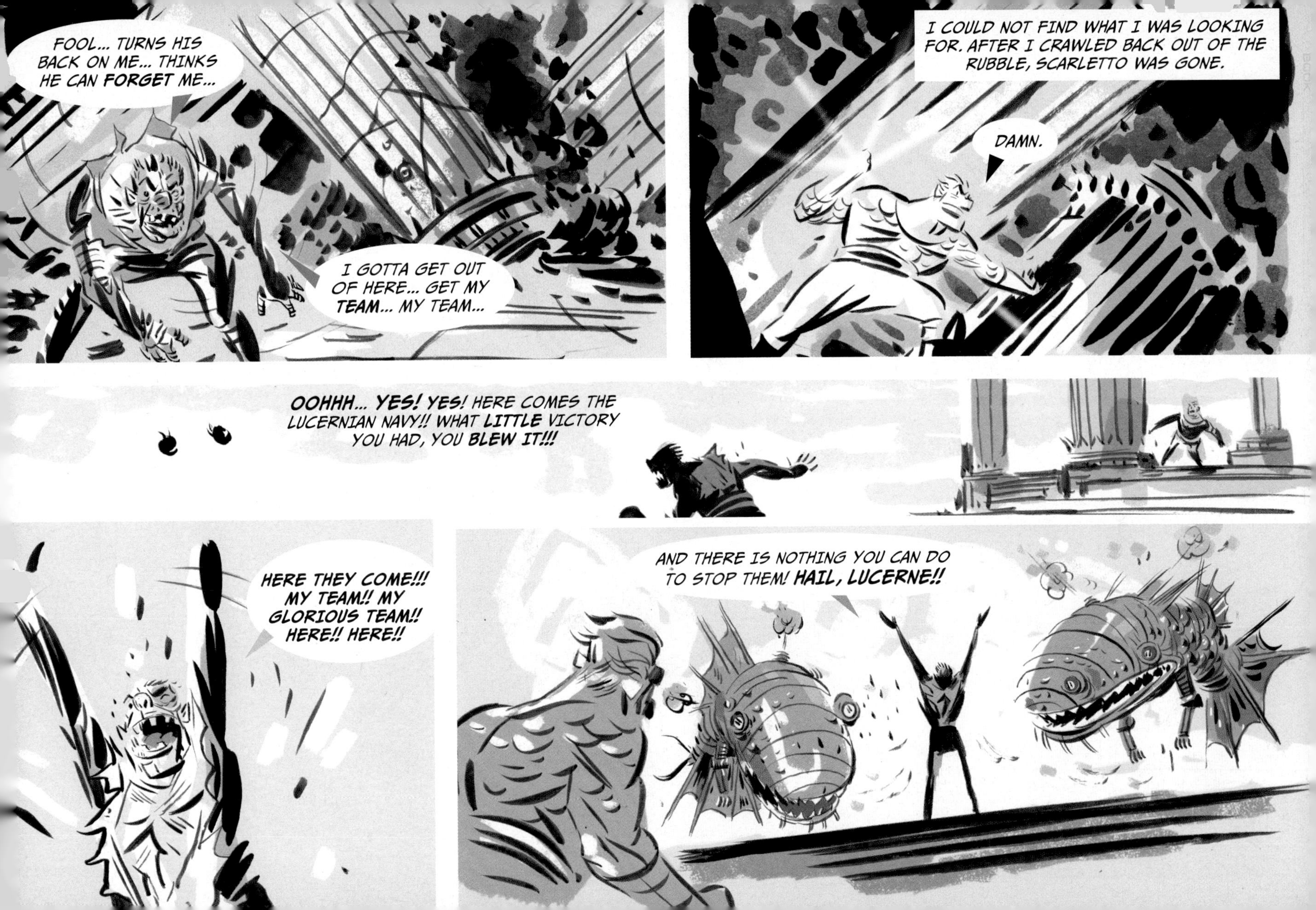
FOOL... TURNS HIS BACK ON ME... THINKS HE CAN FORGET ME...
I GOTTA GET OUT OF HERE... GET MY TEAM... MY TEAM...
I COULD NOT FIND WHAT I WAS LOOKING FOR. AFTER I CRAWLED BACK OUT OF THE RUBBLE, SCARLETTO WAS GONE.
DAMN.
OOHHH... YES! YES! HERE COMES THE LUCERNIAN NAVY!! WHAT LITTLE VICTORY YOU HAD, YOU BLEW IT!!!
HERE THEY COME!!! MY TEAM!! MY GLORIOUS TEAM!! HERE!! HERE!!
AND THERE IS NOTHING YOU CAN DO TO STOP THEM! HAIL, LUCERNE!!

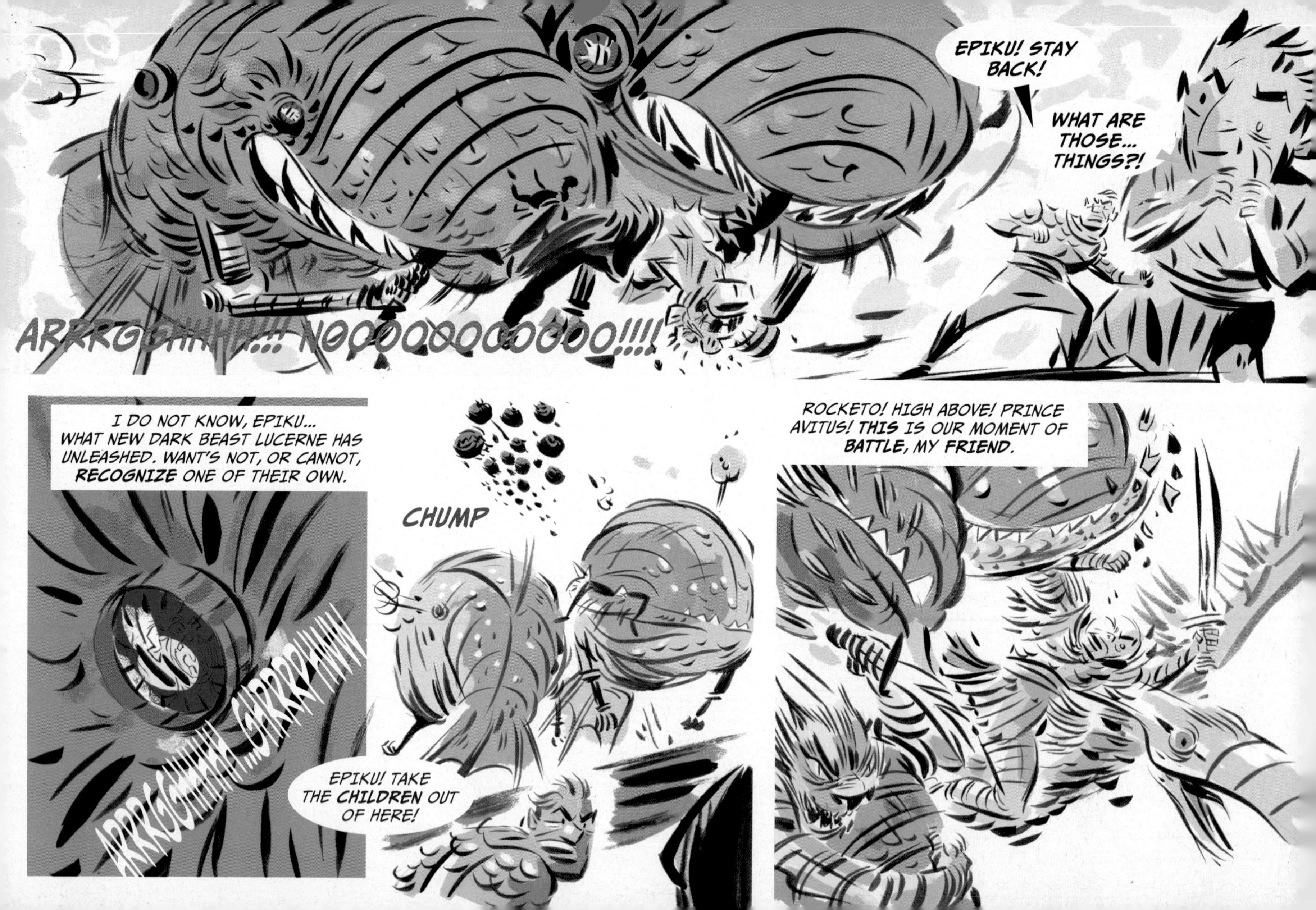
ARRRGGHHHH!!! NOOOOOOOOOOOO!!!!
EPIKU! STAY BACK!
WHAT ARE THOSE... THINGS?!
I DO NOT KNOW, EPIKU... WHAT NEW DARK BEAST LUCERNE HAS UNLEASHED. WANT'S NOT, OR CANNOT, RECOGNIZE ONE OF THEIR OWN.
CHUMP
EPIKU! TAKE THE CHILDREN OUT OF HERE!
ROCKETO! HIGH ABOVE! PRINCE AVITUS! THIS IS OUR MOMENT OF BATTLE, MY FRIEND.

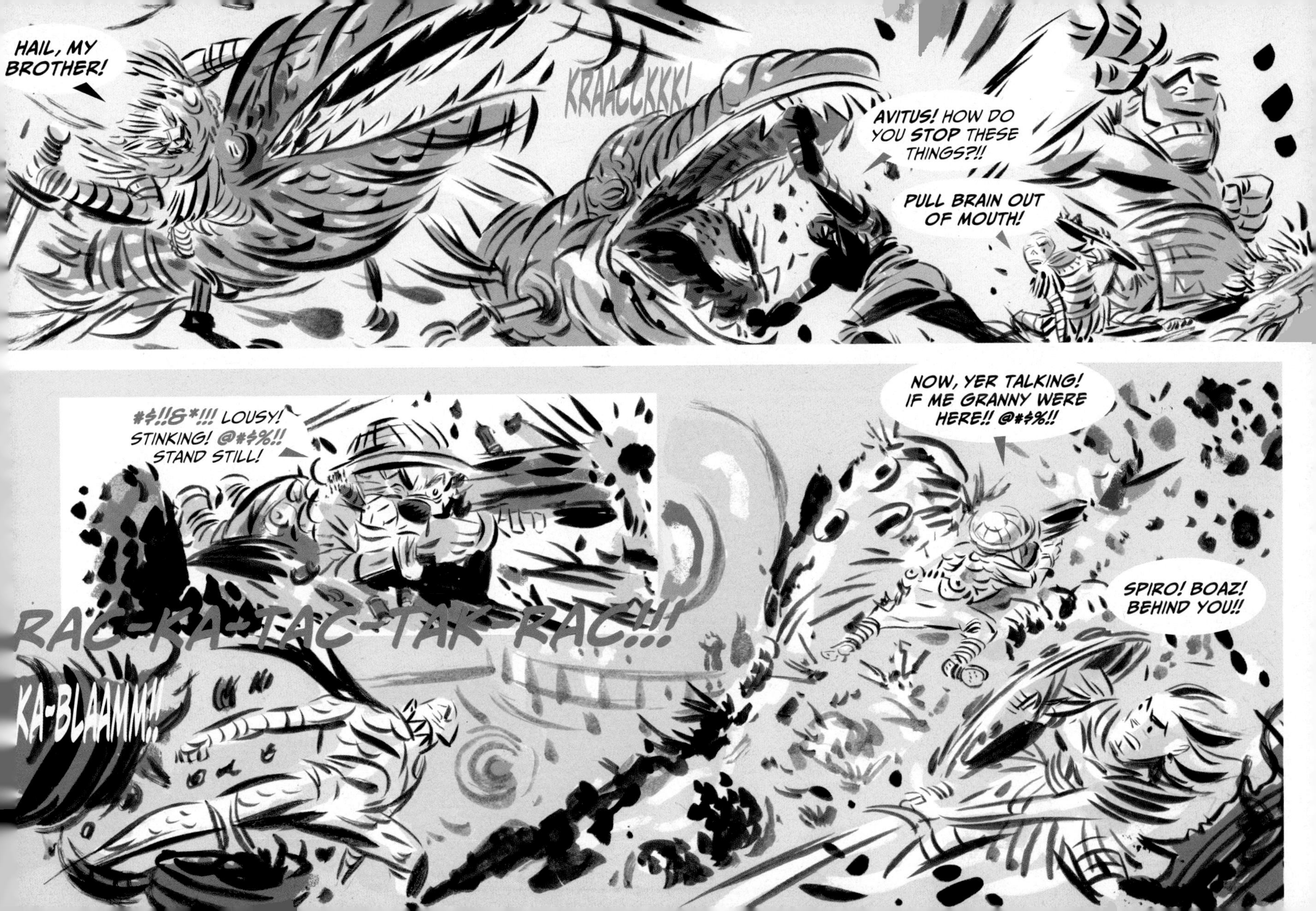
HAIL, MY BROTHER!
KRAACCKKK!
AVITUS! HOW DO YOU STOP THESE THINGS?!!
PULL BRAIN OUT OF MOUTH!
#$!!&*!!! LOUSY! STINKING! @#$%!! STAND STILL!
NOW, YER TALKING! IF ME GRANNY WERE HERE!! @#$%!!
RAC-KA-TAC-TAK-RAC!!!
KA-BLAAMM!!
SPIRO! BOAZ! BEHIND YOU!!

LOOK...OUT.

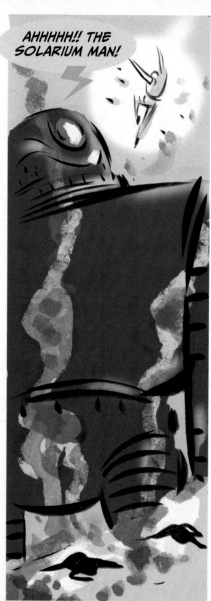

AHHHHH!! THE SOLARIUM MAN!

HOW MUCH TIME BEFORE YOUR SHIELD DIES UNDER A BARRAGE OF LUCERNE'S MIGHTIEST GUNS?!

THE WAY IS CLEARED NOW. MOVE FORWARD THE ARMADA.

EVEN THOUGH THEIR NUMBERS ARE ENDLESS, WE HOLD THIS LINE, MY FRIENDS!

EPIKU! WHE IS ROCKETO

ROCKETO HAS RUN!

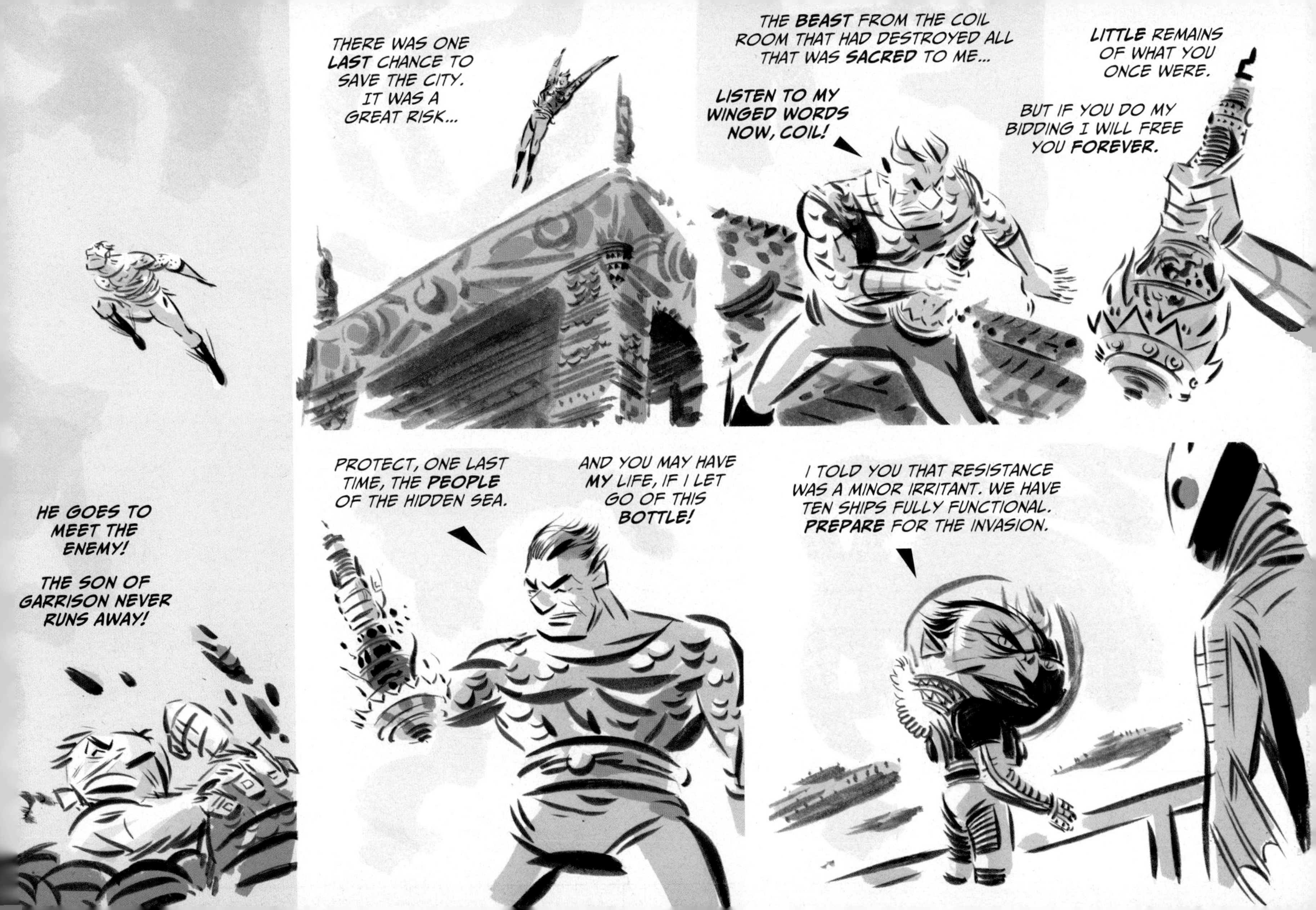
HE GOES TO MEET THE ENEMY!
THE SON OF GARRISON NEVER RUNS AWAY!
THERE WAS ONE LAST CHANCE TO SAVE THE CITY. IT WAS A GREAT RISK...
THE BEAST FROM THE COIL ROOM THAT HAD DESTROYED ALL THAT WAS SACRED TO ME...
LISTEN TO MY WINGED WORDS NOW, COIL!
LITTLE REMAINS OF WHAT YOU ONCE WERE.
BUT IF YOU DO MY BIDDING I WILL FREE YOU FOREVER.
PROTECT, ONE LAST TIME, THE PEOPLE OF THE HIDDEN SEA.
AND YOU MAY HAVE MY LIFE, IF I LET GO OF THIS BOTTLE!
I TOLD YOU THAT RESISTANCE WAS A MINOR IRRITANT. WE HAVE TEN SHIPS FULLY FUNCTIONAL. PREPARE FOR THE INVASION.

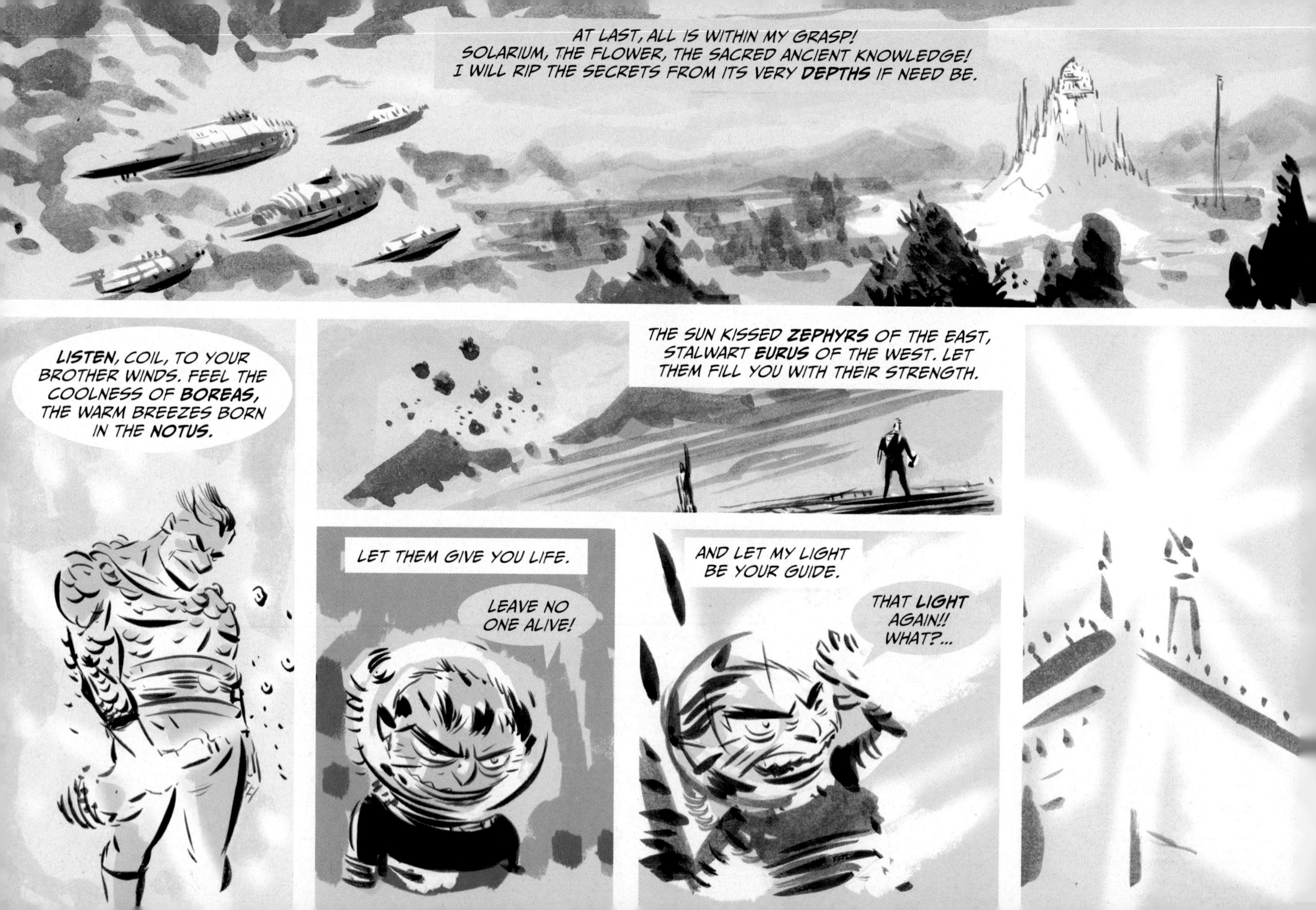
AT LAST, ALL IS WITHIN MY GRASP! SOLARIUM, THE FLOWER, THE SACRED ANCIENT KNOWLEDGE! I WILL RIP THE SECRETS FROM ITS VERY **DEPTHS** IF NEED BE.
LISTEN, COIL, TO YOUR BROTHER WINDS. FEEL THE COOLNESS OF **BOREAS**, THE WARM BREEZES BORN IN THE **NOTUS**.
THE SUN KISSED **ZEPHYRS** OF THE EAST, STALWART **EURUS** OF THE WEST. LET THEM FILL YOU WITH THEIR STRENGTH.
LET THEM GIVE YOU LIFE.
LEAVE NO ONE ALIVE!
AND LET MY LIGHT BE YOUR GUIDE.
THAT **LIGHT** AGAIN!! WHAT?...

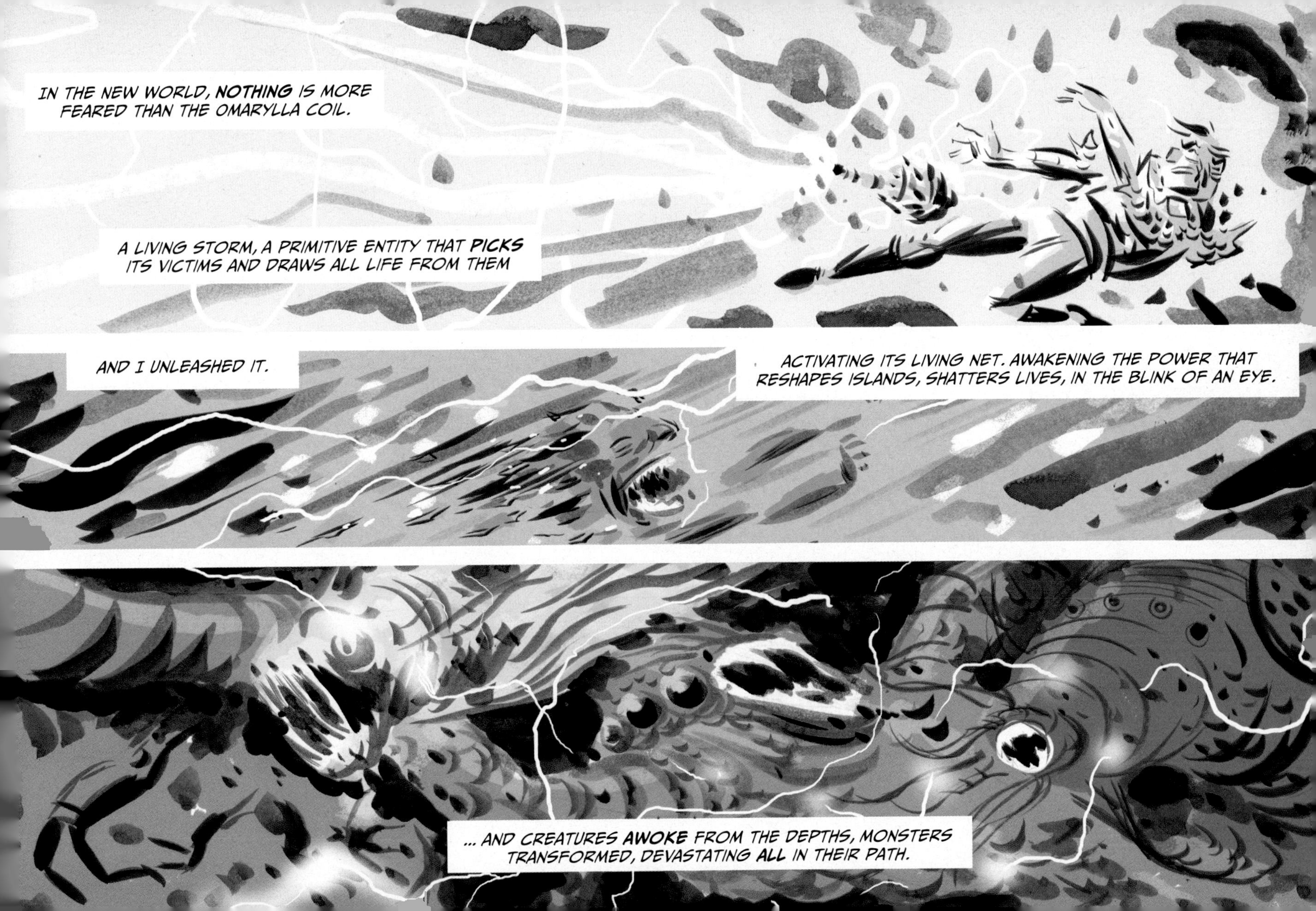
IN THE NEW WORLD, NOTHING IS MORE FEARED THAN THE OMARYLLA COIL.
A LIVING STORM, A PRIMITIVE ENTITY THAT PICKS ITS VICTIMS AND DRAWS ALL LIFE FROM THEM
AND I UNLEASHED IT.
ACTIVATING ITS LIVING NET. AWAKENING THE POWER THAT RESHAPES ISLANDS, SHATTERS LIVES, IN THE BLINK OF AN EYE.
... AND CREATURES AWOKE FROM THE DEPTHS, MONSTERS TRANSFORMED, DEVASTATING ALL IN THEIR PATH.

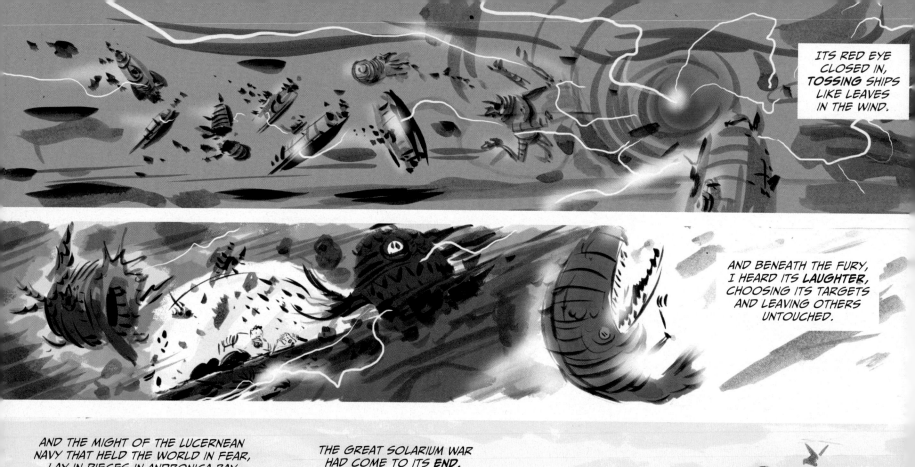

ITS RED EYE CLOSED IN, **TOSSING SHIPS** LIKE LEAVES IN THE WIND.

AND BENEATH THE FURY, I HEARD ITS **LAUGHTER,** CHOOSING ITS TARGETS AND LEAVING OTHERS UNTOUCHED.

AND THE MIGHT OF THE LUCERNEAN NAVY THAT HELD THE WORLD IN FEAR, LAY IN PIECES IN ANDRONICA BAY OFF THE SHORE OF VENEDICTO.

THE GREAT SOLARIUM WAR HAD COME TO ITS **END.**

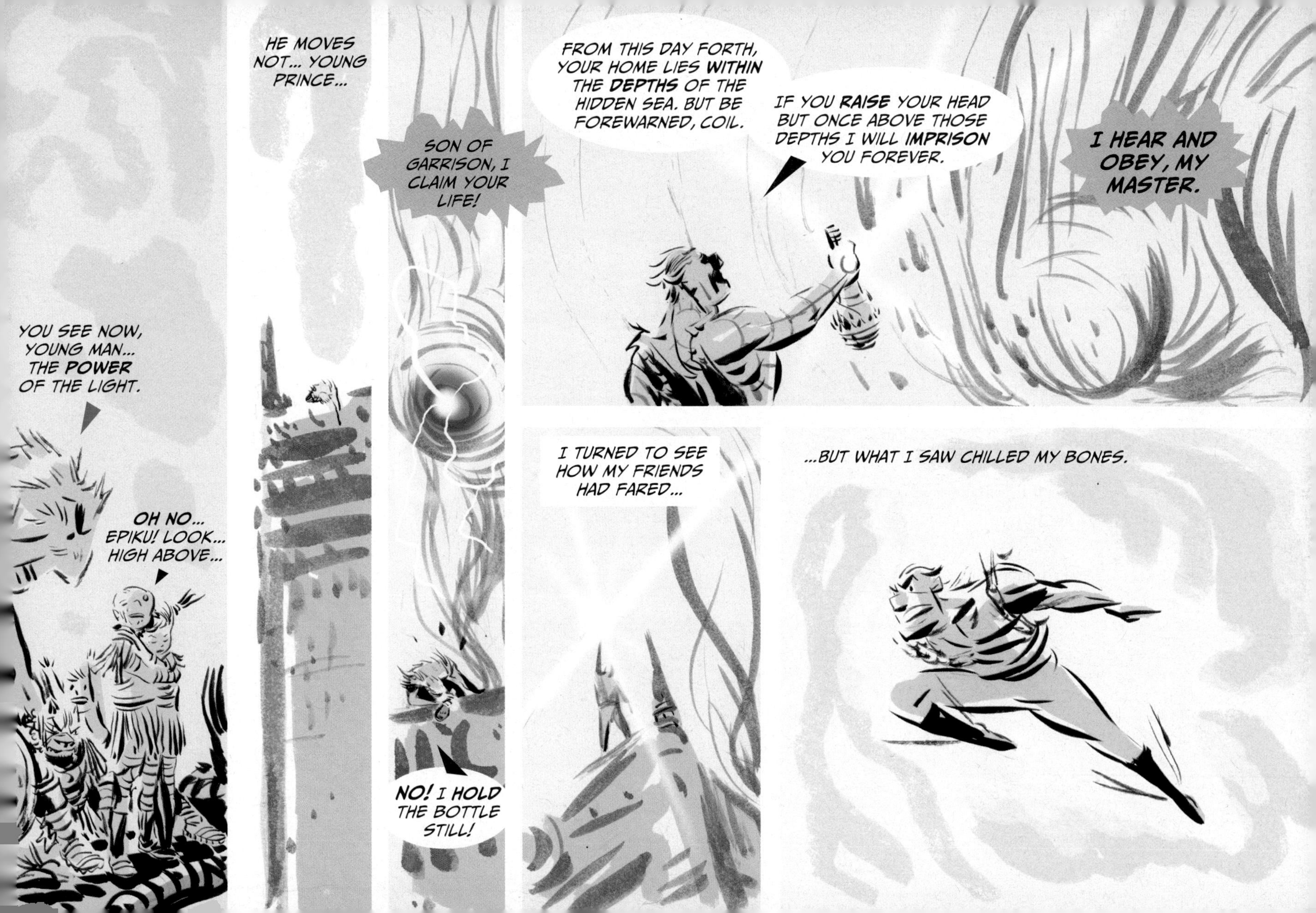

YOU SEE NOW, YOUNG MAN... THE POWER OF THE LIGHT.
OH NO... EPIKU! LOOK... HIGH ABOVE...
HE MOVES NOT... YOUNG PRINCE...
SON OF GARRISON, I CLAIM YOUR LIFE!
NO! I HOLD THE BOTTLE STILL!
FROM THIS DAY FORTH, YOUR HOME LIES WITHIN THE DEPTHS OF THE HIDDEN SEA. BUT BE FOREWARNED, COIL.
IF YOU RAISE YOUR HEAD BUT ONCE ABOVE THOSE DEPTHS I WILL IMPRISON YOU FOREVER.
I HEAR AND OBEY, MY MASTER.
I TURNED TO SEE HOW MY FRIENDS HAD FARED...
...BUT WHAT I SAW CHILLED MY BONES.

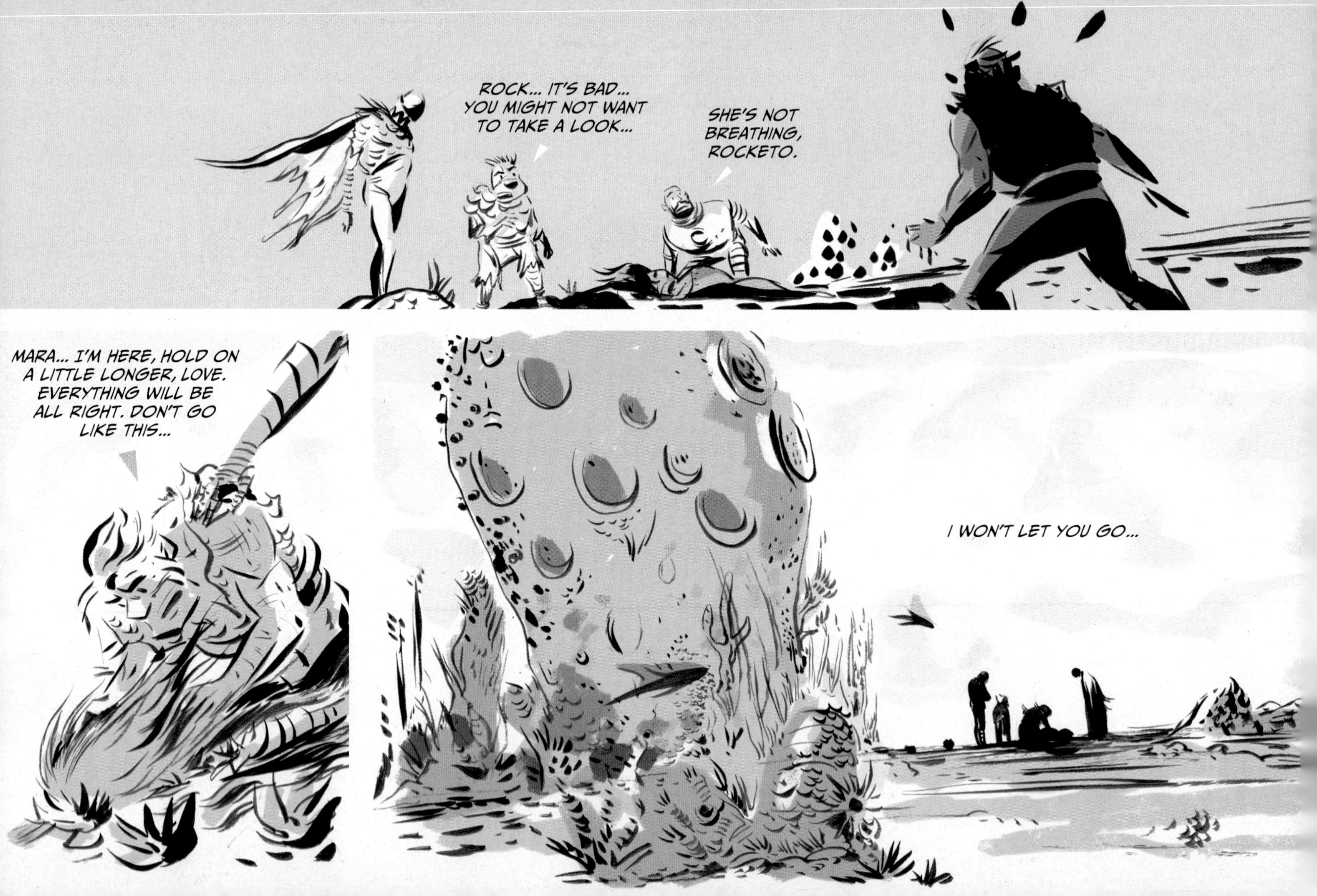
ROCK... IT'S BAD... YOU MIGHT NOT WANT TO TAKE A LOOK...
SHE'S NOT BREATHING, ROCKETO.
MARA... I'M HERE, HOLD ON A LITTLE LONGER, LOVE. EVERYTHING WILL BE ALL RIGHT. DON'T GO LIKE THIS...
I WON'T LET YOU GO...

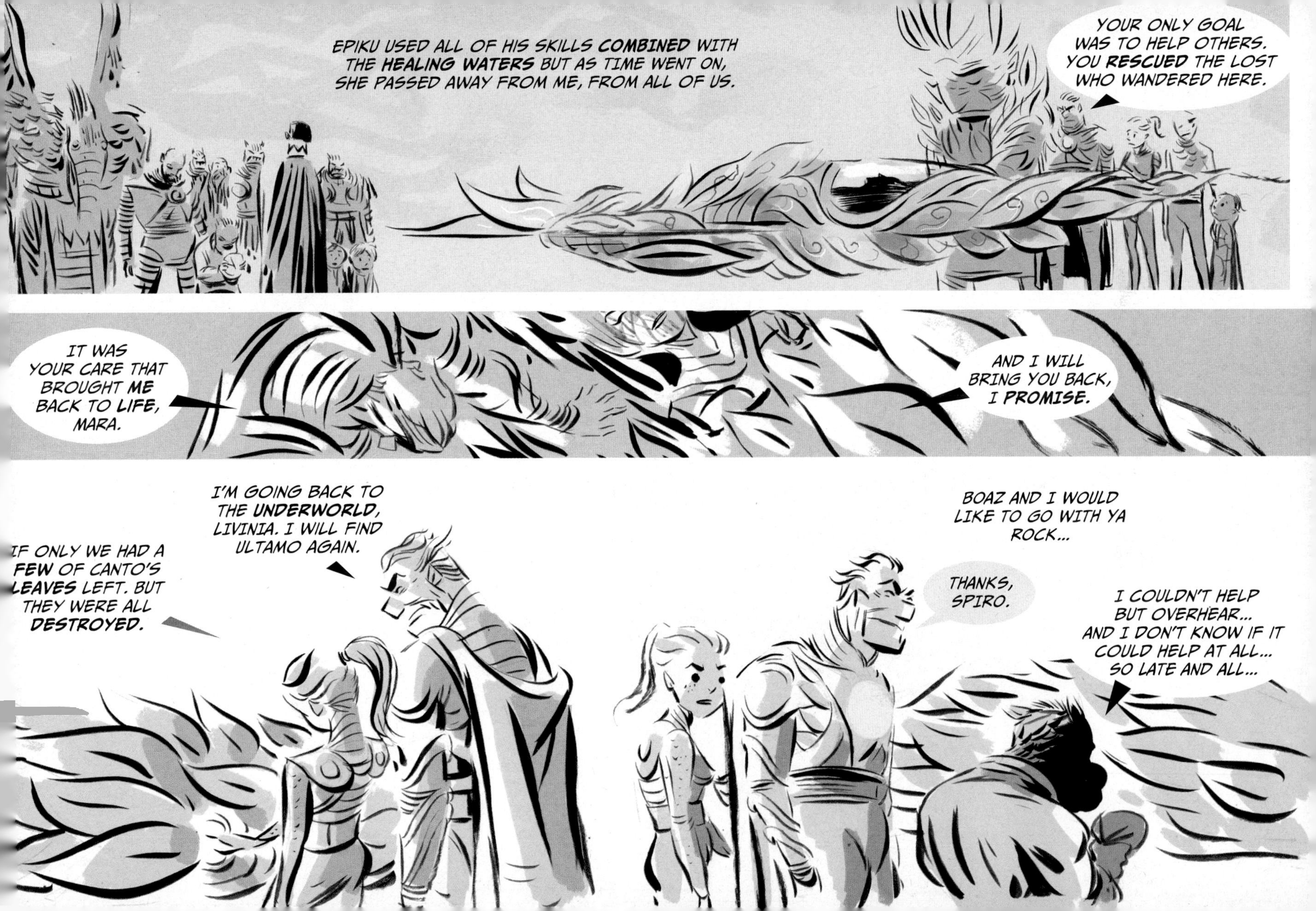
EPIKU USED ALL OF HIS SKILLS COMBINED WITH THE HEALING WATERS BUT AS TIME WENT ON, SHE PASSED AWAY FROM ME, FROM ALL OF US.
YOUR ONLY GOAL WAS TO HELP OTHERS. YOU RESCUED THE LOST WHO WANDERED HERE.
IT WAS YOUR CARE THAT BROUGHT ME BACK TO LIFE, MARA.
AND I WILL BRING YOU BACK, I PROMISE.
IF ONLY WE HAD A FEW OF CANTO'S LEAVES LEFT. BUT THEY WERE ALL DESTROYED.
I'M GOING BACK TO THE UNDERWORLD, LIVINIA. I WILL FIND ULTAMO AGAIN.
BOAZ AND I WOULD LIKE TO GO WITH YA ROCK...
THANKS, SPIRO.
I COULDN'T HELP BUT OVERHEAR... AND I DON'T KNOW IF IT COULD HELP AT ALL... SO LATE AND ALL...

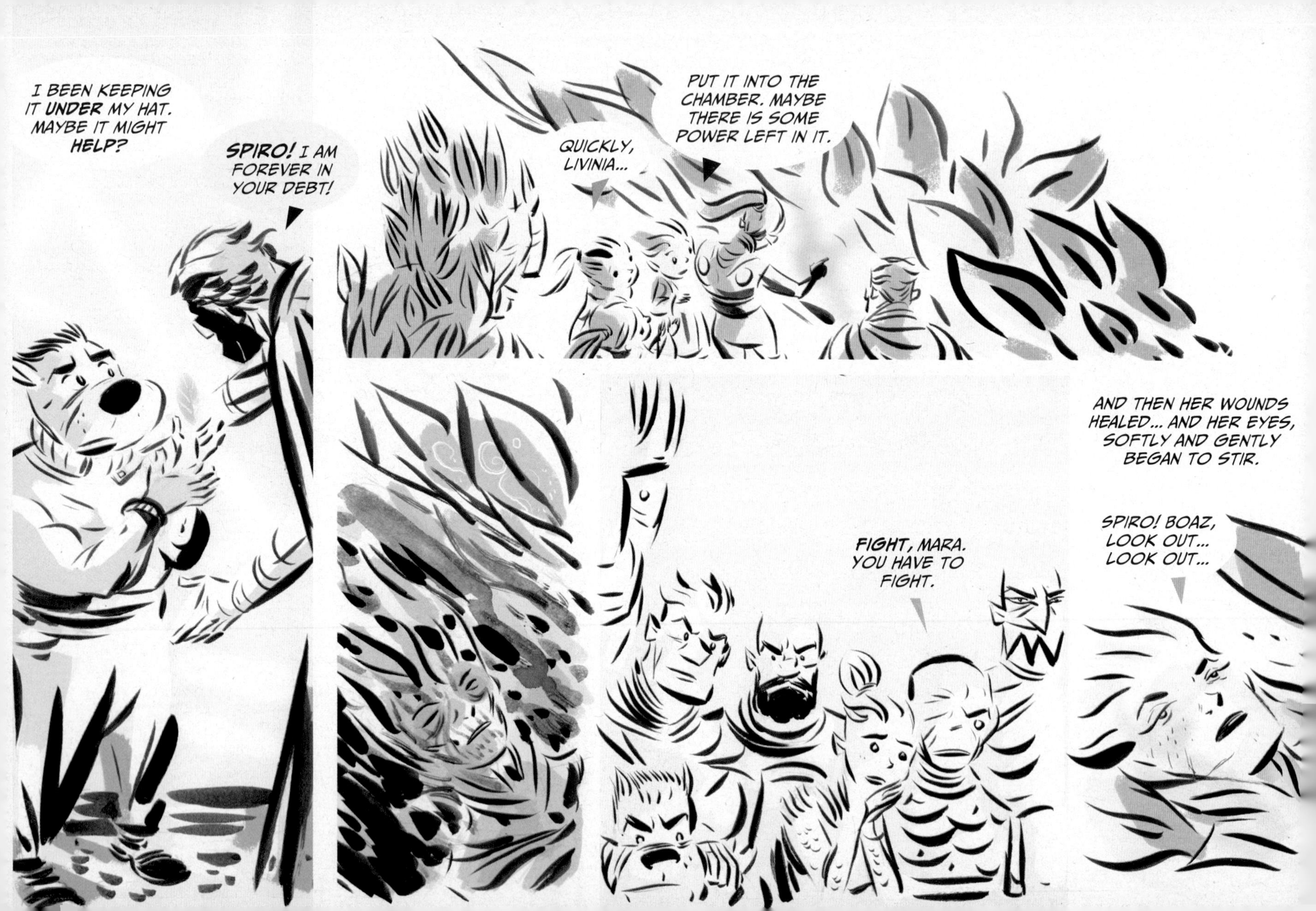
I BEEN KEEPING IT **UNDER** MY HAT. MAYBE IT MIGHT **HELP?**
SPIRO! I AM FOREVER IN YOUR DEBT!
QUICKLY, LIVINIA...
PUT IT INTO THE CHAMBER. MAYBE THERE IS SOME POWER LEFT IN IT.
FIGHT, MARA. YOU HAVE TO FIGHT.
AND THEN HER WOUNDS HEALED... AND HER EYES, SOFTLY AND GENTLY BEGAN TO STIR.
SPIRO! BOAZ, LOOK OUT... LOOK OUT...

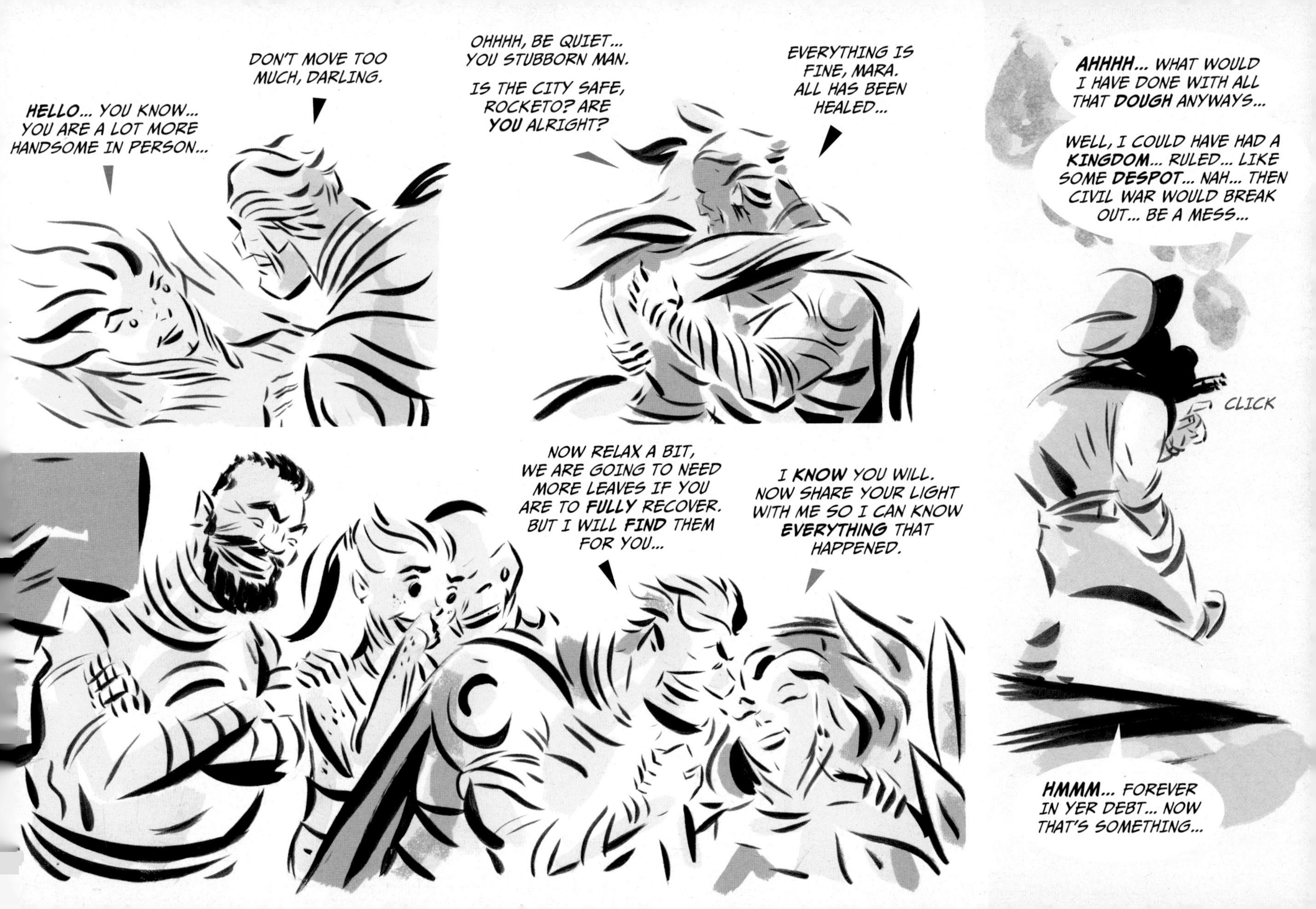
HELLO... YOU KNOW... YOU ARE A LOT MORE HANDSOME IN PERSON...
DON'T MOVE TOO MUCH, DARLING.
OHHHH, BE QUIET... YOU STUBBORN MAN.
IS THE CITY SAFE, ROCKETO? ARE YOU ALRIGHT?
EVERYTHING IS FINE, MARA. ALL HAS BEEN HEALED...
NOW RELAX A BIT, WE ARE GOING TO NEED MORE LEAVES IF YOU ARE TO FULLY RECOVER. BUT I WILL FIND THEM FOR YOU...
I KNOW YOU WILL. NOW SHARE YOUR LIGHT WITH ME SO I CAN KNOW EVERYTHING THAT HAPPENED.
AHHHH... WHAT WOULD I HAVE DONE WITH ALL THAT DOUGH ANYWAYS...
WELL, I COULD HAVE HAD A KINGDOM... RULED... LIKE SOME DESPOT... NAH... THEN CIVIL WAR WOULD BREAK OUT... BE A MESS...
CLICK
HMMM... FOREVER IN YER DEBT... NOW THAT'S SOMETHING...

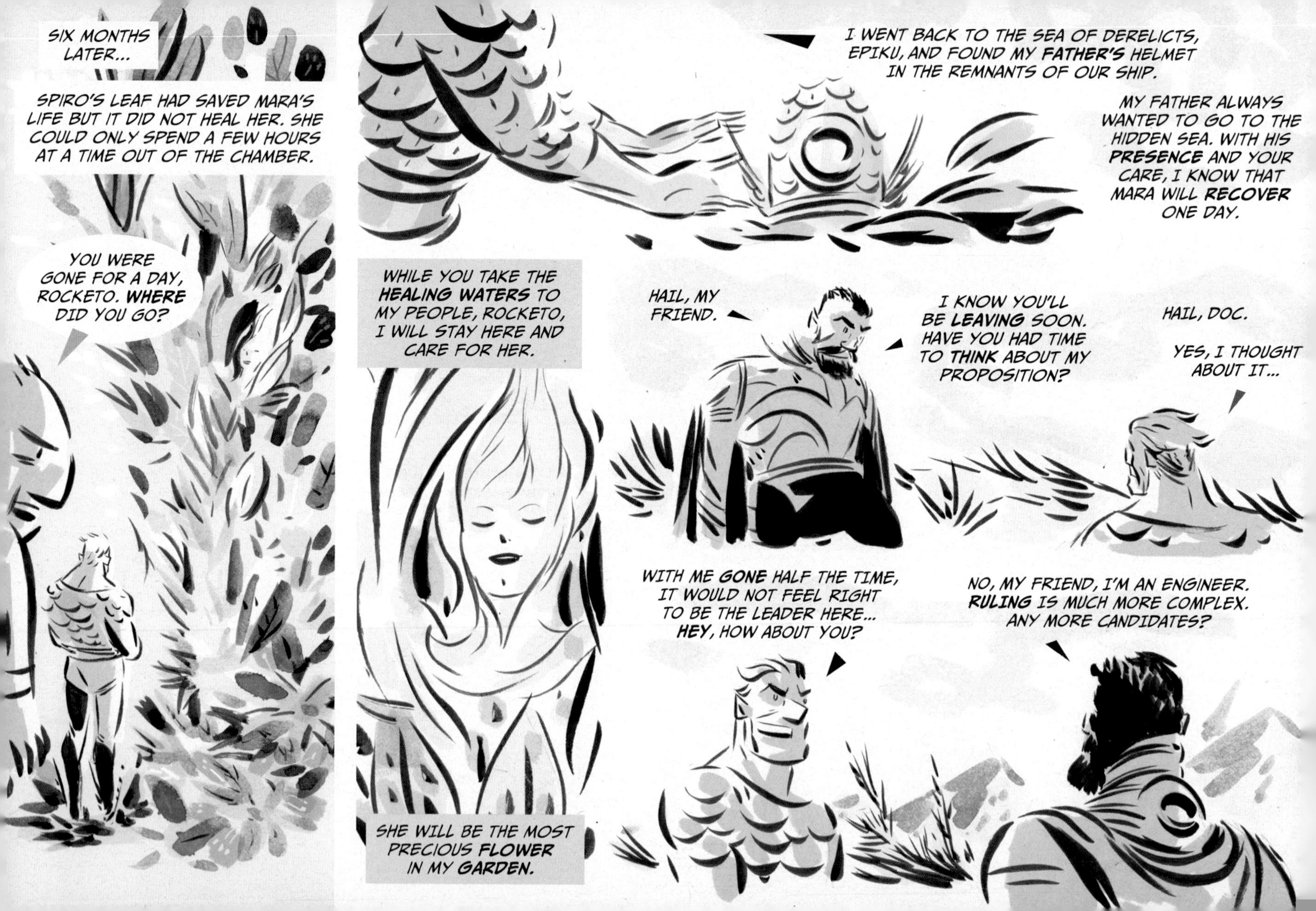
SIX MONTHS LATER...
SPIRO'S LEAF HAD SAVED MARA'S LIFE BUT IT DID NOT HEAL HER. SHE COULD ONLY SPEND A FEW HOURS AT A TIME OUT OF THE CHAMBER.
YOU WERE GONE FOR A DAY, ROCKETO. **WHERE** DID YOU GO?
I WENT BACK TO THE SEA OF DERELICTS, EPIKU, AND FOUND MY **FATHER'S** HELMET IN THE REMNANTS OF OUR SHIP.
MY FATHER ALWAYS WANTED TO GO TO THE HIDDEN SEA. WITH HIS **PRESENCE** AND YOUR CARE, I KNOW THAT MARA WILL **RECOVER** ONE DAY.
WHILE YOU TAKE THE **HEALING WATERS** TO MY PEOPLE, ROCKETO, I WILL STAY HERE AND CARE FOR HER.
SHE WILL BE THE MOST PRECIOUS **FLOWER** IN MY **GARDEN.**
HAIL, MY FRIEND.
I KNOW YOU'LL BE **LEAVING** SOON. HAVE YOU HAD TIME TO **THINK** ABOUT MY PROPOSITION?
HAIL, DOC.
YES, I THOUGHT ABOUT IT...
WITH ME **GONE** HALF THE TIME, IT WOULD NOT FEEL RIGHT TO BE THE LEADER HERE... **HEY**, HOW ABOUT YOU?
NO, MY FRIEND, I'M AN ENGINEER. **RULING** IS MUCH MORE COMPLEX. ANY MORE CANDIDATES?

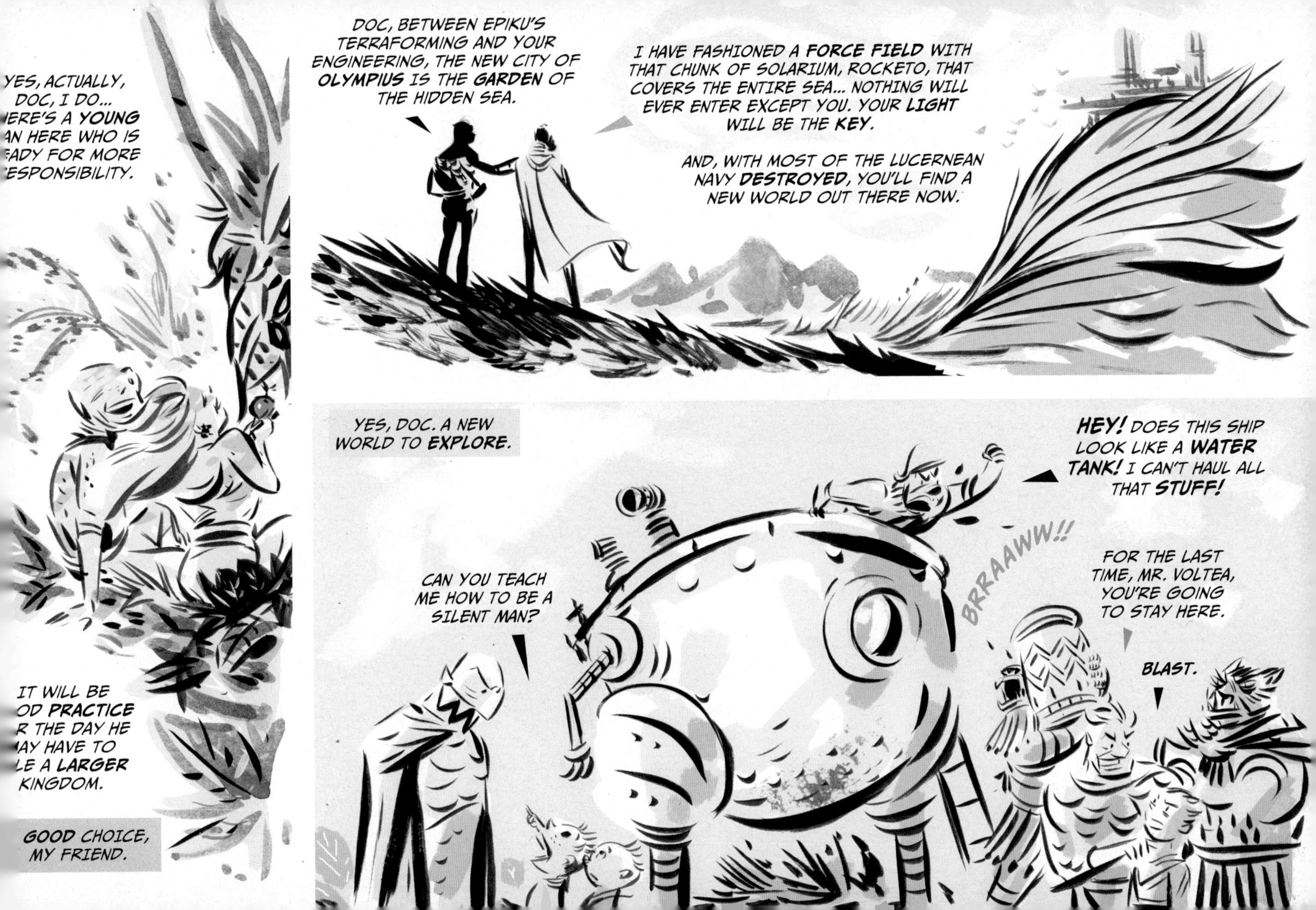

YES, ACTUALLY, DOC, I DO... ERE'S A YOUNG AN HERE WHO IS EADY FOR MORE ESPONSIBILITY.
IT WILL BE OD PRACTICE R THE DAY HE AY HAVE TO LE A LARGER KINGDOM.
GOOD CHOICE, MY FRIEND.
DOC, BETWEEN EPIKU'S TERRAFORMING AND YOUR ENGINEERING, THE NEW CITY OF OLYMPIUS IS THE GARDEN OF THE HIDDEN SEA.
I HAVE FASHIONED A FORCE FIELD WITH THAT CHUNK OF SOLARIUM, ROCKETO, THAT COVERS THE ENTIRE SEA... NOTHING WILL EVER ENTER EXCEPT YOU. YOUR LIGHT WILL BE THE KEY.
AND, WITH MOST OF THE LUCERNEAN NAVY DESTROYED, YOU'LL FIND A NEW WORLD OUT THERE NOW.
YES, DOC. A NEW WORLD TO EXPLORE.
HEY! DOES THIS SHIP LOOK LIKE A WATER TANK! I CAN'T HAUL ALL THAT STUFF!
BRRAAWW!!
FOR THE LAST TIME, MR. VOLTEA, YOU'RE GOING TO STAY HERE.
BLAST.
CAN YOU TEACH ME HOW TO BE A SILENT MAN?

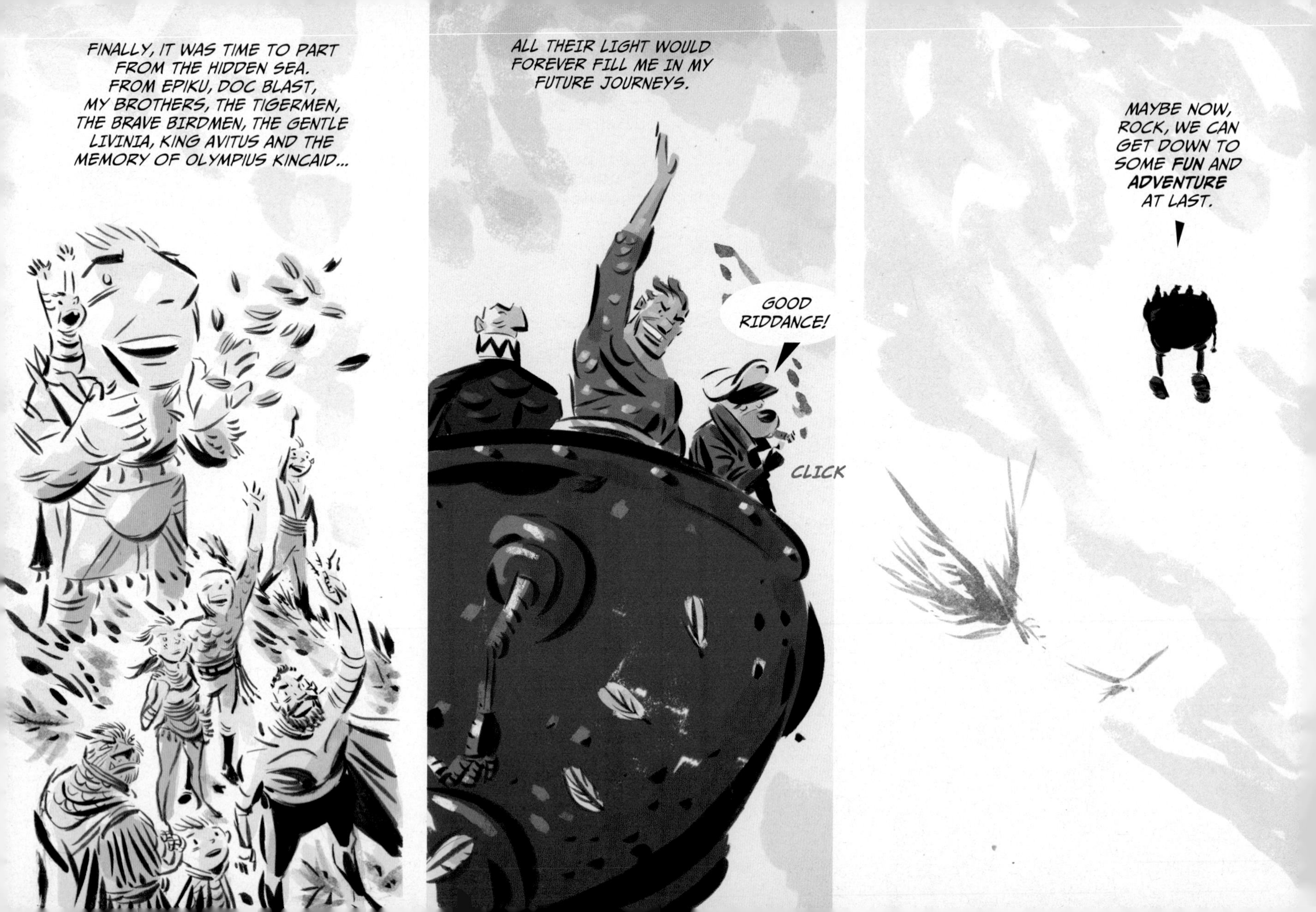
FINALLY, IT WAS TIME TO PART FROM THE HIDDEN SEA. FROM EPIKU, DOC BLAST, MY BROTHERS, THE TIGERMEN, THE BRAVE BIRDMEN, THE GENTLE LIVINIA, KING AVITUS AND THE MEMORY OF OLYMPIUS KINCAID...
ALL THEIR LIGHT WOULD FOREVER FILL ME IN MY FUTURE JOURNEYS.
GOOD RIDDANCE!
CLICK
MAYBE NOW, ROCK, WE CAN GET DOWN TO SOME FUN AND ADVENTURE AT LAST.

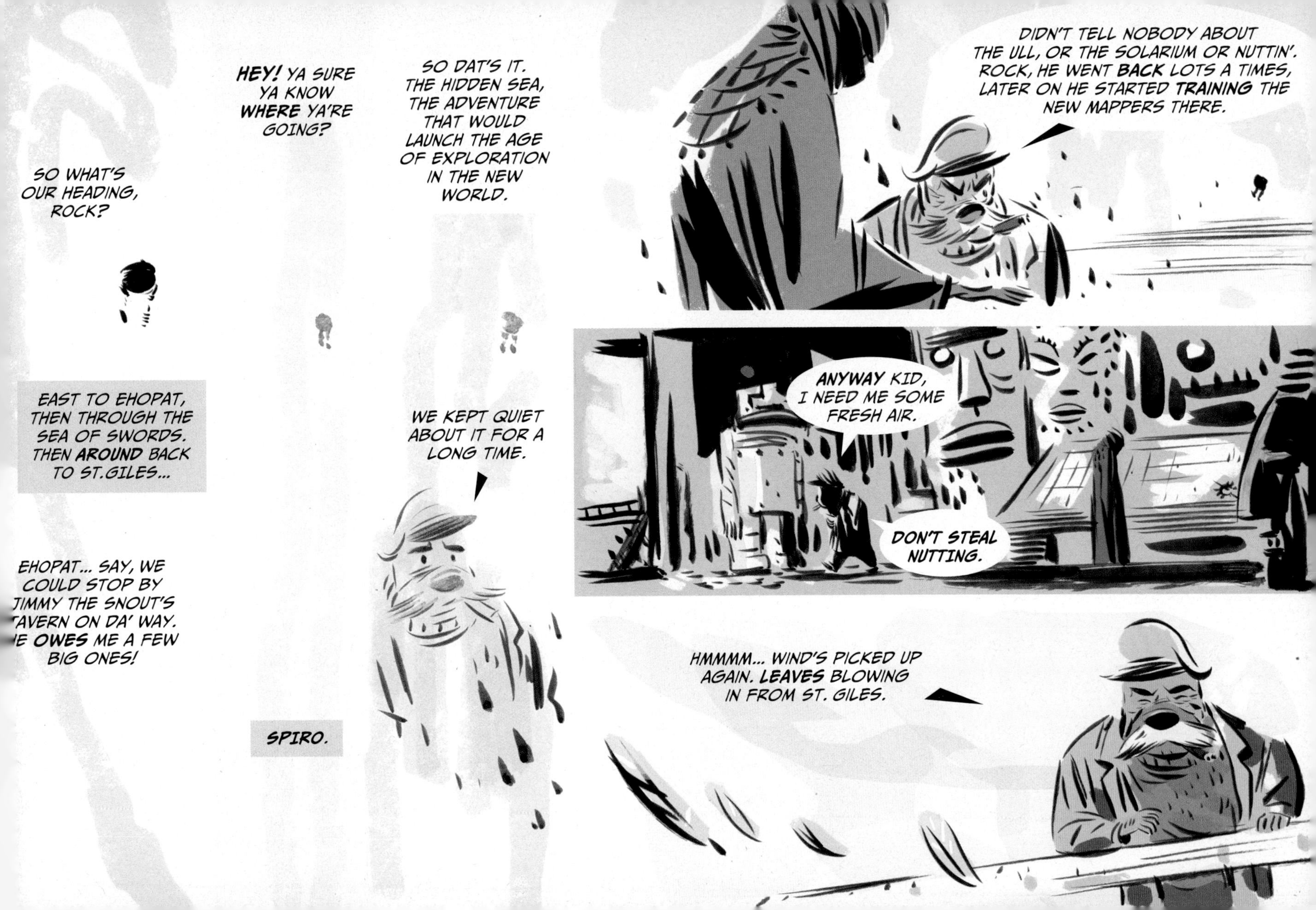
SO WHAT'S OUR HEADING, ROCK?
HEY! YA SURE YA KNOW WHERE YA'RE GOING?
SO DAT'S IT. THE HIDDEN SEA, THE ADVENTURE THAT WOULD LAUNCH THE AGE OF EXPLORATION IN THE NEW WORLD.
EAST TO EHOPAT, THEN THROUGH THE SEA OF SWORDS. THEN AROUND BACK TO ST.GILES...
WE KEPT QUIET ABOUT IT FOR A LONG TIME.
EHOPAT... SAY, WE COULD STOP BY JIMMY THE SNOUT'S TAVERN ON DA' WAY. HE OWES ME A FEW BIG ONES!
SPIRO.
DIDN'T TELL NOBODY ABOUT THE ULL, OR THE SOLARIUM OR NUTTIN'. ROCK, HE WENT BACK LOTS A TIMES, LATER ON HE STARTED TRAINING THE NEW MAPPERS THERE.
ANYWAY KID, I NEED ME SOME FRESH AIR.
DON'T STEAL NUTTING.
HMMMM... WIND'S PICKED UP AGAIN. LEAVES BLOWING IN FROM ST. GILES.

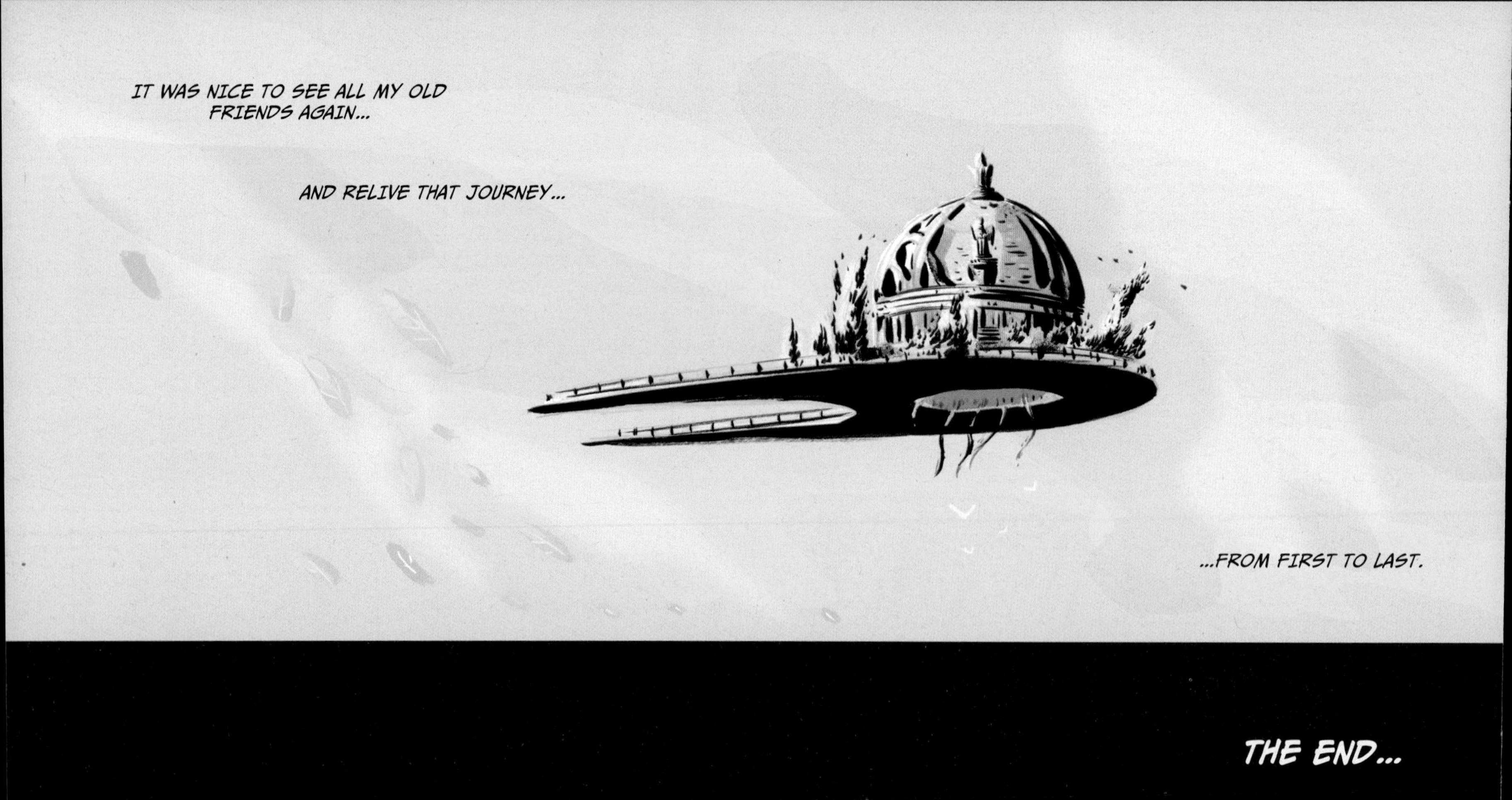
IT WAS NICE TO SEE ALL MY OLD FRIENDS AGAIN...
AND RELIVE THAT JOURNEY...
...FROM FIRST TO LAST.
THE END...

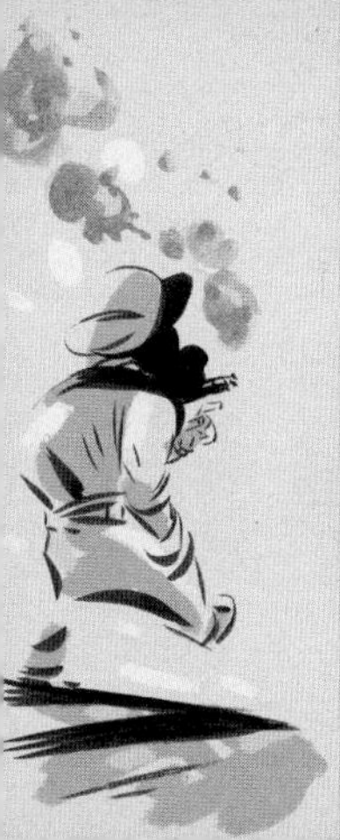

ROCKETO

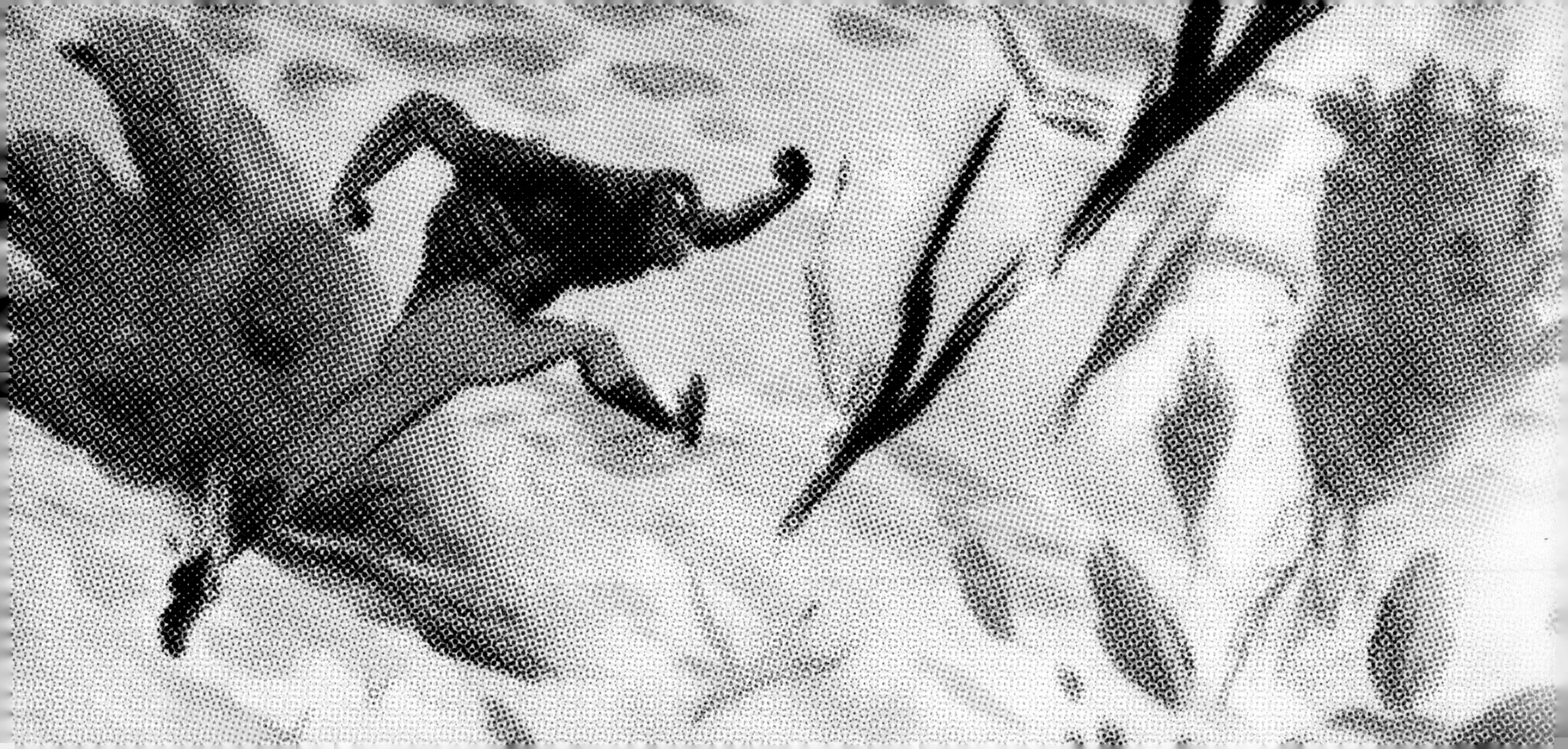

THE ART OF ROCKETO

ILLUSTRATIONS & SKETCHES

A GUIDE TO THE NEW WORLD

ROCKETO PIN-UP

Illustrations

While envisioning the world of Rocketo, one of my great pleasures was taking time out to imagine some of the adventures Rocketo and Spiro would have in between the long journeys. Maybe when the long journeys are fully done I can go back and revisit some of these lost tales. In the process of doing these illustrations the actual locations of the New World came to life, and character designs became more solid in my mind.

Rocketo and the Queen of the Tiger Men

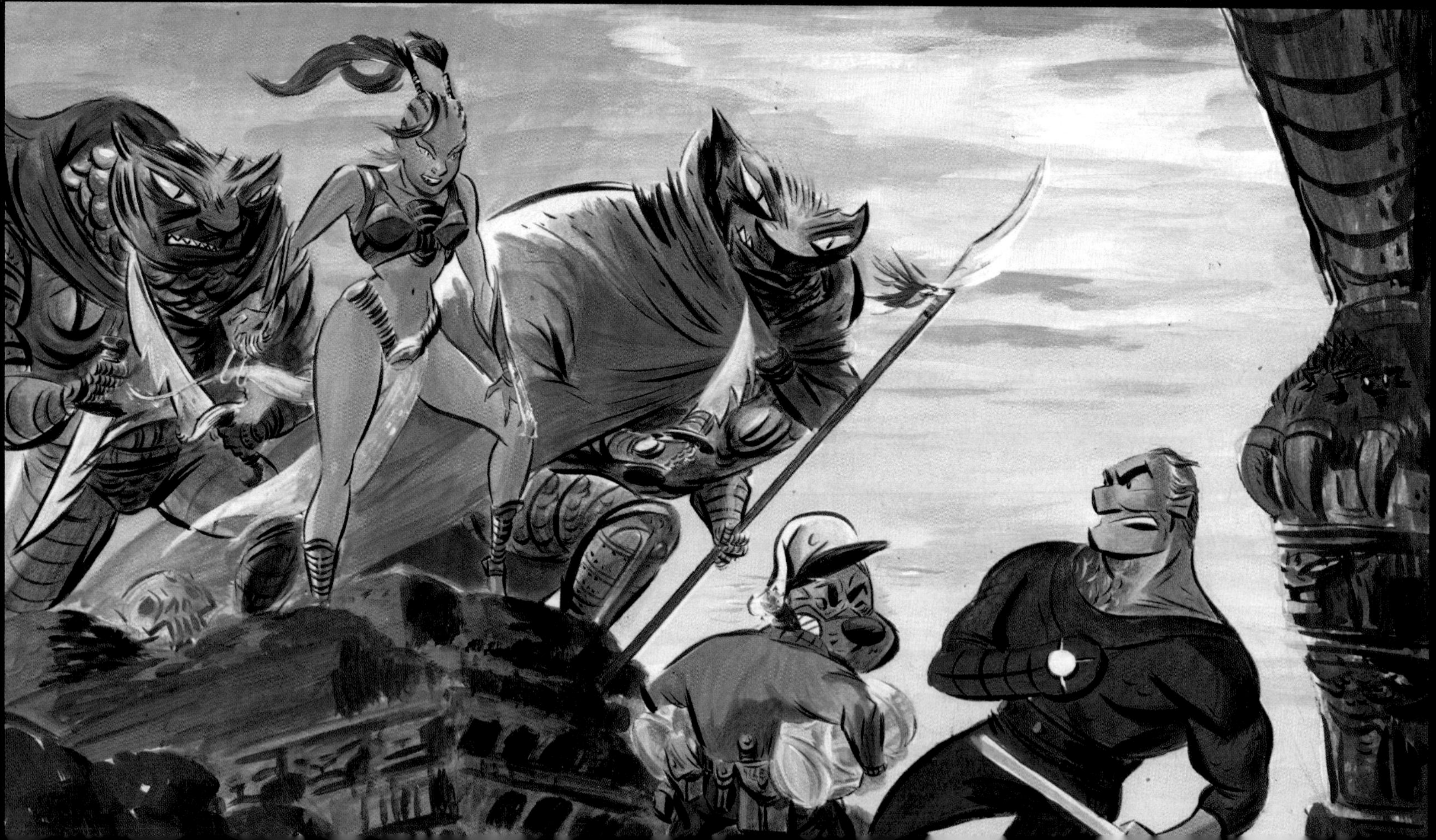

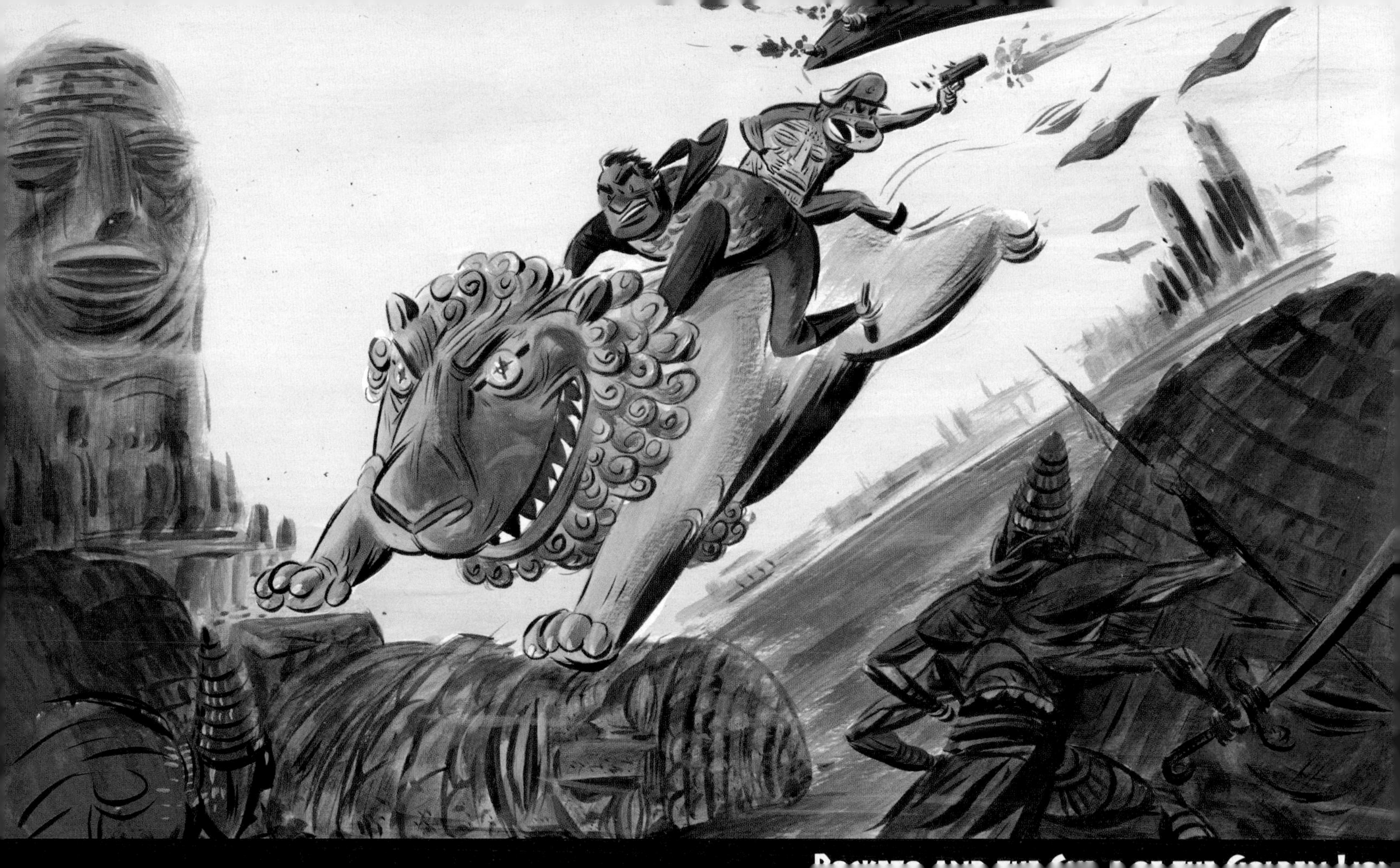

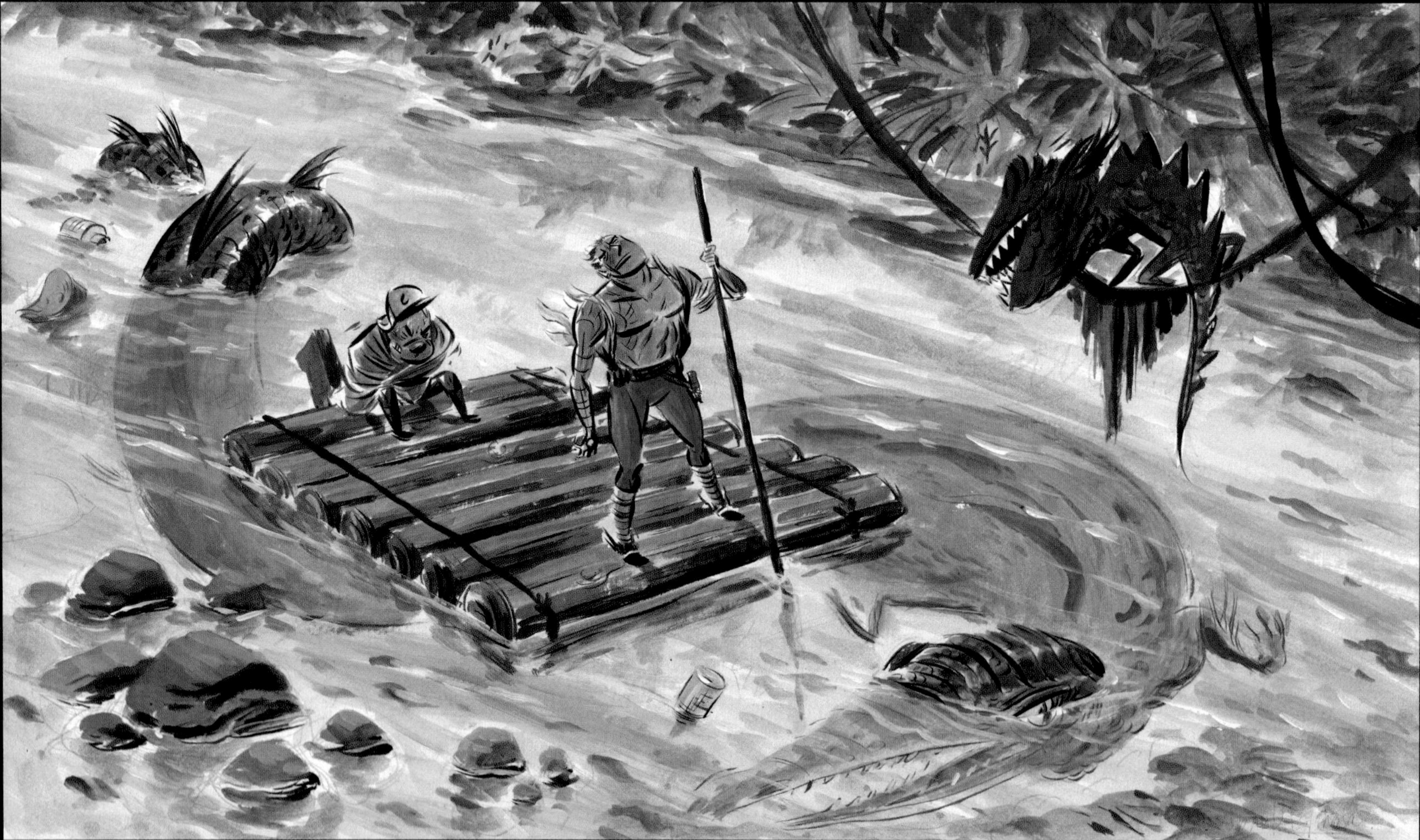

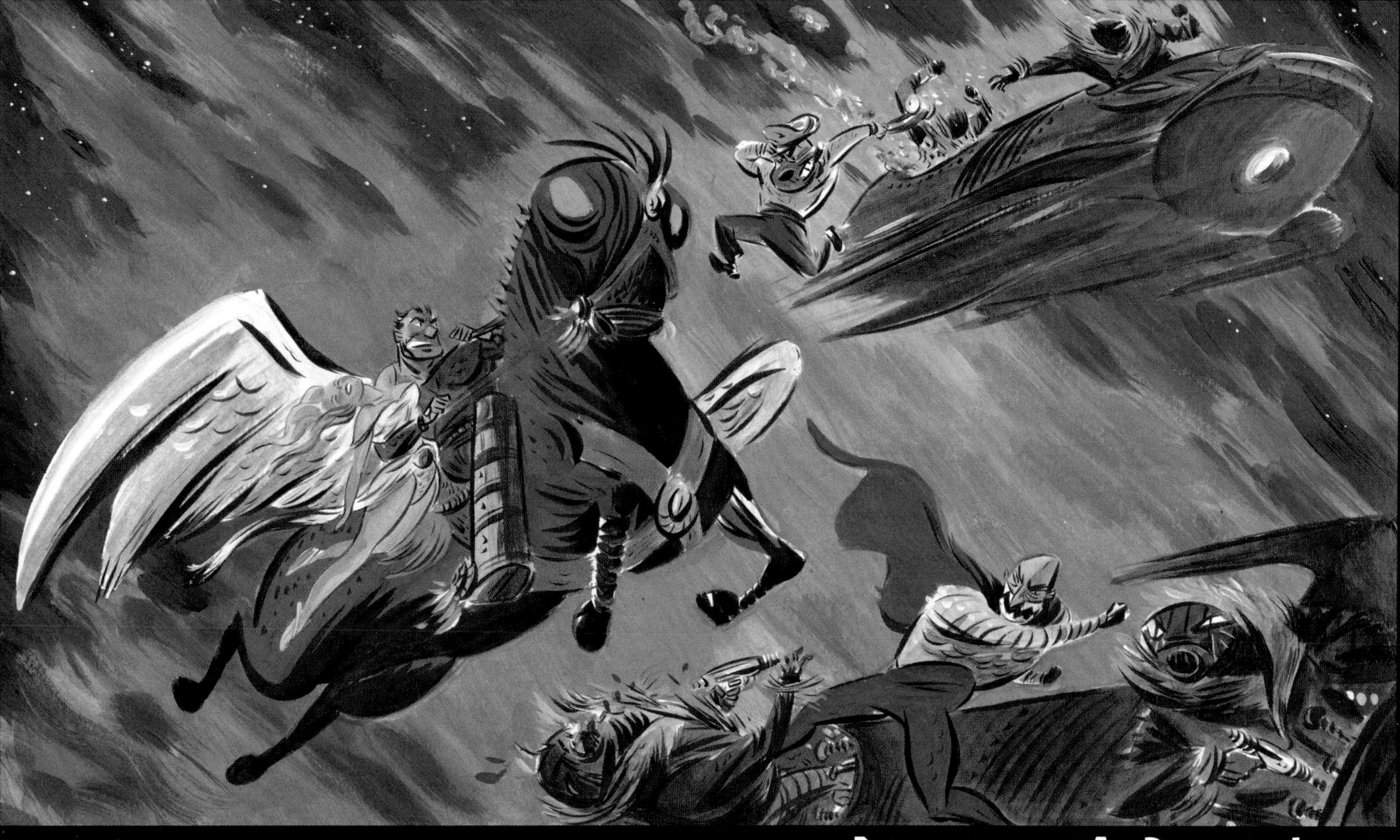

ROCKETO V.S. THE AIR PIRATES OF LUCERNE

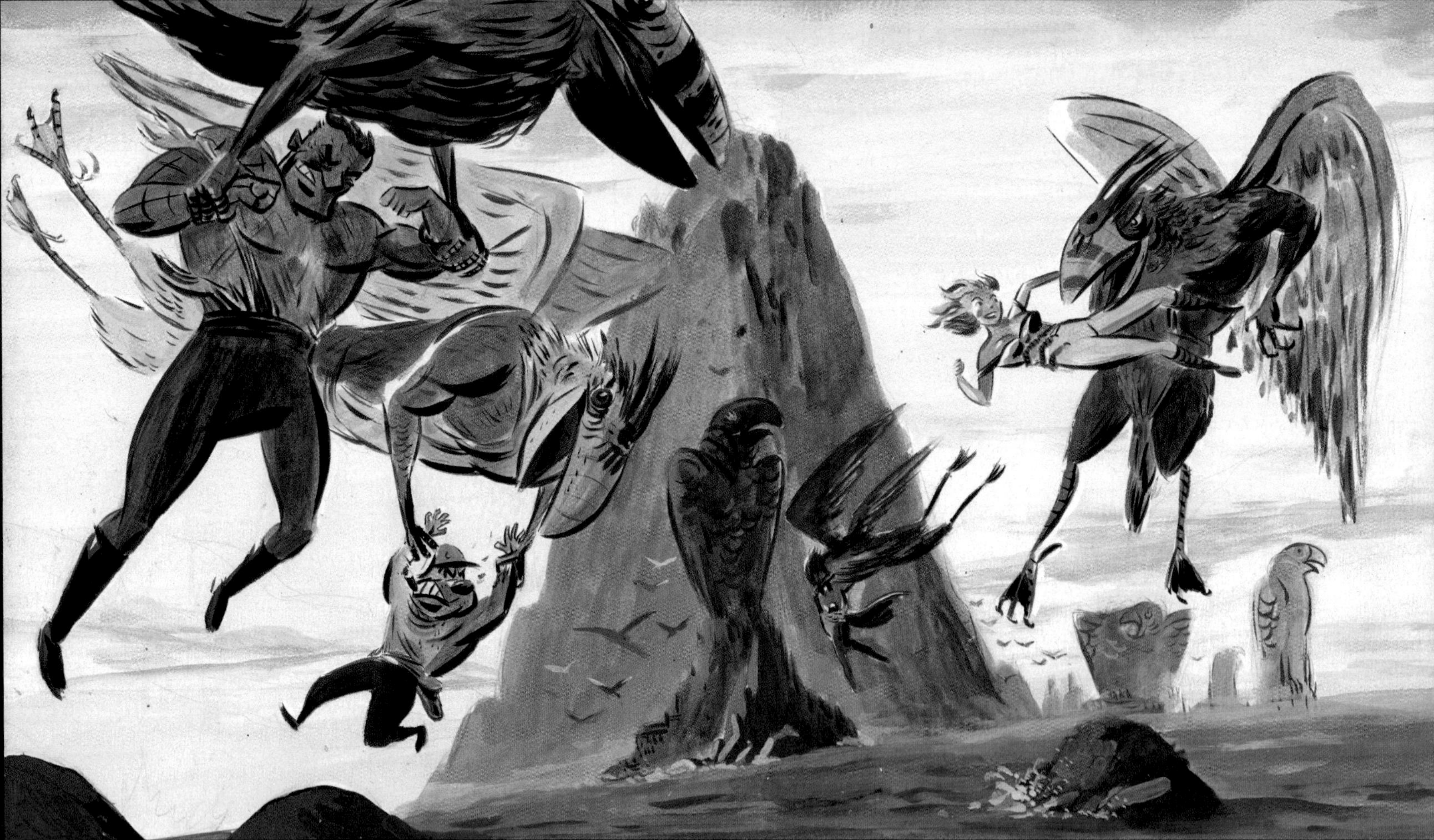

ROCKETO AND THE SECRET OF BELLASANDRO

It shows Rocketo with his jump boots and blue steel going to rescue Spiro and company.

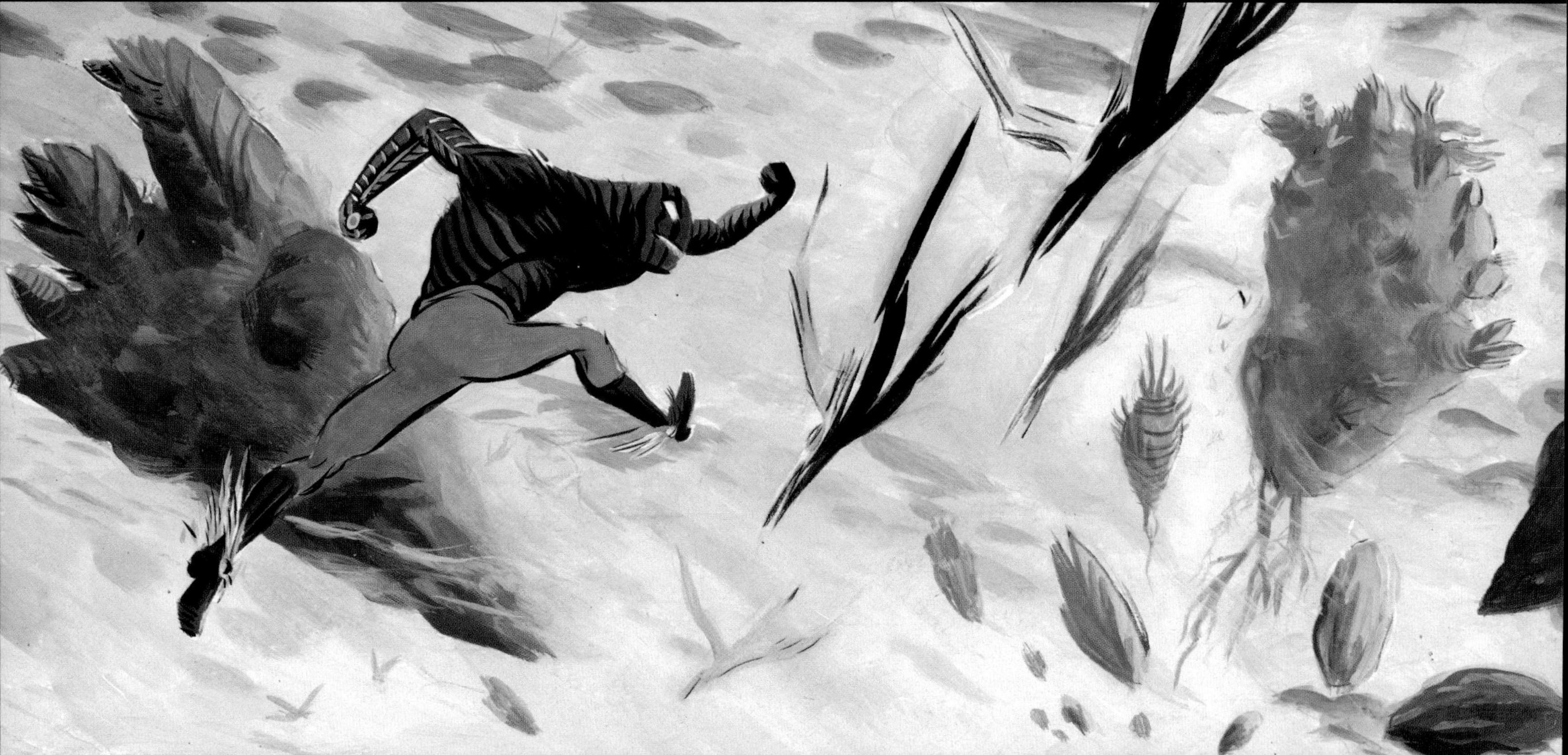

SKETCHES

Some pages from my sketch books that I have kept throughout the development of this project. For me, the early part where it can go anywhere is always the time to play, think, explore.

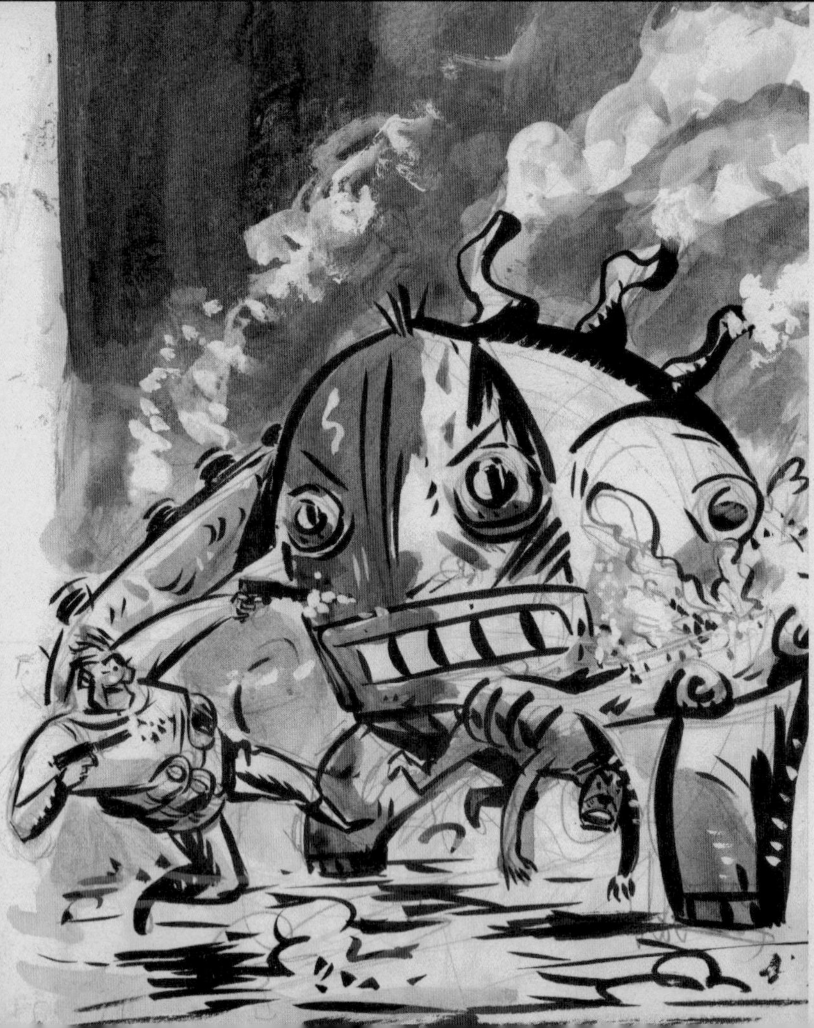

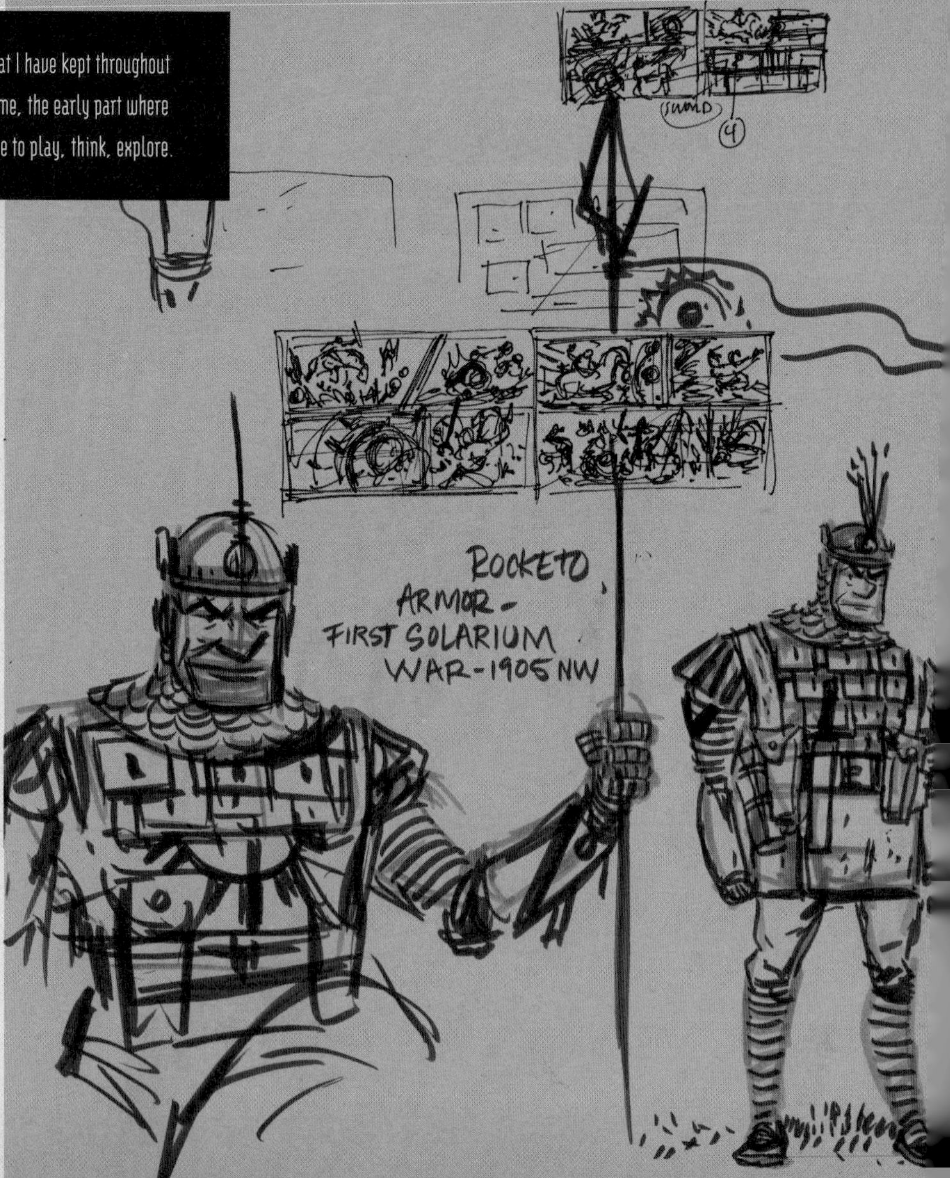
ROCKETO ARMOR -
FIRST SOLARIUM WAR-1905NW

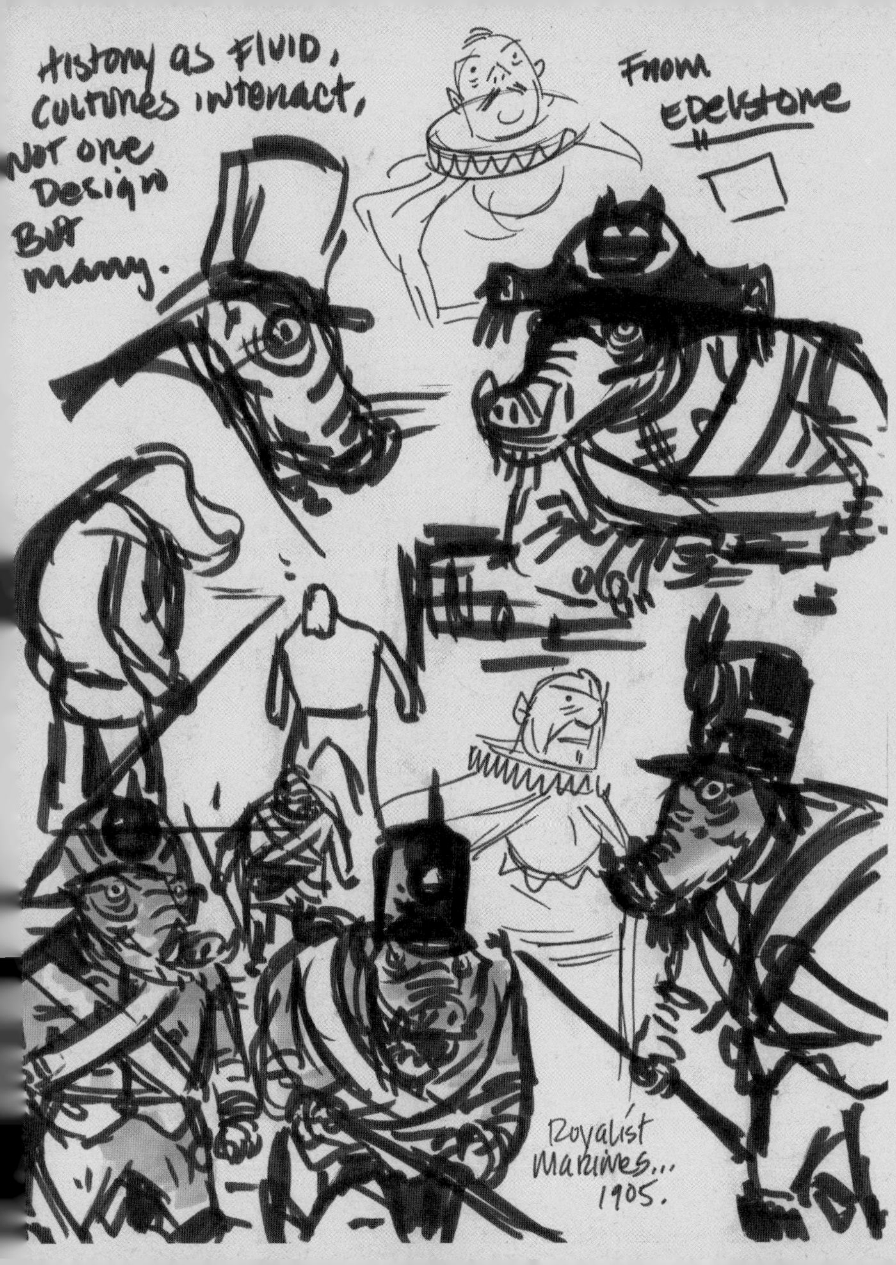
History as FLUID,
Cultures interact,
not one
Design
But
many.
From
EDELSTONE
Royalist
Marines...
1905.

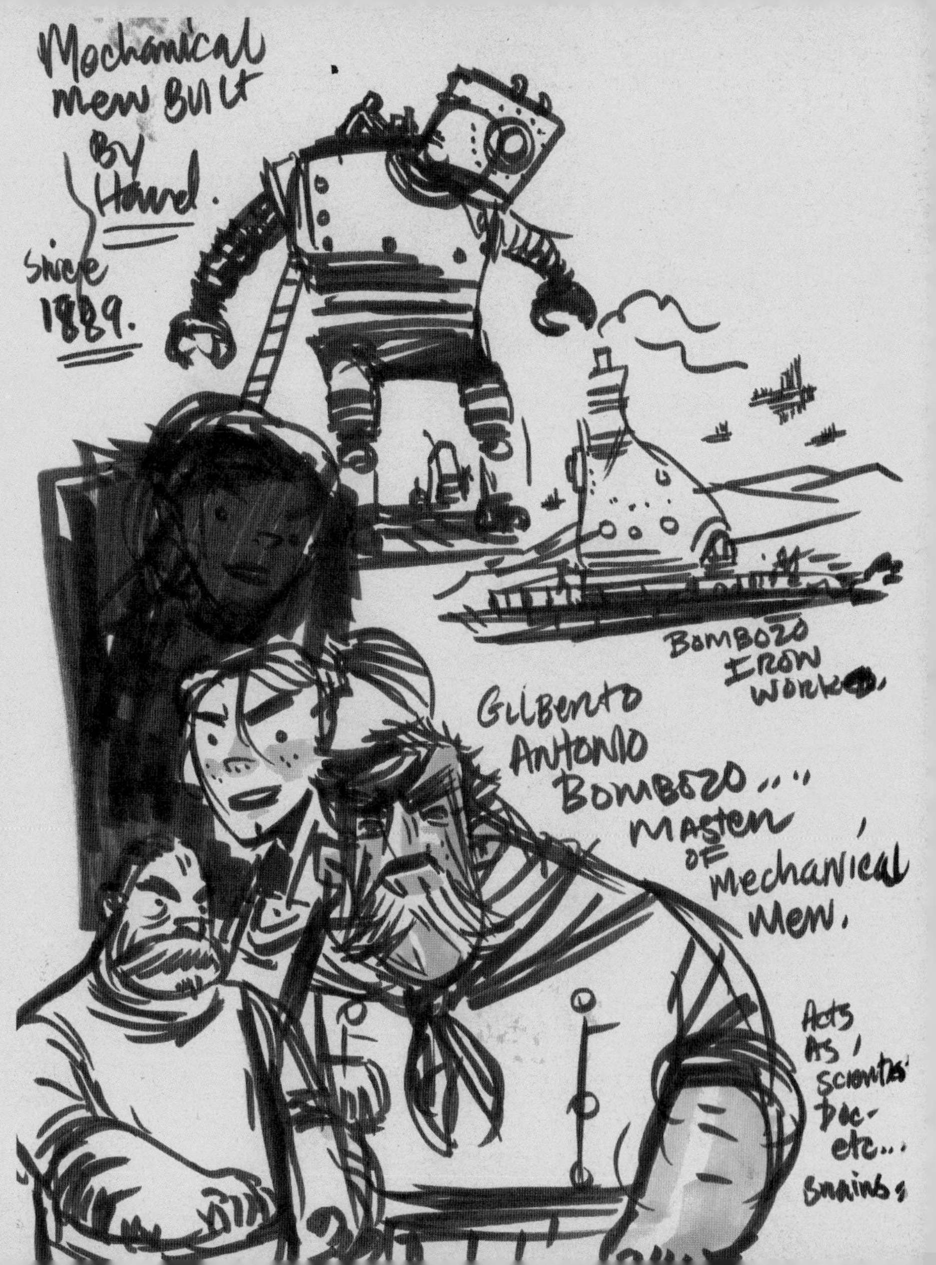
Mechanical
Men Built
By
Hand.
Since
1889.
BOMBOZO
IRON
WORKS.
Gilberto
Antonio
Bombozo...
Master
of
Mechanical
Men.
Acts
As
scientist
Doc-
etc...
brains.

Here are some original sketches for Dr. Hiram Arkwright. I would later use a different design for Arkwright and use the fellow with the giant glasses as another science villian working for Lucerne.

The fellow with all the scars was the early concept for what would later become Prince Avitus. He was originally going to be a fellow comrade of Rocketo during the Solarium wars. I like the design and he will show up in one of the later Journeys.

centon
Lime
Drops
right

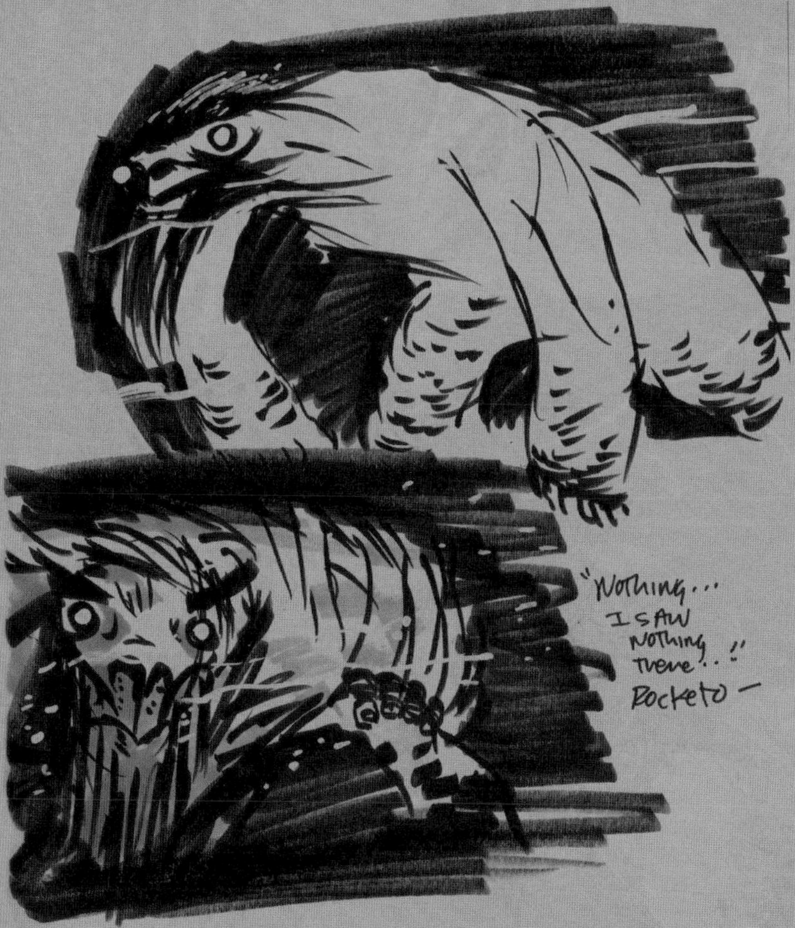
"Nothing...
I saw
nothing
there..!"
Rocketo—

Early SNOWMEN designs. Rocketo was going to the arctic in the Hidden Sea story, I dropped the idea but the the characters will show up in some form in the Journey to the New World.

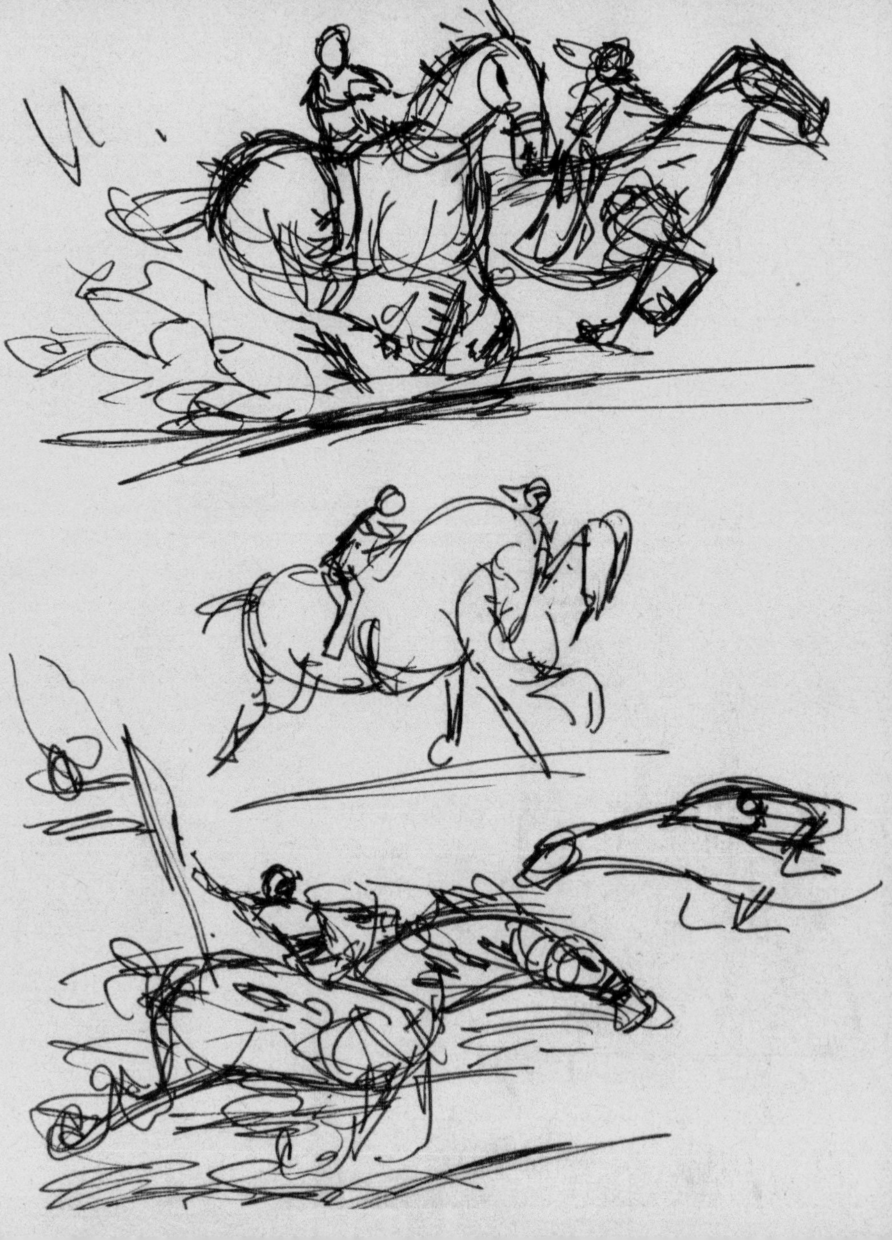

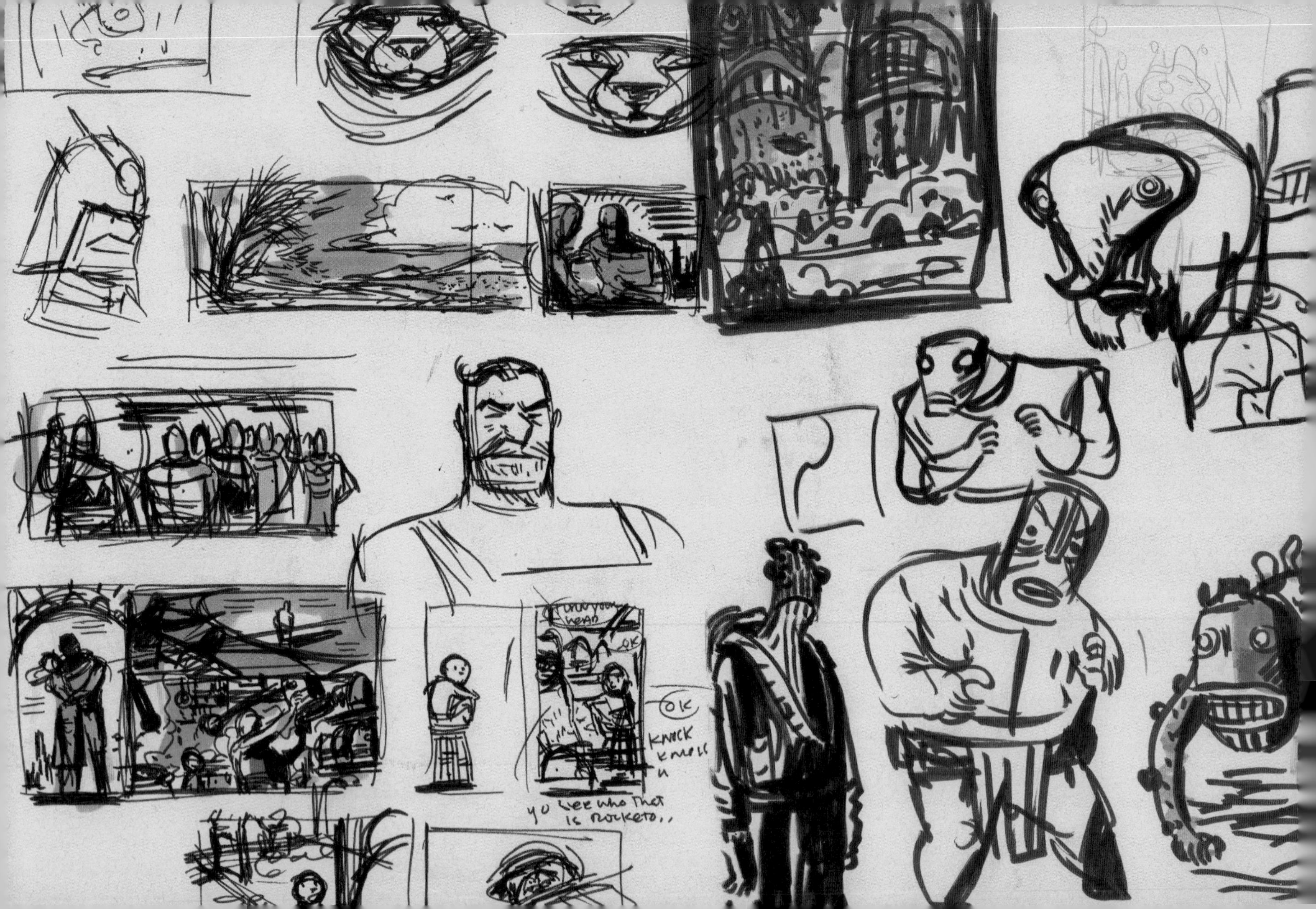
OK
OK
KNOCK

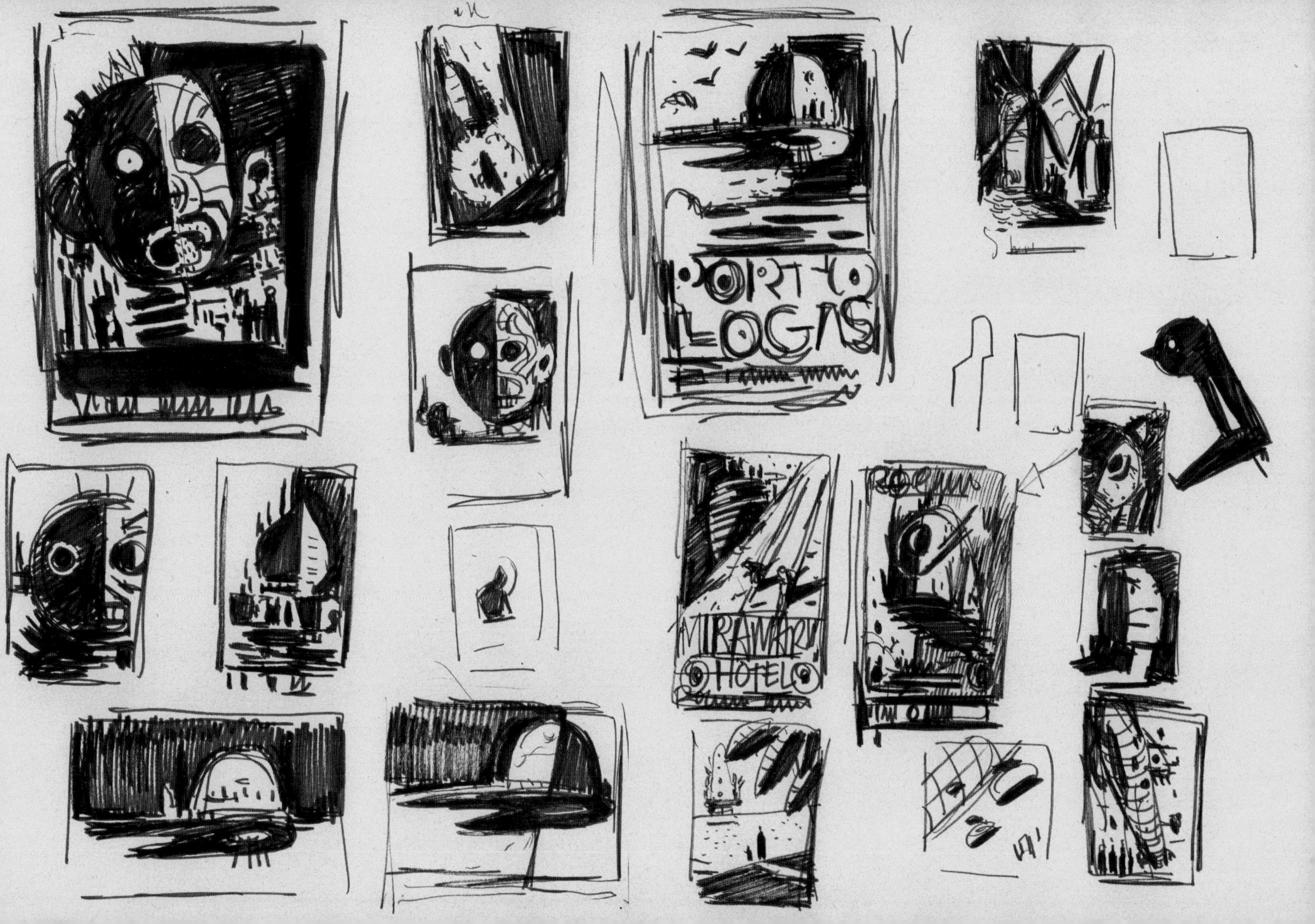
HOTEL

A Guide to THE NEW WORLD

EXCERPTS FROM: THE NEW WORLD GEOGRAPHIC SOCIETY MUSEUM
BY EDITH WELLS

PEOPLE

AGRAMENTE, PRINCE: Prince of the Royal Family of Lucerne, second in line for the throne. Considered the power behind the throne and known for his political machination, duplicity and close association to chief Lucernian scientist, Hiram Arkwright.

ARKWRIGHT, HIRAM: chief scientist of Lucerne and the inventor of the nucleosynthetic vacuum engine which provides condensed energy from solarium, and the infamous Sekmet machine. His extraordinary intelligence and vast political power made Arkwright one of the most feared men of the world. He had the reputation of being able to read people's minds.

AVITUS, PRINCE: Prince of the Royal Family in Lucerne, 4th in line for the throne. Protected since birth by a special armor, Prince Avitus was genetically engineered by Hiram Arkwright during the Solarium War. He reached his full maturity in just two years at which time he was given the same mapping powers used by Arkwright's Sekmet machine.

BIRDMEN OF BELLISANDRO: One of the first genetic experiments that combined the characteristics of humans and birds. Averaging seven feet in height with a fourteen foot wingspan, the Birdmen generally live in mud-based dwellings along the cliff faces of Bellisandro. The flying warriors were some of the fiercest soldiers and were known for their marauding ways.

BOAZ (Silent Man from Ehopat): Date of birth and heritage unknown. Boaz was one of a race of the mysterious men of Ehopat who willingly have their mouths sealed as part of their life-long religious vow of silence. He was known to be quick, powerful and a master in martial arts, some credited him with the unusual ability to become invisible at will. He was thought to have a priceless collection of antique weaponry although no trace was ever found. He was often in the company of Spiro Turnstiles who claimed the Silent Man had vowed to protect him. Boaz returned to his native land in 1955.

CANTO: Also referred to as Canto the Great. Mythical warrior/leader who came to the survivors of mankind after the Great Shattering and led them to the Great Mountain where he taught them the skills they would need to survive in the now-hostile environment.

EPIKU (Earthman): Born in 1851 NW to Mantu and Freen, Epiku was one of the legendary Earthmen of Garuda who are known for their intimate connection to the forces of the earth. A gifted doctor, Epiku could produce natural medicines by growing from his own body. His mission in life was to renew the environment of his homeland which had been poisoned by the extensive solarium mining after the War.

FISH PEOPLE: A species of man genetically bred to survive under water. Mainly inhabiting tropical waters, the Fish People often made their homes among the sunken ships and debris of the oceans. Some say the species once included great leviathans who ruled the depths of the ocean.

GARRISON FAMILY OF MAPPERS: One of the original 12 mapping families whose early members included Volteo Garrison, the Star Maker; Gilberto Garrison, the Light Bringer; Orlando Garrison, Mapper of Kova and the great Rocketo Garrison, the Mutant Slayer.

GARRISON, ROCKETO (Mapper): Born 1887 NW on the Island of Kova to Volteo Garrison, of the renown Garrison family of Mappers, and Princess Tien of Shuxiang. Rocketo Garrison was one of the few survivors of the Omarylla Coil which destroyed Kova in 1895. He was adopted by Horace Ivanov of the Ivanov family of Mappers and lived with him and Horace's son, Saturn, in St. Giles. Garrison defied the Mappers' tradition by joining the forces of the Commonwealth in the Solarium War. He was captured, held at the infamous Rose Karthush, and was part of the final POW release. The first of his famous adventures began in 1917 when he joined Spiro Turnstiles to explore the mysterious Hidden Sea. In succeeding years he opened up many new lands in the New World to exploration and founded the New World Exploration Society. Contemporaries described him as a brave though reserved man whose curiosity and stubbornness made him the great explorer he was. Some claimed he had the legendary mapping ability to temporarily change his genetic structure to survive a hostile environment. His love of horses was seen in many of the metal sculptures he created at his home in Porto Logas. Rocketo Garrison disappeared under mysterious circumstances in 1952 NW. His home at Porto Logas in St. Giles houses his priceless map and chart collection.

THE HARPIES: Half-human, half-beast flying creatures who scour the western shores from Zagorah to venedicto. To feed their voracious appetites, the Harpies have been known to eat men, supplies and even the ships themselves.

IVANOV, HORACE (Mapper & Explorer): Horace Ivanov of the Ivanov mapping family, was born in 1802 to Gregor and Natalie Ivanov in St. Giles. A noted Astrocartographer and Mapper, Ivanov opened new routes into Bellasandro and Hayarsha. He married Petya Fedorich who died giving birth to their son, Saturn. After the destruction of Kova he also adopted Rocketo Garrison and taught him his mapping skills.

IVANOV, SATURN (Commander, Commonwealth Air Force): Born in 1885 to Horace and Petya Ivanov, Saturn Ivanov grew up in St. Giles and was close to his adopted brother, Rocketo Garrison. When his mapping abilities did not mature, he joined the Commonwealth Air Force, rising to the position of Commander. A noted aviator, inventor and leader, he was killed at the Battle of Dargopel in 1915 at the age of 30.

KINCAID, OLYMPIUS (Mapper): King of the Hidden Sea. Born to the powerful Kincaid mapping family, Olympius Kincaid was the greatest and most famous of all of the early, legendary mappers. A great explorer, Olympius Kincaid rid the country of Garuda of mutants creatures and was known for his ability to turn his body into blue steel. Like all early mappers, he had a long life span and at the age of 256 years entered into the Hidden Sea to explore its mysteries, never to be seen again.

KING OF THE ATLAS OCEAN: An ancient, gigantic, sentient life form of the Atlas Ocean who challenged all sailors who crossed his waters. In return for tribute, the King would give sailors advice on the best crossings to their destinations.

MAPPERS: There were 12 original Mapping families created for exploration of the New World over 2,000 years ago. These Mappers have an innate sense of curiosity to explore that has driven some to untimely deaths. Known as Living Compasses, their genetic make-up has magnet-like particles that always point to North. The Mapping Guild lives and trains at the San Pao monastery, a giant rocky island that juts out of the Atlas Ocean near the Black Meridian

PRASAD, ATU "Doc Blast": Born 1895 in Lunaripal to Kaushal and Miral Prasad, Atu Prasad was an engineering genius and one of the first men to experiment with solarium power in the human body earning him the nickname of Doc Blast. Prasad designed and fueled the Esmeralda, the ship used by Rocketo Garrison and Spiro Turnstiles on their exploration of the Hidden Sea. After being in seclusion for many years, Prasad returned to the scientific scene in 1952 bringing with him many unique inventions. Prasad was known for his love of flying and was master chess player.

SCARLETTO, GORDON: Born Gordon Leto of the Leto mapping family, he adopted the name of Scarletto. Although a mapper, his abilities never matured. After a number of early brushes with the law, Scarletto joined the infamous Hand underworld syndicate and quickly rose in the ranks. By age 28, he had taken over the crime family and made a fortune in weapons sales during the Solarium War. He mysteriously disappeared in 1917 and some believe his shady dealings with the Royalist forces led to an early demise.

TURNSTILES, SPIRO (Dogman): Born 1890 NW in Edelstone to Aristotle and Magda Turnstiles, Spiro refused to enter his father's profession of service and by 15 had gone to sea in search of adventure. By his mid-20's, he was the captain his own ship and suspected by many of smuggling contraband and rare antiques. In 1919 he joined forces with Rocketo Garrison to found Porto Logas Enterprises, an exploration, charting and importing company. Quick tempered and not above bending the truth or the law, Turnstiles was always seen with his trademark cigar. He was a competitive sailor and entered his yacht, the Esmeralda, in many competitions. As a result of his long-time friendship with Rocketo Garrison, Spiro Turnstiles became the caretaker of Porto Logas and governed access to all of Garrison's maps, charts and histories.

Locations

BELLASANDRO: Rocky, inhospitable island nation at the southern tip of Venedicto inhabited by the Birdmen.

CHARLEROI: Capital city of the Lucernian empire and center for trade, government and culture.

EDLESTONE: Home of the Volkeshunde, the dogmen. Unlike other genetic experiments in which human were genetically altered with animal attributes, the Volkeshunde were based on the canine species and enhanced by human characteristics such as high intelligence, speech, erect posture and the aposal thumb. The standard multiple birth patterns of canines was overwritten by partial infertility. First used in farming, mining and military (guard and explosives) work, the Volkeshunde experienced a leap in evolution that resulted in a virtual enslavement of the population. While the Freedom Act of 1702 gave the species human status and political standing, the race still suffers from discrimination because of its canine base.

GARUDA: A large island nation north of St. Giles known for its mineral wealth including the precious solarium. The home of the Earthmen, a race of giants who have an intimate understanding of the earth and its inhabitants.

THE GREAT ATLAS OCEAN: Great ocean separating the empire of Lucerne and the Commonwealth of Nations which includes St. Giles, Edelstone, Campanus and Garuda.

HAYARSHA: A rocky, desert-like land east of venedicto and the home of the famous Tigermen.

THE HIDDEN SEA: The Hidden Sea, the Sea of Mists, Haloborko, Ullmarta, Sea of Madness, and also known by many other names is not really a sea of water but a giant crater filled with fogs and mists whose depth has never been measured.

KOVA: Small island near the southern edge of St. Giles that was nearly destroyed by an Omarylla Coil in 1895 NW.

LUCERNE: Empire nation and world-power after the Solarium War.

PERDITION'S POINT: known for its lighthouse built on upon a luminescent sea creature whose light was a warning to ocean-going ships and whose stench could be noticed miles away.

PORTO LOGAS: After the Journey to the Hidden Sea, Rocketo Garrison took up residence at Porto Logas, an obsolete observatory that floats above Perdition's Point in St. Giles. After his disappearance, Porto Logas became a museum to house Garrison's vast store of maps, charts, exploration equipment and memorabilia.

ROSE KARTHUSH: An infamous prisoner of war camp during the Solarium War controlled by the Royalist forces. Karthush, the largest island, has centers for the re-education of political prisoners (Rose Karthush), social misfits (Gold Karthush); and the terminally ill (Green Karthush).

SAN PAU: Secluded city in Kuhastan best known as being the headquarters of the Mapping Guild.

SANSEBO: Island nation to the east of St. Giles known for its ports and commerce.

SEA OF HERAKLES: Inland sea that borders Lucerne to the north, Kurtos to the east, Venedicto to the south and Zagorah to the west.

ST. GILES: St. Giles is the center of the Commonwealth Movement and said to be one of the most beautiful Continents. Its pastoral setting, mild climate and the cultured attitude of its inhabitants, attracted scientists and scholars from around Lucerne, making it the home of more than 300 major universities, libraries, museums and research centers including the Hochenbee Observatory. The Hermitage is a major center for genetic research.

VENEDICTO: A relatively unexplored continent containing several backward countries including Zagorah, Bellisandro, Ehopat and Hayarsha as well as the mysterious Hidden Sea.

ZAGORAH: A land on the north eastern segment of the continent of Venedicto. Comprised mostly of desert, Zagorah was long a land of wandering, warring tribes and deluded mystics. Lucerne established the Fortress of Zagorah to patrol access to the Sea of Herakles.

ULTAMO: An ancient city said to be the most beautiful in the world because of its jewel-like towers and high culture. Known as the Golden City by a Golden Sea, some claim that Ultamo was located on the Moon and acted as a portal to deep space exploration in the years before the Great Shattering.

Events & Objects

BATTLE OF DARGOPEL: Dargopel was a main base of operations for the Commonwealth forces during the Solarium War. When the fortress and its force of two million soldiers were destroyed by the Royalists' deadly Sekmet War Machine, the War ended.

CHANKU EXPRESS: An impregnable fortress and city on wheels that traveled the route from Kuhastan to Charleroi.

COMPASS ROSE: Mysterious and rare flower thought to possess the ability to act as a compass.

DRAGONS OF THE HIDDEN SEA: It is not known who built the four colossal entry points to the Hidden Sea. The Golden Dragon lies in the west, the Jade Dragon in the east, the Ivory Dragon in the north and the Silver Dragon in the south.

FIRE MOUNTS OF ST. GILES: A breed of horses known for their courage, strength and speed. The Fire Mounts were used by the Commonwealth during the Solarium War and were almost completely exterminated. The breed was later brought back by Rocketo Garrison.

THE HAND: Criminal underworld organization run by the ruthless Gordon Scarletto who made his fortune selling arms to both armies during the Solarium War. The Hand was involved in every facet of criminal activity until Scarletto's sudden disappearance at which time it was taken over by Big Red Hannigan.

HOLOGRAPHIC PROJECTION MAPS: These holographic charts and maps are created by the genetic material of an individual Mapper who downloads the memories of the places, sights, smells, sounds and textures of an explored area. The Map is usually narrated by the originating Mapper and projects a three-dimensional view of the Mapping journey around the viewer. Some maps also allow a two-way conversation between the Mapper and the viewer. The maps can only be activated by a Mapper with a lighted compass. Although other people can view the map or chart, only the Mapper can fully experience it as well as gain access to valuable information from history. This safeguard has ensured that Mappers are usually not kidnapped, held for ransom or used by others; as a result the Mappers have a policy of being politically neutral.

JANZOON: A small, secluded country on the eastern edge of Venedicto known for its riches.

NEW WORLD EXPLORATION SOCIETY: The New World Exploration Society was founded in 1919 by Rocketo Garrison, later a world renown Mapper and Explorer, with the goals of promoting world-wide exploration, education and peace. The Society was quickly opposed by members of the Mapping Guild who objected to the Society's political stance, training of women Mappers and promotion of an integrated world culture. Matters came to a head in 1920 when several Mappers were found dead under mysterious circumstances and the Society came under suspicion.

MAPPER'S OATH: "Let your light be a guide to explore this shattered world and lift the eyes of men to the stars and beyond."

SEKMET MACHINE: A solarium powered weapon with mapping abilities designed by Professor Hiram Arkwright of Lucerne. Used in the Battle of Dargopel to destroy xxx men, it abruptly brought an end to the Solarium War.

SOLARIUM: Solarium is a fine dust-like particle that covers the upper atmosphere of the planet Lucerne. It was formed from the explosion that shattered the known world. It is an incredible source of energy and a small handful of the dust can power a ship for years.

THE SOLARIUM WAR 1911-1915: The war as waged primarily between the Royalist forces of Lucerne and the Commonwealth of Islands. At issue were the mining rights to Solarium, the energy source which provided clean power for the nucleosynthetic vacuum (NSV) engine developed by Professor Hiram Arkwright. The Royalist forces were victorious and claimed exclusive rights to all Solarium discovered within the newly established Hundred Island Demarcation.

A GUIDE TO
THE NEW WORLD

Rocketo
Pin-up

There is this wonderful feeling of seeing one's character done by another creative and talented hand. I am lucky to have in this trade a collection of talent that has taken Rocketo to a visual journey he could never have imagined on his own.

ROCKETO BY KEVIN DART

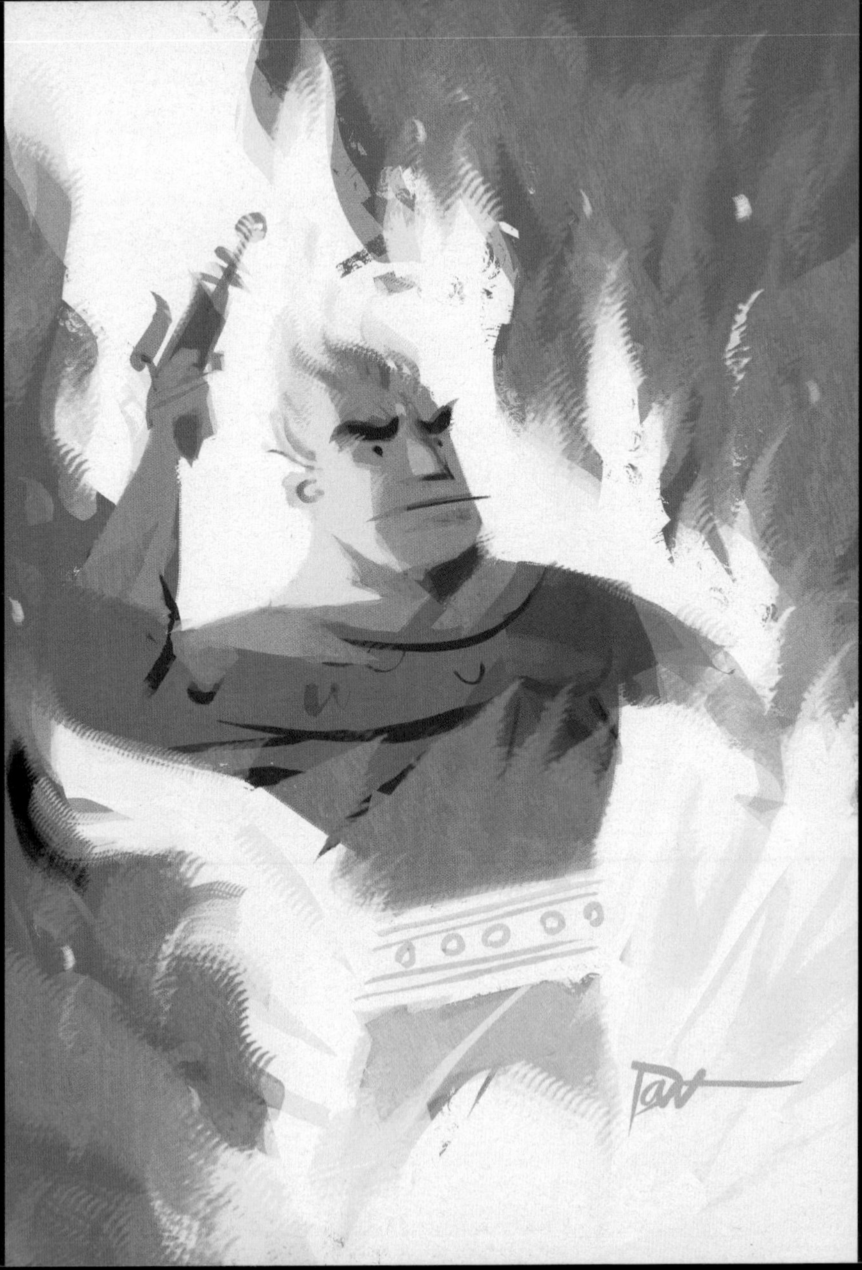

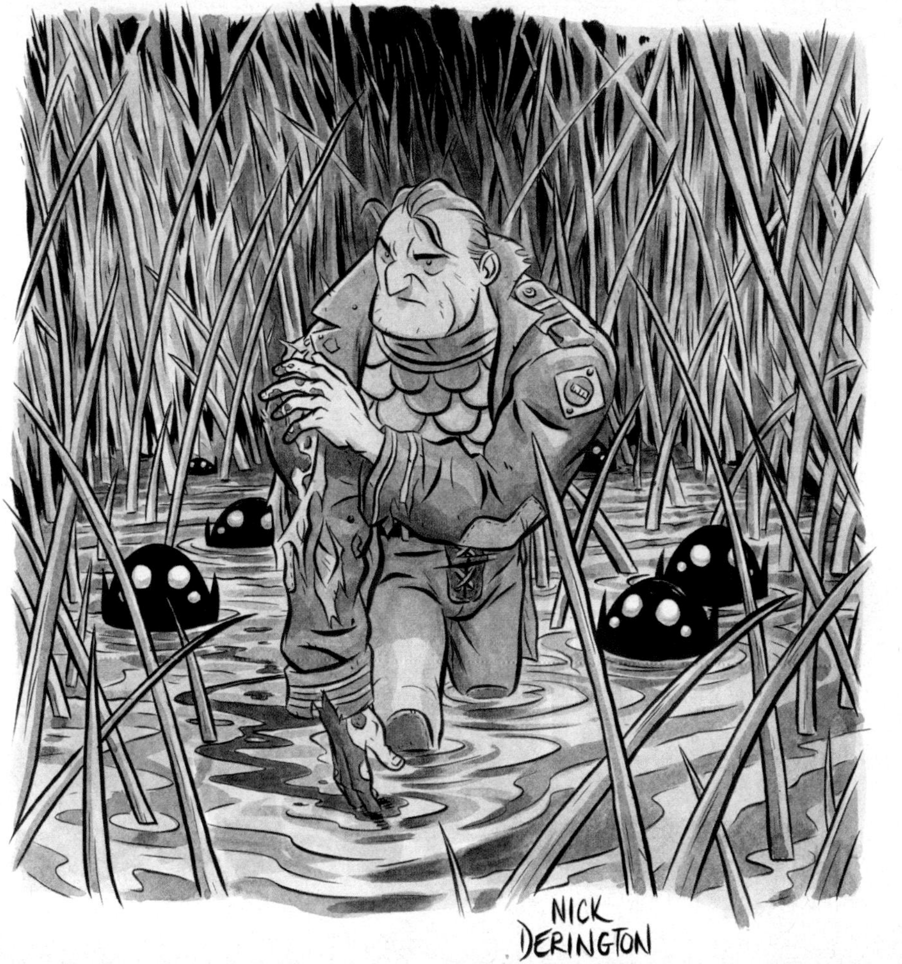
NICK DERINGTON

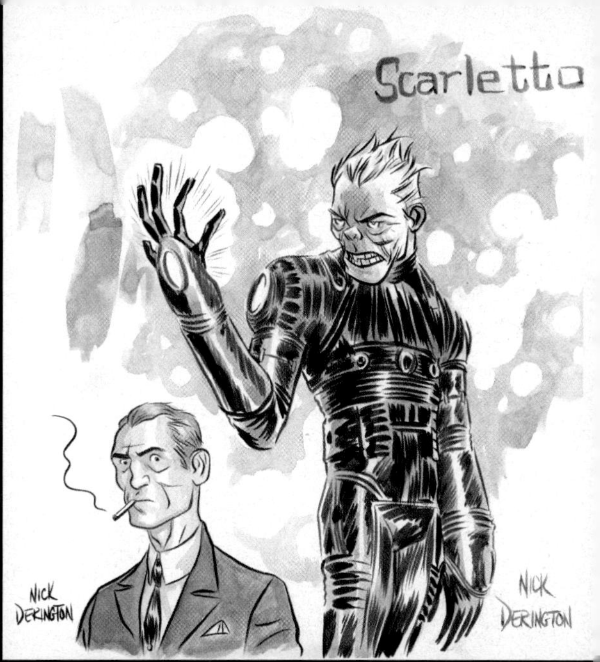
Scarletto
NICK DERINGTON
NICK DERINGTON

ROCKETO BY NICK DERINGTON

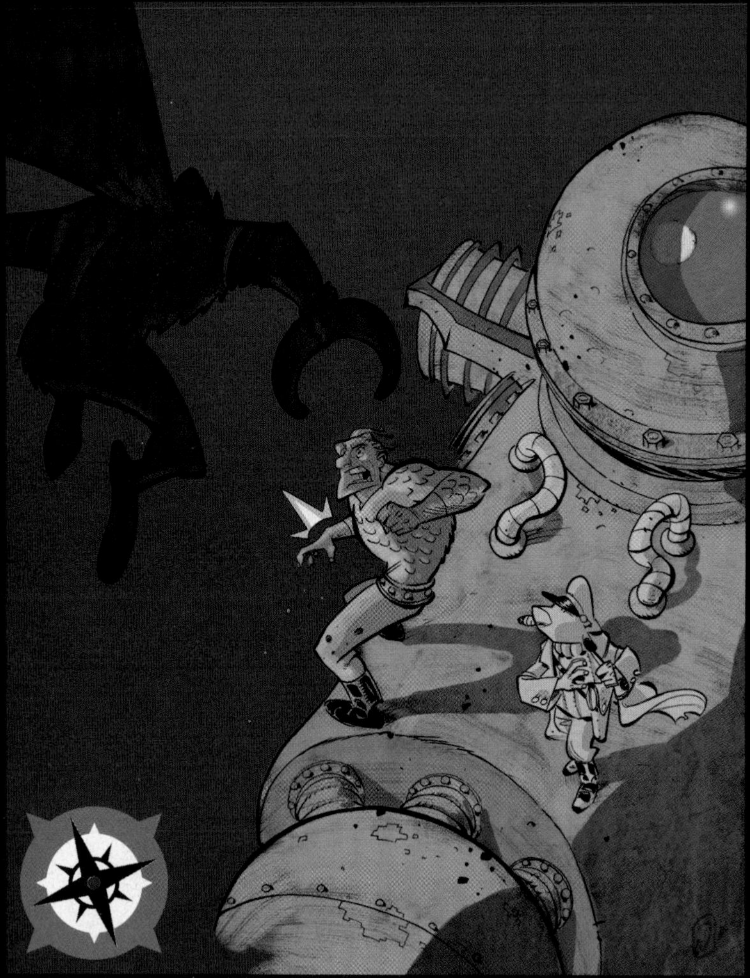

ROCKETO BY PIERRE ALARY

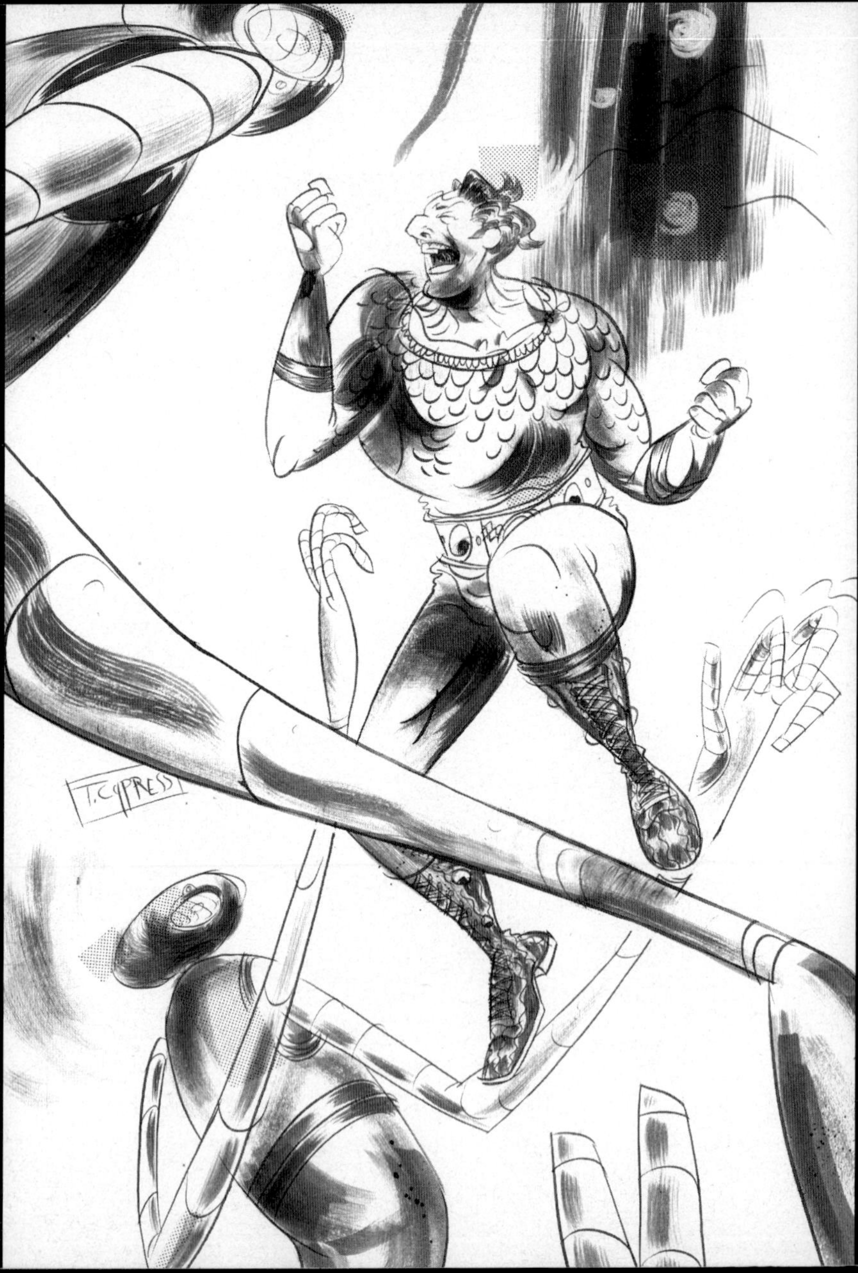

T. CYPRESS

ROCKETO BY TOBY CYPERESS

ROCKETO BY PAUL MAYBURY

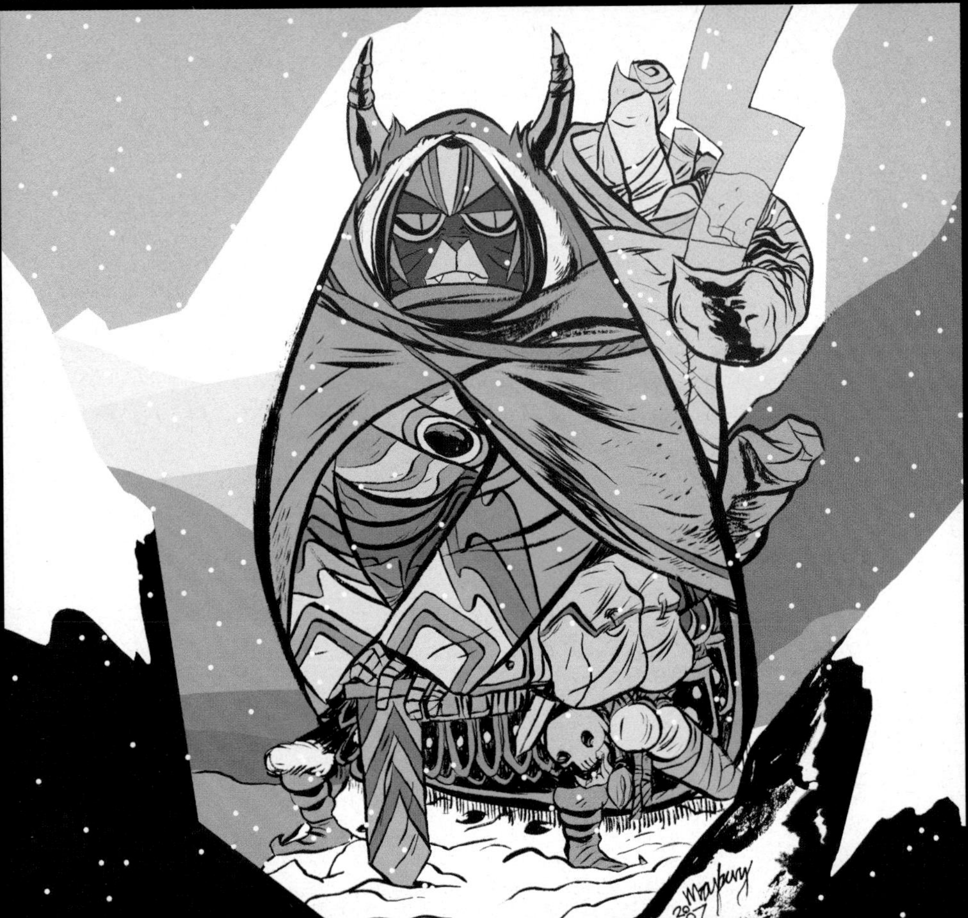

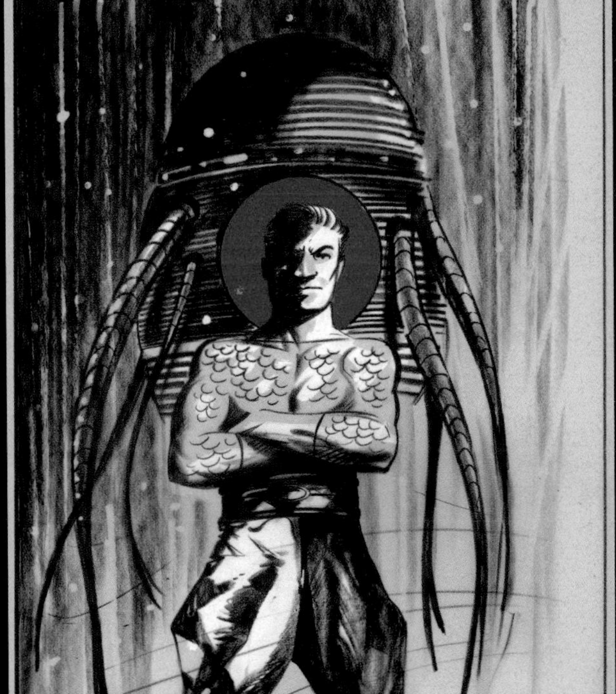
GORING '06

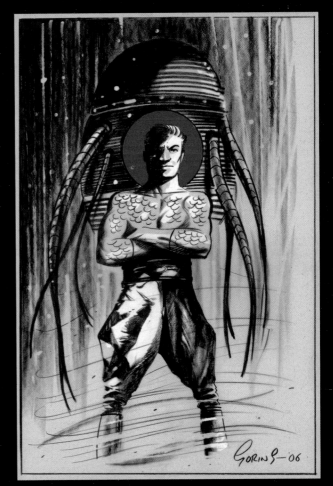

ROCKETO BY TREVOR GORING

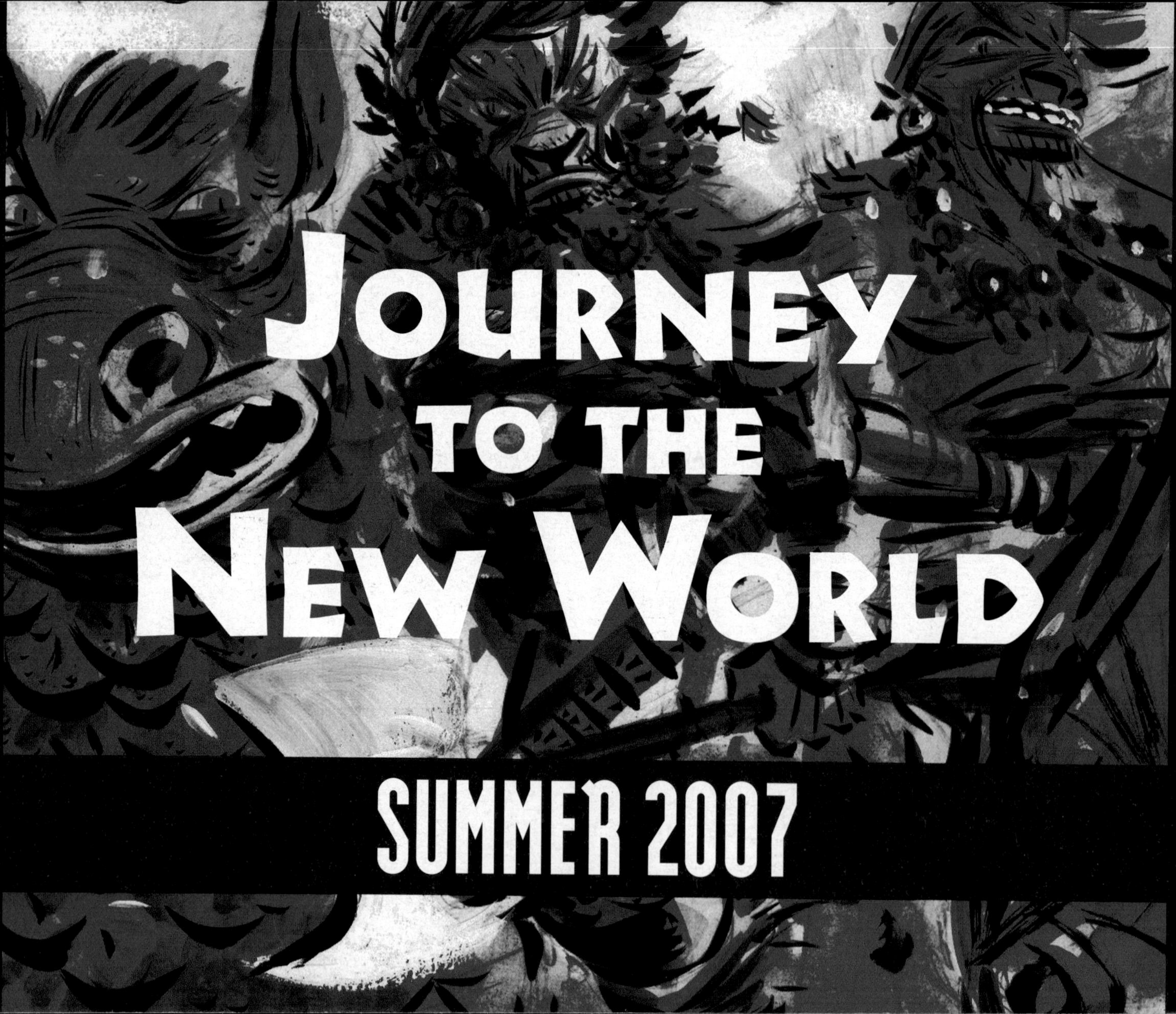
JOURNEY TO THE NEW WORLD
SUMMER 2007

I.

Listen now, while I sing
of the man born once in Kova,
then born again within the Hidden Sea,
who with his friends hurled Lucernean ships
into bottomless mists, and with that blow
released the grip that held men in tyranny.
Four long years have passed since that mighty battle.

II.

One by one, rise the once conquered lands
To challenge Lucerne's pitiless rule.
Fighting for all there worth.
Battles boil underground and across desert sands
on martial fields and the wine dark sea
The New World, balanced on the brink,
fears even a slight breeze may
tip mankind forever into chaos.

III.

The Flower of Man, taken by the Ull
from a world too young to understand,
is pursued by Rocketo Garrison.
Seeking to use its infinite power
to awaken his love that lies sleeping,
Rocketo feels the wind shift, the world shudder.
The Great Shattering, begun in history's dawn,
May at this hour, be concluded unless
one man unites this broken world.

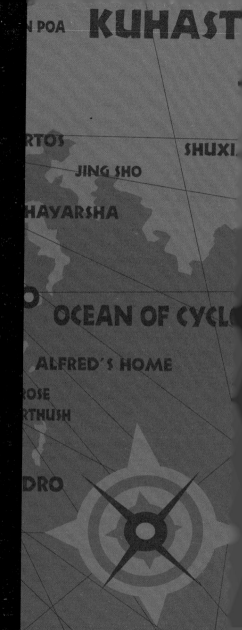

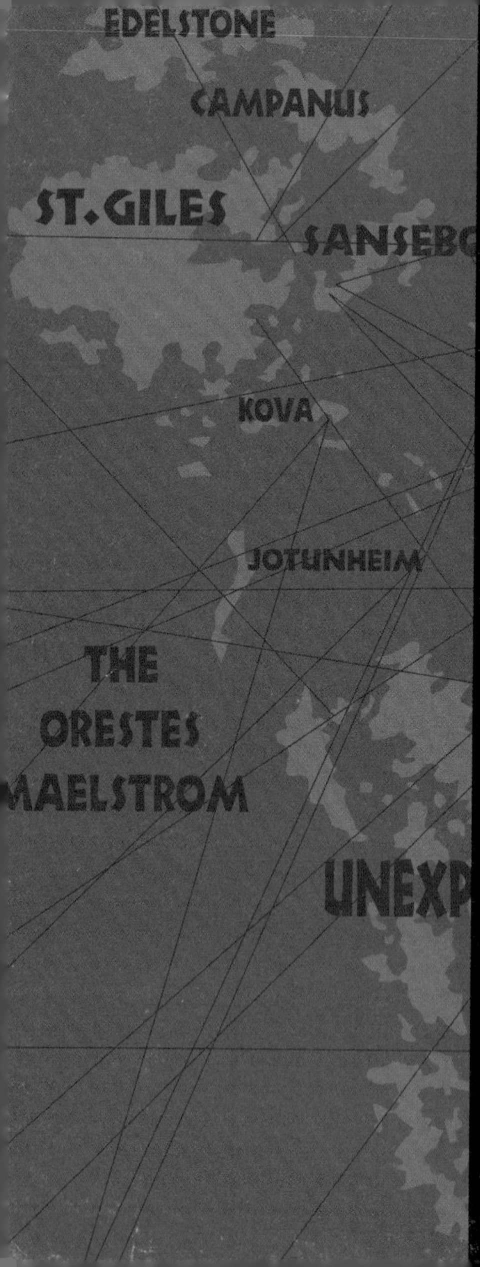

EDELSTONE

CAMPANUS

ST.GILES

SANSEBO

KOVA

JOTUNHEIM

THE
ORESTES
MAELSTROM

UNEXP

N POA

KUHAST

RTOS

SHUXI

JING SHO

HAYARSHA

OCEAN OF CYCLO

ALFRED'S HOME

ROSE
RTHUSH

DRO

YA
741.5
2/08

To Mr. Uly,

Who took the Journey into the Hidden Sea along with me.

Through long walks we saw giant ships get swallowed by swirling mists.

Your nose led to lost scents lingering under the giant Earthmen of Garuda.

With every turn you take, you lead a path into the new world.

Enjoy the cigar, chum.

ZUM ZUM BOOKS offers special thanks to

LISETT TORRES, ALEX ROSS, DARWYN COOKE, ARSHAK NAZARIAN, DAVID WILLIAMS, FRANK BARRON,

KRISTINE HOPPE, GLEN BRUSNWICK, JUNOT DIAZ, MAXWELL CONTON, MANNY TORRADO,

CHRIS MEADE, JONAH WEILAND, NANCY NOVAK, BETSY BRYTOS, DAVID MALAPOE.